ALL FOR THE KING'S SHILLING

C&C

CAMPAIGNS & COMMANDERS

GREGORY J. W. URWIN, SERIES EDITOR

All for the King's Shilling

The British Soldier under Wellington, 1808–1814

Edward J. Coss

Foreword by John F. Guilmartin, Jr.

University of Oklahoma Press : Norman

Library of Congress Cataloging-in-Publication Data
Coss, Edward J., 1954–
All for the king's shilling : the British soldier under Wellington,
1808–1814 / Edward J. Coss ; Foreword by John F. Guilmartin, Jr.
p. cm. — (Campaigns and commanders ; v. 24)
Includes bibliographical references and index.
ISBN 978-0-8061-4105-3 (hardcover : alk. paper) 1. Peninsular War,
1807–1814—Psychological aspects. 2. Great Britain. Army—
Military life. 3. Great Britain—History, Military—1789–1820.
4. Wellington, Arthur Wellesley, Duke of, 1769–1852—Military
leadership. 5. Psychology, Military. 6. Combat—Psychological
aspects. I. Title.
DC232.C67 2010
940.2'742—dc22
2009036980

*All for the King's Shilling: The British Soldier under Wellington,
1808–1814* is Volume 24 in the Campaigns and Commanders series.

The paper in this book meets the guidelines for permanence and
durability of the Committee on Production Guidelines for Book
Longevity of the Council on Library Resources, Inc. ∞

1 2 3 4 5 6 7 8 9 10

To David Chandler (1934–2004),

FRIEND, MENTOR, AND CONSUMMATE HISTORIAN,

AND TO DEB, BEN, AND BRITTANY

(THEY KNOW WHY)

Contents

List of Illustrations · ix

List of Figures · xi

List of Tables · xiii

Foreword, by John F. Guilmartin, Jr. · xvii

Acknowledgments · xxiii

Introduction · 3

1. An Unjust Reputation: The Genesis of the
   "Scum of the Earth" Myth · 29

2. Gone for a Soldier: The Realities of Enlistment · 50

3. Over the Hills and Far Away: Surviving on Campaign · 86

4. A Stick without a Carrot: Leadership and the Soldiery · 123

5. Ordeal by Fire: The British Soldier in Combat · 154

6. Banded Brothers: Combat Motivation and the British Ranker · 191

7. Into Hell before Daylight: Peninsular War Sieges · 211

Conclusion · 235

Epilogue · 239

Appendices

A. The British Soldier Compendium · 244

B. Regression Analysis Using the British Soldier Compendium · 264

C. Nutritional Analysis Using the British Soldier Compendium · 272

CONTENTS

Notes 289

Bibliography 347

Index 367

Illustrations

Worcestershire soldier of the 29th Regiment of Foot in the
    Peninsular War   177
Soldier of the 40th Regiment of Foot   178
Arthur Wellesley, the 1st Duke of Wellington   179
5th Fusiliers in Spain attacking French units   180
94th Foot defending Matagorda, 21 March 1810   181
Assault on Ciudad Rodrigo, January 1812   182
Site of the great breach at Ciudad Rodrigo   183
Ditch and ramparts of Ciudad Rodrigo   184
Terrain and walls of Ciudad Rodrigo   184
Narrow streets of the inner town of Ciudad Rodrigo   185
Obstacles in a siege assault   186
Attempting to take bastions by assault   187
Going through the breach at Badajoz, spring 1812   188
Fortress wall of Badajoz   189
Tower of Badajoz   189
Badajoz fortifications   190

Figures

1. Age distribution of all enlistees   54
2. Age-group distribution of all enlistees   55
3. Height distribution of enlistees   57
4. Age distribution of 1806 enlistees   249
5. Age-group distribution of 1806 enlistees   249
6. Enlistment per year   251
7. Enlistment per month   257
8. Effect of bread prices on enlistment   266

Tables

1. The ten most frequently listed trades in the BSC   69
2. Typical weekly wages for common trades in the
   United Kingdom during the Peninsular War   74
3. Nutritional comparison of standard rations for
   various armies   99
4. Extraordinary caloric expenditures   101
5. Dietary Reference Intakes (DRIs) (%)   102
6. Regimental courts-martial records, 44th Foot, 1778–1784   138
7. Nationality of enlistees by regiment in the BSC
   sample and sources   245
8. Nationalities of enlistees by regiment (%)   246
9. Nationalities of enlistees by branch   246
10. Nationalities of enlistees by branch (%)   246
11. Percent of each nationality's enlistees in each branch   247
12. Nationality of each branch's enlistees (%)   247
13. Disposition of soldiers (when listed)   247
14. Percent of each nationality's enlistees with each disposition   247
15. Age distribution of 1806 enlistees   248
16. Age distribution of all enlistees   248
17. Age distribution by nationality   248
18. Age distribution by branch   248
19. Height distribution of all enlistees (inches)   250
20. Height distribution by nationality (inches)   250

21. Height distribution by branch (inches)   250
22. Height distribution of enlistees aged 18 and older (inches)   250
23. Number and percentage of enlistees not meeting recruiting standards   250
24. Enlistment per year as reflected in the BSC sample   251
25. Regression comparing enlistment and bread prices   252
26. Enlistees with no trade by nationality   252
27. Enlistees with no trade as percent of nationality   253
28. Enlistees with no trade by nationality as percent of whole sample   253
29. Trades by nationality   253
30. Trades by nationality as percent of each nationality's enlistees   253
31. Trades by nationality as percent of whole sample   253
32. Enlistees with no trade by branch   254
33. Enlistees with no trade by branch as percent of branch   254
34. Enlistees with no trade by branch as percent of whole sample   254
35. Trades by branch   254
36. Trades by branch as percent of each branch's enlistees   254
37. Trades by branch as percent of whole sample   255
38. Distribution of trades in 1806 sample   255
39. Trades by type reported in the BSC   255
40. Nationality (%): 88th Foot (1815) and BSC sample   258
41. Height (inches): 88th Foot (1815) and BSC sample   258
42. Age (%): 88th Foot (1815) and BSC sample   258
43. Nationality (%): 6th Foot (1811) and BSC sample   259
44. Height (inches): 6th Foot (1811) and BSC sample   259
45. Age (%): 6th Foot (1811) and BSC sample   259
46. Nationality (%): 58th Foot (1803) and BSC sample   259
47. Height (inches): 58th Foot (1803) and BSC sample   260
48. Age (%): 58th Foot (1803) and BSC sample   260
49. Distribution of trade types (%): 58th Foot (1803) and BSC sample   260
50. Distribution of the most frequently listed trades (%): 58th Foot (1803) and BSC sample   260
51. Nationality (%): 20th Lt. Dragoons (1810) and BSC sample   261
52. Height (inches): 20th Lt. Dragoons (1810) and BSC sample   261

53. Age (%): 20th Lt. Dragoons (1810) and BSC sample   261
54. Nationality of the 1806 sample by branch   262
55. Nationality of the 1806 sample by branch (%)   262
56. Percent of each branch's enlistees of each nationality in 1806   262
57. Percent of each nationality's enlistees in each branch in 1806   262
58. Trades in 1806 sample   263
59. Age distribution of 1806 enlistees   263
60. Regression comparing enlistment and bread prices   265
61. Regression comparing enlistment and multiple economic factors   269
62. Effects of independent economic factors on enlistment   269
63. Characteristics of enlistees in poor economic years   270
64. Characteristics of enlistees in good economic years   271
65. Nutritional breakdown of standard rations for the Roman soldier   275
66. Nutritional breakdown of standard rations for the common soldier serving in the English Civil War   275
67. Nutritional breakdown of rations for 16th-century Spanish officers, soldiers, and sailors aboard galleys   276
68. Nutritional breakdown of standard rations for 14th-century Venetian oarsmen   276
69. Nutritional breakdown of minimal standard rations for 16th-century Spanish galley slaves   277
70. Nutritional breakdown of standard rations for the British common soldier during the Napoleonic Wars   277
71. Vitamin and mineral analysis of Roman soldier's diet   278
72. Vitamin and mineral analysis of common soldier's diet in the English Civil War   279
73. Vitamin and mineral analysis of 16th-century Spanish soldier, sailor, or officer's diet aboard a galley   280
74. Vitamin and mineral analysis of 14th-century Venetian oarsman's diet   281
75. Vitamin and mineral analysis of 16th-century Spanish galley slave's diet   282
76. Vitamin and mineral analysis of British common soldier's diet during the Napoleonic Wars   283

77. Total energy expenditure for an average British ranker   284
78. Total energy expenditure for all plausible body types
     and ages   285
79. Examples of extraordinary caloric expenditure   286

Foreword

"Scum of the Earth!"

The Duke of Wellington's famous categorization of the troops he commanded in the Peninsular Campaign, including the most ferociously effective infantry of the day by soldierly and scholarly consensus, has left a strong imprint. Beyond marking the starting point for most historians' assessments of the character and motivation of the British soldier in the late eighteenth and early nineteenth centuries, it has been taken to validate commonly held scholarly perceptions of the character of soldiers of *ancien régime* Europe in the Age of Reason—perceptions that continue to be applied to today's soldiers. The Comte de St-Germain, French minister of war in 1775–77, used the term *bourbe* (slime of the worst kind, found on the bottoms of ponds) to characterize the ordinary soldiers of his king's army. According to this interpretation, ordinary rankers were, as the Iron Duke had it, scum: thuggish brutes brought into the ranks as an alternative to imprisonment and kept there by a ferocious discipline that made them more fearful of their officers than of the enemy.

The social and political forces unleashed by the French Revolution are generally held to have wrought a dramatic change for the better in the motivation of ordinary soldiers, changing at least French soldiers from automatons to self-motivated citizen-soldiers. It was not that straightforward or simple, of course, as affirmed by specialist military historians, most importantly John Lynn in his path-breaking *The Bayonets of the Republic: Motivation and Tactics in the Army of Revolutionary France, 1791–94*. But the word has not spread far, and the Iron Duke's characterization still holds sway among historians in general, at least insofar as his redcoats are concerned.

These perceptions are uncritically applied to explain the tactical successes, or lack thereof, of both the French and British armies in the wars of the French Revolution and Napoleon. The critical arm was infantry, and the striking effectiveness of British infantry, particularly under Wellington's command, is generally attributed to the iron discipline that he and his officers imposed on unruly ruffians. By contrast, French success is generally attributed to the independence of mind of the French soldier, fighting at first for the success of the Revolution and later for France. Similarly stereotypical interpretations apply to soldiers' excesses off the field of battle. Of particular interest here, the predisposition of British soldiers to pillage and plunder— which is abundantly confirmed by contemporary sources, including accounts of the soldiers themselves—is regarded as a product of their thuggish nature. By contrast, historians have tended to look discreetly away from pillage, rapine, and atrocities committed by French troops. The stark realities portrayed by Francisco Goya in his dramatic paintings of summary executions and his even starker etchings, recording in graphic detail atrocities on both sides during the War in Spain, are left without military context.

Based on extensive mining of records in the British National Archives at Kew near London (formerly the Public Record Office), buttressed by exhaustive reading in the theory and practice of combat motivation, Edward Coss's new and convincing interpretations have a relevance that reaches far beyond our understanding of the dynamics of the Napoleonic battlefield to encompass the behavior of soldiers under the stress of combat in the here and now. The core of his analysis rests on regimental records containing the vital data of some 7,300 men recruited into the king's service during the Napoleonic Wars, some 5,400 of whom can reasonably be presumed to have served in the Peninsular Campaign. The 25th, 53th, and 32nd Regiments of Foot are particularly well represented. In addition to age, place of birth, and height, the records indicate former employment. Effectively all were from the working class, which was the source of Wellington's bias against them, uttered across the abyss of a social divide so wide as to be all but impossible for the modern reader to comprehend. Far from being criminals, petty or otherwise, the vast majority were unemployed agricultural laborers, craftsmen, and tradesmen, forced to accept military service as an alternative to starvation. They were, as Coss shows, the victims of a demographic trend: the enormous upswing in the birth rate in the British Isles, particularly in a broad band running from southeastern England through Wales and southern Scotland, that began in the early eighteenth century as the product of an increase in food production and changes in agricultural land allocation. The result was an excess of population that went beyond the Industrial Revolution's demands for labor. We should note that this was an almost entirely British phenomenon.

Once accepted into service, the redcoat was dependent on the king's shilling for his survival, but, as he learned to his chagrin, pay was erratic and frequently behind and provisions sorely inadequate when he was deployed overseas. From Coss's in-depth analysis of the redcoat's rations and sustenance we learn that Wellington's soldiers in Spain were significantly worse fed than, among others, Roman legionaries and sixteenth-century Spanish galley slaves (the latter a particularly telling indictment). That was true not only of total caloric intake but of essential nutrients. It should come as no surprise that the redcoat turned to plunder to keep body and soul together. To his credit, Wellington frequently complained to his superiors and provisioners about his men's lack of pay and victuals; but that did not vitiate his class prejudice; while valuing their remarkable steadiness in battle, he still saw them as scum. As for his officers, they were (with few if any exceptions) men of the moneyed classes. With independent means, they were able to purchase food and luxuries that their men could only dream of, except on rare occasions in the sack of a city, when military law condoned free pillage if the place had been taken by storm. That the men pillaged on such occasions—with their officers' approval—is hardly a surprise. In a revealing detail, Coss tells us that an officer's personal servant earned nearly twice a redcoat's wage—assuming that it was paid, whereas the servant's assuredly was. What is a surprise is the remarkably low incidence of crimes against persons committed by British soldiers. Theft and looting were commonplace; indeed Wellington's rankers were extraordinarily thorough and good at it. But, in contrast to their French opposites, they committed few physical outrages against the civil populace, a point that Coss documents convincingly. Moreover, their group ethos condemned wanton violence against civilians.

What, then, was it that made Wellington's redcoats—our reference here is to his infantry, the key to his successes—so steady that the French never beat them in battle? Coss's explanation is one of the most valuable parts of the book. In part it was the Iron Duke's remarkable tactical skill and eye for terrain, but the central ingredient was cohesion, the social force that makes the difference between a combat-effective unit and a mob. Rejected by their parent society, thrown together in an inherently inhospitable and frequently lethal environment, under the command of officers who shared their Britishness but who had little empathy for their privations, they banded together and fought not so much for king and country as for one another. Drawing on an impressive list of analyses, beginning with sociologist Charles Horton Cooley's seminal work on the primary group, Coss shows beyond doubt that it was the redcoat's loyalty to his comrades-in-arms that endowed him with unwavering cohesion. His primary loyalty was to his mess, typically six men who marched, camped, and ate together. Next came the men of his company and battalion. They were in it for the duration and depended on one another in and out of combat. Their loyalty to one another was unshakable and held them together in the face of enemy fire, answerable to their officers' commands. Looting and pillaging among the civil populace was endemic; theft from a comrade was rare. When it occurred, theft— like other offenses such as "dogging it" in combat and failing to share the risks of one's fellows—was rewarded with the ultimate sanction: ostracism. It was not pretty, and the degree to which the officers were aware of the mechanism is uncertain, but it worked. Coss's explanation of the way in which the cohesive bond was forged and how it played out in widely varying tactical scenarios is, to my mind, the culminating point of the book.

An important casualty of Coss's scholarship is the notion of the "universal soldier," the mythical creation of intellectuals who presume that soldiers have fought for the same essential reasons and with the same repercussions since time immemorial. In fact, Coss's redcoats are uniquely British creatures of the early nineteenth century, a peculiar product of their social status, time, and place and the strategic and operational choices confronting their ruler and commanders. That their motivations and behavior bear strong similarities to those of American GIs in World War II, physical deprivation aside, is a reflection on the common Anglo-American experience. The similarities are documented by Coss's exchanges with recent American veterans of conflict in Iraq and Afghanistan and by reference to the U.S. Army's massive study of the psychology of combat among soldiers in World War II.[1]

This is an important work that makes major contributions to our understanding of the wellsprings of combat effectiveness, particularly in an Anglo-American cultural context, blending physiology, individual and group psychology, and the tactical demands of combat and their repercussions in a remarkably comprehensive and thought-provoking manner. It is likely to remain the definitive work on the social dynamics of the British Army in the Napoleonic Wars for the foreseeable future.

John F. Guilmartin, Jr.
Columbus, Ohio

Acknowledgments

I am indebted to a number of exceptional people, each of whom has contributed significantly to this endeavor. Any spark of insight comes from the inspiration they collectively and selflessly provided.

First and foremost, I would like to thank Joe Guilmartin, John Lynn, John Rule, and Jack Ahern, my mentors; I don't have the words to express what their continued support, guidance, and infectious love of history have meant to me. Every student of history should be so lucky as to have four such fine scholars and gentlemen as guides.

I have been most fortunate to receive both advice and ongoing encouragement from Greg Urwin, an exceptional editor (University of Oklahoma Press) and friend. His faith in this book has allowed it to come to life. Kathy Lewis, my copyeditor, also made key suggestions and contributions. Her professionalism and skill were noted and much appreciated.

As for support, I have had the great fortune to rely on Faith Anne Hurley. Her mathematical and editorial insights have aided in the development of many concepts found herein. Faith Anne's assistance, in fact, made the appendices possible. In addition, Tim Pray, Josh Howard, Matt Spring, Judy Duguid, Peter Kochem, Phil Fry, Chris Carnes, and Major Scott Kastelic have provided editorial assistance as well as recommendations on content and approach; like Faith Anne, they have done yeoman work on my behalf, all the while offering unconditional support. Special thanks to Philippa Tinsley of the Worcester City Council, Peter Harrington of Brown University, and Richard Tennant for their help with the images in this book. Dave Knack, Alexander Cochran, and Mike Bizer, my supervising professors at the Army's Command and General Staff College, have also offered encouragement and taken an interest in this book, as have Charles Esdaile, Richard Tracy, Christian Keller, Harry Dinella, James Harvey, Eric Katz, Bill Both, Tom Dziegielewski, Dave Lane, and Chris Sasso, all fine colleagues and comrades. Such extraordinary friends are priceless.

The encouragement of David Chandler, a longtime friend and an unmatched genius when it came to military history, has made an important difference over the years. From the genesis of this work, well over a decade ago, to its now completed state, I have shared my ideas with him. When his health deteriorated, we exchanged letters and cards. I regret that I won't be able to present him with a copy of this book, a small token to repay his advice and unfailing kindness.

Finally, this work would never have germinated beyond simple musings without the understanding of my wife, Debra, and my two children, Ben and Brittany. My wife has traveled abroad with me and assisted me in research, from the National Archives in Kew to Les Invalides in Paris. She also helped compile the demographic research contained herein and listened, amused and tolerant, as I shared each aspect of my discoveries. Brittany was also pressed into service inputting data, much to her regret. Both she and Ben have put up with my seemingly endless streams of historical anecdotes and insights with an amazing degree of forbearance. The impact of my enthusiasm has not gone unnoticed: Ben has chosen architecture and Brittany medicine as their professions. History was never in the running. Deb, Ben, and Britt have somehow understood my passion for military history and my need to comprehend and analyze the behavior of men in battle. They have put up with my absences, my need for solitude, and my piles of research notes and books without complaint. They have been my sustaining motivation throughout. My gratitude to all these people knows no bounds.

ALL FOR THE KING'S SHILLING

Introduction

O ne of the most neglected areas of research in the field of Napoleonic studies is the campaign and combat behavior of the common British soldier who fought against the French in the Peninsular War, 1808 to 1814. The British redcoat, the infantryman in particular, performed extraordinarily well in combat, contributing to a series of unbroken battlefield victories in Spain and Portugal. The army's achievements, to a great degree, rested on the combat effectiveness and tactical capabilities of the infantry rank and file. It was their unit cohesion, their ability to act as a unified force during battle, that worked in concert with Wellington's leadership to set Britain's infantry apart from all others that opposed Napoleon Bonaparte's armies in the field, a matter of no small historical importance.

The battlefield triumphs of the British army over its French counterpart, however, are usually attributed to the command genius of Arthur Wellesley—the first Duke of Wellington—and his ability to master and make use of the savage and violent natures of British rankers.[1] Wellington made a number of comments that contributed to this interpretation, and his references to the British rank and file as the "scum of the earth" have been accepted as the definitive evaluation of the men.[2]

Over the past two centuries, as Wellington has risen in eminence as one of the greatest commanders in military history, the enlisted soldiers he led have collectively acquired a reputation as thieves, rogues, scoundrels, criminals, and undesirable outcasts.[3] Such historical assessments, however, appear to be based largely on Wellington's comments and related, but mistaken, assumptions regarding the characters, backgrounds, and motivations of the British rank and file. These flawed appraisals also (of particular interest here) overlook the fundamental role played by the group and group norms in shaping campaign and combat behavior. The contradiction between the portrayals of the ranker as a villainous, thieving brute and as a stalwart combat soldier, unwavering in battle, has never been fully explored. The first implies a predatory instinct and a nature of pure self-interest, rooted in personal gain at the expense of others, while the second requires the selfless ability to function as a member of a small cadre of men whose collective interest is group survival balanced against mission success.

Not one historian who has attempted to unravel the question of how men behave during battle has posited that thugs make ideal soldiers, including those who have analyzed the face-to-face dynamics of hoplite warfare and the Roman cohort, the French Revolution, the American Civil War, and the behavior of men under fire in World War I and World War II.[4] None of the current work on combat psychology, in fact, supports the position that socially isolated individuals with sociopathic tendencies perform well on the battlefield. Rather, the literature has shown that a unit's combat efficiency is largely dependent upon how well its members adapt to and are shaped by small groups whose norms demand active battlefield participation.

In the seminal work on the effects of primary and secondary groups on individual soldier morale, Edward Shils and Morris Janowitz found that deserters, perhaps the most dysfunctional men in the German army during World War II, failed to be assimilated into groups because they exhibited the same antisocial characteristics in military life as they had in civilian life. "They were the men," Shils and Janowitz explain, "who . . . had difficulties with friends, work associates, and their own families, or had criminal records."[5] The problems interacting with fellow soldiers worked to isolate these men, usually emotionally and psychologically but also sometimes spatially, as the deserters placed themselves beyond the boundaries of group influence. Without ties to other men, the deserter had no personal obligation or need to face the dangers of war; thus, desertion became a viable choice for those not constrained by group norms.

Conversely, the British regular by and large behaved extremely well under fire and survived on campaign because of the mutual support he extended to and received from his comrades. His existence as part of a collective epitomizes the social dynamics described by Charles H. Cooley in his groundbreaking work on primary groups. Cooley outlines the process, mindset, and potential power of collectives on the individual: "By primary groups I mean those characterized by intimate face-to-face association and cooperation . . . it is a 'we'; it involves the sort of sympathy and mutual identification. . . . One lives in the feeling of the whole . . . the only essential thing being a certain intimacy and fusion of personalities."[6]

Cooley could very well have been delineating the effects of company and squad life on the individual soldier. Oddly, historians analyzing the Peninsular War have depicted the British redcoat as a social deviant and hardened, predatory individual; his battlefield triumphs are attributed to his inherent callousness and ferocity, and never to the nature of small group dynamics. Such an assessment merits reexamination, as it runs counter to what we know about the connections between group norms, cohesion, and the behavior of men in battle. And, as it turns out, there is very little substantiating evidence to support the accepted, if simplistic, representation of the British ranker as a marauding, selfish, and brutish individual capable of any number of despicable acts.

A careful examination of surviving army enlistment books, journals, letters, memoirs, and regimental records reveals a richer and more telling portrait of the British soldier and the stressors that acted on him. When they are reviewed in conjunction with relatively modern social-psychological studies of men in combat, models of combat motivation, and recent social histories focusing on the effects of cultural norms on human behavior, a broader and more nuanced picture of the British common soldier emerges, one that stands in direct contrast to the currently accepted portrayal.

The men who filled the ranks of the British army were drawn from the working class and were victims of demographic change. Unprecedented increases in population created a populace with a higher proportion of young people than had been the norm. Insufficient occupational opportunities in rural communities combined with years of poor harvests to drive the people toward the cities, where their hopes of employment were dashed by the rise of industrialization, the resulting labor surplus, and the economic dislocation of Napoleon's continental embargo. The image that presents itself is of desperate men driven to enlist because of economic circumstances and the lack of social relief in England, Ireland, Wales, and Scotland. They were mostly manual laborers but also weavers, tailors, shoemakers, tinsmiths, and men of various other trades. Enlistees included boys in their preteens through men in their fifties; they volunteered because they had few alternatives. That they sought refuge in the army, a thoroughly unpopular institution that offered little in the way of long-term economic promise and advancement but much in the way of danger and toil, shows just how hopeless, miserable, and hard-pressed these individuals must have been to enlist. The enticement of the enlistment bounty, regular pay, food, and the chance to find their self-worth—to belong to something and do a day's work for a day's pay—made the army appear promising to men who were displaced and disconnected from society through no fault of their own.

Once in the army and on the continent, men soon learned that the army had great difficulties providing the promised pay and rations. The themes of hunger and want weave their way through almost every enlisted man's account. Pay was usually in arrears, and the soldier's daily ration of one pound of meat (including the bone), one pound of biscuit, and a third of a pint of spirits (usually rum, brandy, or wine) was nutritionally insufficient; in addition, ration deliveries were often sporadic and piecemeal. Men frequently marched for days without adequate food, and on some days with next to none. Such deprivation tended to be part of the everyday experience for the vast majority of British regulars in the Peninsular War.

Often poorly fed, without shoes, and in tattered and dirty uniforms, the men discovered that in order to survive on campaign and on the battlefield they had little choice but to rely on each other. The key to understanding the behavior of the British soldier is an awareness of the rank and file's reliance on what Cooley, and later Shils and Janowitz, referred to as the "primary social group."[7] The British ranker needed the emotional and physical support of the group, perhaps as much as or more than any other soldier of the time; to him, the term "band of brothers" had profound meaning.

The psychological and physiological experiences of campaign and combat bonded the common British soldier to the men with whom he lived, suffered, and fought. Their ongoing desperation strengthened the bonds that connected them. This mutual reliance is reflected in scores of primary-source narratives, and it is in these documents that we find repeated descriptions of group dynamics as the basic mechanism governing the men's behavior. The soldier's deep-seated need to belong to the group allowed the collective ethos of this small but essential social organization to establish norms of acceptable individual conduct. These standards applied to intragroup dynamics, such as the sharing of food and behavior under fire, and to group interactions with civilians and enemy soldiers beyond the boundaries of the battlefield. Behaviors that enhanced the chances of group survival—such as maintaining one's place in line during battle, giving one's best during the fight, and sharing food—were reinforced. Other actions that endangered the unit—such as fleeing from combat, conveniently lagging behind under fire, or hoarding provisions when other soldiers had none—were condemned, with the ultimate punishment being ostracism.

Behavioral norms existed in all Napoleonic armies, varying by regiment and nationality due to campaign experiences and cultural constraints. Men in war have an inherent need for the support offered by their companions, the fellow soldiers with whom they endure the privations and dangers of military life. Thus, group-based values take on significance. But for the British regular, group norms may have carried a greater emotional weight. Unlike the men of other armies, the British soldier was a volunteer who probably enlisted for life.[8] And unlike the majority of conscripted soldiers of other nationalities who had experienced varying degrees of social value and stability, the British ranker was also a societal outcast, for economic reasons largely beyond his control. The campaign lives of conscripted soldiers from France, Prussia, and Austria were anything but easy; their tribulations paralleled those of their British counterparts. These men, however, held hope that war's end meant discharge from the army. Even if fate offered the British redcoat a reprieve from the rigors of army life, he realized that a return to civilian society would only place him in the same circumstances that he had enlisted to escape. To understand the psyche of the British soldier, we must realize that he never knew when or if he would be discharged. As far as the soldier could make out, the army was the last home he was ever going to have.

Living day-to-day as a member of a regiment and its more intimate subdivisions, the British soldier turned to the group for support and guidance. These formal and informal assemblages shaped his attitudes, values, and self-image. The loyalty and mutual trust developed over time among British redcoats became a driving force, compelling men to assimilate group standards as part of their personal codes, with normative compliance being the regulating instrument. Thoughts of patriotism, religion, home, family, and enduring battle in order to end the war and return to Great Britain are rarely mentioned in the writings of the common British ranker as sustaining campaign or combat incentives.[9] It was the group, as American soldiers of today willingly confirm, that governed the conduct of the rank and file when danger was at hand.[10]

We cannot presume with any certainty that the ties binding British soldiers together were of greater emotional importance than those between soldiers in other European armies of the time, for it is impossible to quantify emotion. These bonds were remarkably strong, however, and it is far more likely that primary group interaction, rather than significant character flaws, was one of the underlying reasons for the combat effectiveness of the British redcoat. A measured investigation of this question must look beyond Wellington's negative judgments and focus more on the soldiers' backgrounds and motivations in order to understand how groups affected individual behavior.

Two types of primary sources, properly juxtaposed, allow a substantive evaluation of the British soldier: firsthand accounts and demographic data. The words of Peninsular War participants, preserved in journals, letters, and reminiscences, offer the essential human perspective. Scores of such accounts, often partial in nature, were left by enlisted men. While far less numerous than those left by soldiers in the American Civil War, these personal recollections provide a corpus of firsthand information regarding life in the British army. The number of these accounts is somewhat surprising, given the low estimated literacy rate among British soldiers. François Furet and Mona Ozouf have shown that there is a high correlation between signing one's name and the ability to write, at least at a minimal level.[11] Using soldiers' signatures as a guide, Alan Forest has concluded that just under half of Napoleon's soldiers could read and write.[12] Since Napoleon's men were conscripts, drawn from a much wider portion of the socioeconomic spectrum than were British soldiers, we can reasonably surmise that the literacy rate of British common soldiers was probably lower than the 50 percent estimate for the French.[13] That so many men felt the need to put their thoughts on paper verifies that the events they described more than likely were deemed of significant emotional value and worthy of preserving. While we have been deprived of hearing the voices of illiterate soldiers, with two exceptions, their more learned counterparts do offer insights into soldier motivations in general.[14] Whether or not the backgrounds and perceptions of soldiers who could not write were different from those of the rankers who recorded their thoughts is open to debate.[15] The surviving accounts of the two illiterate soldiers appear to align fairly well with the tales provided by better-educated redcoats who recorded their observations.

A general word of caution is warranted regarding the use of personal chronicles. As Forest points out in his analysis of the men who served Napoleon, such narratives are not written with a common purpose. Reflections in the form of memoirs are vastly different in design and value than hastily scribbled diaries or letters home. Memoirs often contain degrees of conceit and deceit, both unintentional and purposeful, as the writer sometimes feels compelled to "set the record straight," usually to his benefit. Forest correctly argues that memoirs are written for posterity, as historical records of sorts, with the final goal being acquired respectability.[16] This applies to the memoirs of enlisted men, but more so to the accounts of officers, who felt a greater need to enhance and protect their reputations.[17] Despite these qualifiers, memoirs still have value. Considering the words of not one but many men who experienced the same campaigns, battles, hardships, challenges, emotions, and horrors allows comparative evaluations to be made. The myriad perspectives and memories provide context and verification for one another.

Journals, diaries, and letters, on the other hand, have a kind of spontaneity or, as Samuel Hynes puts it, "the virtues of immediacy and directness."[18] While such first-person accounts can be empty, rambling narratives, they can also be intensely personal. Running the gamut of human emotions, they are often filled with aspirations, fears, grief, and more humor than we would imagine. While some private forms of communication are poignant and others inevitably filled with misinformation, most are simple recollections of the reality of soldiering. As Forest summarizes, such personal accounts, "unlike the more heroic of war memoirs, concentrate heavily on the immediate experience of soldiers, on their own units, the men around them, [and] the men with whom they shared so much more than they would ever have had to do in civilian life. . . . Often, of course, the day-to-day experiences they describe are petty and banal, yet that very banality gives their accounts a degree of veracity which otherwise they would lack."[19]

Less fettered by the desire to voice an opinion on the events of the day and removed from any hope of glory, the journals, diaries, and letters of enlisted men supplement and confirm the insights into day-to-day existence provided by memoirs. The soldiers felt a psychological need to consign their thoughts to paper, with little intent beyond sharing and preserving these life moments; in the process, their writings left a record of their social and psychological experiences. Whether naïve or worldly, dull or witty, these personal chronicles reveal men stripped of their social veneer, allowing the forces that drive them to be seen more readily.

Yet it must be remembered that much of what can be gleaned from firsthand accounts (even the most reliable varieties) may not always be that which the authors consciously wish to relate. An anecdote in a letter home describing the shame a soldier felt about stealing freshly baked bread from a Spanish household may reveal more about the commissariat's inability to feed the troops than it does about the character of the individual composing the letter. Likewise, an officer's journal entries that are dominated by descriptions of dinners, women, and the countryside—but never mention the men under his command, the difficulties of long marches and short rations, or the ugly aftermath of battle—tell much about the difference in campaign experiences between enlisted men and some officers; such letters also help us understand how well-fed officers of independent means might fail to grasp why their men felt the need to steal food or drink themselves into oblivion in order to dull the pain. Again, the ability to compare scores of accounts allows a collective overview to emerge, one that looks past the intent of individual authors. It is from such a summative view that patterns of the soldiers' prejudices, values, beliefs, and *raison d'être* become more obvious. Common concerns come to the surface, mostly dealing with survival and shared hardship, group demands and constraints, the relationships among men, the fear and recollections of battle, and the all-too-uncomfortable reminders of mortality. This collection of thoughts and musings can yield much information regarding how British soldiers viewed their experiences of army life on the continent.

The second important type of primary source—demographic information compiled from enlistment records—adds quantitative support to the first-person chronicles described above. The heretofore mostly ignored enlistment records housed in the National Archives at Kew (formerly called the Public Record Office), outside London, are an important source of personal background data for British soldiers. Regimental description books that summarize individual enlistment statistics provide a wealth of information on the backgrounds of the men who volunteered to serve King George III, such as country of origin, age at enlistment, height, previous occupation, and attestation date. These data, which I collected in the form of a 7,300-man database, help dispel previously held suppositions about the men's backgrounds and criminal natures, substantiating their portrayal as out-of-work men of many occupations forced into the army because of economic necessity. The British Soldier Compendium (BSC) consists of data drawn in 50- to 75-man groupings from randomly chosen pages within the regimental description books.[20] The BSC includes information covering fourteen British line regiments, four cavalry regiments, and the artillery corps; these are the only units for which information could be found.[21] These individual statistics, once compiled into a database, offered a rare opportunity to investigate the British volunteer. Dates of enlistment, for example, were analyzed in relation to economic indicators, such as bread prices, fluctuations in real wages, and seasonal employment. Height and age information led to related research on body mass index (BMI), which allowed for a thorough nutritional investigation of the macro- and micronutritional effects of standard British rations on the common soldier. This, in turn, permitted an assessment of the ranker's nutritional needs relative to energy expenditure in the field as well as a comparison of British rations with those of other armies over time. Additionally, occupational data made it possible to examine trades in general across the BSC sample; this information was also broken down by nationality and scrutinized by year, in an effort to determine possible correlations between enlistment and the effects of economic disruption on various trades.

Unfortunately, information on the remaining British infantry regiments (originally over 100 in number) and on the numerous cavalry regiments has been largely lost. The extant regimental data are of varying quality, as other researchers have noted. Glenn Steppler, one of the few historians to delve into these records in search of information regarding the British soldier, best sums up the idiosyncratic nature of regimental records. "The record keeping of the British army," he explains, "was an extremely haphazard affair, in which each regiment went its own way, good, bad, or indifferent."[22] Steppler's portrayal is apt, as the battalion description books differ in the types of information recorded, in the organization of data, and even in accounting practices. The final records are almost as diverse as regimental histories; the British penchant for regimental individuality, with the regiment rather than the army being the center of military life, is most evident here.

In an effort to meld the collective first-person chronicles with the demographic information contained within the BSC, the narrative of this monograph revolves around the life and memories of an actual soldier, William Lawrence. Though illiterate, Lawrence was quick-witted, largely diligent in his duties, and possessed of a reflective and keenly observant mind. His account was first dictated to a semiliterate soldier. Its grammar was later polished by George Bankes and published in its present version.[23] In many ways the quintessential British soldier, Lawrence enlisted at a young age due to family economic hardship and dissatisfaction with his apprenticeship. Recruited in a year of high economic stress, he declared that his previous occupation was as a laborer, the most commonly stated vocation of the British soldiery. Lawrence worked the bounty system to his benefit and embarked on a long, eventful, and often difficult military career.

Lawrence rose to the rank of sergeant, surviving a lashing of 400 strokes, a severe wound, and not one but two siege assaults. Army life forced him to become as skilled a plunderer as he was a combat soldier. His recollections are filled with the insights of a man who experienced both the cruelties of war and the sustaining camaraderie of his fellow soldiers. Lawrence speaks repeatedly of his messmates and the group-based ethos that guided his actions and theirs. The degree to which he depended on these men is evident throughout his auto-biography. His life of privation as a member of a primary group en-compassed well more than a decade of military service. Lawrence fought in most of the major Peninsular War campaigns and at Water-loo. He was cast aside by his government soon thereafter, though he was later brought back to serve in Ireland.

Lawrence's age at enlistment, his occupation, and his experiences in the army mirror those of the British soldiery writ large, making him a more than adequate representative of common British rankers in general. The breadth of his experiences (from his time as a way-ward young apprentice who initially found the army more attractive than civilian life to his days surviving long marches on short rations and his ordeals in combat) provides a framework against which other first-person accounts can be compared. Many of Lawrence's general observations are confirmed in sources left by the British rank and file. Only the longevity of his career, surviving over fourteen years of ac-tive service, sets him apart from the majority of his peers. Lawrence's honesty and his willingness to relate tales that often show his per-sonal failings as well as those of his comrades make his chronicle a reasonably reliable source of information. His story also acts as a guide through which demographic information can be presented and analyzed. Lawrence's tale is quite similar to that of Claude Le Roy, the common soldier used by historian John Lynn in his account of the French Revolutionary army. The Comte Saint-Germain, the French minister of war from 1775 to 1777, expressed feelings very much like Wellington's toward the soldiers from the lower classes. Saint-Germain called men like Le Roy the *bourbe* (slime) of the nation. His remarks reveal that prejudices toward the rank and file were not re-stricted to the British army.[24]

An in-depth, socially and culturally sensitive investigation, guided by Lawrence's experiences, helps transform the British ranker from a faceless thug into a real man made of flesh and blood. Such an approach is necessary in order to dissect the separate but related aspects of soldiers' motivation. It will assist us in understanding the factors that worked on the British civilian, causing him to enlist;

those variables that helped to sustain him on campaign; and the mechanism that allowed him repeatedly to face and withstand the demands of combat.[25]

Here Steven Westbrook provides the analytical tool necessary to examine the entire range of variables that impacted campaign behavior and combat efficiency. His three-tiered model of compliance theory breaks motivation down into three general categories: coercive, remunerative, and normative. Westbrook defines coercive force as "actual or threatened application of physical standards." Remunerative power "rests on the control of material resources and rewards." Finally, normative power, also referred to as persuasive, manipulative, or suggestive power, is "based on the allocation and manipulation of symbolic rewards and deprivations."[26]

Westbrook's methodology reveals that all three types of power shaped the motivations of the British soldier. Initially, the British recruit was drawn to service for remunerative reasons. His enlistment was most likely linked to economic stressors,[27] although patriotic enthusiasm may have played a limited role, as did the potential to escape undesirable apprenticeships and the drudgery of everyday life.

While on campaign, the British soldier received little in the way of physical or psychological support. Meals and pay were infrequent, while rewards, advancement, and hopes of an improved situation were almost nonexistent. Thus, remunerative forces as wielded by his superiors soon lost their influence. Likewise, the ranker learned that the army was not interested in persuading him to behave in a certain fashion by providing medals, praise, or other rewards. Army life, in large part, was patterned by military authority on external, punitive discipline: the lash was a constant reminder to the soldier of what lay in his future should his conduct not measure up to the army's code of conduct. Moreover, the kind of ideological indoctrination common in the French army (perpetuated by songs, pamphlets, and bulletins regularly distributed to the men) was unheard of in the British army.[28] In addition, the civilians he protected—be they British, Spanish, or Portuguese—rarely, if ever, expressed appreciation. Even letters from family were rare; very little in the way of correspondence (similar to that sent to soldiers in the American Civil War approximately a half-century later) was delivered to the British enlisted man. The ranker may have been proud of his country, but he received little external encouragement that contributed to his morale while on campaign.

The British regular soldiered on because his self-image and core values were tied to his primary social group. Isolated from civilian society, the common soldier reordered his world around the small cadre of men with whom he endured campaign life and combat. The standards of the group became the most compelling mechanism in his life, providing both guidelines and behavioral incentives. Westbrook's most influential type of controlling force, normative power, is based on the distribution and denial of abstract rewards, such as group status, honor, and respect.[29] Self-esteem, generated by the garnering of group-based incentives, drove men to adhere to norms that enhanced the chances of group survival. By meeting the expectations of the primary social entity, the British soldier was incorporated into this small family unit. Concern for and support from the group became the fundamental sustaining consideration, which made life endurable.

Survival on campaign and success in combat created unit pride; the British ranker accepted rules of conduct, especially those that applied on the battlefield, because of the normative power of the group. Rewards and sanctions meted out by the group helped to dictate the bounds of acceptable behavior. Discipline—here defined as the willingness to submit to a system of rules and regulations (both formal and informal)—helped turn individual soldiers into competent fighting teams. The British soldier developed self-control on campaign (expressed in his efforts to endure hard marches without falling out and his acquiescence to military law) and in battle (where he maintained his place in the ranks as French columns approached) because his personal needs and those of the group coincided with the behavior required of the soldiers by military leadership. In this way, a sense of honor and pride developed; the soldier's self-image became entwined with that of his group, company, battalion, brigade, and the army in general. Perceived values related to courage, discipline, and comradeship became internalized standards that worked to guide behavior.

It was from the perspective of a group member that the British ranker perceived the world and himself. That he fought with unequaled ferocity to safeguard his adopted family and behaved in ways consistent with maintaining his place in it should hardly be surprising, for the regiment was all the family he would ever have. The soldier might take a Spanish, a Portuguese, or even a French wife while on campaign. He might father children, who would become an extended part of the regimental retinue, following in the army's wake as it tramped across the continent. But no matter what other attachments he formed, the British soldier would never be part of a social group more intrinsically tied to his survival and self-image than the one composed of his messmates, the core cadre of men he leaned on every day.

Moreover, the group provided the individual soldier with a sense of control, which had emotional and physiological benefits. As Stephen Rosen points out in his work on human responses to stress, "The idea that soldiers under fire make decisions about whether to continue fighting the same way shoppers do may not be correct." Using various studies testing the physiological reactions of men under great duress, Rosen found that perceptions had a profound effect on the body's reaction to uncertainty: "If the subjects feel they are in control, the presence of stressors in the environment creates high levels of adrenaline . . . and is associated with the subjective feelings of excitement and arousal, not anxiety." Perceived helplessness, however, creates elevated levels of cortisol (a stress hormone), which is related to distress and depression. This distress-induced depression, Rosen argues, is "cognitively, behaviorally, and biochemically similar to, if not indistinguishable from, the disease known as depression."[30] Such depression is almost contagious in its effects on men under fire and can lead to unit disintegration in battle.

The group and the presence of comrades altered the British soldier's perceptions in a way that increased his ability to deal with the combat environment; his trust in the group and its capacity to take actions that acted to safeguard its members became a self-fulfilling prophecy. The workings of the small group allowed for the creation of a belief system based on perceptions of control rather than helplessness, which had real mental and physical advantages and augmented unit capacity to function in combat.

Internal mechanisms are rarely referenced, though, when the soldiers under Wellington are considered. Instead, draconian discipline is frequently presented as one of the reasons behind the success of the British rank and file. But fear of the lash was at best a secondary concern for the British soldier. Coercive, external discipline can act as a controlling mechanism, but its effectiveness during extreme conditions is limited. Fear of potential punishment pales as a motivating force when a soldier is faced with imminent starvation or the immediate realities of shot and shell. Even the open cordon of sergeants and officers that was positioned behind the men to prevent soldiers from running away during combat posed only a potential threat to men hoping to skulk away. In the confusion of battle, the rankers could often evade their superiors, who represented a real but less lethal risk for soldiers who weighed their chances of rebuke and possible harm from an officer's sword or sergeant's spontoon against the absolute dangers of the battlefield. Rosen concludes that, while external discipline "is a necessary and useful part of all military organizations, it cannot and does not eliminate at the level of individuals the neuropsychological behavior induced by uncontrollable levels of stressors in the environment."[31] Fear will often paralyze a man, not galvanize him to take action other than flight. The threat of punishment might cause a soldier to pause and consider the consequences of outright desertion during combat, but only concern for the group and his place within it would cause him to participate actively in battle. On campaign, self-preservation and group norms motivated the redcoat to risk a flogging in order to procure food in the amounts denied him by the army; this act was sanctioned by the group as long as the spoils were duly shared.

As for the quality of leadership, the men at the top—Sir John Moore and especially the Duke of Wellington—were talented and perceptive professionals who helped the British soldier discover his worth on the field. Wellington's tactical nuances were particularly effective, building the men's confidence in him and in themselves in a string of battlefield victories. Other commanders, such as Rowland Hill, Thomas Picton, and Robert Craufurd, were also consummate professionals who knew how to instill pride and motivate men. And while the middle- to lower-level leadership ran the gamut from talented to ineffectual, tactical competence at the battalion level and below appears to have been consistently good.

The primacy of the small group, particularly the six-man mess unit that ate together and stood side by side during combat, is most evident in the soldiers' expectations of how men were to conduct themselves. Their memoirs, letters, and journals convey that each soldier understood that his actions during battle were founded on preserving the group during times of danger. Adherence to group values was also the consistent catalyst guiding the men's reactions to short rations. Firsthand accounts show that the British ranker tolerated and even encouraged plundering, what the men referred to as "reconnoitering," because it played a large role in the primary group's collective survival. Men stole because the army continually failed to provide for their basic needs, forcing them to look after themselves. The army's neglect of the men, in the form of commissariat failures and the nutritional inadequacy of the rations, resulted in widespread food thefts by malnourished soldiers who had little choice; such acts were so prevalent that individuals gained respect within their units based on their abilities to gather various foodstuffs and other shared valuables. Major-General George Bell remembered infantryman Tom Tandy as being especially esteemed, for he carried his own reaping hook and always left room in his backpack "for anything Providence might send on the way."[32] William Grattan, a subaltern in the 88th Regiment of Foot—which was nicknamed "the devil's own" and deservedly earned a "taking away with them" reputation—recalled stealing items from abandoned Portuguese houses. "Every nook was searched with anatomical precision," he wrote. He matter-of-factly called such theft "a slight breach of discipline."[33] That an officer viewed such a practice as acceptable, even necessary, reinforces the point that common theft was not always seen as an overtly criminal act.

Stories of the British soldier's skill at plundering are legion; the soldiers' reputation as consummate looters is well deserved. Countless tales describe the toil and misery they faced almost daily, yet their looting is remembered while the reasons for it are not. There are two telling constants in all the narratives. First, as noted above, the men plundered food and alcohol (and money in order to purchase both) in large part because of dietary shortages and the need to seek temporary respite from the difficulties of army life. William Surtees, a private in the 56th Regiment of Foot and later in the 95th, pinpoints the motivation behind these violations of the army code of conduct. He describes how constant hunger drove the men to scrounge or steal whatever food they could find and how they shared the spoils with each other. The consequence, Surtees reasons, was "innumerable robberies of potato fields and gardens . . . and many were the men that got punished for this crime, but it could not be put a stop to, for hunger is not easily borne."[34] On the subject of harshly judging the men because they chose to steal and live rather than follow orders that ignored their plight, James Anton, a sergeant in the 42nd Regiment of Foot, eloquently reminds us: "Soldiers are not philanthropists, and the questioner would perhaps be inclined to relax a little from the laudable principle which may actuate his conduct when sitting comfortably at home, were he placed under similar circumstances in a hostile country, after months of half-fasting and half-feeding on bare bones and moldy ship biscuit."[35]

The British soldier stole because he was often desperately hungry and because he sought escape from his unending daily misery in inebriation. Drunkenness and the ability to plunder did, in fact, become two learned avocations in which the vast majority of enlisted men put great stock. In this the British varied little from other soldiers of the Napoleonic Wars. These traits, however, must be considered within the context of the soldiers' life of hardship and with some understanding of how their shared values were shaped by behavioral constraints, as defined by the men's primary and secondary social groups.

The second constant found in primary sources relates to the degree to which group norms applied to actions such as looting: the spoils were not secreted and consumed by the soldier lucky or enterprising enough to find them. Personal chronicles reveal that food, liquor, or apparel items were routinely shared with the soldier's messmates, with very few exceptions. This collective altruism was in effect even when it meant dividing a small portion of food into a half-dozen or so minute shares. This process applied equally to the sharing of plundered foodstuffs and material items, just as it did to the distribution of daily rations.[36]

It is significant that all the firsthand accounts examined for this work contain a score of references to men sharing their meager findings but only three incidents in which a British soldier is accused of stealing from his compatriots.[37] In one of these cases, the soldier awoke to find that his haversack had been pilfered and with it his remaining rations. He then stole bread from a drunken, unconscious comrade but shared the spoils with another soldier who had been temporarily blinded.[38] Thefts among comrades seem to have been remarkably few in number, a view confirmed by Anton.[39] The penalty for such an action was almost always the permanent loss of the perpetrator's place in the group. For the British redcoat who lived and functioned within the concentric spheres of the mess group, company, and regiment,[40] such a fate was the equivalent of being declared anathema; it is difficult to avoid positing a causal relationship between behavior and group status.

Behavioral norms not only governed actions with respect to the group; they also extended to the soldier's interactions with civilians and the enemy. A common thread running through a great many firsthand sources (one usually ignored by historians rushing to condemn the character of the British soldier) is the existence of a limiting code of conduct among the rank and file related to what Grattan euphemistically described as slight breaches of discipline. The code was simple: stealing was acceptable; armed robbery or any accompanying acts of violence were not. (The exception to this rule was after assaults during sieges, as addressed below.) Men shunned comrades who were seen committing such acts or were suspected of doing so. This restraining set of rules applied to interactions with peasants as well as noncombat situations involving French soldiers. Anger, often tinged with collective shame, was directed at men who stepped outside the behavioral boundaries agreed upon by the group, violating the established norms.

The men lived by a set of principles, different from those held by civilians eating regularly and sleeping under a roof, as Anton reminds us, but ideals nevertheless. The soldiers expected each other to adhere to them and would not accept less from any other person they encountered. The British soldier might steal food or invade a home in pursuit of alcohol, but he rarely tolerated armed assault and wanton acts of cruelty or violence. In Lawrence's account of his many years as an enlisted man and sergeant of the 40th Regiment of Foot, he flatly admits that the men of his regiment stole; he also confirms that the British soldier would only go so far in his efforts to procure food and drink. He posits that the men rarely allowed events to escalate to the point where bloodshed was involved.[41]

The legal records of the British army during its Peninsular and French campaigns substantiate the existence of such a limiting behavioral code. The records reveal surprisingly few trials and convictions for armed assault, murder, and rape, all of which were capital offenses. According to F.S. Larpent, the judge advocate general during the Peninsular War, only 41 men were shot or hanged from 1812 to 1814, most for desertion.[42] This was in an army whose numbers exceeded 70,000 men by 1813.[43] Army courts-martial records also do not support the position that violent offenses were routinely committed by common soldiers.[44]

No proof has yet been uncovered that the British failed to prosecute serious crimes. Such a position taken by any regimental commander would have run counter to Wellington's efforts to avoid the kinds of frictional relationships with the civilian populace that so inhibited French strategy and would have been dealt with severely had he discovered officers turning a blind eye to offenses committed by British soldiers. Civilians did complain to Wellington about offenses but were sometimes too frightened or intimated or possessed insufficient proof to provide proper evidence to a court-martial. The difficulties of producing witnesses or even written depositions while the army was on the march proved an additional impediment to prosecuting cases.[45] While this implies that some criminal acts went unpunished, it is likely that the incidents mentioned in Wellington's letters were probably related to theft and not bodily assault or murder. But given Wellington's frequent use of the word "outrages" in his dispatches, it is difficult to identify for certain the types of crimes to which he was referring.[46]

Armed assaults, rapes, and murders were certainly committed by British regulars. Such crimes exist in all societies, across socioeconomic boundaries. It would be naïve to think otherwise. The Marqués de la Romana, for example, recalled with a fair degree of certainty that redcoats "killed three magistrates and various other inhabitants" during the retreat from Corunna. And though Charles Esdaile may be correct that Sir John Moore "pushed the men onwards [during the retreat] at a rate that was quite disproportionate to the danger," that would not excuse the soldiers for committing murder.[47] The question is whether such acts were typical or atypical behavior for British redcoats. In that regard, no substantiating evidence has yet been produced to support the claims that the British common soldier routinely committed such crimes with the frequency that has been assumed. Thus, without hard data it seems unfair to speculate that violent criminal acts were perpetrated in great numbers by the British rank and file. Such crimes were, most likely, fairly uncommon actions, carried out by a relatively small number of men. The case against the British soldier, it seems, rests more heavily on inferences than it does on evidence.

Considering Wellington's appraisal and the way in which historians have universally used his words to judge the character of the British soldier, there is more than a touch of irony in comparing the campaign behavior of British and French troops. Their actions have been interpreted in almost opposite fashions. The French seemingly committed the kinds of atrocities wrongly associated with British troops, while the British soldiers showed relative restraint. Oddly, historians have tended to excuse the behavior of the individual French soldier while excoriating the British ranker.

The French army often stole and burned and sometimes raped and murdered its way across the Iberian peninsula; the price of occupation extracted by the invading French forces varied by locale, Spanish resistance, and the availability of provisions. Mass executions of Spanish citizens believed to be guerrillas were probably carried out by various methods, including garroting, hanging, and firing squads.[48] The degree to which these acts can be verified is challenging: it remains uncertain how many were real atrocities and how many were part of the Spanish propaganda campaign against the French.[49] The French acts, however, were recorded in a great many letters and diaries and recalled in memoirs by stunned British soldiers, shocked at the ferocity and repeated violence against civilians. Unlike the vast majority of questionable evidence presented against British soldiers, we have much more documentation against the French, corroborated by British soldiers, by Spanish and Portuguese survivors, and by French combatants and observers. While somewhat vague in nature (with no quantifiable verification of the crimes committed by French soldiers), the evidence is considerably more substantial than that presented against the British ranker.

A description of one of the most disturbing episodes was provided by Sergeant Joseph Donaldson of the 94th. In 1811 he came across a chapel at Porto de Mos. Almost 200 townspeople, including children, had been herded inside before it was set afire, burning the people alive. Donaldson summarized the experience by noting: "The wanton cruelty of the French soldiers, on this retreat, defies description." He later discovered a "convent or chapel" in which the French had assaulted an entire Portuguese family. They shot the father, slit his wife's throat, then tied up the son and repeatedly beat and raped his sisters in front of him because he would not or could not reveal where the family's money was hidden. The reaction of Donaldson, who was apparently calloused by similar scenes across Spain and Portugal, tells us something about the common views as to the culprits: he commented with certainty that "such were the tender mercies of the French soldiery."[50]

George Simmons of the Rifles adds a tale concerning French troops under André Masséna inflicting revenge on their Portuguese hosts as the army evacuated Santarem in 1811 and marched toward the Spanish border. He writes: "Two young ladies had been brutally violated in a house that I entered, and were unable to rise from a mattress of straw. . . . It is beyond horrid. . . . Almost any man they [the French] get hold of they murder. The women they use too brutally for me to describe."[51]

The measured account of John Carss, a lieutenant in the 53rd during the peninsular campaign, leaves little doubt as to the nationality or purpose of the assailants. He wrote home in 1809, describing French barbarity toward Portuguese peasants. His letters outlined the resulting escalation of cruelties exchanged by the Portuguese and the French occupying forces, detailing how the Portuguese gained revenge on captured French soldiers. "They burned them," Carss recalled, "or hung them on trees naked. The French did the same with the Portuguese and burned almost every house on the retreat. Some villages they destroyed, and men, women, and children. No person would believe the cruelty of the French except they saw it."[52] It must be noted, however, that Carss does not provide unassailable proof or list the names and accounts of witnesses. Thus, in passing judgment on the conduct of French soldiers, we must be careful not to judge them by the same standards that have been unfairly applied to British regulars in the Peninsula.

Such excesses, though, were partially verified by a French naval captain, Pierre Baste, who saw French soldiers "sack Córdoba and deliver it up to all the horrors of a town taken by assault," even though the town was not defended. "Murder and pillage," he remembered, "were soon joined by the rape of women, virgins, and nuns, and the theft of sacred vessels from the churches."[53] The same occurred at Gamonal.[54] A French infantryman, François Lavaux, writing about the French occupation of Alcañiz, openly declared: "Having murdered everyone and looted everything in sight, we stayed on for another six weeks."[55]

Another French soldier, the cavalryman Marquant, questioned the effects of such a strategy of destruction. He was not surprised that Spain and other nations "take us for hordes of barbarians and brigands, that they should prefer their masters to our laws and that they should take every opportunity to defeat us. . . . If we are defenders of humanity and property, let us not violate them on the soil of others whom we are seeking to convert to the status of free men."[56]

Moreover, we have the visual weight of the paintings and drawings left to us by the Spanish painter Francisco Goya, an eyewitness to the events in Spain. Although a type of propaganda, Goya's works forever captured the horrific essence of French cruelty in the series entitled *The Disasters of War.* His scenes vividly presented manifestations of French violence and Spanish retaliation, in all its disturbing barbarity, depicting butchery in a fashion never before put to canvas.[57]

Esdaile, one of the most prominent scholars examining Spanish efforts against Napoleon, confirms that such underlying hatred and related atrocities—based on gross mistreatment of civilians by the French and reciprocating acts by the citizenry—marked Spanish-French interaction across much of Spain.[58] He describes wounded French soldiers in the hospital at Manzanares being beaten, thrown into ovens, hung in chimneys, burned and boiled alive, and hacked to death by Spanish locals. Laure Junot, the beautiful wife of the French general, corroborates the self-perpetuating nature of this destructive environment: "The most revolting injustices were being committed by our men, often in reprisal for atrocities that had been inflicted on us, and these outrages were being avenged in their turn so that a chain of disasters had been unleashed of which there was no hope of seeing the end."[59]

Esdaile also writes of British regulars discovering French soldiers mutilated and nailed to barn doors and angry mobs of peasants demanding the right to murder French prisoners under British guard.[60] French violence was so extreme that concomitant civilian retribution rose to levels that threatened French communication, affected strategic choices, and worked to lower French morale precipitously, seriously threatening unit cohesion.[61]

The French plundered their own compatriots with the same zeal and efficiency during their retreat in 1814, although the soldiers did not savage the populace as they did the common folk of the Peninsula. The letters of Arthur Kennedy, who saw much of Spain and France while making the transition from infantry officer of the 24th to cavalry lieutenant of the 18th Light Dragoons, record his surprise at the degree to which the French stripped their own people of every edible, potable, or salable commodity. Kennedy noted that the French had not been paid in 20 months but nevertheless expressed great pity for the French peasantry, who were left with nothing.[62] Kennedy's recollections are noteworthy because they illustrate that the French could be selective with their violence, limiting their conduct with French noncombatants but not with Iberian peasants.

In contrast, Edward Heeley, a batman to Lieutenant-Colonel Sir George Scovell, the assistant quartermaster general to the army, recorded in his journal that during the British pursuit of the French army through southern France: "All the good behavior of the British soldiers quite endeared them to the inhabitants."[63] This was a time, no doubt, when the men were receiving their rations and pay on a fairly regular basis.

Despite the evidence of French misconduct, historians have not used terms such as "rogue," "thug," "criminal," or "scum" to describe Napoleon's soldiers. Often needing food as much as the British soldier he fought against, the French enlisted man stole to live; but in his looting endeavors he appears to have been more inclined to rape and murder to take what he needed than was his British counterpart. His behavior was predicated on a set of group standards markedly different than those of the British soldier, at least on campaign in foreign lands. This is especially evident in French army songs, which implied not only that military service made French soldiers irresistible to women in other countries but that the potential for rape was an expected bonus and part of campaign life. As Michael Hughes puts it, "In addition to the baubles awarded by Napoleon, songs offered sex in exchange for military service. The camp songs communicated an unmistakable message through the repeated descriptions of the sexual adventures of the *grognards*."[64]

Often the French soldier viewed violence off the battlefield as a tool necessary for his survival and, perhaps, one that granted him access to the spoils of war as he saw them, his rewards being justified by his efforts and his position as conqueror. His offenses, though, are attributed to cultural frictions, privations, desperation, and the natural enmity that arises between victor and vanquished, played out with increasing angst and resentment over an extended period; they are never ascribed to the French soldier's failings as an individual. In addition, it is worth observing that while such offenses against civilians were considered crimes in the French army, they were not likely to be prosecuted.

In contrast, the British ranker, constrained by group values (much more than by the threat of the lash and gallows), usually treated civilians with a comparatively high degree of respect. He plundered his Spanish and Portuguese hosts because the army failed to feed him properly and regularly. He looted their hidden valuables and ran off with their bread and wine, but he rarely accosted their persons, viewing such assaults as outside the norms of acceptable behavior. Yet it is the British regular, not the French soldier, who has acquired a reputation as an unsavory and reprehensible fellow, undaunted by either conscience or an appreciation of societal values. Admittedly, the French were at war with the Portuguese and Spanish, while the British were not. But the dichotomy between their reputations and their conduct toward noncombatants is striking; despite Esdaile's claim that British rank and file committed crimes "at least as bad as anything perpetrated by the French,"[65] the two sides clearly interacted with civilians in significantly different ways.

It would be disingenuous, at this point, not to address the behavior of the British soldier after successful siege assaults. Here the behavioral constraints enforced by the group were abandoned during post-assault rampages, such as at Badajoz and Ciudad Rodrigo (both in 1812) and San Sebastian (in 1813).

In order to appreciate fully why usual standards of behavior were abandoned after siege assaults, it is necessary to understand the nature of such attacks. Storming bastions required soldiers to negotiate the glacis, the ditch, and then the breach; the men were exposed to heavy and direct fire the entire time. Casualty rates for assaulting troops during these nighttime attacks were horrific, often approaching 100 percent for lead units.

In spite of the odds, the soldiers under Wellington made a series of attacks, usually forcing their way up and through the breaches and into the various citadels, gaining him the quick but costly victories that he needed to maintain his strategic initiative. Those redcoats who survived the assault—motivated by revenge, relief, and the opportunity to fulfill their desires for alcohol, women, and loot—imposed themselves on the citizenry. They committed the kinds of transgressions (such as assault, armed robbery, rape, and even murder) that deservedly earned Robert Blakeney's description of them as "a pack of hell-hounds vomited up from the infernal regions."[66] Blakeney, an officer of the 36th, is often unfairly critical of the men, but in this case his description seems appropriate. The soldiers' behavioral excesses during these limited and special circumstances are also the basis for much of the misjudgment and disapprobation of historians ever since. (Siege assaults are dealt with in more detail in chapter 7.)

Still, even at their worst, it appears that the misdeeds of the British soldier only approximated those of his French counterpart; the British ranker never engaged in the mass slaughter and ongoing depredations that vilified the French soldiery in the eyes of the Spanish and Portuguese. Rather than serving as proof of the base nature of the British infantryman, the soldiers' actions during postassault rampages are the outcome of a series of complex, interwoven motivations based on group dynamics, siege assault rules, the experiences and expectations of the attacker, and the British soldier's life of deprivation.

The siege behavior of the rank and file, though, has all too often been presented as an example of the British ranker's conduct and character in general. Wellington's words, unquestioned as to their accuracy, seemed to reinforce this judgment. A close examination of primary-source documents, however, presents an alternative explanation underlying the redcoat's deportment and motivations. The British regular of the Peninsula campaign, despite his unjustly acquired reputation, was no more a criminal than any other soldier of the Napoleonic Wars. He was a man, common in almost every respect except for his ability to adapt and survive under extremely difficult circumstances. Excluded from a civilian society that had no need for him, the ranker joined the army mostly for economic reasons. Once in the army, he found in the primary and secondary groups of his unit a new home and family. Adherence to group norms enabled the soldier to garner esteem and personal value; the group also enhanced his chances of survival. That he desired membership in such groups and was successfully able to function therein is evidence that he was not an antisocial individual, alienated from his fellow soldiers and all those with whom he had contact. His actions, even when looting, were those of a man very susceptible to normative constraints.

The British soldier lived and fought as a member of a small, tightly knit band of comrades. His need to give and receive support as part of this component of the regiment engendered exceptional cohesion, which gave him a small but significant advantage in battle. By adopting the group's shared values, the soldier learned to fight to preserve himself and the integrity of his unit. The ability of the British regular to withstand the demands of close combat and privations of campaigning was not founded on his flawed and cruel character, supposedly revealed in his propensity for plundering and fondness for drink and violence. He may have earned his daily shilling in the service of the king, but his allegiance, behavior on the march, and battlefield performance were shaped by the close relationships to the men with whom he lived, fought, and often perished. The British ranker's need to belong, not his base nature, allowed him to become one of the steadiest and continuously successful combat soldiers of the Napoleonic Wars.

1

AN UNJUST REPUTATION

The Genesis of the "Scum of the Earth" Myth

It is not difficult to trace the origins of the myth of the British soldier as "scum" or to see how, through repetition, the idea evolved
into the established view of the common redcoat's background and
traits. Ascertaining why Wellington made such derogatory judgments (when he clearly knew that supply shortages were as often as
not the cause of the solders' misconduct) and why his comments
have been accepted at face value, without examination, is much more
challenging.

The myth grew into collective memory because Wellington made
a series of contemptuous remarks over an extended period regarding
the British rank and file.[1] Scholars, not unreasonably, have assigned
great weight to Wellington's running commentary, quoting his negative appraisals of the men's character in numerous works on the Napoleonic period.[2] Perpetuated over time, these judgments have colored analysis of the British soldier, the reasons behind his success on
the battlefield, and his conduct on campaign. As a result, the ranker's
motivations and achievements have been either misunderstood or
overlooked entirely, largely obscured by Wellington's observations.

Alone and unanalyzed, Wellington's words, particularly taken in
colorful snippets, do not provide a sufficient evidentiary basis to as-

sess the nature of his soldiers. A measured examination of the complex issues regarding human behavior, especially in the often harrowing and chaotic circumstances of campaign and combat, requires more than just one eyewitness; even an observer with the knowledge and experience of Wellington cannot be ceded sole authority on the issue without collateral findings to support his observations. His writings regarding the soldiers, their conduct, and the reasons underlying their actions are, in fact, sometimes contradictory. Wellington's motivations and the impetus behind many of his comments were more multifaceted than has been acknowledged. Looking beyond the individual observations made by Wellington, and investigating the background and circumstances related to his assessments of the men, confirms that he was well acquainted with the adversity faced by the men but was also restricted from openly recognizing the difficulties that affected his men by command issues and financial conditions in many cases and by his own social standing and experiences in others. Wellington's perceptions appear to have caused him to attribute soldiers' behavior to innate character flaws, rather than to the extenuating challenges of campaign life.[3]

Wellington's letters and conversations regarding the character of the rankers he led portrayed them as the dregs of society. Because these vivid and damning appraisals have been quoted so widely, they serve here as a starting point in examining Wellington's assessments and the constraints under which he labored.

The earliest recorded occasion on which Wellington openly expressed his contempt for the men under his command was in a letter to the Earl of Bathurst, written near the end of the war (2 July 1813) from Huarte, Spain. Wellington lamented: "We have in the service the scum of the earth as common soldiers." He complained of efforts in England to stop flogging: "And as of late years we have been doing everything in our power both by law and publications to relax the discipline by which alone such men can be kept in order." Wellington then added to the insult: "It is really a disgrace to have to say anything to such men as some of our soldiers are."[4]

Wellington expressed similar sentiments almost 15 years after Waterloo: "The man who enlists in the British army is, in general, the most drunken, and probably the worst of his trade or profession to which he belongs, or the village or town in which he lives."[5]

In letters composed in April 1829 and March 1832, Wellington further impugned the rank and file: "In ninety-nine cases out of a hundred, soldiers enlisted on account of some idle or irregular, or even vicious motive." He went on to state that iron discipline alone could "remove those irregular or vicious habits."[6]

One of Wellington's most well-known appraisals came almost two decades after the conclusion of the Napoleonic Wars. In conversations with the Earl of Stanhope, enthusiastically and surreptitiously recorded by the earl, Wellington again derided the British soldier. He reiterated his position in an exchange on 4 November 1831: "I don't mean to say that there is no difference in the composition or therefore the feeling of the French army and ours. The French system of conscription brings together a fair sample of all classes; ours is composed of the scum of the earth—the mere scum of the earth. It is only wonderful that we should be able to make so much out of them afterwards. The English soldiers are fellows who have enlisted for drink—that is the plain fact—they have all enlisted for drink."[7]

Wellington communicated his disdain in an even more scathing, though very similar, assessment during another conversation with Stanhope a week later. In that exchange, Wellington first spoke emphatically for a strong system of military punishment and then commented on the difference between the French and British armies:

> Oh, they [the French] bang them about very much with ramrods and that sort of thing, and then they shoot them. Besides, a French army is composed very differently than ours. The conscription calls out a share of every class—no matter whether your son or my son—all must march; but our friends—I may say it in this room—are the very scum of the earth. People talk of their enlisting from their fine military feeling—no such thing. Some of our men enlist from having got bastard children—some for minor offenses—many more for drink; but you can hardly conceive such a set brought together, and it really is wonderful that we should have made them the fine fellows they are.[8]

While he is fairly consistent in his pejorative evaluations of the soldiers, at least in the later years of the struggle in Spain and Portugal and after the war, Wellington's writings during his command years also describe many of the reasons that caused the men to plunder. His letters present an astute understanding of the factors, mostly economic, that worked to prevent him from feeding and caring properly for the army. Throughout the peninsular campaign, the British, Portuguese, and Spanish armies were plagued by logistical shortfalls. A large number of Wellington's communications disclose the degree to which the armies under his command suffered. In three such letters written in August 1809 right after the battle of Talavera, he complained about the lack of supplies. To J.H. Frere he wrote: "In the meantime, with all these movements, we are horribly distressed for provisions. The soldiers seldom get enough to eat, and what they do get is delivered to them half mouldy, and at hours at which they ought to be at rest."[9]

Wellington openly described the dire straits in which the British-led forces found themselves regarding rations to Marshal William Beresford: "We are starving, our men falling sick, and we have nothing to give them in the way of comfort for their recovery. . . . We have not had a full ration of provisions ever since the 22nd of last month [a span of 28 days]; and I am convinced that in that time the men have not received ten days' bread, and the horses not three regular deliveries of barley."[10]

In a letter written three weeks later to the Duke of Richmond, Wellington described the deteriorating situation faced by the soldiers under his command: "Starvation has produced such dire effects upon the army, we have suffered so much, and have received so little assistance from the Spaniards, that I am at last compelled to move back into Portugal to look for subsistence. . . . They cannot say we were compelled to go therefore by the enemy, but by a necessity created by the neglect of the Spaniards of our wants."[11]

Wellington wrote repeatedly to authorities and peers in Great Britain, Spain, and Portugal, cajoling officials to provide both gold and provisions to the forces fighting the French on the Peninsula.[12] He complained openly in May 1810 to Charles Stuart (later the 1st Baron Stuart de Rothesay) about the difficulties of campaigning without sufficient logistical and financial support: "It has rarely happened that an army . . . has been obliged to carry on operations in a country in which there is literally no food; and in which, if there was food, there is no money to purchase it." The situation was grave enough that Wellington considered withdrawing the army and returning to Great Britain.[13]

In a dispatch to Brigadier-General Robert Craufurd dated 20 May 1810, Wellington voiced his displeasure with administrative limitations that hindered his ability to look after his men and make use of them as soldiers. "The Commissary General is forbidden," he noted unhappily, "to give money in lieu of rations, to give back rations, &c. &c." Expressing his concern for the Portuguese army in a letter to Stuart, Wellington later argued that he was responsible for his conduct and that of the armies under his command, but the Portuguese Regency government appeared less concerned about how its lack of action affected the troops. He asked the Regency to acknowledge the legitimacy of his requests, especially regarding funding for the army defending Spain and Portugal.[14]

Wellington's anger at the continued governmental neglect of the army, and the resulting misbehavior of the soldiers who were forced to plunder because they were not fed, surfaced in his correspondence with Stuart. "It is impossible," he reasoned, "to punish soldiers, who are left to starve, for outrages committed in order to procure food; and, at all events, no punishment, however severe, will have the desired effect of preventing the troops from seizing what they can get to satisfy their appetite, when neglected by those whose duty it is to supply their wants."[15]

The situation remained unresolved by Wellington's standards in the summer of 1811, when he made yet another stern complaint about Portuguese governmental failures and their effects on the Portuguese army. Responding to Stuart, he expressed his exasperation:

> In respect to the papers and returns forwarded in your letter, I shall not even take the trouble of reading them, because I know they are fabricated for a particular purpose, and they cannot contain an answer to the strong fact stated by me, viz., that owing to neglect, deficiency of arrangement, and omission of the Government to supply the means, the army and their equipments were starved during the winter, and that, when the moment of action came, the soldiers and animals were unable to perform the service; the former deserted or went to the hospital, and the latter died.[16]

This oft-repeated set of circumstances harried Wellington and his soldiers throughout the Peninsular War. The sheer number of his letters on this topic leaves little doubt that Wellington recognized the deleterious effects of short rations on soldiers in the field. His peninsular correspondence differed only in details from dispatches that he sent during his years in India, in which he praised the men for their conduct in battle, cajoled the government for adequate funds to feed and pay the soldiers, and castigated the rankers for their willingness to plunder when they were not fed. He stated his concern for the soldiers in a letter composed while the army was encamped at Senboogaum. Writing to Colonel John Murray in August 1803, Wellington declared: "Every attention must be paid to economy, but I consider nothing in this country so valuable as the life and health of the British soldier, and nothing so expensive as soldiers in the hospital. On this ground, it is worth while to incur almost any expense to preserve their lives and their health. I also request you to pay particular attention to their discipline and regularity, and to prevent their getting intoxicating liquors, which tend to their destruction."[17]

Thus, it is clear that Wellington had a sound understanding of the campaign realities encountered by the rank and file. He even acknowledged the hardships faced by the soldiers' families back home and how distressed families contributed to desertion rates. In an 1811 letter to Lieutenant Colonel Henry Torrens, military secretary to the commander-in-chief,[18] Wellington articulated his concern regarding the lack of benefits extended to families of line soldiers. Detailing the inequities of line service over militia duty and the related practical considerations of recruiting, Wellington identified one of the most significant problems confronting men who volunteered for regular service: the families of soldiers in the militia were provided for, while those of men serving in line units were not. He suggested that this arrangement be reversed and concluded that better men would enlist and that desertion would decrease if financial support was afforded to dependents of recruits who signed up for service in the regular army.[19]

Wellington also addressed the unfairness of paying noncommissioned officers (NCOs) little more than privates, noting that the old pay proportions were not retained when soldier pay increased to one shilling. In order to preserve the distinction and status of corporals and sergeants, whom Wellington rightly identified as the foundation on which army discipline rested, he suggested to Lord Liverpool (Robert Jenkinson) that pay increases be instituted for all noncommissioned officers.[20] While this may have been purely an administrative suggestion to enhance disciplinary control, it still illustrates Wellington's cognizance of the details of daily life as they affected the soldiery.

Hence it cannot be said that Wellington was unaware of or unconcerned about the difficulties faced by his men. Yet his dispatches and later commentary regarding the characters of the men often focus almost solely on the soldiers' plundering, while disregarding the inadequacy of rations, which was the dominant catalyst that drove the redcoat to steal and added to his zeal for drink. The inconsistency in some of Wellington's letters reveals a growing frustration with the men's behavior, the governmental neglect that forced the situation on him, and, perhaps, his emerging and final perception of the issue. He appears to have viewed the continued looting (of food, alcohol, and other items) as an ongoing command problem; if the government made it impossible to feed the men, then the soldiers would just have to endure the privation. No excuses would be accepted and no exceptions granted.

Writing to Lord Liverpool in the spring of 1810, Wellington complained: "We are still much distressed for money, and I shall not be able to pay the troops on the 24th of this month."[21] In the same letter he railed against what he called the "disgraceful outrages" of plunder and expressed his determination to have rankers who were convicted as thieves executed, as a means of inducing the officers, noncommissioned officers, and men to curtail theft, regardless of circumstances.

That same month Wellington bemoaned rising desertion rates in a letter to the adjutant general of the forces. He attributed the increased desertion "in a great measure to the bad description of the men . . . who have been received principally from the Irish militia," the inattention of those in command, and the "irregular and predatory habits of the soldiers."[22] He then went on to state strongly that the men had no real cause for desertion. In direct contradiction of his letter to Lord Liverpool, Wellington claimed that their duty was light, their quarters good, their pay regular, and their accounts balanced and that "there had been no distress for provisions since the month of August."[23]

Less than a year later Wellington admitted to Dr. James McGrigor, the director general of the Army Medical Board, that "pecuniary dis-

tresses of this army" prevented the soldiers from being paid monthly;
but he refused to acknowledge the effects of short rations and no pay
on the men. Wellington explained the oddities of the system that
prevented him from settling accounts but never addressed the severe
impact on the men resulting from such limitations: "The pay of the
army is seldom less than three months in arrear; but no more than one
month's pay is ever issued at a time, and the balance due on one
month's account only can be given at one time." The men's diet was
nutritionally insufficient even when issued regularly (see chapter 3
and appendix C). Without pay, the soldiers could not hope to buy
supplemental food, which was a physiological necessity, given the
physical demand of campaigning. Pay shortages therefore greatly increased the likelihood that the rank and file would turn to plunder in
an effort to avoid malnutrition and sometimes starvation. The missing monthly paydays also affected desertion rates: some men left their
units in search of food and other soldiers quit the ranks entirely, dis-
pirited by an institution that demanded much but delivered little. In
addressing McGrigor's report on army mortality, Wellington appears
to forget his previous letters describing starving soldiers; he dismisses
the correlation between McGrigor's statistics on deceased soldiers
and the nutritional deprivation resulting from inadequate provisions
and pay, claiming that the men's "rations are invariably delivered to
the soldiers daily, except on marches."[24]

As logistical difficulties continued to create disciplinary issues,
Wellington refused to acknowledge that the root cause of much of the
men's misbehavior was the lack of food and pay. In his famous order
to all brigade and divisional officers under his command, issued in
November 1812, his disgust with his leaders and their failure to control the soldiers is most evident. He contends that the inattention of
the officers allowed the men to commit "irregularities and outrages
of all descriptions . . . with impunity," stating bluntly that the soldiers had no reasons to misbehave: "This army has met with no disaster; it has suffered no privations which but trifling attention on the
part of the officers could not have prevented, and for which there
existed no reason whatever in the nature of the service; nor has it
suffered any hardships excepting those resulting from the necessity
of being exposed to the inclemencies of the weather at a moment
when they were most severe."[25]

While Wellington may have been referring strictly to the campaign season of the summer and fall of 1812, his other letters and the personal accounts of British regulars affirm that food shortages and missed paydays were common experiences throughout the Peninsular War. Wellington may have been dealing with the problem by attempting to influence the only variable he felt he could control outright: the men's reaction to the army's inability to provide for their needs. He viewed plundering as more than just a matter of discipline. The French had mistreated the people of the Iberian Peninsula, with looting, rape, assault, and sometimes murder becoming all too common. In doing so, the French turned the Spanish and Portuguese populations against them; the fierce episodes of retribution from both sides altered French strategy and greatly impaired operations. For Wellington, it was a command imperative to prevent his men from alienating the populace in a similar manner. Perhaps, in this regard, he began to look upon the men more as instruments that needed rigid management and less as human beings in need of food, care, and rest. As the peninsular campaign unfolded, Wellington discovered that logistical problems remained a constant, as did the soldiers' need to steal in order to eat, despite his best efforts to use harsh discipline as a deterrent. Thus, his negative comments regarding the men's characters may be attributed in part to his growing frustration with a set of circumstances that he could not manage to his satisfaction, yet which threatened to upset the army's tenuous relationship with the people of Spain and Portugal.

The possibility also exists that class perceptions shaped Wellington's sensitivity to the soldiers, their needs, and their reactions. He never addressed this directly, so we are left to conjecture, putting his views into a social context. While we would not expect Wellington to be conscious that his perceptions and class norms were not absolutes or admit that such a top-down perspective might be flawed, we must consider his judgments within the larger social picture.

Wellington was an unusually discerning and gifted individual. Still, his attitude toward the lower social orders—which included the soldiers, who were primarily drawn from the laboring class—may reflect some of the prejudices of the affluent and powerful societal groups in Georgian England. Rural and urban laborers were often viewed as threats, lying in wait to upset societal order, abscond with stolen goods, and overthrow those who held power. This was especially true after the events of the French Revolution, which seemed to confirm the worst fears of the aristocracy and landed gentry regarding the negative traits and inherent failings of working-class people in general.[26]

Wellington's writings seem to reflect a certain impatience and dissatisfaction with—and later outright distaste for—common soldiers. His repeated references to the men's baseness and what he saw as their innate tendencies toward reprehensible behavior do not align with the campaign challenges that he knew existed and that compelled the men to act as they did. Nor did his pejorative opinions of the redcoats extend to their behavior under fire; the British regulars never let Wellington down on the battlefield, and his comments reflect this. Perhaps the rankers' repeated refusal to adhere to his strictures regarding plundering—when food, drink, and pay were not provided regularly—reinforced his prejudices regarding the supposed character failings of men from the lower rungs of the social order. Additionally, his role as commander forced Wellington to view mission success as all important; if the actions of his men, however justified by events or commissariat failures, jeopardized operations, he may have had little choice but to attempt to rein in the soldiers. He could hardly do so if he acknowledged the legitimacy of their complaints. All we can say for certain is that something colored Wellington's vision of the men who served under him.

Some of Wellington's officers were perhaps equally limited by such perceptions. The majority of his officers were sons of professional men (doctors, lawyers, businessmen, and so forth) or country gentry; a select 2–3 percent came from the aristocracy and the upper echelons of society.[27] The social and economic differences between officers of what today might be called middle-class or upper-middle-class origins and the men they led may have made it difficult for many of the officers to understand the men, their motivations, and their daily tribulations. The struggles of men who could find no employment and were castoffs of the economy were foreign to officers who had spent hundreds of pounds purchasing their commissions. This was especially true in regard to the effects of the commissariat failures on the lives of the common soldiers. The ranker suffered terribly when rations were not delivered; he learned to plunder rather than starve. The majority of officers, meanwhile, ate not only regularly but well in the officers' mess, purchasing their food locally with discretionary personal income.

Sensitivity to their roles as defenders not only of culture but of the social caste system of Georgian England may have predisposed some officers to view the men as inferiors. In treating the rankers as unsavory and wayward miscreants who required the occasional reminder of the lash to keep them in order and in their place, officers followed the established norms of British society, which regarded the lower classes as dangerous and corporal punishment as necessary for their control. In his work on the armies of Revolutionary France, Samuel Scott provides a cautionary note regarding the frequency and validity of soldier appraisals viewed through such a social lens. "It is more likely," he argues, "that claims about the number of beggars and criminals in the [French] army are based on prejudice both contemporary and subsequent, and partly on the identification of the unemployed members of the lower classes with social derelicts."[28] Scott's words certainly apply to most examinations of the British army as well. When trying to reassess the behavior and character of the British soldier, the possibility of such prejudices must be kept in mind.

In addition, the collective memory of the ranker as a distrusted, violent thug evolved in part because the memoirs, journals, and letters of the officers were considered more valuable than accounts by common soldiers. Many of the writings left by officers provide an almost idealized view of campaign life and warfare. Details regarding the sufferings of the rank and file on the march and the men's psychological reactions to the carnage and human loss that accompanied battle are glaringly absent. In their place are references to the countryside, interesting encounters, the beauty of native women, hunting, difficulties with servants, leisurely life, and the full bounty of the officer's mess (often including price lists of the various foodstuffs purchased to ensure that the evening meal was up to standards). Lieutenant-Colonel John Leach's account is a case in point. He portrayed campaigning as something of a sportsman's holiday, describing the joys of hunting hares, partridges, quails, and rabbits with hounds.[29]

Moyle Sherer, an officer in the 34th, was more attuned to the tribulations of the men, often noting the positive quality of their characters. Nevertheless, he provides us with another example of the contrast between the soldier's view of army life and that of the moneyed officer. Sherer wrote of doing frequent business with the sutlers that followed the army. His depiction of army experiences on the march stands in contrast to the tales of want and misery that fill so many enlisted men's accounts. "Thus we were often well . . . supplied with many comforts," he recalled, "such as teas, sugar, brandies, wines, segars [sic], &c." He said that army life only lacked "books and the society of women." Sherer and officers of his means also bought food from peasants: "We paid liberally for everything . . . [and the peasants] brought us constant supplies of bread, milk, eggs, poultry, honey, and excellent country wine."[30]

Nineteenth-century Britain, perhaps seeking to justify its colonial endeavors and its rightful place as the dominant world power, saw in certain officers' accounts war as civilians often wish to see it: as a necessary and fairly comfortable endeavor. Few people enjoy the ever-present reminders of war's enduring ugliness; the cruelties and degradations so often described in the chronicles of common redcoats may have been too painful to merit full remembrance. For this very reason, after every war the hardships and the personal sufferings of the everyday soldier are usually forgotten by the general public but never by the men in arms.

Moreover, the experiences of the officer class in Spain and the war's outcome provided a parallel with world events that unfolded during Britain's imperial expansion. The officers' tales may have been perceived as examples of gentlemanly behavior and an affirmation of sorts that the hierarchical British social system produced leaders with a natural affinity for governing the less fortunate lower classes, a concept easily extended to exercising authority over indigenous peoples in foreign lands. The officers' chronicles to a great degree reflected the values of the upper levels of society and thus were granted distinction, while the more telling first-person accounts of enlisted men were overlooked.

Most historians inevitably have followed suit, allowing Wellington's evaluation and those of select officers to shape current works on the subjects of the British army and the common soldier.[31] While their descriptions vary, writers of British military history almost always depict the British regular as a feckless rogue, thief, scoundrel, criminal, and undesirable.[32] He is accused of being gathered from the darkest, most dangerous streets and from jail cells and herded straight into the army, where brutal discipline curbed his baser tendencies and allowed him to be of some use to his country.[33] A few examples illustrate how writers analyzing the Peninsular War have done little more than echo Wellington's judgment on the subject.

Richard Glover's assessment of the British ranker serves as the prototypical case of using Wellington's words, sometimes with artistic license, to create a colorful if inaccurate portrayal of the men. Glover describes the rank and file of the British army as "appalling thugs" who required flogging to be controlled. He argues that they were successful on the battlefield because "these drunken thugs were tough with a ruggedness unknown and scarcely conceivable in the decorous modern England of today." Glover further claims that men were willing to undergo a flogging for a bottle of rum and surmises that "either men or rum are not today what they were in the robust eighteenth century." As a last judgment, he asserts that the soldiers regularly committed acts of "robbery and murder" when not in sight of their officers and that these officers had some effect only because their presence reminded the men of the lash and military justice.[34]

Glover's contentions are as specious as they are dramatic. He provides absolutely no substantiation to support his claim that the British ranker was a brute or a murderer. Nor does he offer any evidence for his assessment that men today are any less capable or have less grit than those of the eighteenth and nineteenth centuries. In addition, his conceptualization of combat success being dependent on the thuggish nature of the men runs against all the literature on the behavior of soldiers in combat. His remark on the robustness of men and rum is amusing but inane.

Arthur Bryant, a biographer and admirer of Wellington, also does not mince words in his description of the British ranker: "His [Wellington's] regiments were still recruited from the national rag-tag-and-bob-tail: penniless, drunken Irish peasants, village bad characters, slum bullies and pimps, and balloted ploughboys with a penchant for drinking and roving."[35] Like Glover, Bryant provides nothing in the way of documentation to substantiate his claims. His evaluation seems in large part to be a clever rewording of Wellington's compiled thoughts on the rankers in general.

C. T. Atkinson also reiterates Wellington's position, arguing that his "scum of the earth" characterization "was not without justification." He then claims that the army showed its good character in France by its "abstention from plunder" only because flogging had "taught it how to behave."[36] Atkinson does not seem to consider it pertinent that the men were regularly being fed during their advance across France, which was the exception rather than the rule for the British army on the march.

Such unsupported opinions, reiterated by a great number of writers, have added little to our understanding of the British soldier. Moreover, the collective opinions of so many scholars have acted to limit more thorough investigation into the lives and motivations of the common redcoat. The result has been the perpetuation of the "scum of the earth" myth, an invention that has left us with marginal insight into how the men perceived and dealt with the ordeals of life on campaign and the awful, stomach-turning tests of the battlefield.

The disconnect between the uneven evidence provided by Wellington's dispatches (and the willingness of historians to condemn the character of the British redcoat based solely on his opinions) and the realities of soldier life on campaign and in combat is even more pronounced in view of the large number of positive commentaries regarding the soldiers' character and capabilities. Many of his contemporaries considered this widely disparaged British ranker to be one of the most reliable combat soldiers of the Napoleonic period, renowned for his courage, discipline under fire, professional competence, compassion for his comrades, and ability to endure hardship. Even Wellington, usually stinting when it came to praise but not condemnation, did not deny their fighting capability. While his remarks in public dispatches, which often had political and leadership implications, did not always align with his personal views, he often seemed to take delight in the rankers' steadiness on the field of battle. John Carss, a lieutenant in the 53rd Regiment of Foot, related his pleasure in the infantry's recognition by Wellington after the battle of Talavera (28–29 July 1809). In a letter home, Carss proudly stated that "Sir Arthur sent down to General A. Campbell commanding our brigade to say we were the bravest fellows in the world and he had not the words to express how highly he was pleased with our conduct."[37]

In May 1811 Wellington further marveled at his soldiers' abilities after the battle of Albuera, which was primarily a contest of infantry: "It is impossible by any description to do justice to the distinguished gallantry of our troops; but every individual nobly did his duty; and it is observed that they . . . were lying, as they fought in the ranks, every wound in the front."[38] He also commented in a letter on the costly nature of the battle and the reason the British emerged victorious: "Another such battle could ruin us, and Soult claimed he had won a victory but, they [the British soldiers] did not know it and would not run."[39]

In a letter dated 18 July 1813, Wellington added to his praise: "It [the British army] is . . . an unrivaled army for fighting."[40] Less than a week later George Woodbury, an officer in the 10th Regiment of Foot and later the 18th Hussars, was gladdened to hear Wellington express similar praise regarding the men's fighting abilities. "Thank God we are not stigmatized with cowardice," Wellington exclaimed, "if we are for plundering."[41]

Approximately two years later Wellington expressed similar sentiments during a conversation with the Radical member of parliament Thomas Creevey on 24 April 1815. During their talk, Wellington tried to allay Creevey's fears concerning Napoleon's chances of victory in his Belgian campaign. When asked if he might need the support of Louis XVIII's royal French troops, Wellington scoffed and replied: "Oh! Don't mention such fellows! No: I think Blücher and I can do the business." Pointing to a British infantryman standing nearby, he said: "There, it all depends upon that article whether we do the business or not. Give me enough of it, and I am sure."[42] Elizabeth Longford, Wellington's most capable biographer, argues that Wellington meant these words as atonement for his "scum of the earth" epithet.[43] It is unlikely, however, that Wellington intended to make amends. He was probably simply stating his opinion of their combat value, something he saw as having little or no correlation with their character.

No less a figure than Napoleon seemed to agree that the outcome of battles between the French and the British hinged on the steadiness of the British soldier. The Corsican had some measure of respect for the British infantrymen, even though their effectiveness in combat had cost him dearly. The emperor once told General Maximilien Foy, sent to him in Paris by Marshal Masséna to explain the series of defeats inflicted by the British, that the reason for the repeated French defeats was fairly simple: the French were afraid of the British soldiers. "Well, you see," Napoleon commented, "the English have always beaten them."[44]

The record of British victories explains why Napoleon made disparaging remarks about the British soldiers and Wellington before the battle of Waterloo; his expressed sentiments were intended to boost the morale of his generals, who were cowed to some extent by the prospect of facing the British army on that last, desperate campaign in June 1815. "Just because you have all been beaten by Wellington," Napoleon sneered, "you think he's a good general. I tell you Wellington is a bad general, the English are bad troops, and this affair is nothing more than eating breakfast." Marshal Nicolas Soult, who had experienced the battlefield competence and ferocity of the British infantry in numerous battles during his long years in Spain, may have thought otherwise. He replied wishfully: "I earnestly hope so."[45]

During his final exile on the island of St. Helena, Napoleon was doubtless freer to express his true judgment. There he opined: "If I had had an English army, I would have conquered the universe."[46]

Sir William Napier, who served during the Peninsular War as a captain and then a major in the 43rd Regiment of Foot and who commanded the men in question, wrote an extensive and influential history of the campaign. He disagreed vehemently with Wellington's infamous "scum" evaluation. Napier openly praised and defended the British regular:

> The whole world cannot produce a nobler specimen of military bearing, nor is the mind unworthy of the outward man . . . he is observant, and quick to comprehend his orders, full of resources under difficulties, calm and resolute in danger, and more than usually obedient. . . . It has been asserted that his [the British soldier's] undeniable firmness in battle is the result of a phlegmatic constitution uninspired by moral feeling. Never was a more stupid calumny uttered! Napoleon's troops fought in bright fields, where every helmet caught some beams of glory, but the British soldier conquered under the cold shade of aristocracy; no honors awaited his daring, no despatch gave his name to the applause of his countrymen; his life of danger was uncheered by hope, his death unnoticed. Did his heart sink therefore? Did he not endure with surpassing fortitude the sorest of ills, sustain the most terrible assaults in battle unmoved, and with incredible energy overthrow every opponent, at all times proving that no physical military qualification was wanting, the fount of honour was also full and fresh within him![47]

Captain John Kincaid of the 95th Rifles perceived the same stead-fastness and courage in the men under his command. He wrote proudly, amazed at "their constancy under the most desperate cir-cumstances . . . though they might be destroyed, they were not to be beaten."[48]

Sherer, as noted, also found the British common soldier to be most admirable. He believed soldiers were as virtuous as any other members of civil society: "It will be remarked by those who live among soldiers, that they are charitable and generous, kind to chil-dren, and fond of dumb animals; add to this, a frequent exposure to hardship, privation, and danger, make them friendly and ready to assist each other . . . the worthless characters who are to be met with in every regiment (and society) are generally shunned."[49]

Sherer later waxed poetic on the British soldier's sense of duty and determination during combat and captured his matter-of-fact at-titude regarding danger in battle: "I am one who suspects that three hundred British grenadiers would have held the pass of Thermopylae as stoutly as the Spartans; and would have considered it as the simple discharge of a perilous and important duty, to die on the ground on which they fought."[50]

A similar appraisal of the men's character comes from a regimen-tal surgeon, Dr. William Ferguson. He had seen the men in action and in camp and did not doubt their worth: "While a regimental surgeon I have been among the common soldiers, and I can vouch that I have never in any walk of life fallen in with better men; they certainly could not be sober men, but they were of excellent temper, cheerful, patient, always ready to assist, and bearing the severest hardships with equanimity that could not be surpassed."[51]

Such positive firsthand appraisals are fairly common, with a good many coming from officers, showing that the ranker was well re-garded by many who knew him. While in the field, he stole to sur-vive. Yet even under dire circumstances, the redcoat shared his looted food, plunder, and coin with his messmates and sometimes even with the wives of fallen comrades. Moreover, the British regular appeared to treat the French and the indigenous peoples he encountered with a surprising degree of civility.[52] Sir Robert Porter, a freelance artist who accompanied Sir John Moore to Spain and Portugal, wrote home about a declaration made by the Portuguese wife of an army muleteer. The woman proclaimed that she had seen "more charity exercised by

heretics [the British soldiers] than she had ever met with in any religious assembly that Portugal produced."[53] Porter's anti-Catholic
bias may have colored his version of the story to the point of gross dis-
tortion. The woman's evaluation of the rankers just might be based
on their conduct, however, independent of Porter's religious prejudice. The point is that redcoat adherence to group restrictions apparently limited certain behaviors, so that soldiers' actions were in some
measure distinguished from those exhibited by gangs of real brutes
and criminals.

The redcoats' exemplary conduct under fire was also not engendered by their base natures. Courage, defined as the conscious and
willing decision to face death in order to preserve themselves, their
comrades, and their unit as a whole, was their combat motivation.
Courage and related cooperative actions have no meaning for vagabonds, rogues, and sociopaths disconnected from society on every
level. The behavior and character of the British soldier earned him the
esteem of many eyewitnesses who watched him on campaign and in
the field. Observations filled with praise, recorded in numerous accounts, describe a combination of courage, group cohesion, and related behavioral standards that belies the negative characterizations
of the enlisted man.

T.H. McGuffie, one of the few researchers in this period to disagree with the standard interpretation of the British ranker, found
Wellington's assessment to be short-sighted. McGuffie's take on the
soldiers, and Wellington's inability to see the men's true qualities,
cuts to the heart of the matter: "His lack of sympathy failed to discern, under the filthy layer of their obvious vices, the deep, sincere and inherent virtues of loyalty, patience and courage which per-
sisted in them even under the temptations of their enforced periods of
idleness."[54]

Finally, Major-General F.M. Richardson, in his book on the fighting spirit of soldiers, concurred with this positive assessment of the
British soldier, providing a distilled summation: "The British soldier . . . [was] judged by Napoleon to be the bravest in Europe and
by Wavell to be 'the finest all-around fighting man the world has
seen.' "[55]

These testimonials are offered as circumstantial evidence to cast
doubt on Wellington's "scum of the earth" assessment and similar
judgments by historians who have conveyed his words as established

fact. Often it seems improbable that the writers of these firsthand tributes are describing the same men so vilified by Wellington. These positive evaluations of the British soldier, countering Wellington's observations, should at least give the reader pause to reflect.

One further example suffices to show how preconceptions on the part of even careful and astute historians have worked to perpetuate the mistaken image of the common British soldier, further burning it into the public consciousness. Charles Esdaile, writing about Moore's retreat to Corunna in 1809, states: "From the very beginning of the retreat its passage was marked by a trail of burnt villages and homeless inhabitants. Brutalized stragglers [British soldiers] took what they wanted by force, whilst there were also outbreaks of mindless vandalism."[56] He cites the accounts of a Rifleman, an infantry officer, and a cavalry captain as evidence. Examined in detail, however, these chronicles provide important additional information that presents the retreat incidents in a totally different vein. Robert Porter, the infantry officer, wrote of the unbelievable privation of the retreat and the fasting diet of the men, what he termed "dieting with the gods." Calling the British soldiers "starving wretches," he described the friction between the soldiers and the Spanish people they had come to protect. Porter revealed the resentment felt by the rankers against the Spanish, who ignored the men's basic needs, failing to provide even the smallest portions of food to the fleeing army. The soldiers felt that the Spanish had abandoned them to their fates and the pursuing French. "All these things," Porter wrote, "excited an indignation in their breasts which, luckily, for the people we were amongst, wreaked itself on their chairs and tables instead of their heads."[57]

Cavalryman Alexander Gordon confirmed this, noting in his journal that the Spanish secreted provisions and "pretended to be unable to supply our necessities." He also asserted that the British regulars knew this. While admitting that the men stole anything they could find, Gordon also added a significant bit of evidence against Esdaile's claim that the burning of houses was the result of the British soldier's propensity to pillage and destroy, writing that the villages were intentionally set afire to prevent the French from benefiting from them.[58]

Finally, the recollections of Rifleman Harris do not support Esdaile's position. Filled with details of human suffering, Harris's memoirs paint the forced-march retreat to Corunna as a desperate venture in which British soldiers (as well as their wives and children) and officers alike fought the elements and the French cavalry, all the while being without provisions; the soldiers and their loved ones perished by the hundreds in one of the most agonizing retreats in British military history. Harris describes "pallid men, way worn, their feet bleeding . . . now near sinking with fatigue . . . [reeling] as if in a state of drunkenness, and altogether I thought we looked the ghosts of our former selves; still, we held resolutely."[59] His chronicles do not depict the British redcoat as a hardened villain, intent on wanton destruction.

The Porter, Gordon, and Harris accounts illustrate how much of the testimonial evidence offered by historians against the British soldier does not stand up under cross-examination. When more carefully inspected, these documents contribute subtle but significant details that attribute the British ranker's behavior to factors other than those that have been repeated so often.

The common belief in the vile nature of the British soldier is also at odds with the uncontested opinions of both Wellington and scholars concerning the exemplary combat behavior of these same men. Wellington's successes were not based solely on his ability as a commander. His decisions were carried out by enlisted men, who continuously exhibited the courage and tenacity necessary to win battle after battle. The soldiers were expected to hold their positions with unswerving resolve until the last second, when the opposing French columns were often only tens of yards away. As the columns began forming into line, the British soldier stood, fired, and charged, closing with the bayonet on the French formation suddenly stricken by the close-range British fusillade. The steadfastness, discipline, and audacity required to execute such a maneuver successfully (so often lauded by observers of all kinds) are not characteristics of the social misfit and troublesome, self-concerned, hardened ruffian described by most historians as the archetypal British soldier. On the contrary, the British soldier's allegiance to others and his desire and need to adhere to the values of his primary group enabled him to adopt these specialized tactics that Napoleon's other adversaries were unable to duplicate.

Historian Linda Colley has recognized the need for an analysis that addresses the discrepancy between the collective memory of the ranker as a reprehensible individual lacking in values and bereft of a moral compass and the actual behavior, motivations, and deeds of the British soldier. She writes: "Although the impact of mass arming in revolutionary and Napoleonic France has been analyzed with great skill . . . the hundreds of thousands of Britons who joined the ranks of the regular army and the militia and volunteer corps during these wars have been comparatively little studied . . . we still fail to see these men as they really are."[60] Given the lack of evidence presented by scholars in support of their negative depictions of the British rank and file and the number of accounts espousing the worth of the British redcoat, perhaps it is time to reconsider the British ranker and lay to rest the "scum of the earth" myth. The common British soldier deserves the chance to be seen for what he was and not what we have supposed him to be.

2

GONE FOR A SOLDIER

The Realities of Enlistment

In his attack on the idea of a "universal soldier" who exhibits essential continuity throughout the ages, John Lynn argues that soldiers differ in ways specific to their eras and environments. They are both the products and the producers of cultures specific to them. Lynn advocates that we "replace the unchanging, faceless warrior with real flesh and blood," cautioning historians "to question assumptions and [to] take care in generalizing about war and warriors." He makes a compelling case for analyses based on cultural norms and perceptions, which, in a military environment, grow out of social and economic factors, hardship, logistical considerations, and leadership demands; these circumstances are unique to particular armies. "A cultural interpretation," Lynn contends, "is most likely to grant individuals and people their full personal, social, and cultural character."[1]

Ultimately the behavior of the British infantryman on campaign and in battle is best understood in terms of the culture of the soldier group; but to understand the unique intensity of that culture, we must start with the social realities of the soldier's life, beginning with his status in the civilian world and his rationale for "going for a soldier," as explained in this chapter.

Lynn's call for analyses based on an understanding of societies, economies, and a soldier's connections to a specific "time, place, and culture" is especially germane when it comes to the British regular of Peninsular War fame, an individual who has long suffered from the generalized universal soldier approach.[2] The two-dimensional portrait of the British ranker—which colors all the British soldiers who fought in the wars against Napoleon as rogues and thugs, miscreants by nature and by choice—has emerged as part of collective memory because the very nuances of historical investigation delineated by Lynn have been largely ignored. While it is of course impossible to extrapolate with absolute certainty how any number of social, economic, physiological, and psychological considerations affected countless individual soldiers, a more detailed investigation does allow a subtler and evocative image to emerge. In an effort to illustrate the effects of such variables on soldiers' lives and personalize British Soldier Compendium (BSC) data,[3] one soldier's experiences are used in this study as a vehicle for understanding army life. William Lawrence of the 40th Foot, who survived years of campaigning in the Iberian Peninsula and France, acts as a guide of sorts in this endeavor. His background and military experiences, recalled in his autobiography, provide a frame of reference against which events, motivations, and the demographic insights can be considered and compared.

One of seven children, Lawrence was born in 1791 in the English county of Dorset. His father, an agricultural worker turned laborer, was forced to give up the family farm in order to provide for his burgeoning family. Lawrence began work at a very early age in order to help meet the needs of his family; he worked at various agricultural jobs for pennies a day until his teens. Given the circumstances, education was out of the question.

When Lawrence reached the age of 14, his father borrowed the rather large sum of £20 in order to pay a builder to accept his son as an apprentice.[4] This seven-year commitment would provide Lawrence with room and board, training, and clothing, but no wages. He soon found, however, that his new master was difficult to please. When the man started rationing Lawrence's food, the apprentice began to consider ways of escaping the situation. Nine months after being apprenticed, Lawrence made an abortive attempt to flee.[5] He was caught by the builder, who used a bullwhip to administer punishment.

Undeterred, Lawrence soon filched a seven-shilling coin and some food from his master and, though unable to find the documents detailing his indentured servant obligations, made another attempt at escape. He was given a reprieve by his master's wife after being caught again, and off he went a third time. Unable to find work except for a few menial jobs, Lawrence was hungry and tired when he chanced upon a recruiting party of artillerymen. He was an easy mark for the recruiting sergeant's palaver and willingly accepted the king's shilling as well as the five-guinea enlistment bonus. Paraded from one public house to the next, along with other recruits, he quickly spent most of the bounty. Unfortunately for Lawrence, an acquaintance revealed to the sergeant that the young man was an indentured apprentice. Unable to repay the recruiting bounty (as he only had a bit more than 17 shillings remaining), he was remanded to his parents' custody, and the money was confiscated. He was taken before a magistrate, who gave him the choice of fulfilling his apprenticeship or going to jail.

Given strict orders to conduct himself immediately back to his master, Lawrence exhibited the same kind of stubbornness and instinct for self-preservation that would later allow him to survive as a regular line infantryman. Rather than return to the untenable situation with the builder, he took himself to a nearby town and straight into a public house. There he found another recruiting sergeant, this time of the 40th Foot. He quickly enlisted again, accepting the sergeant's word that he would merit a 16 guinea bounty. Lawrence was given coach fare to Somersetshire, where he signed his "X," took the oath, and told the colonel that he was a laborer. The officer replied that was just fine, "for laborers made the best soldiers."[6] Later, after being sworn in, Lawrence was given a bounty of two and a half guineas, rather than the promised 16. More than a little dissatisfied, he considered enlisting in the marines to collect the full 16 guineas. But unable to find a way to Portsmouth, where the marines were quartered, he returned to the barracks of the 40th Foot and began a military career that would span parts of two decades. Although the dates in Lawrence's account are imprecise, he would have been about 15 years old at the time, and the year was most likely 1806.

Lawrence's situation and resultant recruiting adventure were perhaps not atypical for the time. British Soldier Compendium (BSC) data show that most recruits for 1806 were, like Lawrence, English, accounting for just over 77 percent of the sample for that year; the Irish (13.7 percent), Scots (7.8 percent), and foreigners (1.0 percent) round out the recruiting class for 1806.[7] (In the British regimental recordkeeping system, Welshmen were included under the category "English" in general returns. All nationality data for this work follow this format.)

The year Lawrence enlisted was a particularly grim one economically. Continued economic stress brought on by Napoleon's continental blockade, the impact of increased industrialization on the hand-looming and hand-weaving trades, and the decision by the government to divest itself of the volunteer system may have had a pronounced effect on English enlistment, particularly in the industrialized centers in the north around Manchester.

The BSC sample for all years, 1790–1815, offers a broader and more precise look at enlistment in general. For the years leading to and including the Peninsular War, Englishmen constitute slightly less than 53 percent of the total sample. The Irish make up nearly 30 percent of volunteers, while the Scots represent almost 16 percent; foreigners constitute the remaining 2 percent of recruits.[8]

Only 48 percent of infantrymen were English (including Welshmen), which means that the majority of British infantrymen were not of English decent; the Irish and Scots together made up the largest proportion of this branch (at 33.7 and 17.1 percent, respectively), for a total of almost 51 percent.[9] The percentage of Irish recruits is not surprising; it has been estimated that as many as 160,000 men from Ireland may have served in the British army between 1793 and 1815.[10] As would be expected, Lawrence's enlistment in the infantry coincided with the choice of most recruits from this period. The percentages of Irish (84.9) and Scottish recruits (80.6) volunteering into this same branch, however, were higher than the percentage of English recruits (67.7).[11]

At 15, Lawrence was younger than most enlistees, the average age of recruits being about 22.5.[12] The most common age for army enlistment, though, was 18. Lawrence was not, in fact, an unusually young recruit, being part of the most common age group: 15 to 19 years. This pattern of youthful volunteers was consistent both in 1806 and across army returns for the Peninsular War.[13]

In addition, Lawrence's youth is in keeping with the norm for English recruits, who were on average slightly less than 22 years of

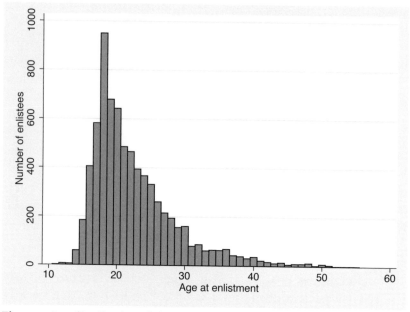

Figure 1. Age distribution of all enlistees.

age. This made them a year younger than Irish volunteers and two years younger than Scottish enlistees.[14] Approximately 72 percent of British army recruits, in fact, were less than 25 years old. This number aligns fairly well with Samuel Scott's data on French line troops in 1793. While Scott's figures record the ages of veterans rather than recruits, they still show that nearly 60 percent of French infantry privates were under the age of 25.[15] Jean-Paul Bertaud's work on the soldiers of the army of the French Revolution reveals that 50 percent of line infantry recruits from 1789 to 1791 were 18 to 25 years old; about 75 percent of the volunteers of 1792 were younger than 26, a number very much in agreement with the BSC figures.[16] André Corvisier's data for French soldiers of all ranks in 1716 reveal that about 34 percent of the army was less than 26 years old.[17]

The similarity in the age data of French and British volunteers of the late eighteenth and early nineteenth centuries (from Corvisier's numbers on the army of Louis XV to the BSC information covering British volunteers from 1790 until 1815) suggests that some common influences may be at work. While it is impossible to pinpoint precisely the factors shaping enlistment ages, it is feasible that the popu-

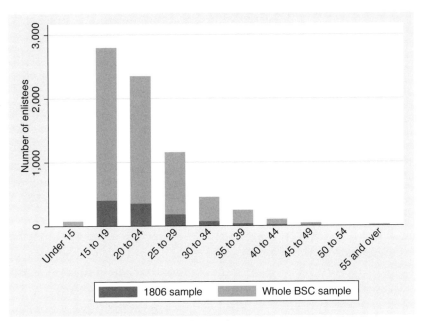

Figure 2. Age-group distribution of all enlistees.

lation surges experienced throughout Europe at the time in question played an important role. Excess population would have made jobs scarce, especially for rural laborers tied to finite plots of land. Data from Corvisier, Betraud, Scott, and the BSC confirm that a significant portion, often a majority, of enlistees came from small, rural communities.[18] The simultaneous need to find gainful employment in times of economic crisis—created by too many people competing for too few jobs—and the necessity of relieving family stress by reducing the number of mouths that needed feeding could have forced lads coming of age to consider army enlistment an attractive possibility. Limited occupational opportunities may have combined with the allure of adventure to drive young men in both Britain and France toward military service.

Lawrence's youthful age at enlistment is not as odd as it may first seem. Young boys appear to have been accepted as recruits if they were of a minimum height of five feet. The regimental description records on minimum age are sometimes difficult to interpret, as most boys were accepted as drummers and marked as such. Some boys of sufficient height, however, were listed as full recruits in the description books, with 11 being the youngest age in the army sample. A.W. Cockerill estimates that in 1811, at the peak of the Peninsula campaign, there may have been as many as 3,600 boys in the army under age 16.[19] Cockerill observes that the Militia Amending Act of 1811 allowed one-quarter of all militia recruits to be 14 to 16 years old. The total number of men raised that year exceeded 21,000, meaning that perhaps as many as 5,000 boys entered the militia over one year. How many of these boys transferred to line units is unknown. John Fortescue's numbers from general army returns, however, show that no fewer than 1,497 boys joined the army each year, with a high of 3,806 in 1807.[20] Given the young age of so many recruits, Cockerill argues that the army was not filled with grizzled "scum" but rather with the "very flower of the nation."[21] While this statement may be an exaggeration, there is still some truth behind it; the tender age of so many recruits works against the standard portrait of the ranker as a hardened *grognard* (literally, "grumbler," meaning a veteran).

In regard to physical stature, Lawrence never mentions his height at enlistment. Considering his age, he was probably around 63 to 64 inches, which was the average height for 15-year olds in the BSC sample.[22] Lawrence reached an adult size of 73 inches, however, so his enlistment height may have been above average. His full-grown size, in fact, was greater than that of 99.5 percent of the volunteers studied.[23]

If Lawrence's stature was typical for a recruit, it would not have put him at a great disadvantage compared with older men: the average height for English enlistees was 66.3 inches tall.[24] The physical stature of volunteers differed little by nationality; the Scots were the tallest at 66.6 inches, while the Irish were the shortest at 66.18 inches. Inadequate nutrition probably explains the slight Irish height deficiency.[25]

The heights reported in the BSC are consistent with other data on the size of adult males from 1810 to 1819 and those of urban and rural criminals from the decade after Waterloo.[26] Both these estimates put the average height of men around 66 to 67 inches. André Corvisier's very detailed analysis of the French army at the end of the seventeenth century reveals a range in heights from 1.624 meters (64 inches) to 1.896 meters (75 inches), with the most common height being between 1.678 meters and 1.732 meters (66 inches and 68 inches) for soldiers in 1763.[27] Covisier's numbers show that 60 percent of French soldiers in 1763 were less than 68 inches tall. Bertaud notes

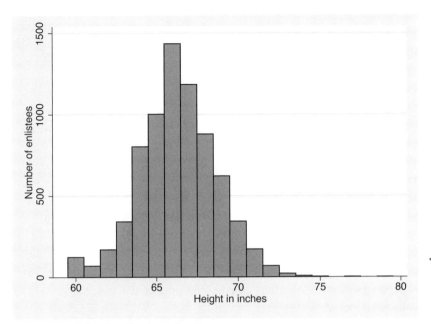

Figure 3. Height distribution of enlistees.

that height minimums for enlistment sometimes were as high as
70 inches even as late as 1791. By 1792, though, 64 percent of recruits
were shorter than 66 inches. The *levée en masse* of 1793 brought
a less-select cross section of the populace into the army. Heights
dropped to 60 inches on average, with 65 percent of men entering the
infantry being 66 inches or less.[28] Scott's figures on the heights of line
soldiers in the French army circa 1793 substantiate Bertaud's numbers and match the BSC sample: Scott's data set and the BSC both
indicate that approximately 70 percent of soldiers were less than
68 inches tall.[29]

The heights for the British population and British soldiers in the
BSC sample also coincide with the estimated average stature for adult
males in Roman times, between 64 and 67 inches, although it should
be noted that the Roman army had height requirements above this
range.[30] Comparing heights from the time of the Roman Empire to
the Peninsular War also confirms, in a small way, that heights increased through medieval times but regressed through the Little Ice
Age, which lasted from the sixteenth through the nineteenth centuries. Richard Steckel notes that heights of skeletons from the ninth

through the eleventh centuries averaged about 68 inches. He argues that "average height measures a population's history of *net* nutrition."[31] Steckel contends that the warm period from AD 900 to 1300 and the benefits to health, nutrition, and height related to the isolation of villages and towns from each other (as noted by anthropometric historians) account for this increase in stature.[32] He argues that urbanization in preindustrial Europe, with the resulting increased exposure to disease, poorer diets, and more arduous working conditions, reduced the heights of European men and women.

By 1600, as Steckel notes, "when the coldest two centuries of the little Ice Age began," unpredictable climate shifts and lower temperatures resulted in reduced food production.[33] The fluctuations and warmer intervals caused people to continue to use standard agricultural methods that proved unsatisfactory during the colder stretches.[34] The outcome was a gradual decline in average heights. By the eighteenth century, during the end of the coldest period of the Little Ice Age, heights for adult males had fallen to about 65 inches.[35] The gradual warming of temperatures worldwide at the end of the eighteenth and beginning of the nineteenth centuries, however, worked to increase agricultural yields and helped contribute to a gradual recovery of height. A combination of factors, including nutrition, a decrease in disease and disease virulence, and smallpox inoculation, probably played a concomitant role.[36] The BSC confirms that heights were in fact on the rise by the nineteenth century: for all enlistees aged 18 and over the average height was 66.6 inches.[37]

Recruiting regulations stipulated minimum height, minimum and maximum age, and nationality requirements: "none under five feet seven and a half except for growing lads" and "no Frenchmen or deserters nor any man upwards of twenty-five or under fifteen years of age."[38] The rules go on to specify that "growing lads [are] not to be under five feet five inches, and Certificates of their Age [must be obtained] from the Minister and Churchwardens of the parish they were born in."[39] Yet another regulation from 1796 stipulates that "all healthy lads under sixteen years of age, who are likely to grow, may be taken as low as five feet one inch."[40] Recruiting sergeants were cautioned "not to enlist any man, whose height and person does not correspond with the above Instructions in every particular, as he will be obliged to the disagreeable necessity of rejecting them."[41]

The British army's need for soldiers, though, superseded regulations. Almost one volunteer in four did not meet the age requirements (most of them being too old), while more than one enlistee in five was beneath the height standard.[42] A recruiting poster for the 7th Light Dragoons under Lord Henry Paget, dated 1809, confirms that men under the minimums were regularly sought after: the poster encourages lads that they "will be taken at Sixteen Years of Age, 5 Feet 2 inches, but they must be active."[43] A Horse Guards' memorandum from 1808 reveals that of 106 recruits, randomly chosen, 41 were shorter than 65 inches.[44] By 1806, the year Lawrence enlisted, the official height restriction had been lowered to 64 inches.[45]

Lawrence, underage and possibly undersized, found his way into the ranks during a year of economic panic. The collapsing economy of 1803, three years before he enlisted, had been followed by two years of inadequate harvests, resulting in a dramatic rise in food prices. Fears of invasion rose, and another bad harvest came on the heels of the mechanization of the spinning, carding, and weaving industries.[46] Five industrial textile mills housing about 100 shearing frames had been established in northern England by 1806; within a year 72 textile mills and between 1,000 and 1,400 such frames would be in existence,[47] signaling another phase of the Industrial Revolution. Of equal importance was Napoleon's continental blockade system, initiated in 1806. British exports would remain stagnant until 1808, when the combined effects of the French and American embargoes would drive them precipitously lower; exports would rise significantly in 1809 before falling off by 1811–12 due to the ongoing conflict with America, the related loss of American markets, and the tightening of the continental embargo.[48]

The effect of the French blockade, coming as it did at the time when much of the textile industry was making the transition to machines, should not be underestimated.[49] This confluence of variables led to economic dislocation that resulted in the continuous decline of real wages and increased unemployment, especially among hand-frame and hand-loom textile workers.[50] In his work on the standard of living in Britain during the Industrial Revolution, Rufus Tucker presents price indices and real wages showing that when wages were considered against the cost of living British workers suffered worst in 1805–1806.[51] His numbers on the total diet cost in Oldham during this period reflect the struggle of workers to feed themselves in light of the rising costs of essential foodstuffs.[52]

Real wages would rebound by the end of 1806, when fears regarding the effects of the blockade and another bad harvest proved to be exaggerated, but not before having a disruptive effect on urban and rural workers. As Geoffrey Best notes in his work on war and society, the outcome for many workers and their families was economic misery. "In a country enormously taxed," he argues, "with food dear, subject to common harvest hazards, undergoing a population explosion and all the jumps and jolts of the first industrial revolution at the same time, the results were awful and dramatic. For the work force of textile industries above all, but not for them alone, it meant unemployment, privation, humiliation, and a prospect of starvation."[53] The government responded to the glut of unemployed workers by increasing the numbers of army recruiting parties operating in Britain from 405 in 1806 to 1,113 a year later.[54]

One further variable possibly affecting army enlistment in 1806 and the years that followed was the demise of the volunteer force. This movement was an attempt to provide able-bodied citizens with military training and was at first an armed response to the events of the French Revolution, particularly the Terror. Originally conceived as a force capable of staving off local political uprisings,[55] the volunteer movement began drawing men to its ranks as early as 1793; 100,000 men were serving by 1801.[56]

The secondary purpose of the volunteer system was as a home-guard static defense against invasion, pitched to the masses as a kind of middle-class civic-mindedness. In his article on the subject, J.E. Cookson calls it an "outgrowth of counter-revolutionary loyalism."[57] Training was minimal, far below militia standards, and responsibilities few. The need for such a force to be mobile, however, kept many men of property from participating, as most preferred to remain near their homes, farms, and businesses. The poor, naturally, took up the slack.[58] Volunteers were paid for drill time as compensation for any lost wages and were made exempt from the militia lottery.[59] The major problem with the volunteer system was that service was not compulsory or for any specified term, meaning that men could resign at any time. The effect this had on military discipline can be imagined. The threat of French invasion in 1803–1804, however, brought more than 400,000 volunteer enlistees into the ranks, as fear drove men from a wider social and economic spectrum into service. Vice-Admiral Horatio Nelson's naval victory at Trafalgar in 1805 over the combined fleets of France and Spain, though, removed the immediate need for such a force. The government, realizing that funding an armed civilian force over which it had little control was less than ideal, allowed the system to fall slowly into disuse. From 1805 to 1807 the corps of volunteers lost over 25 percent of its strength,[60] and the system was gradually phased out over the remaining years of the war. At least a portion of the 100,000 men who left the volunteers around 1806 may have found the army a viable option, especially considering the economic stressors at work in that particular year.

The crisis of 1806 was a continuance of the economic downturn and harvest problems that began to erode living standards in the years 1799–1800, the first back-to-back failed harvests of the Napoleonic Wars. (The second series occurred in 1811–12.) Inflated food prices reduced real wages in 1801 to a level only slightly less devastating than during the crisis of 1555–57.[61] From 1797 to 1801 the cost of wheat went up 200 percent, barley 255 percent, and oats 231 percent.[62] For the masses, existing mostly on cereal-based diets, the rapid rise in grain prices set the stage for a decade of fluctuating misery; for many, daily existence often slipped from subsistence to starvation. A four-pound loaf of bread, for example, went from six pence in 1792 to one shilling five pence by 1812.[63] Skyrocketing food prices, increased taxation and unemployment, adverse trade balances, and near-famine conditions substantially, if temporarily, reduced living standards for the majority of British workers.[64] Thus, 1807 had the single highest recruiting totals for the war.[65]

Concomitantly, mortality rates soared through 1804 and begging reached "monumental proportions," as Roger Wells points out in his work on famine in England during this period. "Desperation," he suggests, "rather than exploitation, surely underlay the noted increase in belligerent, aggressive begging. Scavenging was seen on unknown scales with 'children picking Potato parings on the Dunghill to boil for Food' at Wolverhampton. Manchurian urchins fought off stray dogs competing for bones thrown from the kitchens of the affluent."[66]

In addition to the confluence of economic disruptions in 1806, other variables had a concurrent influence on daily life and the increased attractiveness of enlistment. A poor harvest in 1808, in combination with lagging imports, led to rising prices. Working men rallied together to plead for a minimum wage. When none was forth-coming, strikes followed. Moreover, the American embargo against Great Britain (1807–1809) had a substantial impact.[67] The real value of imported goods from America declined 73.2 percent, from £6.5 million to £1.7 million.[68] Exports to the United States fell from £11.8 million to £5.2 million during this time, a loss of 56.2 percent.[69] Most of this loss was compensated for by increased exports to non-U.S. ports in the Americas, but the shock to individual industries was still felt. Cotton imports from the United States, crucial to Great Britain's textile industry, fell from £44 million to a little more than £12 million.[70] In the case of cotton, the difference could not be made up elsewhere. Because of the embargo, cotton imports from British plantations in the New World also fell almost 13 percent, resulting in a devastating 32.8 percent loss of textile production.[71] Textile factories were idled and workers discharged. Adding to this already devastating situation, the overall effect of the embargo drove up prices on other commodities in Great Britain, none of which were easily absorbed by working-class families already on the brink of financial ruin.[72]

Two years of adequate harvests followed in 1809 and 1810, and an industrial boom was spurred by the redistribution of trade to new ports and positive speculation based on the potential of economic growth. The boom, however, peaked in 1810. When the blockade tightened in summer, goods become difficult to obtain, prices fell, and the economic upturn collapsed. Unemployment on a grand scale followed, with the textile industry being especially hard hit. England experienced a true depression, which was exacerbated by two consecutive harvest failures in 1811 and 1812.

Another disruptive economic force was the introduction of machines on a large scale, especially in the textile industry. These machines were wonderful inventions, representing a real technological breakthrough, but they threw thousands out of work. The new machines became more than tools in the hands of workers; they replaced many workers altogether. The jennies and water frames provided a huge mechanical advantage over handwork (from six to one to twenty-four to one for jennies and up to several hundred to one for frames). In addition, machine performance quickly improved to make use of these advantages. Early machines were not much faster than traditional handlooms, but by the mid-1820s the technical advantage was approximately 7.5 to 1.[73] This meant that one boy on two power looms could do the work of 15 handwork craftsmen. Most of these hand-weaving and looming artisans discovered that their skilled trades no longer guaranteed a livable wage or steady employment, and many fell on hard times. Thus, the effects of the Industrial Revolution not only provided Britain with the wealth to exert its power internationally but also, as a third-order effect, supplied the able bodies needed to fill the ranks of the army that conducted Britain's campaigns worldwide.

The transition from handmade textile products produced by thousands of independent knitters, weavers, and spinners to machine-manufactured goods created on power looms is too complex a story to address here.[74] It suffices to say that this period of technological innovation took a toll on hand craftsmen; and as workers lost their jobs, resentment grew.[75] Those lucky enough to be employed in the mills often found the harsh realities of factory labor not to their liking.[76] The work was unhealthy, dangerous, and poorly paid. Isolated incidents of people rising together to destroy the machines that took their jobs or made such occupations so ill-paying that life became unbearable occurred as early as 1803.[77] The first hanging related to destroying a mill took place in Salisbury that year.[78]

The first large-scale riots started in 1811, the result of long years of suffering, declining wages, lost jobs, and hopelessness. Beginning in rural villages, the outbreaks were the manifestations of rioters' dissatisfaction with their employment situations. Using violence to call attention to their plight, the machine breakers wanted what could not happen: a return to the past. Machine breaking soon spread to Nottinghamshire and similar locales with long histories of hand-textile trades. Riots were spontaneous and evolved from break-ins to large-scale machine destruction. Owners were naturally outraged and offered rewards, but public sentiment always went with the machine breakers, who became known as Luddites.[79] Machine destruction then spread to cotton mills. The army was soon called into the three Midland shires of Leicestershire, Nottinghamshire, and Derbyshire to quell the disturbances. The poet Percy Bysshe Shelley summed up the popular attitude toward such official reaction, lamenting to a friend that "the military are gone to Nottingham—Curses light on them for their motives if they destroy *one* of its famine wasted inhabitants."[80]

The presence of troops had little effect on the machine breakers, however, as the nocturnal groups easily evaded the soldiers and continued about their business. It is estimated that between November 1811 and January 1812 approximately 2 percent of all frames in the Midlands were smashed; about 175 machines a month were destroyed during this three-month period,[81] amounting to about £100,000 of machinery and property damage.[82] Machine breaking would continue throughout the war as the economy fluctuated and automation slowly replaced hand-textile workers.

At just this time, more disagreements with the United States surfaced. Problems involving European trade and foreign impressments of American sailors would eventually lead to war in 1812, resulting in the loss of important New World markets and further depressing Great Britain's economy. The English Parliament had issued its Orders in Council (1807) as a response to Napoleon's Berlin Decree.[83] These orders forbade French trade with Britain, its allies, or neutral countries, such as America. The United States issued an embargo on foreign trade in 1807 in hopes of convincing both Britain and France to respect American neutrality.[84] The American Non-Intercourse Act of 1809 was the next U.S. effort to induce Britain and France to alter their policies regarding impressments and neutral shipping. This law allowed American ports in the United States to admit ships from every country except Great Britain and France. The act failed to convince England and France, however, that their policies were in error.

These attempts at economic coercion, while hurting the American economy more than its British counterpart, did impact exports from Great Britain, which fell 33 percent by 1811, down to £26 million; exports to the United States fell to £2 million by that same year.[85] As Best again summarizes, with Napoleon's blockade, American troubles resulting in the War of 1812, and the failed harvests, Britain's merchants "now found supplies of raw materials irregular, stocks piling up unsaleable, and their credit . . . over extended. 1808 was a bad year, almost disastrous. 1811, after the temporary recovery year 1810, was entirely so."[86]

The loss of harvests was especially daunting given the increasing population of Britain. Economist B.A. Holderness provides the crucial comparison: "broadly speaking, output from English agriculture rather more than doubled between 1750 and 1850," whereas the population of England and Wales rose approximately 165 percent.[87] Thus, any disruption in agricultural output resulted in a bleak existence for numerous working-class men and women, many of whom were already existing on subsistence diets. Fully blown crop failures were catastrophic under any conditions; but for the masses, already living day-to-day with little nutritional margin for error, the outcome was one of nightmarish proportions and forced starvation diets. In his work on the connections between economic pressures and crime in eighteenth-century Britain, Douglas Hay notes that in good years about 10 percent of the population could not buy enough bread for a whole year (given no other expenditures); in a bad year 20 percent could not purchase enough bread; and in a very hard year the number rose to 45 percent.[88]

The consequences of these successive jolts to the British economy are reflected in Poor Law expenditures. While the population had grown an alarming 15 percent during the first decade of the nineteenth century, Poor Rates rose over four times this amount, increasing 65 percent.[89] By 1812, for example, almost 15,000 persons in Nottinghamshire (almost 50 percent of the population) needed economic relief.[90] In Liverpool the Poor Rate doubled to over 15,000 townsfolk; in Bolton 3,000 of 17,000 inhabitants were in need, but only 10 percent of that number received any aid.[91] According to parliamentary returns, of the estimated 200,000 persons living in manufacturing districts, "no less than 50,000 received only the two pence half-penny per day for food."[92] Although "changes in the levels of unemployment and under-employment are probably doomed to remain among the imponderables of this problem,"[93] as M.W. Flinn states, the swelling numbers of Poor Rate recipients give some idea of the increasing scale of economic need during this time. It is estimated that nearly 1 million men, women, and children needed poor relief at the peak of military mobilization.[94]

British army enlistment must be considered against this economic backdrop. It is impossible, of course, to ascertain with certainty exactly why so many men chose to volunteer during the years in question. Various social, political, and even patriotic forces may have been at work, in addition to the more overt economic pressures. Yet the surges in enlistment do seem to coincide with the hard economic times, making them too compelling a possibility to ignore.[95]

One major question that the BSC was designed to investigate is how economic factors in the United Kingdom at the time of the Napoleonic Wars affected army enlistment. The underlying hypothesis is that enlistment rates rose as economic conditions worsened. A regression analysis of monthly bread prices and enlistment using BSC data drawn from the years 1790 to 1815 reveals a statistically significant correlation between the cost of bread and recruitment numbers.[96] These numbers show that when bread prices rose even one penny per four-pound loaf over a thousand men joined the army who in other circumstances most likely would not have enlisted. The impact of bread prices on recruiting becomes clear when we consider that the cost of bread nearly tripled between 1792 and 1812. Corvisier points out similar connections between harsh winters, failed crops, bread prices, and enlistment in the French army during the early eighteenth century: "One will say, perhaps, that this is a good effect of an evil cause, and that recruits are so plentiful because of misery in the provinces."[97]

Since bread prices only reflect information about a very small portion of the economy, it is logical to compare enlistment rates to a wider range of economic data. A separate regression was run, taking into account real wages, imports, and the anomalous economic stressors particular to 1806. The results indicated an even greater correlation between economics and enlistment. Real wages were compared to those of 1900, the year that Rufus Tucker used to evaluate the earning power of artisans in London from 1729 to 1935. The regression data confirm that when real wages fell by one-hundredth of what they were in 1900,[98] all else being equal, as many as almost 2,000 men would have enlisted. When imports fell by £1 million per year, all else being equal, the regression model estimates that over 800 men would have sought refuge in the army.[99] Finally, when variables regarding the three coinciding economic stressors of 1806 are considered (the initiation of the continental blockade, the mechanization in the textile industry, and the beginning of the disbandment of the volunteer system), the model estimates that approximately 7,000 more recruits joined the ranks than would otherwise have done so.[100]

The economic stressors used in the regressions indicate hardships as they applied to the lives of everyday British citizens. They are not meant to imply that the war had a long-term negative effect on the British economy. Those industries geared toward the war effort prospered, particularly copper mining and production, gun making, and shipbuilding and related dock work. Coal mining, brick making, iron making, hardware and plate goods manufacturing, and glass making bore the brunt of curtailed trade and increased duties; these industries experienced limited growth, if any. The building industry was also depressed as a result of taxes on houses (house, window, income, and local rates) and taxes on building materials.[101] The textiles industry, though, was hardest hit by the combination of war and industrial transition. Wages collapsed, and unemployment soared. Three examples illustrate this effect. Weekly wages for hand weavers in Bolton were around 25 shillings a week in 1805; by 1809 they had fallen to 16 shillings; and in 1812 they were down to 14 shillings.[102] Similar losses in earning power occurred at Stockport, where wages for weaving 24 square yards of cambric dropped from 25 shillings in 1802 to 10 shillings in 1811.[103] Likewise, wages for hand-loom weavers fell from 1 shilling 4 pence a day in 1802 to 8 pence in 1806 and 7 pence by 1807,[104] a loss of 56 percent by 1807. Frank Darvall shows that weavers who once made 31 shillings had to be content with 10 shillings for a six-day week by 1812. He also notes that potatoes and oatmeal became the only dietary staples that many such men could afford.[105]

The effect of falling wages and loss of employment opportunities on weavers can be ascertained by noting that the weaving trade constituted the number one occupation in the BSC other than laborer, nearly three and one-half times as common as the next occupation (shoemaker).[106] In 1806, the year Lawrence enlisted, the number of textile workers nearly equaled that of laborers, making up one-third of all listed occupations and more than all other jobs combined. For the entire BSC sample, 29.1 percent of soldiers listed textile work of one variety or another as their previous occupation.[107]

The economic fluctuations caused by the episodic, punctuated equilibrium progress of the Industrial Revolution, in conjunction with war-related economic variables, hit the people on the lower end of the socioeconomic continuum hardest.[108] Rural and urban manual laborers, unemployed textile workers, and even tradesmen such as shoemakers, smiths, and carpenters found the downturns difficult to weather. For many men unable to make adjustments or find a new employment situation, the army provided an option during what Flinn terms "short-term crisis peaks."[109] Again, the BSC provides insight. A comparison of enlistment during specific years in which such "crisis peaks" were prominent (1800, 1806, and 1812) with years in which the economic indices were positive (1803, 1810, and 1813) illustrates that a higher percentage of recruits listing an occupation other than "laborer" chose the army over penury, emigration, or crime in difficult years. The number of such volunteers increased almost 35 percent during the bad economic years in question.[110] These were men with real trade expertise and experience. Moreover, such men were most likely older than the average enlistee; the percent of recruits 30 years of age and older rises by almost 51 percent to over 12 percent of volunteers during the three years of major economy decline.[111]

Workers with marketable skills would be expected to find jobs fairly easily in both urban and rural settings. That such men struggled to find work and were forced to consider army enlistment as the answer to their employment difficulties says much about the severity of the economic downturns. It also casts doubt on the myth portraying the British soldier as a perpetually unemployed and unemployable rogue or street scum whisked from jails into the armed services. Recruits appear to have enlisted not because the army provided them an outlet for violence but because economic circumstances diminished their occupational opportunities or eliminated them all together; compared with the hardship and deprivation brought on by long stretches of unemployment, the army emerged as a palatable choice.[112]

Fred Anderson, in his work on the British army and society in provincial Massachusetts, acknowledges that British enlistment was often directly tied to economic conditions. Writing on the army of the late eighteenth century, he argues that army ranks were filled with "people cast adrift by enclosure and industrialization: farmers and laborers from depressed rural areas, artisans whose skills were obsolescent, and other poor but respectable folk whose positions in society had been eroded in an era of rapid economic change. For such men military service offered an alternative to a bleak proletarian life —or even starvation."[113]

The BSC sample provides data regarding the type of trades previously practiced by army enlistees as well as the numbers of men without an occupation. The total for the latter is remarkably small, given the pejorative descriptions by which the British soldier is usually, if unfairly, remembered. Less than 3 percent of enlistees did not provide a previous occupation, with the Irish making up the largest

Table 1. The ten most frequently listed trades in the BSC

Trade	Number	Percent of BSC sample
Laborer	2,943	40.59
Weaver	1,307	18.03
Shoemaker	377	5.20
Tailor	234	3.23
None	195	2.69
Smith	145	2.00
Carpenter	123	1.70
Servant	76	1.05
Spinner	76	1.05
Baker	63	0.87

national segment; 1.4 percent (or just over half of all volunteers without a previous trade) came from Ireland.[114] Looking at soldiers who fell into the "no trade" category by country, the Irish were more than half again as likely to lack a trade as English recruits and three times more likely than Scottish recruits.[115]

In choosing "laborer" as his previous trade, Lawrence fell into the largest single segment of recruits: almost 41 percent of volunteers listed "laborer" as their occupation.[116] By nationality, the Irish again took the lead: about 48 percent of Irish volunteers registered as laborers, reflecting the lack of industrialization in Ireland. Just over 39 percent of Englishmen and 37 percent of Scots did the same.[117] BSC totals substantiate previous estimates regarding the percentage of manual laborers in the civilian workforce.[118] Contrary to suppositions that the recruit was somehow unusual and outside the employment patterns of British society, he was thus in fact very much part of the norm.

Table 1 shows the most common listed occupations.[119] In addition to laborers, almost one volunteer in five was a weaver, and more than one in twenty was a shoemaker.[120] Tailors, smiths, carpenters, servants, spinners, and bakers round out the top ten trades. The BSC data support arguments put forth by Arthur Gilbert, who contends that "the recruiting records examined show that during wartime the army did attract men who had identifiable trades, men who had a vocation, but who . . . could not make a go of it."[121]

The reliability of the process by which enlistees communicated the name of their occupation prior to joining the army is naturally a bit suspect. Being asked for such information could be construed as intrusive or embarrassing by men who were experiencing occupational distress and the humiliation of unemployment. Thus, it might be expected that some of these men, when pressed by the recruiting sergeant to give an occupation, may have exaggerated or falsified their trade. This certainly applies to "laborer," which may have been the default choice of men too ashamed to admit they had held no significant employment during their recent past. Conversely, men who had achieved success as blacksmiths, schoolmasters, or tinsmiths may have been hesitant to admit that economics or circumstances had caused them to lose their positions.[122] Some of these recruits may also have opted to list their prior trade as "laborer," as did Lawrence, who was a runaway apprentice.[123] In the end, we are left to trust the men's word on their prior occupations. The total numbers and varieties of trades listed in the BSC (230 separate occupations) lend a certain credibility to the sample. Given that very few data exist for this topic, the information in the BSC sample is assumed to be a fairly accurate representation of army recruits and their previous trades.[124]

During the eighteenth and nineteenth centuries, seasonal unemployment was the norm for agricultural laborers and many other workers. It was the disruption in these seasonal patterns that threw many people already existing on the brink of destitution over the edge into abject poverty. As previously noted, the lack of hard data on unemployment makes precise analysis difficult. BSC regressions, however, illustrate that the sequence of economic variables outlined above did negatively impact employment, forcing many men to choose army enlistment over indigence.

An analysis of monthly enlistments appears to reveal a correlation with seasonal employment, a pattern similar to that presented by André Corvisier in his work on French soldiers of the late seventeenth century.[125] Both Corvisier's findings and the BSC statistics show increased recruitment during winter months, when little agricultural work was available, and declining enlistment during planting and harvesting seasons. The French army under Louis XV recruited primarily when the army was in winter quarters, while the British recruited year round in the Peninsular War, even though the army campaigned seasonally. Nevertheless, seasonal variables related to agricultural employment may have played a role in recruitment for both armies.[126] This seasonal recruiting focus is noteworthy, as more than 40 percent of army enlistees in the BSC listed "laborer" as their trade, but only 0.3 percent (21 recruits) listed "farmer" as their occupation.[127] I conjecture that the small number of recruits listing "farmer" as their occupation must have owned the land on which they farmed and that the acreage may have been of sufficient size to distinguish them from small-plot farmers or those who worked on other people's land. In this case, the sharecropping farmers, listed as laborers in the BSC, would have been employed on the land of men similar to those who listed "farmer" as their previous occupation. Since approximately 35 percent of workers were agricultural laborers during this period,[128] it might be assumed that the BSC sample would reflect this proportion; if this was so, the numbers of men in the BSC sample who farmed would be about 2,500.

While the numbers do not allow us to distinguish rural laborers from their urban counterparts, it is possible to surmise that the majority of those men who told the recruiting sergeant that they were laborers were rural agricultural workers. Corvisier shows that from 1753 to 1763 between 61 and 73 percent of French soldiers were from small rural villages, a figure that would produce numbers of agricultural workers in line with BSC estimates for farm-related occupations.[129] Scott's figures for French soldiers in 1793 corroborate Corvisier's numbers, with almost 64 percent of the men coming from villages with less than 2,000 inhabitants.[130] Using the numbers from three French provinces for the year 1793, Bertaud presents similar findings: approximately 63 to 68 percent of recruits were peasants, with half of them being agricultural employees, servants, or day workers.[131] The level of industrialization in Britain was significantly greater than in France, with resulting differences in demographics, yet farm work was still the occupation of a large portion of British society, and thus the BSC "laborer" statistics would be expected to reflect the predominance of this occupation.

Lawrence was not a rural agricultural laborer, and his enlistment was not related to a dependence on seasonal work. Whether or not his situation was directly or indirectly related to the economic stressors at work in 1806 is open to debate. What is certain from his account is that he could find no suitable employment other than his apprenticeship; dissatisfaction with his circumstances and a dash of potential adventure also may have played a role in his decision to volunteer.

Lawrence never mentions patriotism, ideals, or any other abstraction as the motivation behind his choice. Even at the tender age of 15, the thought of life outside the county parish in which he had lived his entire life offered a glimmer of hope and more promise than returning to a situation he detested, which provided the potential of financial remuneration only after six more years of labor as an apprentice.

Lawrence and his family would have found little succor in the British system of poor relief. It was a patchwork of stop-gap measures stitched together across the centuries. The Poor Laws laid most of the responsibility of looking after the impoverished on local (parish) governments, and two principles guided all relief: relief should never be generous and should never be too easy to accept. Efforts to improve local conditions and encourage the needy somehow to rise above their troubles and remove themselves from the poor rolls included forcibly resettling them back to the parishes of their birth;[132] "badging the poor" (making them wear two-letter badges designating the first initial of their parish and a "P" for poor);[133] renting local houses where the penniless could be housed, supervised, and made to work;[134] and instituting "outdoor relief" in the form of agricultural labor.[135] The Poor Relief Act of 1782 also authorized groups of parishes to set up common workhouses for indigents. Able-bodied adults were ineligible, however.[136] Perhaps the most useful of the Poor Laws was the Speenhamland system authorized by the Poor Relief Act of 1795. This initiative, again aimed at the local level, endeavored to supplement the wages of the needy, force local business owners to hire them, or, as a last resort, put the destitute on the public payroll doing roadwork or hauling gravel.[137] None of the Poor Laws were intended to deal with emergency relief on the scale needed during the first decade of the nineteenth century; it is not surprising that they failed to make any substantial impact on the plight of the countless poor.

Given this system of assistance, enlistment in the army offered a less demeaning variety of economic relief, though most men and their families viewed volunteering for the military as a desperate measure. The army was a thoroughly unpopular institution among all the classes, and service therein was viewed as anything but desirable. For the propertied, wealthy, and powerful, the army was an unpleasant reminder of the threat it posed to English liberties; memories of Charles I and II, Oliver Cromwell, and James II remained fresh.

The typical commoner also had no love of the army, which was seen as the tool of a repressive government. Utilized as a surrogate constabulary force,[138] the army protected property and limited dissent among the disadvantaged. Its use in stemming the urban and rural food uprisings beginning in 1800,[139] the part it played in quelling the numerous machine-breaking incidents and rallies during the Luddite Rebellion (beginning in 1811), and its later role in the "Peterloo massacre" of 1819 exemplify just why the army was resented by the people. More troops (about 12,000 men), for example, were used for Luddite repression in 1811–12 than sailed for Portugal with Wellington in 1808 (about 9,000 men).[140] The Riot Act of 1715 permitted the use of military force against crowds that refused to disperse, and local magistrates were not hesitant to put the act to use.[141] The Irish, for obvious reasons, had even less affection for the British army and the government it embodied, particularly after the crushing of the 1798 Rebellion.

Moreover, army life offered little in the way of long-term enticements. For the common soldier, army pay was low: one shilling a day minus deductions.[142] Comforts were also nonexistent, advancement potential limited, and the discipline harsh. Enlistment, at least until 1806, was for life, which meant that an enlistee was accepting the potential of a difficult and dangerous existence with few comforts. The term "gone for a soldier" remained a mother's or wife's lament, a grief-tinged phrase describing the whereabouts of a son or husband likely lost forever.

Yet, despite these failings, the army remained a viable alternative during hard times and bad harvests. It continued to be viewed as an opportunity, in part because of the promise of employment but mostly due to the bounties used to entice men into taking the king's shilling. The size of the bounty fluctuated with the economy, inversely mirroring living standards; the emolument ranged from two guineas in times of plenty to a high of £23 17 shillings 6 pence by 1812.[143]

To men facing continuing unemployment and unending want, any chance was better than none, and the size of the bounties was a significant factor in their decision-making processes. This is especially apparent when the bounties are compared with typical weekly wages (table 2). Wages varied, of course, by profession, time, and locale.

Table 2. Typical weekly wages for common trades in
the United Kingdom during the Peninsular War

Profession	Weekly wages
Agricultural worker	8–10 shillings,[a] 12 shillings by 1812[b]
Silk worker	12 shillings[c]
Knitter	14 shillings or more[d]
Clay digger	15 shillings (six days' labor)[e]
Carpenters, masons, bricklayers, and plasterers in England	18–30 shillings[f]
Carpenters, masons, bricklayers, and plasterers in Scotland and Ireland	15–18 shillings[g]
Printer in Scotland	20 shillings[h]
Hand weaver in Bolton or Lancashire	25 shillings[i]
Dockyard worker	28 shillings (six days' labor)[g]
Fine-work hand spinner	18–44 shillings[k]

[a]Bowley, "The Statistics of Wages (Part I)," 104.
[b]Holmes, "Introduction," in *Redcoat*, xxi–xxii.
[c]Darvall, *Popular Disturbances and Public Order*, 32–33.
[d]Ibid.
[e]Holmes, "Introduction," in *Redcoat*, xxi–xxii.
[f]Bowley, "The Statistics of Wages (Part VIII)," 104.
[g]Bowley, "The Statistics of Wages (Part VII)," 488.
[h]Bowley and Wood, "The Statistics of Wages (Part V)," 713.
[i]Darvall, *Popular Disturbances and Public Order*, 54–55. Wages would fall as low as 14 shillings by 1812. Wood, "The Statistics of Wages in the United Kingdom (Part XVIII)," 432.
[j]Holmes, "Introduction," in *Redcoat*, xxi–xxii.
[k]Wood, "The Statistics of Wages (Part XV)," 129.

It must be kept in mind, though, that the number of workers earning these wages was limited; finding work was the problem. To a man unemployed, down on his luck, and with no money in his pocket, the £12 to £23 enlistment bounty must have seemed a small fortune. For an unskilled laborer, agricultural or otherwise, such figures constituted anywhere from half a year's wages to almost a year's wages. Even to a man with building-trade skills, the bounty equaled three to six months' earnings. Lawrence was certainly pleased with his first £5 bounty and a bit less with the second bonus of two and a half guineas. Since he earned no wages as an apprentice, the sums were a fair amount to have in hand. Lawrence was more than willing, however, to accept the inherent risks of bounty jumping to procure the £16 bonus offered by the marines. Only the lack of transportation (as has been described) prevented him from collecting the larger prize and putting out to sea.

The army recruiter plied his trade in an environment of economic depression and hopelessness. Recruiting parties, led at times by officers and on other occasions by sergeants, would frequent street corners and public houses, making their presence known. Dressed in new uniforms sometimes fitted with more-than-regulation amounts of braiding and ribbons, the party was a striking sight to the unemployed and the sometimes malnourished inhabitants of any town through which the party paraded. Charles O'Neil, later of the 28th Regiment of Foot, recalled just how recruiting parties were perceived in Ireland: "The sight of so many well-dressed soldiers presented strong inducements to the ragged, half-clad children of poor unfortunate Ireland, to leave her shores at least for a season. Then there was the hope of returning with a pension. . . . These inducements carried desolation to many a home, but they filled our ranks."[144]

Those areas hardest hit by economic distress, such as Manchester, where only 9 of 84 cotton mills were in full operation by 1809, were prime targets for recruiting parties. "Twenty thousand people are there [in Manchester] said to be out of employ," an article in the *Newcastle Chronicle* reported, "but recruiting sergeants stand ready day and night to offer them 'ready pay and good quarters.'"[145] William Rowbottom from Oldham left a wealth of information in his diaries about his district and its reaction to war. He noted a "universal pant for glory" accompanied by stark economic distress as the reasons weavers enlisted.[146] A commentary in the *Times* of London supports this position: "Men enter as substitutes in the militia, or as recruits in the Line, because they want employment."[147]

John Macfarlane, a weaver and son of a weaver, enlisted in 1807 because of unhappiness with his job and home. He described the presence of eager recruiters: "There was a great demand for the army. Drums and fifes were heard on every street in Glasgow. If a person was walking on the street or looking in through a window, you would not be there long till there was a soldier asking you to enlist."[148] A Scottish recruiting sergeant corroborates the need to single out prospective recruits but goes on to add a bit of sophistication to his method: "Set a Glasgow man, and a Glasgow weaver to that [recruiting] to lure recruits out of Glasgow mills."[149]

In those districts less economically depressed, the recruiting parties resorted to various methods of persuasion, most involving drink and false promises. A recruiting sergeant for the Royal Artillery, for example, plied Alex Alexander, a potential volunteer, with numerous reasons to enlist: "We [the Royal Artillery] have superior pay, superior clothing, little marching, always riding with the guns on expedition, &c. Then you always have marching money, no musket or kit to carry, just a sword such as you see the party wear. Besides there is no flogging in the Royal Artillery, but every encouragement is held out for young men of every description, and much more to such fine-spirited, well-educated, young fellows as you." The sergeant then went on to promise that Alexander "would be a sergeant in six months, and an officer in a year or two at the very farthest."[150] Alexander took the man at his word and enlisted for life. He soon discovered that he had been sold a bill of goods and that army life was nothing as promised: "The first man I saw punished [flogged] my heart was like to burst. It was with difficulty I could restrain my tears, as the thought broke upon me of what I had brought myself to. Indeed, my spirits sunk from that day, and all hopes of bettering my condition in life fled forever. I had hitherto only seen the pomp of war—the gloss and glitter of the army; now I was introduced into the arcana of its origination, and under the direct influence of its stern economy. I felt how much I had been deceived."[151]

When military spectacle and promises failed, recruiters resorted to less subtle means. One recruiting sergeant, Joseph Donaldson of the 94th, was a Scotsman and an expert at his trade. He explained his approach to dealing with potential recruits: "Your last resource was to get him drunk, and then slip a shilling in his pocket, get him home to your billet, and next morning swear he enlisted, bring all your party to prove it, get him persuaded to pass the doctor. . . . Should he pass, you must try every means in your power to get him to drink [again], blow him up with a fine story, get him inveigled to the magistrates, in some shape or another, and get him attested; by no means let him out of your hands."[152]

This same sergeant also took the time to explain his technique for dealing with men of different professions. While possibly exaggerated for effect, the sergeant's words appear to reflect his acquired experience in dealing with potential recruits:

The truth is, you could scarcely ever catch a weaver contented. They are always complaining. Therefore, you would never have much trouble enticing them to enlist, if you knew how to go about it. . . . Ask him how a clever handsome-looking fellow like him could waste his time hanging see-saw between heaven and earth in a damp unwholesome shop, when he could be breathing the pure air of heaven . . . and have little or nothing to do if he enlisted for a soldier,—that the weaving was going to ruin, and he had better get into some berth, or he might soon be starved. This was generally enough for a weaver; but the ploughboys had to be hooked in a different way. When you got into conversation with them, tell how many recruits had been made sergeants, when they enlisted—how many were now officers. If you saw an officer pass while you were speaking, no matter whether you knew him or not, tell him he was only a recruit a year ago; but now he's so proud he won't speak to you. If this won't do, don't give up the chase—keep after him—tell him that in the place your *gallant honourable* regiment is lying, everything may be had for almost nothing. . . . As you find him to have the stomach, strengthen the dose, and he must be overcome at last. You must keep him drinking—don't let him go to the door without one of your party with him, until he is passed the doctor and attested. . . . To be sure . . . some of the sentimental chaps might despise all this, but they were the easiest caught of all. You had only to get into heroics, and spout a good deal about glory, honour, drums, trumpets, applauding worlds, deathless fame, immortality, and all that and you had him as safe as a mouse in a trap![153]

The enterprising Duke of Gordon allegedly used his family and the beauty of his wife to lure recruits into the ranks in the late 1790s. Accompanied by bagpipes, his daughters would dance a reel for any man who joined the newly formed Gordon Highlanders (92nd Regiment of Foot). According to Philip Haythornthwaite, it was the duke's wife, Bonnie Jean, who sealed the deal by placing the king's shilling between her lips and offering it with a kiss to any man who would take the shilling and enlist.[154]

Still, despite the financial lure of the bounty and all the machinations of recruiting parties, recruitment remained a problem. The demand for men nearly always exceeded supply.[155] Losses due to disease, battle, and desertion never fell below 16,000 men a year, reaching a peak of over 25,000 soldiers in 1812.[156] British army and navy fatalities during the Napoleonic Wars totaled approximately 225,000 soldiers,[157] when the army as a whole averaged about 144,000 men and the navy about 64,000.[158] The total of nearly a quarter-million deaths makes a higher ratio of fatalities per number serving than in World War I.[159]

Yearly enlistment numbers, however, never exceeded much more than about 19,000 men, which meant that replacing losses was a constant concern and sometimes unattainable goal.[160] The government considered a number of improvements to the army to encourage enlistment; as Best notes, the only practical solution not attempted was to make "military life less forbidding and impoverishing."[161] The British government even resorted to enlisting Spanish volunteers into British line regiments in an effort to fill the ranks. This limited experiment produced about 300 soldiers, who appear to have served with some distinction.[162]

In a further attempt to entice men to serve, British militiamen were allowed to volunteer directly into the regular army starting in 1805.[163] Because these soldiers could not be compelled to serve beyond the boundaries of Britain, large bounties were offered to volunteers willing to exchange into line units. A series of militia acts between 1808 and 1812 made militia service compulsory for all men between 18 and 30 years of age, simultaneously increasing the numbers of soldiers available for island defense and the pool of potential full-service recruits.[164] An additional bill was introduced in 1813, permitting militia regiments to volunteer for service on the continent. The results were disappointing, however, as less than 8,000 of the expected 30,000 militiamen took advantage of the opportunity.[165] Eventually, though, over 94,000 militiamen transferred to the army between 1807 and 1814.[166]

It has been suggested that the quality of the British soldier may have improved dramatically from 1806 on, when men from all walks of life and socioeconomic levels were drafted into the militia.[167] This "upgrade" argument has two fundamental flaws. First, as has been shown, British recruits were more respectable than has so often been asserted. Their average age and occupational backgrounds at enlistment present a picture of probably decent and fairly young men, driven into the army because of economic circumstances. The second and more telling problem with the idea that the militia brought a better caliber of individual into the service relates to the practice of substitution. While the militia theoretically drew on the entire spectrum of British males, a clause in each militia act permitted men being drafted into the militia to send a substitute in their place. The rates for securing a replacement averaged between £20 and £30 and in some districts rose to the princely sum of £60.[168] These fees usually exceeded the standard bounties offered for line service. Those enterprising substitutes who then volunteered into the regular army stood to receive a bounty in addition to their fees as militia replacements.

The substitutes who accepted these large sums naturally came from the disadvantaged classes, the same stratum of mostly poor and unemployed men who were the targets of regular army recruiters.[169] As John Fortescue points out, it was the substitutes who composed the militia, not the drafted men. In Bute in 1804, for example, not a single balloted man entered the militia ranks; all were paid surrogates. The Middlesex militia likewise filled its 1803 quota with 4,499 substitutes and one originally drafted man. When the drafted man's time expired in 1810, as Fortescue humorously recalls, "the Lord Lieutenant begged to be allowed to keep him as a curiosity."[170] The ballot for the year 1807 illustrates the widespread nature of substitution: for all of Britain only 3,129 principals were raised from a draft of 26,085 men (12 percent). All the rest were replacements. Hence Fortescue concludes that "these substitutes were precisely the men, who but for the heavy bounty which they gain from serving comfortably at home, would gladly have enlisted in the army."[171] Thus, it can safely be said that the influx of men from the militia into line units had a negligible effect on the overall quality of the soldiers in the regular army.

Even allowing militiamen to transfer into line units did little to ameliorate the recruiting situation, and shortages remained an ever-present problem. Crimps (middlemen in the recruiting process) soon rose to importance, especially during times when the economy improved and recruiting was hardest. Many crimps were tavern keepers, which gave them ready access to potential volunteers.[172] Recruiting sergeants would pay the crimps a fee in return for handing over a certain number of recruits. The crimps were often unscrupulous characters who shanghaied men by whatever means necessary, including knocking them unconscious or helping them drink their way into a comparable state. Though similar to naval press gangs, the crimps did not have the legal authority to abduct and hold men; this legal obstacle, however, did little to inhibit them from procuring men for the army through questionable means. Some crimps instructed men in the art of desertion and reenlistment, thereby increasing the profit margin for both but exposing only the recruit to the threat of death should he be caught in the act. Further pressing the legal boundaries, crimps sometimes worked deals to have men released from local jails; the men would be shepherded directly to recruiting sergeants and into the army with little heed paid to their wishes. The crimps prospered even after Parliament passed the recruiting bill of 1796, which organized recruiting and assigned quotas to counties.[173]

The myth of the British recruit as criminal may have originated here, as crimps did funnel a small number of men from local jails into the military. It is unknown exactly how many civilians chose armed service over jail time; given the lack of documentation and first-hand accounts confirming the practice, the number appears to be limited. It is crucial to remember, however, that the men released from prison and allowed to join the army were mostly jailed as debtors and had not been convicted of serious crimes, as Arthur Gilbert has pointed out.[174]

Roger Buckley, in his study of the British army in the West Indies, demonstrates that convicted criminals and deserters were only accepted into the penal corps, the Royal West Indian Rangers (established in 1806), and the Royal York Rangers (1808), which were formed with drafts from the Royal African Corps and transported to India, West Africa, or, as was most often the case, the West Indies. He confirms that magistrates had the statutory authority to pardon criminals and paupers only if they would serve in the West Indies,[175] a strategically important theater but a frequently lethal environment for soldiers sent to serve there, due to yellow fever, malaria, dengue, dysentery, and other diseases. Of the 80,000 soldiers sent to the West Indies between 1793 and 1798, 40,000 died.[176] Data from 1793 to 1815 show an astounding 424,000 casualties, including 75,000 deaths.[177]

Buckley concludes "that the army [on the continent] was maintained primarily with men untainted by crime," pointing out that not a single study supporting the British-recruit-as-criminal supposition exists for the period in question (1792–1815).[178] Historians often allude to the criminal background of the British ranker but rarely produce supporting evidence, perhaps, as Buckley states, because it does not exist.

Buckley praises Silvia Frey for being one of the few scholars who has gone against the grain and questioned the theory that British recruits were predominately lawbreakers, convicted or otherwise. He cites Frey's summation that "it is a misconception to suppose that such men [convicted criminals, highway robbers, thieves, smugglers, and rogues] were a majority in the British army."[179] Gilbert, on whose limited demographic work Frey based her argument, took the first position against the widely accepted characterization of the soldiers' backgrounds. Referring to Middlesex enlistment records, he concludes: "These figures do suggest that when the army expanded during wartime, this was not accomplished simply by sweeping the jails and that when rewards of a reasonably attractive kind were offered workers would enlist." Gilbert goes on to state that "a closer examination of the eighteenth century is in order, one that calls for close empirical work rather than simply accepting the comments of those whose views were coloured by the prejudices of the time."[180]

It is important to provide a context within which the label "criminal" and the nature of crime in England 200 years ago can be analyzed. An understanding of the British legal code and the relationship between crime and economic distress affords us insight into what constituted crime in Great Britain during the Napoleonic period, how British society dealt with those who broke the law, and how the misperception of the soldier-as-criminal may have originated.

From the seventeenth century onward, the propertied classes of Great Britain caused the enactment of a plethora of capital crimes statutes, the vast majority of which were related to crimes against property. This collection of crimes became known as the Bloody Code, and it underlay the English system of criminal law from 1688 to 1815. Under this code, 225 offenses brought capital punishment, including sheep stealing, pick-pocketing more than a shilling, cutting down trees in an avenue, or maiming cattle.[181] Even children could be hanged or transported for small thefts. The result was a steady increase in the number of convictions and a rise in prison populations.[182]

The mounting crime rate in Great Britain during the late eighteenth and early nineteenth centuries was in great measure related to economic hardship; as real wages fell and employment opportunities vanished, people stole to survive.[183] While population increases must be considered when analyzing crime rates, Douglas Hay's work on Staffordshire from 1800 to 1803 shows that spikes in prosecutions for theft were undoubtedly driven by economic pressures. He contends that "petty thefts were committed in dearth by people who were not committing them before, or that those who had done so were obliged to increase the frequency with which they stole because of the higher price of food." Hay goes on to argue that evidence for these crimes shows that they were committed by families or individuals without planning and "for very small amounts of property, even food." Other serious offenses, such as highway robbery and assault, showed little fluctuation, being "insensitive to price changes." These crimes, Hay says, "were often the work of men and women who committed such crimes with regularity, and who were exempt from the pressing concerns of the necessitous poor."[184] J.M. Beattie supports this hypothesis by correlating patterns of prosecutions across time with the Schumpter-Gilboy Price Index. He argues that the correspondences between prosecution rates and increases in crime are tied to "fluctuations in the changing price of food and in other indicators of economic wellbeing."[185]

Robert Stewart, Lord Castlereagh, the secretary of war under William Pitt the Younger and later the foreign secretary under Lord Liverpool, addressed the connection between want and crime rates. Speaking on the two types of crime as he saw them, crimes of "deep moral depravity" (such as murder, manslaughter, and rape) and crimes of property, Castlereagh noted that during the period from 1810 to 1818 the first did not rise, while the second did. "The causes of this undisputed rise in the incidence against property," he argued, "were purely economic and transitory; more than half of all persons committed for trial in 1818 in England and Wales came from Lancaster, Warwick, York, Middlesex, and Surrey, notoriously the most populous and manufacturing districts in the kingdom."[186]

Such crimes of property increased during the winter, as fuel and shelter needs increased at the very time when seasonal employment dried up.[187] Thus, many of the idle and disorderly men culled from the jails by crimps, and probably a great many of the pretrial felons released by magistrates to serve in the penal corps, were driven by such economic pressures to commit property crimes. Felonies, it must be remembered, included the theft of wood, vegetables, fruits, and clothing.

Stephen Nicholas and Richard Steckel note that historians have by and large rejected the concept of a separate underground criminal class existing during the nineteenth century.[188] Citing works by George Rudé and David Jones,[189] Nicholas and Steckel make a convincing summary of crimes and those who committed them during the late eighteenth and early nineteenth centuries: "These studies argue that the great majority of crime was committed by ordinary men who worked jobs . . . but who also stole articles on occasion. Though not 'honest men,' the convicts were employed people who supplemented their income by theft in times of stress."[190]

Rudé's work on crime in Sussex, Gloucester, and London during the nineteenth century confirms the relationship between economic downturns and the types of crime they engendered. In Sussex the most frequently stolen item was food, with clothing being the next most popular choice.[191] In Gloucester money and valuables were the most selected items, with clothing and food rounding out the top three items.[192] Further data from Surrey and Southwark and the rural parishes outside Surrey corroborate Rudé's findings. In Surrey clothes were stolen most often, with food being the second most pilfered item; these categories were reversed in the rural areas of Surrey. In Southwark the stolen items of choice were clothing, household goods, worked metal, and food.[193]

As Rudé points out, this gives us "some preliminary idea of prisoners' priorities." He calls these offenses "survival crimes" and argues that "such crimes tended to respond directly to short-term economic factors such as a rise in prices or a fall in wages, whereas the more serious and more violent crimes, or those most susceptible to capital punishment, were not so responsive to economic motivation."[194] Rudé notes that 75 to 80 percent of all the crimes in Sussex and Gloucester through 1850 fell under the category of larceny.[195] As his data show, it was not difficult to acquire the label of "criminal": of the 2,000 people tried in Sussex and Gloucester between 1805 and 1850, 70 percent committed to trial were found guilty.[196] As to the types of people committing crimes, Rudé found that 89.2 percent of convicted criminals in Sussex from 1805 to 1850 were laborers and servants. For Gloucester it was 69.2 percent, and for London in 1810 it was 32.5 percent.[197]

It seems fairly likely, then, that even those few men forced into the army by magistrates for committing offenses were not hardened criminals by nature; they appear to be individuals who turned to crime during times of desperate need. The crime data also illustrate, quite poignantly, the wretched circumstances that drove men to consider army enlistment as their last hope.

One further crime-related occurrence may have adversely affected perceptions of the British ranker, adding the final touch to the criminal stigma associated with soldiering. Crime levels dropped when men went to war, while indictments (particularly for theft) rose during the first years following peace.[198] These patterns created general expectations that peace meant increased crime and that war caused crime rates to diminish. It was assumed that the logical culprits responsible for the change in crime rates were the men who enlisted. This natural, if skewed, perception was enhanced when crime rates jumped following the discharge of large numbers of soldiers back into civilian life. That the men who enlisted because they could find no employment came home by the hundreds of thousands to find the bleakest possible employment situation seems not to have been incorporated into public memory. With no means to support themselves, many of the men turned to begging and crime, as did many civilians in the depressed economic times following the war. Over 300,000 soldiers and sailors were released in 1815, flooding an already precarious economy with surplus laborers.[199] As H.V. Bowen notes, "Not only did this represent somewhere between 1 and 3 percent of the entire population, but also it included a very significant proportion of the most vulnerable adult male laboring classes."[200]

Perhaps the most touching display in the Napoleonic collection at Britain's National Army Museum is the solitary mannequin of a former British soldier, one-legged and leaning on an old crutch, reduced to mendicancy. Bedraggled and miserable, the soldier wears his Waterloo medal pinned on what remains of his uniform tunic and stands, cup in hand, begging to survive. That he has been perceived to be a malcontent with violent and criminal tendencies is both a misperception and a travesty. His motivations and his contributions have been misinterpreted and largely forgotten, even as Wellington has risen to be regarded as perhaps the greatest soldier ever produced by Britain.

The demographic information revealed in the BSC, however, coupled with economic analysis, presents a new perspective on the British regular. Rather than being a despicable rogue with a vile nature and a background to match, the typical British army recruit during the period 1803 to 1815 was most likely a young man driven to enlist through a combination of demographic, technological, and political forces that melded to create an untenable employment situation. Unable to find work or even feed himself, the volunteer chose the army out of need. Like Lawrence, the recruit may also have been unsatisfied with an apprenticeship, if he was lucky enough to have one, and perhaps enamored enough with the opportunities purportedly offered by the army to consider the advantages of leaving home. Few volunteers mention patriotic ideals as the reason behind their choice. It was the bounty and the hope of employment that appealed to most recruits, and this returns us to economic necessity as the primary motivation behind enlistment. The British volunteer may not have been the "very flower of the nation," as Cockerill has suggested,[201] but no proof exists that he was "scum" herded from jail and forced to serve his country. Unfortunately, accepting the king's shilling did not mean an end to the recruit's days of desperation and despair. In fact, his times of want were only beginning.

3

OVER THE HILLS AND FAR AWAY

Surviving on Campaign

Recruits soon learned that daily life in the service of the king was anything but easy and that nothing in the army was free. After he appeared before a magistrate and put his mark on his recruitment papers, William Lawrence's life as a soldier of the king officially began. Being shortchanged on the enlistment bonus may have enlightened Lawrence, who was always quick to assess situations, that not everything about army life would measure up to the recruiting party's promises. If his two recruiting experiences were the norm, he also quickly found himself parted from the bounties he received. The first efforts to separate a volunteer from his money were usually initiated by members of the recruiting party, who shared with every enlistee the traditions that must be upheld by each new soldier: loaning money and buying rounds at the public house.

Joseph Donaldson remembered the warning he received upon enlisting in the 94th Regiment of Foot. When asked by one of the recruiting party, a fellow from Aberdeen, if he had received his bounty, Donaldson replied in the affirmative. "Then," cautioned the soldier, "you'll no want for friends as long as it lasts." Donaldson's experience confirmed the truth underlying the soldier's words of advice. He recalled: "So, I found; for every little attention was paid to me they could devise. One brushed my shoes, another my coat; and nothing could equal the professions of good-will and offers of service I received. There was a competition amongst them who should be my comrade, each supporting his offer by what service he could render me."[1]

Donaldson was informed that it was the custom for new recruits to treat the soldiers of his new battalion who were present, so he did, even giving in to their pleas for loans. Moreover, each recruit was coerced to provide the sergeant conducting the party to barracks with a dinner and an accompanying present, showing the recruit's appreciation and goodwill. As the group progressed from public house to public house, the men of the recruiting party ordered rounds of whiskey, each offering to contribute when the bill came due. When it came to actually paying the tab, each soldier made a half-hearted attempt to borrow from his comrades. In the end, the bills all went to Donaldson. He was similarly besieged that evening, the next morning, and the evening after, until his funds were spent. After his money ran out, Donaldson approached those to whom he had loaned shillings. He was laughed at, ridiculed, and even threatened, but not repaid. "This," he noted, "opened my eyes a little."[2]

In addition to these overt methods of siphoning off the volunteer's enlistment bonus, the army had further surprises in store for the enlistee. A varying amount of the bounty, from £2 and 2 shillings to £4,[3] had to be returned to pay for the soldier's kit, which included shoes, socks, gaiters, shirts, cap, and knapsack.[4] If the recruit had already spent the entire bounty, the cost for these necessities was deducted monthly from his forthcoming pay.

Lawrence's bounty was probably consumed in a similar fashion; he does not mention this ordeal, perhaps because time, disappointment, or possibly having been in a state of inebriation prevented him from recalling all the details. It was a common occurrence, in any case, and only the first hint that army life would prove harsher than expected. General John Burgoyne's dictum "The life of a soldier is the property of the king" certainly applied,[5] and the recruit soon understood that the sovereign did little to preserve his royal possessions.

It first struck Lawrence that the men's lives were no longer their own when he and his regiment were hurried to a ship leaving for Rio de Janeiro, after receiving his kit but no real training. More than a little bewildered by events, Lawrence witnessed what he called "the most disheartening spectacle." As the regiment was boarding, he could not help but notice the heart-wrenching scene, played out again and again, of soldiers being separated from their wives and children, perhaps for the last time. Only 6 wives out of each company of 100 men were officially allowed to accompany their husbands, and the magnitude of the distress greatly dismayed Lawrence. He recalled this brush with the realities of army life: "I could not see a dry eye in Portsmouth, and if the tears could have been collected, they might have stocked a hospital in eye-water for some months . . . it was indeed dreadful to view."[6]

Lawrence did not realize it at the time, but army life for the soldiers who served George III was most often an experience that fluctuated within fairly narrow bands, from barely tolerable to miserable. Time in winter quarters, when the physical and psychological demands of campaign and battle were drastically reduced, was comparatively easy on the ranker; rations were usually regular and sleeping quarters more substantial than during time in the field. And while the food received by the rank and file at best barely covered their needs during relatively sedentary times, the demands on the soldier were fairly light, so barracks life was bearable.

Existence on campaign was a different story. Living in the field is rarely pleasant for any soldier, regardless of the period, but the Napoleonic soldier tended to experience mostly hardship; the British ranker was no exception. Pay, clothing, and rations became irregular, even rare, commodities for all soldiers in the field. The most pressing issues for the redcoat were those that sapped both his strength and his motivation during the daily grind of campaign life. Lawrence had not been long with the army before he identified the critical issues that became daily tribulations, opining that the army greatly suffered during a march from Oropesa due to "the heat of the weather, the long exposure, the insufficient food, and bad roads, and illness being very prevalent."[7] This was not the last time that he would have reason to complain.

For much of the Peninsular War, the British regular camped under the stars with little for protection.[8] Blankets were issued to the men in 1809 and tents to the officers; the men learned to make a tent of sorts with two blankets, two muskets, and four bayonets.[9] The effects of exposure in severe weather, from storms to frigid cold, took their toll on the men. The issuing of tents to the rank and file in 1813 helped reduce exposure, but the soldiers all too often found themselves without adequate food or clothing.

Lawrence reminds us, though, that living under the stars was not always so uncomfortable. Good weather allowed the soldiers some degree of relief. Moreover, sometimes the men were quartered in decent buildings and had "plenty of our own supplies," usually during the winter and spring seasons when the troops were billeted on a semipermanent basis. These rare times of ease and comfort, however, did little to stop the men from exploring their housing in search of plunder; perhaps they did so out of habit or in an effort to fill their bellies and their pockets in anticipation of the hard times they knew would come. In the case in which he mentions having "plenty," Lawrence and his mates discovered and dug up a jar hidden in the cellar; the vessel contained about 7,000 Portuguese dollars. The men, as always, divided the shares equally and then successfully contrived to keep the theft hidden from the owner and their officers who were sent to investigate the incident. Lawrence and his fellow redcoats, determined to keep their ill-gotten gains, boldly declared their innocence to the officers who arrived on the scene and eventually hid the loot in pumpkins to avoid the mandatory searches that followed the complaint.[10]

Unfortunately, Lawrence never relates how or on what he and his accomplices spent their purloined cash. Most likely they spent it on drink, women, and food, and probably in that order. The rankers might have used the money to purchase clothing or shoes, as the lack of boots and replacement uniforms was a constant source of aggravation. Long marches, lack of shelter, and difficult terrain made short work of the soldiers' original issue. Large numbers of men quickly discovered that their shoes were disintegrating and could find no substitutes. Being without shoes was so prevalent that the men coined a term for it: "padding the hoof." James Anton of the 42nd Highlanders stated sadly that it was "impossible to describe the painful state that some of those shoeless men were in, crippling along the way, their feet cut or torn by sharp stones or brambles."[11] Rifleman Harris offers a similarly vivid picture of these men on the march: "I have seen officers and men hobbling forward, with tears in their eyes from the misery of long miles, empty stomachs, and ragged backs without even shoes or stockings on their bleeding feet."[12] In his letters home, Major-General F.P. Robinson asserted that being barefoot was the norm for the men. Writing in July 1813 near San Sebastian, he declared: "Our whole Division are nearly barefoot. . . . Many of my poor fellows have traversed the Pyrenees without either shoe or stocking to their feet; yet no complaint is heard . . . all we want is food and clothing."[13] The nightly slaughtering of bullocks offered the men some respite: they took strips of the raw hides of the slaughtered beasts and wrapped them around their feet.[14]

As for uniforms, the men wore them until they were threadbare, tattered, filthy, and closer in color to brown or black than to red. They found and wore any type of clothing in an effort to cover themselves. Collectively they looked more like a roaming band of stragglers or bandits than an army.[15] William Grattan, who served in the Connaught Rangers,[16] described the men as being "without any distinguishing mark of uniform."[17] The soldiers learned to preserve what they did possess, while discovering tricks such as baking their jackets in ovens to remove the vermin.[18] On the rare occasion when new clothes were issued, the cast-off uniforms were burned in an effort to rid the soldiers of their insect companions.

Even the elite Coldstream Guards did not receive their yearly shipment of uniforms on time. In April 1814, for example, only the first battalion's uniforms were delivered, and those were too few and too small to outfit the men. When the shipment came for the second battalion in 1815, after the battle of Waterloo, the uniforms were all too large. The remedy in both cases was formulated by Benjamin Selway, a regimental quartermaster. He organized groups of men to cut and sew pieces of the new uniforms together to make proper-sized regimental coats and pants. Given the numbers of tailors, weavers, and other textile workers in the army, finding men with appropriate skills would not have been difficult.[19]

Often without real shelter, a soldier would count himself lucky if at the end of the day's march he found some type of hovel whose only occupants were vermin; these creatures, mostly lice and fleas, soon took up residence in hair or clothing. The men's hair, daubed with dirty grease, soap, and flour for braiding, also proved attractive to rats and mice, which, as Anton recalled, were often found at night "scrambling about our heads, eating the filthy stuff."[20] The men hated the queuing of hair and (for numerous reasons) were pleased when the standing order was discontinued in 1808.[21] Even this caused distress, though, as the regimental wives feared for their status, because one of their responsibilities was dressing the men's hair each day.[22]

The difficulties of exposure and the lack of uniforms paled, however, when compared to the greatest aggravation facing the British soldier: the inability of the commissariat to feed the men adequately. The regular's daily ration of one pound of meat (including the bone), one pound of biscuit, and a third of a pint of spirits (usually rum) was nutritionally deficient (see the discussion below). In addition, from the rankers' accounts it appears that the commissariat experienced ongoing problems in delivering full rations to the men in the field. In fact, it seems that failed ration deliveries were something of the norm.

All soldiers complain about campaign rations, and the soldiers of the Napoleonic Wars were no different. Each national army faced logistical challenges that it could not overcome, at least not on every operation. The French army suffered extreme privation and casualties on the retreat from Napoleon's disastrous Russia gambit, for example, that exceeded anything the British experienced in Spain; only in the brief withdrawal to Corunna in 1809 did the redcoats face a similar nightmare of supply shortages, harsh weather, and determined enemy pursuit. Napoleon's retreat from Russia, however, lasted only about two months. The logistical shortcomings in Spain and Portugal affected the British army for over six years, just as it did the French. The duration of Wellington's struggle to feed his soldiers, coupled with his edicts against plundering, put the common ranker in a tenuous position. It is difficult to read the soldiers' accounts, almost all of which tell similar tales of commissariat breakdowns and episodes of near-starvation, without feeling some degree of pity for the men. The number of such anecdotes gives a certain degree of credence to the rankers' complaints.[23] A few examples will suffice to convey the degree of suffering to which the redcoats became accustomed.

John Douglas, an NCO in the Royal Scots, grumbled about a three-day march from Ciudad Rodrigo to Campillo in the fall of 1812, during which "not a toothful in the shape of eatables was served out."[24] Without supplementing their diets, Douglas and his fellow soldiers would have lost about four pounds a man.[25] William Wheeler of the 51st wrote of a similar experience, stating that he recalled many days of marching with no food and on one occasion existing for four and a half days on a half-allowance of biscuit.[26]

Colonel John Leach remembered a two-week march during which the men received only their daily meat ration and a mixture of coarse flour, bran, and chopped straw.[27] The meat alone was insufficient; the effects of the bread replacement can only be imagined, as the concoction's high-fiber, high-roughage content would have greatly diminished the body's ability to absorb calories from the flour and maybe the meat as well.

Such experiences caused the men to become resourceful when it came to obtaining additional nourishment. John Green of the 68th Light Infantry describes how the men, carrying their camp-kettles, would assail the battalion butchers in hopes of procuring leftovers from the bulls slaughtered for the day's meal: "It was a common practice with us to catch the blood, which we boiled . . . and this served as a substitute for bread." Green goes on to depict the men, covered with blood, falling over one another as they scrambled to obtain a share.[28] Lawrence also mentions the practice, writing that blood "was caught in our kettles and boiled and eaten, and was found to be very good." He recalls with amusement watching as a Corporal Burke cooked bullock's heels. Too impatient to boil the heels or heat them properly, if such a thing was possible, Burke tossed the heels into his frying pan, hair and all. He then nibbled at them as they sizzled, repeatedly throwing the uncooked segments back into the pan until all was eaten.[29]

Gathering where the bullocks were killed appears to have been a common method of attaining additional nutrition, even if the parts obtained were not the most desirable. John Cooper, a sergeant of the 7th, wrote of jostling with other soldiers in order to obtain the liver, tail, and blood of the animals.[30] Hard-pressed officers did the same; George Bell, an officer in the 34th who would rise to major-general, curried favor with the brigade butcher in order to gain access to these items without having to fight for them. The butcher occasionally rewarded him with a bullock's or sheep's head. Bell called these commodities "luxuries," for the "army was long unpaid and our credit low."[31]

A highland soldier openly acknowledged that food was in short supply. Given the position of feeding biscuit scraps to Wellington's hounds, the young man realized that his status could not have been much lower, for the canines ate better than he did. "I was very hungry," he reflects, "and thought it a good job . . . as we got our own fill [of biscuits]. . . . I sighed, as I fed the dogs, over my humble station, and ruined hopes."[32]

Two comments, one by Major Charles Napier and another by a common soldier, best sum up the soldier's point of view regarding the trials of army life. In a letter to his mother in 1811, Napier complains: "We are on biscuit full of maggots, and though not a bad soldier, hang me if I can relish maggots. We suffer much in point of food."[33] The ranker, complaining to a mate, provides the viewpoint from the bottom. "Bill," he grumbles, "the parliament and the great men at home . . . don't know anything about individjals [*sic*] . . . they don't know that you are damned tired, and that I hae [*sic*] got no pong [*pao*, which is Portuguese for bread]."[34]

Colonel Leach captures the impossibility of surviving under the difficult conditions of campaign life with little food; he also reveals the soldiers' black humor regarding their predicament. With a bitterness born of experience, he wryly comments that "if any corpulent person despairs of reducing his weight . . . I strongly recommend a few week's change of air and scene [with the army] . . . taking especially good care to observe the same rules and regulations for diet. . . . If that fails to have the desired effect, I give him up."[35] Cooper concurs with this assessment, remarking: "When a man entered upon a soldier's life . . . he should have parted with half his stomach."[36]

Men joked about their daily misery, but their letters, journals, and memoirs often contain resentful passages complaining of their treatment, with the lack of food being their chief concern. The account of Moyle Sherer, an officer in the 34th, is representative. His explanation for why men plunder is surprisingly astute. Given that many officers had the financial means to buy supplemental food from the locals and thus removed themselves from the common soldier's daily food struggles, Sherer's insight is that much more remarkable: "Setting aside assault or battles, the soldier is often harassed with toil and hunger, impatient and penniless. . . . when troops are neither fed, clothed, or paid with regularity, they are tempted beyond their strength. . . . the military man, who has served, learns how and when to make allowances for their disorders, which the world is ever too forward to characterize as barbarous and licentious."[37]

These sad and telling accounts, while sometimes humorous, illustrate a serious logistical problem that affected the redcoat's health and fitness as a soldier. Provisions were all too often sparse, and their quality was also uneven at best. Robert Knowles, a lieutenant in the 7th Royal Fusiliers, was disconcerted when he examined the meat provided by the army. He wrote home that "the meat is so poor that it would be burnt if exposed for sale in Bolton Market."[38] Rifleman Kincaid grumbled that his meat ration was often "enough to have physicked a dromedary."[39] Green was equally disgusted with the quality, referring to the two pounds of meat he was given as "carrion."[40] One of Costello's friends in the 95th voiced a similar concern about provision quality after a bout of food poisoning induced by army rations: "when I came into it [the army] I had a stomach like any Christian; but now, oh God, have mercy on my poor stomach, that for want of Christian food is turned into a scavenger's cart, obliged to take in every rubbage."[41] Donaldson complained that the bullocks often went unfed and were marched to exhaustion, just like the men. As a result, the meat was "as tough and stringy as a piece of junk."[42]

Given these considerations, it is understandable that the ranker turned to theft in order to supplement his diet. The ability of the British commissariat to feed and clothe the men was no worse and in many ways better than that of other armies of the time. Still, relative merits aside, it was the common redcoat who suffered when supplies were not delivered. Under the circumstances, the British ranker's reputation as a thorough and consummate plunderer and thief certainly appears well earned. The common soldier was as ingenious as he was systematic in his quest to acquire rations of the type and quantity denied him by the commissariat. In this regard, at least, the collective memory is accurate.

John Macfarlane of the Highland Light Infantry fondly reminisced about the time he and six messmates were boarded with a Spanish family near Astorga. The family made large loaves of bread daily but watched the soldiers carefully to guard against theft. The men contrived to divert them and successfully made off with a six- to eight-pound loaf, which was quickly divided into shares. Macfarlane's account exudes the men's joy at devouring the hot bread.[43]

Anthony Hamilton, an officer of the 43rd, found the men of his battalion equally enterprising. One or more of them distracted the regimental bakers while comrades, using their bayonets, made holes in the backs of ovens and "liberated" loaves for personal use.[44] Lawrence writes of obtaining fresh bread in the same fashion. He and his mates amused the Spanish woman who ran the bakery, regaling her with "Peninsular tales" as the bread was baking. On a given signal, other soldiers broke open her oven and absconded with all the loaves. Lawrence adds: "We did all we could to reconcile her loss to her . . . but this pity did not detain us long." The men then met up and shared the bread, which was "a greater luxury than meat . . . [and] smoking hot, though not very well done; but if it had been dough we could have eaten it at that time."[45]

Green, a longtime veteran, adds an interesting side note to these capers, admitting that when he was on sentry duty he was forced to chase such men but did so with little zeal. "I ran after the bread-stealers," he conceded, "without having the least intention of catching them, knowing myself what is was to be hungry."[46]

Lawrence offers us another telling episode detailing the risks that the rankers took in obtaining food. When encamped near Portalegre, Portugal, in March 1811, the men were billeted in a chapel. In a nearby farmyard the redcoats discovered a quantity of pigs, which the "company had not tasted in some time." After using a sergeant's halberd to skewer a select swine and allow it to die in the field, ensuring that blame would not be directed his way should the incident be discovered, one of the men snuck into the field and dragged the animal back to the chapel. Despite this precaution, the owner of the hog observed the theft. When he appeared at the chapel demanding the pig, the soldiers, who outnumbered him, denied him satisfaction. Knowing that the farmer would return with the colonel, Lawrence and his comrades took the novel approach of hiding the still-warm carcass under the cloth gown of the chapel's statue of the Virgin Mary. The men correctly assumed that neither the farmer nor the colonel would ever search such a sacred shrine. That night "every man of the chapel company had a small portion [of pork] in the pot."[47]

Interestingly, Lawrence states that they expected no serious punishment if the theft was discovered. He believed that the only consequence would have been stopping the men's grog for a time, which, while serious enough to the British ranker, was hardly comparable to the short dance on the gibbet.[48] When it came to plundering, Wellington often threatened the redcoats with this punishment and sometimes imposed it, but the offenses apparently were so frequent that such a disciplinary method would have stripped the army of men in a very short time had it been the norm.

Douglas pitied the peasants who drove their flocks of sheep and goats through the town in which his unit was billeted, but that did not stop him from taking advantage of the situation. "We had nothing more [to do]," he recollects with pleasure, "than to stand at the door and choose either sheep or goat, lay hold of him and drag him in and pop him into the kettle."[49] Such days of easy pickings were rare, however, and exposed the soldier to possible disciplinary actions.

Charles O'Neil of the 28th Regiment of Foot remembered hunting wild pigs after a march; he knew it was against orders, "but we were literally starving to death." Successful in his hunt, he carried the pig back to camp. When his adjutant discovered the pig, he offered a doubloon for it instead of reporting the theft. "But food, in our condition, was far more precious than money," O'Neil recalls, "and we refused his offer." He wisely sent a quarter of the pig to the officer in appreciation for ignoring the indiscretion.[50]

A Sergeant Johnson of the Scots Greys recorded in his journal that he and his comrades had been without food for two days before Waterloo. Writing the night before the battle, he stated that the "keen tortures of hunger" forced the men to pilfer swine and poultry from a nearby farmhouse whose owner had refused to sell them any food. He notes that his commanding officer, Colonel Inglis Hamilton, joined the Greys and men from a number of highland infantry regiments around the campfire and shared the plunder, with Hamilton supplying the brandy.[51]

Like Colonel Hamilton, other officers were often forced to ignore Wellington's strict edicts regarding looting and look the other way, because they realized that the men were in extremis. Macfarlane writes approvingly of his colonel's actions: when the colonel "saw a field of turnips, he came back and called a man of each mess for turnips and water. Our Colonel knew that we had to have something to eat. Wood was sought after, and fires kindled. Afterwards, we got some flour served out. We made dumplings, or round balls, and boiled them. This was done as soon as possible for we were hungry."[52]

Even officers who were strict disciplinarians, like "Black Bob" Craufurd, were forced to bend a little, as they recognized that the plight of the men was beyond human endurance. Harris recorded with amazement how Craufurd feigned ignorance at what the men were doing right under his eyes during the retreat to Corunna: "Craufurd was, I remember, terribly severe, during this retreat, if he caught anything like pilfering amongst the men. As we stood, however, during this short halt, a very tempting turnip-field was close on the side of us, and several of the men were so ravenous, that although he was in our very ranks, they stepped into the field and helped themselves to the turnips, devouring them like famishing wolves. He either did not or would not observe the delinquency this time."[53]

A thorough nutritional investigation provides quantitative proof that the redcoats' tales regarding short rations, food shortages, and constant hunger were not exaggerations. The value of British army rations, in fact, was so low that even when regularly supplied the daily diet was insufficient to maintain a soldier on campaign. Nutritional deprivation left the redcoat prone to fatigue, diseases, and sometimes the physiological and psychological effects of near-chronic malnutrition.

The calculation of caloric needs for an individual depends on gender, height, weight, age, and activity level. For men in the British army in this period, we can estimate the typical heights and ages from the British Soldier Compendium sample. No information on weight is given in the description books, but weight can be calculated approximately from height, based on the body mass index (BMI) typical of men at that time. Estimates based on population studies show that the average BMI for men in the period from 1800 to 1819 was about 20.7.[54] Since BMI fluctuates within fairly narrow ranges for a healthy population, it is relatively safe to assume that the BMI of these men was between about 20 and 22.

When the caloric needs are calculated for men aged 15 to 40, of varying heights from 61.5 inches to about 71 inches and with body mass indexes of 20 to 22, the minimums needed to preserve body weight range from 2,500 to almost 3,500 calories, with an average just slightly under 3,000 calories. For the prototypical British recruit of 66.5 inches and 22 years of age weighing about 136 pounds,[55] the minimum caloric requirements are approximately 3,040.[56]

The British ration, however, provided only about 2,466 calories.[57] Thus, even when supplied, the provisions of the ranker fell almost 19 percent below the absolute minimums needed for men not facing the stresses and exertions of campaign and battle (or carrying the 70- to 80-pound pack that bent every soldier under its burden).[58] Food quantities varied considerably, however, due to campaign and logistical difficulties. Douglas complained that his rations never matched the proscribed amounts. He claimed that whoever was weighing the food back in the shipyards was taking advantage of the men.[59] It is therefore possible that the nutritional values of received rations were even lower than the numbers outlined here.

When compared calorically to the actual victuals distributed to imperial Romans, English Civil War combatants, sixteenth-century Spanish soldiers and sailors, Venetian galley oarsmen, and even sixteenth-century Spanish galley slaves,[60] the British soldier's fare comes in dead last (see the dietary data tables in appendix C for specific breakdowns).[61]

The British ranker marched, fought, and expended energy in a manner not unlike that of the soldier in the English Civil War, yet his diet was substantially less in every way. And while the Roman soldier used a portion of his energy expenditure fortifying his camp every night,[62] such an effort would not require food intake that supplied over two and a half times the calories, twice the protein, and almost three times the amount of carbohydrates and fat furnished to the British regular. Plain and simple, the rations of the Roman soldier were intended to keep him fit and available for active duty, while those of the British soldier were woefully inadequate and worked to debilitate him in relatively short order. The fact that the redcoat was fed a diet that was commensurate with the diet of Mediterranean ship slaves says a great deal about how the ranker was valued by the nation he served and why he found it necessary to steal food to supplement his rations. It is nothing short of miraculous that the Portuguese troops under British command somehow survived on even fewer rations (whatever was left after the British army was supplied).[63]

Jonathan Roth makes a key point, though, that is applicable to this investigation of soldiers' diets. He notes that vegetables are "seldom attested in the historical record."[64] Various legumes and beans were probably an important source of protein and nutrients for the soldiers of different eras, as they were for the poor. So while it is assumed that vegetables of some sort were at least an occasional part of each soldier's diet, the lack of historical evidence precludes their inclusion in this analysis except when specifically referenced. In regard to the dietary intake of the British soldier, however, little can be taken for granted. In the case of vegetables, for example, John Cooper

Table 3. Nutritional comparison of standard rations for various armies

Daily allowance	Imperial Roman soldier[a]	Common soldier (English Civil War)[b]	Spanish officer, soldier, or sailor (16th c.)[c]	Venetian galley oarsman (14th c.)[d]	Spanish galley slave (16th c.)[e]	British common soldier (Napoleonic Wars)
Calories	6,407	4,541	3,654	3,434	2,581	2,466
Carbohydrates (grams)	915	624	496	506.4	523	305
Fat (grams)	111	111	39	64	16	48
Protein (grams)	198	177	105	87	76	101

[a]Goldsworthy, *Roman Army at War*, 291. Goldsworthy states this was the smallest daily ration recorded.
[b]Young and Holmes, *English Civil War*, 50, citing Sir James Turner, who fought with the Swedish, Scots, and later Royalist armies. All army values were for rations actually issued, not for "suggested amounts" listed in regulations.
[c]Approximately 23 percent of these calories came from the 34 fl oz daily wine ration. While this was the same as the amount received by the Roman soldier, he received more bread, making the calories from wine only 13 percent of his diet. These data are for officially supplied food. Compiled nutritional data from this work and notations identifying the primary sources were generously provided by Dr. John Guilmartin. *Colección Navarrete* and *Colección Sanz de Barutell (Simancas)*, cited in Guilmartin, *Gunpowder and Galleys*, 223.
[d]Lane, "Venetian Merchant Galleys."
[e]*Colección Navarrete* and *Colección Sanz de Barutell (Simancas)*, cited in Guilmartin, *Gunpowder and Galleys*, 223.

specifically states that his Peninsular War rations never included any vegetables.[65] The British soldier's diet was clearly insufficient, by modern medical standards, to maintain the ranker's health.

When total energy expenditures (TEE) are figured in, it becomes readily apparent that the British soldier's rations fell well short of meeting his daily needs. The diaries, journals, letters, and memoirs of enlisted men provide enough specifics related to the exigencies of campaign life and the breakdown of the commissariat to construct mini–case studies; these examples of the physical demands placed on the British soldier in the field can be analyzed in conjunction with the caloric values of the partial rations received. Together, they demonstrate the untenable nature of army life for the ranker and the impossibility of trying to preserve health on army rations alone. The ranker often faced huge potential caloric deficits, sometimes almost 7,000 calories in a day of extreme marching and exertion and as much as 50,000–60,000 calories over a two-week span. The men would be physiologically and psychologically hard pressed to accept the related weight loss passively, even if these examples were anomalies, which they are not. The expenditure of calories that will result in a man losing a pound of body fat is usually calculated at about 3,600.[66] A march rate of 20 miles per day is assumed in the calculations shown in table 4.[67] The nutritional value of the British ration, coupled with reoccurring logistical difficulties, made finding sufficient food an ongoing challenge for the redcoat. The men were often forced to forage to supplement their rations.[68]

The evidence is fairly ample that these were not isolated cases.[69] The numbers at least partially explain why the redcoat plundered every turnip patch or potato field he encountered and why Spanish and Portuguese households were stripped of bread, chickens, pigs, or any food item that could be uncovered by the British ranker on the march, with a bit of initiative.

The data concerning micronutrients bring to light the reason why the soldiers were so enterprising and apparently relentless in their theft of food.[70] While the redcoats were not fully aware of the nutritional components of rations or the consequences of deficiencies, they were well acquainted with the physical side-effects of malnutrition. When the standard rations of the armies previously analyzed are compared (see table 5), the shortcomings of the British diet are immediately apparent. The lowest intake level is indicated with underscoring, 100 percent being the recommended level.

As can be seen, the Roman and English Civil War soldiers fared the best: their diets came up short in about half of the 22 categories. In many instances, however, they were still receiving better than 50 percent of the recommended amounts in many of the below-standard micronutrient categories.

In contrast, the diet of the British regular during the Napoleonic Wars was deficient in 17 of the 22 dietary essentials that were examined. The British enlisted men's rations, in fact, were ranked last or tied for last in 13 of 22 of the nutritional categories. The Spanish military on board ship also came up short in 17 categories, as did the Venetian oarsmen; their individual category totals, though, still exceeded those of the British ranker in most areas. The Spanish galley slaves, by comparison, come up short in 18 categories. Their diet, however, came in last in only 10 categories, which puts their rations slightly ahead of those served to the British soldier in a head-to-head

Table 4. Extraordinary caloric expenditures

Campaign experience	Total energy expenditure (calories)	Rations	Calories provided	Approximate caloric deficit	Potential weight loss (lbs)
12 days on the march[a]	23,400 marching plus about 36,000 normal daily expenditure	3 lbs biscuit and bean tops	4,368 plus bean tops	55,032	15.3, plus effects of protein deficiency
Five days in camp[b]	About 15,000 if at rest	1 lb biscuit and some acorns	1,456 plus 110 per oz of acorns[c]	12,664 assuming 8 oz of acorns	3.5, plus effects of protein deficiency
Marching 16 hours in a day[d]	6,240 marching plus about 3,000 normal daily expenditure	Standard	2,459	6,781	1.9
Two-week march without bread[e]	27,300 marching plus about 42,000 normal daily expenditure	Meat and coarse flour mixed with bran and chopped straw	9,282 from meat, little to none from bread replacement[f]	60,018	16.7
A three-day march without any food[g]	5,850 marching plus about 9,000 normal daily expenditure	None	None	14,850	4.1, plus effects of protein deficiency

[a]Green, *Vicissitudes of a Soldier's Life,* 154. He states that they ate any green herb or vegetable they could find.
[b]Knowles, *War in the Peninsula,* 42.
[c]Values for "acorns, raw," in U.S. Department of Agriculture, *USDA National Nutrient Database.*
[d]Morley, *Memoirs of a Sergeant,* 59. He wrote that the men marched eight hours, rested four, then marched eight again. This allowed the officers to press the march for two-thirds of any given day.
[e]Leach, *Rough Sketches,* 95.
[f]Because of its high fiber content straw would lose most of its nutritive value and possibly impair absorption of calories from the meat as well. See *Energy and Protein Requirements,* 118–20. A high concentration of roughage would have increased the rate at which the men eliminated the food.
[g]Douglas, *Douglas's Tale,* 63.

Table 5. Dietary Reference Intakes (DRIs) (%)

Nutrient	Imperial Roman soldier	Common soldier (English Civil War)	Spanish sailor, soldier, or officer (16th c.)	Venetian oarsman (14th c.)	Spanish galley slave (16th c.)	British common soldier (Napoleonic Wars)
Calcium (mg)	29	180	37	48	15	9
Copper (mg)	0	0.2	0.1	0.1	0.1	0
Iron (mg)	320	196	174	158	131	140
Magnesium (mg)	110	78	72	65	48	37
Manganese (mg)	411	252	259	259	239	125
Phosphorus (mg)	298	343	194	169	124	132
Potassium (mg)	68	38	46	33	21	26
Selenium (µg)	846	606	467	412	407	329
Sodium (mg)	17	10	55	84	17	10
Zinc (mg)	243	195	103	75	55	151
Folate (µg)	86	71	48	87	85	30
Niacin (mg)	170	110	84	63	54	85
Pantothenic acid (mg)	133	103	87	70	63	52
Riboflavin (mg)	103	124	68	47	25	52
Thiamin (mg)	146	98	91	104	74	58
Vitamin A (IU)	0	252	30	48	3	0
Vitamin B-6 (mg)	157	84	92	59	22	77
Vitamin B-12 (µg)	8	6	4	1	0	6
Vitamin C (mg)	0	0	0	0	0	0
Vitamin D (IU)	0	14	1.4	2.5	0	0
Vitamin E (mg)	50	9	4	6	8	4
Vitamin K (µg)	29	9	3	6	8	4

Source: Food and Nutrition Board, Dietary Reference Intakes.
Note: µg = micrograms; IU = International Units.

comparison. The slaves' diet was better than the redcoats' in 12 of the categories; the British rations were superior in 8 micronutrients (with ties in 2 nutrients: vitamins C and D).

The most glaring deficiencies in the British diet were in calcium, sodium, copper, and vitamins A, C, D, E, and K. The absence of adequate levels of such micronutrients caused long-term physiological effects, including bone weakness, muscle cramps and debilitation, circulatory problems, poor vision, slowed reflexes, increased susceptibility to excessive bleeding and bruising, rickets, scurvy, and a markedly diminished ability to heal.[71] The redcoats' diet and daily exposure to the elements also left them vulnerable to common ailments such as dysentery, stomach ulcerations, influenza, pneumonia, diarrhea, fevers of various sorts, and respiratory infections.[72] In addition, Major Reva Rogers of the Army Medical Department notes that the alcohol in the rum ration not only provided negligible amounts of key nutrients but worked to "reduce storage levels of several vitamins [in the body] including vitamin A."[73] Thus, even if the British rank and file never appeared on the battlefield, military life took its toll.

The effect of nutrition on immune function is a crucial consideration when analyzing the short- and long-term effects of malnutrition on the British soldier, because his rations were supposed to keep him at fighting strength and available for duty. Disease resistance and disease severity, though, are directly related to nutrition, as recent medical literature confirms. As A. Marcos et al. write in their treatise on nutrition and disease, "the adequate functioning of this [immune] system is critically determined by nutrition, and, as a consequence, so is risk of illness." Moreover, "nutritional deprivation, such as protein energy malnutrition (PEM), often causes immunodeficiency leading to increased frequency and severity of infection, thymus atrophy, and wasting of peripheral lymphoid tissue." They conclude that high-intensity physical activity works to "suppress immune response parameters . . . and that improper nutrition and psychological stress increase the negative effects of heavy exertion upon the immune system."[74] Research by Philip Calder and Samantha Kew supports this thesis. They write that "undernutrition impairs the immune system, suppressing immune functions that are fundamental to host protection against pathogenic organisms."[75]

Another important consideration affecting the British soldier's susceptibility to disease was the deleterious effects of physical and emotional stress on the body. The various stressors and individual responses make this a complex issue to untangle. As Danielle Merino has pointed out, however, "chronic stress experienced by soldiers in wartime leads to immunosupression." Her study of French soldiers undergoing three weeks of conditioning and a five-day combat course provides evidence that extreme physical exertion "induces alterations in the immune system."[76] Merino also cites a study showing that a restricted diet enhances this effect.[77] Immunosuppression can occur in a relatively short time: cellular immune responses were impaired in soldiers after just eight weeks of training.[78] Stress also affects protein and electrolyte metabolism; adrenal hormones alter the rate of both these processes.[79] Extreme fatigue, cramping, and diarrhea can result. Mention of these symptoms appears frequently in accounts left by British soldiers. Additionally, basal caloric needs may increase 200 percent in times of stress and as much as 1,000 percent in severe trauma. Tissue repair and antibody formation may increase anywhere from 60 percent to 500 percent during stress and physical duress.[80]

While somewhat dated (medically speaking) and unlikely to be repeated for ethical reasons, the study of human starvation by Ancel Keys et al. provides further insight into the effects of slow starvation on the human body and psyche. They point out that increased morbidity from all infectious diseases was a by-product of the starvation diets of concentration camp victims.[81] This finding is corroborated by Gayle Chapman et al., who found that patients with fistulas who received optimal nutritional support had nearly an 89 percent healing rate and less than a 12 percent mortality rate, while those receiving minimal nutritional support had only a 37 percent incidence of healing and a 55 percent mortality rate.[82] Linda Russell also provides evidence that proper nutrition is essential to wound healing; when such nutrition is absent, the healing process is slowed, and problems such as infection and scarring are more frequent.[83]

The effects of ongoing nutritional neglect and physiological stress on disease rates are borne out by the British army medical records covering the Peninsular War period. Army Medical Department sick returns for 1810 through 1813 show that on average approximately one-quarter (23.78 percent) of all effectives were in regimental hospitals. Typhus, dysentery, and various fevers were particularly effective in laying men low;[84] weakened by malnutrition and hard campaigning, soldiers fell by the thousands.

For those years, 1810 had the lowest rate, with an average loss to all diseases of 18.8 percent; in 1812 losses reached 29.43 percent of all soldiers in the Peninsula. During this period, British monthly sick rates dropped below 12 percent only once, in July 1810. Monthly rates exceeded 30 percent eight times, with the worst month being October 1812, when 37 percent of the men were on sick call.[85] These numbers only include men who were incapacitated and in need of extended treatment. Soldiers who were mildly ill and debilitated remained in the ranks and did the best they could, usually with the help of their comrades. The end result was 580,000 hospital admissions from 1810 to 1814, leading to 55,000 disease-related deaths during the Peninsular War.[86] Even when the effects were nonlethal, disease still removed men from frontline duty in surprising numbers.[87]

Time in hospital, it should be noted, was not taken lightly. When a soldier entered the hospital, his pay stoppages were increased to pay for rations and medical treatment.[88] The redcoat had precious little pay after regular stoppages; he would not give up a large portion of what remained unless he had no choice. The condition of hospitals and the uneven level of care, highlighted by men's experiences with purges, blistering, bleeding, and surgeons' work after battles, made hospital stays all the more unattractive for the rank and file.[89] Donaldson summed up his experience with medical treatment as "blister, bleed, purge . . . and purge again." As for surgeons' skills, he wrote: "In the field they did more mischief, being totally ignorant of anatomy."[90] While his assessment might seem unfair, it does reveal how the men felt about hospital stays. Moreover, absence from comrades could result in a loss of reputation. As Quartermaster-Sergeant James Anton of the 42nd Regiment of Foot elucidated, prolonged time away from the unit could be perceived as "a desire of avoiding hard duty and field danger. Thus the absentee is considered a scheming dissembler . . . until death proves him a liar."[91]

The key to understanding the British soldier's well-earned reputation as a plunderer can be found in the nutritional analyses above and in the obvious consequences of near-starvation. For this study of the British regular, the most cogent aspect of Keys's examination of starvation deals with the psycho-physiological effects of chronic malnutrition. He notes that the first symptoms of food deficiency (semi-starvation) are languor, extreme fatigue, loss of coordination, muscle soreness, and general debilitation, with instances of fainting and just giving up.[92] All these symptoms closely resemble descriptions of the British ranker on the retreat to Corunna and elsewhere.[93] The manifestations of physiological deterioration included a slowing of autonomic functions, slowed reflexes, loss of sensation in the extremities, intolerance toward noise and cold, and a loss of ambition.[94] These symptoms also made their way into soldier accounts. A summation of the near-starvation experience by a hospitalized survivor of the Warsaw ghetto of 1941–43 also matches characterizations of the effect of severe malnutrition on the British regular of the Peninsular War: "The strength melts away as the wax of a candle."[95]

Keys contends that cognitive functions, beginning with perception but soon including the more complex thought processes that control moral reasoning and social interaction, are slowly altered during the stages of starvation. The thoughts and efforts of the starving turn increasingly toward the acquisition of food.[96] A type of lethargy and apathy, usually first exhibited in regard to personal appearance, gives way to irritability and outbursts of anger as food becomes the sole motivating force.[97] As normal activities and pursuits are curtailed, meaningful social interactions are reduced and moral restraints are lost.[98] Keys points out that as demand for food escalates, so do instances of thievery and violence.[99] G.B. Layton, a captured British medical officer who witnessed the short- and long-term effects of slow starvation in a number of German prisoner-of-war camps during World War II, confirmed the impact of prolonged nutritional deficiency on the human psyche. "None of the other hardships," he recalled, "suffered by fighting men observed by me brought about such a rapid or complete degeneration of character as chronic starvation."[100] Such driving forces may explain, to some degree, the redcoats' actions regarding the acquisition of food and drink.

These starvation-induced processes affected the soldiers' wives on campaign, just as they did their husbands. In fact, the women were even worse off: they struggled not only to keep up with the army but to feed themselves with little or no money and without army support. Those women who were officially on army lists (six per company) were usually given half-rations for acting as battalion launderers, cooks, and nurses and watching the army's cattle and sheep.[101] At times they received full rations and at others nothing at all, depending on the logistical situation. The children of "official" wives received one-quarter of a ration per day (about 530 calories). No food was allotted for the wives or children not on the books. Some women resorted to stealing food, not surprisingly, and some were forced to sell themselves sexually to avoid starvation, to the great distress of their husbands.[102] "Was it to be wondered at, then," lamented Donaldson, "if many of them [the wives] were led astray, particularly when it is considered that their starving condition was often taken advantage of by those who had it in their power to supply them, but who were villains enough to make their chastity the price?"[103] Paul Kopperman, writing about the British army in America during the Revolution, comments that some officers, either unable to understand the circumstances or powerless to change them, "believed that army women debauched the troops and, worse, spread venereal disease."[104]

While the British soldier only rarely reached the threshold of actual starvation, prolonged periods of nutritional deprivation certainly pushed him near enough to the edge to experience many of the physical and psychological symptoms. His actions regarding food and drink and the lengths to which he would go to obtain them certainly make sense in this context. Driven by physiological and psychological impulses over which he had limited control, the British regular had little choice but to become a consummate plunderer, forever on the lookout for food of any kind and drink. It is obvious that the redcoat would have perished without individual initiative in this regard. Ration quality and delivery difficulties were the crucial elements affecting the ranker's health and were probably the primary determinants in shaping his attitude toward looting. Lynn argues that similar supply inconsistencies and failures led Bourbon troops of the mid-seventeenth century to seize food and goods within French borders indiscriminately, a practice he labels the "Tax of Violence."[105] Men simply will not voluntarily starve when food is available and can be stolen or taken by force.

The theft of victuals or valuables that were quickly converted to food and drink might have been justified nutritionally, but such acts came with other costs: regret and the ever-present threat of military punishment. Feelings of shame, more than fear of punishment, surface in many of the first-person chronicles relating instances of food theft. William Surtees remembered his remorse for stealing a cabbage from a field: "It is impossible to justify such an act, but the reader will be convinced, I trust, that sheer hunger alone urged me to the perpetration of this crime." He also wrote of his embarrassment at having stooped to "such disgraceful means of satisfying . . . hunger" and made clear that he was forced to steal because "hunger is not easily borne, accompanied by incessant fatigue."[106]

Green of the 68th expressed similar regret for stealing raw wheat from a Spanish peasant and fighting another Spanish commoner over a bag of flour. "Hunger often caused us to do things," he explained, "which we should have been shamed to do, if we had plenty." He added: "I could not help reflecting on the misery and horrors of war: it was hunger, and that alone, that drove many of us frequently to take what was not our own. Had we been found out, we should have been severely punished . . . but hunger is a sharp thorn, and few would have acted otherwise."[107]

In most circumstances, the soldier's fate if his plundering was discovered probably depended upon his officer's interpretation of the act and (as in O'Neil's case of the stolen pig) willingness to share the spoils. Costello of the Rifles was often in the thick of things when it came to plundering for food; he once shot a goat near a Spanish village, knowing his actions could be as fatal to him as they were to the goat. He was in the process of cutting it up when Wellington rode by. "I felt as if the noose were already around my neck," Costello later recollected, still haunted by his close call. Wellington, for whatever reason, ignored him. Costello's colonel then rode up and congratulated him, tacitly sanctioning the act. Much relieved, Costello shared the goat with him.[108]

Lawrence also had a close call in this regard, which could have led to his hanging. Having purloined a chicken from a nearby farm, he gave it three swings by the neck and put it out of sight under his regulation stovepipe hat. As he returned to camp, parade was called. Just as his captain was walking by, the still-living chicken let out a terrible squawk, to the astonishment of the captain and the horror of Lawrence. When asked for an explanation, Lawrence elucidated as calmly as he could that he had a chicken under his cap that he had purchased while foraging. Luckily for him, his officer laughed it off, commenting that he had no doubt that Lawrence "offered four, but took it with five," referring to the proverbial "five-fingered discount." Amazed at his luck, Lawrence wrote that "he was perfectly right, but I did not think it would have passed off so smoothly, as many in the Peninsula were hung for plunder."[109] He soon became an accomplished pillager of pigs, wheat, sausages, bacon, and any foodstuffs he could search out. He was also not averse to stealing hidden money for food and drink when he was lucky enough to find it, temporarily relieving want.[110]

Officers who lacked a source of outside income often suffered like the common soldiers. Knowles, writing home in September of 1812, recorded: "The officers are extremely ill off, not having a farthing to purchase the comforts which are necessary to men nearly reduced to skeletons by wounds and sickness . . . [some] have sold their horses, asses, or mules; others their epaulettes, watches, rings, etc., and to the disgrace of John Bull, others have perished for want." His letters include numerous requests for additional funds from home, pleading for money so that he could buy necessities. In a little over a year he asked for £85.[111]

Douglas similarly asserted that many of the junior grade officers were financially unable to participate in the officers' mess, commenting that in 19 cases out of 20 these young men "were, in respect of food, worse off than the private soldier." He implied that officers "whose eyes were not always open" would be taken care of by the men in a *quid pro quo* arrangement.[112] Some less affluent officers came to depend upon this process to provide the food that the army could not. Captain John Harley, for example, openly relied on his servant, Pat Dolan, to provide supplies by any means. He wrote that this bothered his conscience, "but necessity had no law, and we could not starve."[113] Such arrangements, however, did not protect the soldier from possible disciplinary action should he be caught scrounging by another officer.

The British regular's daily pay of one shilling a day gave him few choices when it came to purchasing additional food. From this meager amount, the army withdrew money for meat, bread, brushes, pipeclay, losses, and other sums, such as the mandatory contribution to the old soldiers' homes at Chelsea and Kilmainham. John Fortescue has figured that such stoppages left the British private the astonishingly small amount of approximately six shillings a month,[114] often not enough to purchase even a loaf of bread locally. An empty purse prevented the ranker from supplementing his diet; instead he turned to more inspired ways of procuring what the commissariat failed to supply.

Desperate soldiers sometimes resorted to the "calms," a type of confidence game involving illegal trading with peasants. The scam entailed exchanging blankets or some military-issue item for local currency. At some point during the deal, a comrade wearing fake sergeant's stripes on his arm would interrupt the proceedings, declaring them illegal and demanding that the soldier return the money. In the confusion, the soldier would give back flattened uniform buttons, passing them off as shillings. The peasant, feeling lucky to have avoided legal entanglement, would go on his way unaware that he had been taken. The soldier and his comrade would then divide the loot and spend it on food and drink.[115] Using flattened buttons as shillings appears to have been a common ruse, as Major Gordon of the Royal Scots discovered much to his regret. Gordon sent his servant among the men to get change for a guinea and was shocked to discover that 17 of the 21 shillings he received in exchange were soldiers' buttons. He then paraded the men and fined those who were missing buttons.[116]

Even the presence of the French did little to stem the men's "reconnoitering." James Gunn of the 42nd describes gathering potatoes in a field near Pamplona in 1812 just as a French picket was doing the same. They ignored each other and took all the potatoes they could carry.[117] Grattan also saw no reason to pass up a meal just because the French were nearby. He related the tale of how a skirmish with French light cavalry at Burgos in 1812 was interrupted when a large portion of the British army appeared to be retreating en masse. Grattan and the French turned and watched in amazement; they quickly realized that the British army was not in retreat but in pursuit of hundreds of wild swine. He called the pursuit a success, as "scarcely one in a hundred [swine] escaped unhurt." After securing the pigs, the British contingent returned to the ranks to resume the skirmishing. Grattan described the episode as being "the most curious that came within my knowledge during the Peninsular campaign."[118]

Likewise, Robert Blakeney, an officer in the 28th, recalled being so desperately hungry that he and his company sat down to dinner when they discovered a small outbuilding filled with potatoes and fowls, even though the French army was preparing to attack.[119] Macfarlane also wrote of being so fatigued from want of food that he fell asleep in a house that was partially ablaze. He awoke in time to scrounge hard potatoes in the ruins and sat down to scrape flour from a blanket, eating the flour and potatoes even as the French approached. He managed to escape, noting: "I went forward, but very weakly, for the want of food. . . . I could scarcely stand on my feet."[120]

Cooper provides an additional anecdote that illuminates how even a firefight did little to dissuade the men from searching for and sharing food and drink. During the battle of Orthez (27 February 1814), the men broke into a house and discovered a large store of wine. It was quickly handed out, as Cooper explains, "so that the game was 'Drink, Fire, and Drink.'" Other soldiers "engaged in stoning and bagging the wandering poultry."[121]

The sharing of acquired victuals in all circumstances helped establish the authority of the small group and played a crucial role in determining soldier behavior. The mess group was a voluntary assemblage in which men from the same company gathered to receive army rations. These six soldiers also stood by one another in battle and on the march. Naturally, an allegiance grew among these men, just as it does for all combatants who share hardship, danger, and provisions over time. Group norms were founded on simple survival: locating and sharing food on campaign and actively participating in battle. Such actions improved the survival chances of individual group members and thus the group as a whole. Adherence to group norms earned the soldier esteem from his comrades and secured his place within the group. Failure to measure up meant rejection by his mates; this was a serious outcome for every soldier, who relied extensively on the group for emotional support, camaraderie, and the nourishment of the communal camp kettle.

The strength of this military version of the primary social group was founded on mutual support, which, out of necessity, included the equitable distribution of all items acquired while looting. Reciprocity was both an action and an expectation. A great number of redcoat accounts illustrate the sanctity of this act and its commonplace nature.[122] William Grattan of the 88th recalled how food and spoils found in Fuentes d'Onoro after the battle were partitioned, noting "the scrupulous observation of etiquette" practiced by the men as they shared.[123] Rifleman Harris remembered selling his last shirt in order to buy bread, which he then shared with a comrade. Harris writes of the act as a routine part of campaign life.[124] A highland soldier behaved in a similar fashion. Taking some bread from an unconscious comrade, the young man shared it with another ranker, matter-of-factly explaining his rationale: "In relieving his wants, I felt less my own."[125] This statement says a good deal about the rankers and their attitudes toward comrades.

Great finds discovered while plundering were also shared by common soldiers. Costello of the 95th Regiment of Rifles stumbled across the baggage of Joseph Bonaparte and his wife, Spain's French-imposed king and queen, after the battle of Vitoria in 1813. Costello found £1,000 in coin and became very possessive of it, even threatening fellow plunderers from other units. Making it clear that the coins were his, he took all that he could carry and found his way to his company, which was elsewhere; he eventually distributed the loot among many of his comrades. Costello was not always able to keep his knapsack with him, so he went so far as to entrust his remaining treasure to a friend named Bandle. Bandle never let him down or stole even a portion and at times left his own knapsack behind in order to safeguard Costello's.[126] It is worth observing that the process of dividing loot, in whatever form, was a risky endeavor for the soldier supplying the pilfered items, as exposure increased the chances of discovery and possible punishment by military authorities. Thus, the desire to share plunder with squad mates must have been fairly compelling for the soldiers to put themselves routinely in such peril.

Lawrence, naturally, provides us with a number of comparable tales.[127] He captures the essence of the collective practice of sharing food and its benefit to the group as a whole. On one occasion he returned with bread given to him by a Portuguese man in whose home he was quartered: "On my arrival my comrades seemed to smell out my bread, and they came and hovered round me like bees while I divided it was well as I could . . . and it was soon devoured."[128] Lawrence also relates the story of coming across a wagon loaded with boots after Vitoria. His shoes had been reduced to nothing: "the chief part of the sole is my own natural one belonging to my foot." Lawrence disobeyed orders and left the ranks to dig through the cart. Other soldiers had the same intent; after finding himself a pair of boots, he succeeded after two tries in fighting his way through the men and taking some shoes back to his comrades.[129]

Understandably, given the enduring hunger and nutritional and material deficiencies that were part of everyday life for the ranker, and driven by a desire for drink and the escape it brought, plundering in order to survive became a physiological imperative. The sharing of the loot evolved into one of the expected group norms for the redcoat. Under such dire circumstances, the British common soldier's conduct regarding civilians can be understood, although not explained away. Men motivated by hunger are wont to commit crimes in order to acquire food, drink, and valuables. But it is difficult to ascertain with certainty how willing the men were to use violence to obtain their loot and the extent to which they abused Spanish and Portuguese citizens.

Many historians are adamant that British regulars were uncontrollable thugs with a penchant for indiscriminate and wanton destruction of both property and person. That is the legend that has been perpetuated, at least. The records are not so definitive. F.S. Larpent, the judge advocate general during the war, admitted that Wellington occasionally hanged men in an effort to curtail plundering. Larpent also expressed an admiration for the rankers; he campaigned with them and experienced a small sampling of their daily hardship and circumstances. Despite the difficulties of the commissariat and the poor quality of rations, the soldiers provided Larpent less work than their reputation would suggest. Between Christmas 1812 and 5 May 1813 he tried only 80 cases in all, about four a week.[130] Larpent's journals often mention food costs, the men's suffering, and the occasional plundering case, but they rarely refer to soldiers being brought up on the more egregious types of charges for violent offenses.

Army courts-martial records support Larpent's journals. In his analysis of these records covering the six years of the war, Sir Charles Oman found only 80 cases related to plundering. These must have been serious cases involving assault, as minor offenses would have been handled at the regimental level. Oman discovered that during the war 57 enlisted men were condemned, and 24 hanged, for armed robbery with violence, a low enough total given the war's duration and the number of British soldiers in the field. He noted that many of those executed had taken comparatively little from the peasants and had done them little harm, recording that "no more than a blow with the butt-end of a musket had been given in many cases."[131] Walter Henry, a surgeon, recalled one such case; it shows that British military authorities acted swiftly when a transgression was committed and the culprit identified. Henry remembered finding a badly beaten peasant in a Spanish house as he and another officer were searching for food. After a short inquiry, the peasant was able to recognize his assailant, who was hanged.[132]

Most of the time, though, it appears that the rankers exhibited a fair amount of restraint when it came to Portuguese and Spanish citizens. Lawrence admitted that the redcoats took everything they could from civilians but did not harm them. "I am sorry to say," he lamented, "that we ourselves were not quite free from the charge of depredations, though we did not carry them on to the extent of bloodshed."[133] The judicial evidence seems to corroborate Lawrence's contention.

The soldiers were not always unkind to noncombatants, even though they willingly stole from them. A code that established group standards regarding treatment of civilians appears to have been in place. In a general sense, restrictions on abuse—including assault, rape, and murder—allowed the redcoats to take goods but not to inflict physical pain. The rank and file usually adhered to these rules; their conduct could even be exemplary. The first-person accounts contain numerous stories of the redcoat exhibiting concern for civilians and French soldiers alike. Such incidents appear to be more the norm than the exception.[134] Walter Henry even relates the tale of British soldiers showing "great kindness, tenderness, and inviolable respect" for a group of nuns passed on the road during the retreat from Maya in 1813. He comments that the men helped carry the nuns' bundles and assisted them every way they could, noting that "assuredly it was a high compliment to the character and discipline of the British Army."[135] These assessments reinforce commentary by Sherer, the officer of the 34th Regiment of Foot, who states that those who know soldiers believed that "they are charitable and generous, [and] kind to children."[136]

The reality is probably somewhere between Sherer's evaluation and the host of degrading appraisals that paint the rankers as predatory brutes. The intent here is not to absolve the redcoats for all the offenses they may have committed, for dire circumstances and countless interactions with Spanish and Portuguese civilians were a potent combination that surely engendered some misuse of the native populations. Many Peninsular War memoirs, in fact, make reference to the small core of "bad characters" in every regiment, whose conduct was often appalling. Oman referred to them as "irreclaimables" and (quoting Sir John Colborne) believed that 50 or so men (out of 500 to 1,000 soldiers in each battalion) met this description. According to Colborne, "neither punishment nor any kind of discipline could restrain" these miscreants. Oman was likely correct when he identified this "small proportion of the whole . . . always swimming to the top when there was mischief to be done" as being disproportionately responsible for the vast majority of offenses attributed to the soldiery.[137]

This small cadre of malcontents and misanthropes was scorned by fellow soldiers. Donaldson, a sergeant, called such men "bruising fellows" and bullies who were fond of abusing and terrorizing other enlisted men. Describing the aftermath of Badajoz, Donaldson pointed his finger at this group of "cold-blooded villains" as being accountable for the outrages against the townsfolk, while noting that these toughs were reluctant to participate in the actual attack.[138] Sherer, while emphasizing the kindness of British soldiers, had nothing but contempt for "the worthless characters who are to be met with in every regiment (and society) and are generally shunned."[139]

The actions of these good-for-nothings may have caused some soldiers to exhibit derision for their comrades, writ large, although such judgments are small in number. Cooper, an NCO like Donaldson, commented that Wellington needed to be "severe" in order to restrain an army populated by men of the "lowest orders," many of whom were "ignorant, idle, and drunk."[140] A private in the 71st wrote a similar assessment, stating that he "could not associate with the common soldiers; their habits made me shudder." This same soldier, however, later described an incident that runs counter to his negative depiction of the men; the episode provides corroboration that the rank and file had a code of conduct that reflected positively on the character of the man in question and the ranker in general. The highland private remembered seeing a young Spanish woman walking down a road, carrying a bundle. She was set upon by a Portuguese muleteer, whose attentions concerned both her person and the bundle she was carrying. The soldier of the 71st intervened on her behalf and attempted to fend the man off. The muleteer objected to this interference and drew a knife on the soldier, who responded by knocking the muleteer down with his rifle and escorting the young woman beyond his reach.[141]

The disparity in these opinions regarding the character of the ranker illustrates that, like all societies, the British army was populated with men of varying quality who possessed different moral standards. The majority of redcoats, though, appear to have conducted themselves fairly well, except for the theft of food and alcohol. In this, we can be more generous than the Spanish and Portuguese citizens who were robbed. The evidence also seems to suggest that the numbers of violent offenses against civilians may have been exaggerated over time, as Wellington's pejorative commentary on the soldiery melded with the horrors of war in the Peninsula to create an unjustifiably negative image of the rank and file.

The British regular's conduct toward enemy combatants was also fairly measured and governed by group mores. When not on the battlefield, the ranker tended to treat his French counterpart with a professional respect and sometimes with a practical eye toward shared plunder. Lawrence provides a steely and realistic, yet not inhumane, example of interaction with a wounded French soldier. He discovered the Frenchman after the battle of Vitoria in June 1813; the poor fellow had lost both his legs to a cannonball but was still conscious. Noting the man's condition and ascertaining that his death was imminent, Lawrence searched him carefully and came away with pork, a large loaf of bread, and a sum of Spanish and English currency. Despite his statement that the wounded man "could not last long, and very little sympathy could be expected from me then," Lawrence nevertheless "emptied the beans out of my haversack, which with the bread and meat I left by his side."[142] He also returned one shilling to the Frenchman. Lawrence's kindness exemplifies the type of behavior of which the ranker was capable. Behaving otherwise was not without consequences.

Donaldson relates the story of how he and his mates were sharing wine with a French soldier and a few other stragglers after a cooperative looting of a Portuguese home. Donaldson and his men left but discovered that one of their number was missing. Upon returning, they saw that the British soldier and the French private were amicably giving the Portuguese house one last search. When the French soldier found a purse hidden in a chest, the British enlisted man demanded a share of its contents. When the Frenchman balked, the redcoat suddenly produced a knife and stabbed his French counterpart to death. Donaldson and his comrades rushed to the Frenchman's aid but were too late. Appalled, Donaldson called it "a horrid, cold-blooded murder." According to his account, the men had nothing but disdain for the assailant, for he "had perpetrated the murder for the sake of money. He offered to share it with us; but not one of us would touch it; and from that time forward he was shunned and detested by all who knew of the murder."[143]

Green wrote of a similar incident involving a captured French officer during the pursuit of the French during the Walcheren campaign in 1808. When the officer refused to surrender his sword, a ranker of the Royal Scots quickly closed with the Frenchman and ran him through with a bayonet. Green recalled: "Our officers did not approve of this savage act of cruelty." He agreed with this judgment, calling the killer a "hardened monster, and no man of a right mind or true bravery would say that heroism consists in such conduct."[144] As in the Donaldson event, the men probably ostracized the perpetrator for committing what they viewed as a heinous act.

These episodes demonstrate that group values did exist and that they affected soldier behavior. The banishment of men who violated accepted standards exemplifies the mechanism that Steven Westbrook describes in his work on compliance theory.[145] Normative control, he contends, works on the principle of allocation or withdrawal of status and esteem. This group process fashioned the British regular's morals and self-image and guided his conduct. Not every soldier, of course, fully assimilated group ideals. Each ranker adopted the unwritten norms to a varying extent, believing wholeheartedly in some and less so in others. The tie between group survival and behavioral codes, though, gave an immediacy and gravitas to certain deeds and prohibited others. Each soldier understood well enough which actions brought him praise or censure. The fear of "not letting the other man down" was a compelling force in the British mess groups;[146] this dynamic has played an important role in establishing and maintaining group cohesion in most armies throughout history, as it does today.

In nonlethal environments, the bonds of primary social group members and group strictures could sometimes be subverted, however unintentionally. No account of the behavior of the British soldier in the Peninsular War would be complete without referencing the role of alcohol in determining the behavior of the rank and file. In a life that mixed hardship, misery, fatigue, iron discipline, terror, and a certain amount of hopelessness in equal measures, alcohol was an escape. Men craved it and went to great ends to obtain it in any form.

The redcoat had an unerring ability to ferret out hidden alcohol, no matter how well concealed by the locals, for temporary enjoyment and a release from daily privation. As cavalry commander General John Slade remarked, "drunkenness may justly be looked upon as the chief source of almost every crime of which a soldier is guilty."[147]

The British soldier's penchant for hard drinking was both the cause of much of his misbehavior and a symbol of army neglect. The horrors of war have caused many men to seek succor in alcohol to alleviate chronic hardship and stress. But had their lives on campaign proved less harrowing, with food, shelter, and adequate clothing being regularly available, the men's propensity for drinking to excess might have been diminished. T.H. McGuffie also argues, with good reason, that some of the responsibility belongs to the army that supplied alcohol as part of the soldier's regular rations. Green adds an important note: the rum ration was normally distributed around midnight, hours after the soldiers' last meal. He was unsurprised at the effects of alcohol on men with empty stomachs. Drink became the ranker's greatest vice, dispensed by the very government that wished to control the men and did so little to meet their needs.[148]

When the British regular found alcohol in abundance (such as at Villafranco, on the retreat to Corunna, and after successful sieges), discipline broke down as the men sated themselves. Alcohol worked to lower inhibitions; combined with privations and need, it had a deleterious effect on the men's behavior. Binging evolved in many cases into full-blown alcoholism, which made the men dependent on drink and drove them to extreme measures to acquire it. Men fell out on marches due to a combination of fatigue and intoxication; they fired houses and committed various crimes, mostly with alcohol, food, or women as their objectives. These same behaviors were repeated and often exceeded after successful siege assaults, although it is far from clear that the rankers did great harm to civilians. If the British soldier sometimes behaved in ways that brought him no honor, alcohol probably played a role in many of these indiscretions.

With the barest minimums of food, shelter, and clothing—key elements necessary to sustain physical health and morale—the men were pushed to their limits and beyond. One alternative was desertion, a problem that plagued the British army throughout the French Wars. It constituted no less than 20 percent of all tried offenses in the British army in 1809 and almost 52 percent in 1812.[149] Desertion was also a bane to the French army throughout the war, despite Napoleon's efforts to inculcate his soldiers with proper military ideals. As Michael Hughes points out, "One of the sentiments that emerges the most frequently in the writings of French troops is misery."[150] The

French differed from the British in this regard only in their leniency toward deserters.[151]

Desertion frequently had fatal consequences for the British soldier who was caught or captured; it also stigmatized those lucky enough to run away and return without arousing official notice. The men in the deserter's unit were rarely deceived (even if their officers occasionally were), and ostracism usually followed. Desertion was a difficult choice under any circumstances, but doubly so in a foreign land for men without the ability to speak the language. Some soldiers, willing to take whatever risks were necessary, ran away regardless, hoping to cut their ties with the army forever. Many men, however, deserted to look for food; others became lost or were successful in finding alcohol and were too inebriated to make their way back to their units. William Surtees—a veteran quartermaster of the 3rd Battalion, 95th Regiment of Foot—watched with pity as seven deserters were shot after the bloody siege of Ciudad Rodrigo in January 1812. The soldiers had fled the ranks and been caught fighting with the French defenders. All seven men pleaded that they were forced to desert by lack of food and clothing. This attempt to extenuate their circumstances, while probably founded at least to some degree in truth, did not explain their active collaboration with the French; thus, no mercy was shown. Surtees recorded that he "felt sick at heart; a sort of loathing [for the spectacle of the execution] ensued."[152]

In his study of the eighteenth-century British soldier, Arthur Gilbert has discovered that approximately 30 percent of prosecuted desertion cases involved men trying to rejoin their units.[153] This is in keeping with the picture of men deserting to look for food (one motivation for desertion that Gilbert omits in his analysis). Deserting was an extreme measure in any case. Most men instead reacted to the forces that seemed intent on sapping their wills by literally closing ranks and bonding with their messmates. Attempts to share what food there was and withstand the never-ending hardships of campaigning became a collective endeavor.

The common soldier and the officers who led them were for the most part distinctly different types of men, with backgrounds and experiences divergent enough to allow coexistence without a real understanding of the demands and pressures of each other's daily lives. British regulars expected their officers to be gentlemen, with education, manners, incomes, and leadership capacity—all of which the rank and file assumed to be natural endowments of well-born men.[154] That was how common men viewed their social superiors within the stratified societal hierarchy of Georgian Britain. Most officers, in turn, were restrained by cultural norms from perceiving the common soldiers as equals and treated them accordingly. The social chasm between the officer corps and the enlisted men seems to have left many officers disconnected from the experiences, needs, and attitudes of the men they led. Thus, while the ranker sought drink for pleasure and to escape from the daily grind of military life, his officer marveled at what he perceived as folly and weakness of character.

The discrepancy between the men's sufferings and officers' perceptions is exemplified in one series of parallel incidents on the retreat to Corunna. Harris gives us the particulars. Toward dusk one night on the terrible retreat, he came across a man and a woman, clasped in each other's arms, dying in the snow. He knew them both, understood that the march, the elements, and lack of food had caused their demise, and grieved that he could do nothing for them.[155] Blakeney, an officer, witnessed a similar scene: a man, woman, and child all expired in the snow, clinging to each other. Seeing a cask of some sort in their midst, he assumed that the three had drunk themselves into a stupor. He chalked their deaths up to "exhaustion, depravity, or a mixture of both" and exhibited neither concern nor compassion.[156]

Not all of the officers were inured to the men's plight, but most appeared to consider the health and well-being of the men to be the responsibility of the army as a whole and not something with which they should be personally concerned. Two exceptions stand out, showing how the quality of the soldiers' lives might have been improved had concerted efforts been made. Surtees records with gratitude the efforts of a new officer who somehow procured for the men "plenty of oatmeal and milk" in place of the daily ration of bread and meat. The diet had a positive effect, as Surtees recalled: "Our wasted bodies began shortly to resume quite another appearance."[157]

An even more ambitious plan was put into action by Major-General Robinson, who was perceptive enough to note the sick-rate differences between officers and enlisted men and concerned enough to try to alter the men's diets in order to remedy the problem. Taking his "Kitchin physick" solution to Wellington, Robinson boldly proposed that it was feasible on a divisional level. He proudly noted how improved nutrition made a difference:

> The Army has been dreadfully sickly until within the last fortnight, the men are now recovering fast—One Battalion of Guards [1st Regiment], that joined the Army in October last in front of Salamanca, has buried near seven hundred men in the course of the winter [actually 800]—my old Regt [38th] buried 150 in this town, yet in no place are the Officers sickly, on the contrary they are very healthy, & therefore as young and old underwent the same hardships and privations as the men during the retreat, the cause of such a difference must be a striking one; I ventured my opinion upon Lord W—and I think clearly proved to him that Kitchin physick was what the men wanted to restore their constitutions, that the ration was not enough with men who required every possible means to recruit their strength, & who had not money to purchase little comforts.... The first thing I did on joining my Brigade was to examine the state of the Men's Messes, and the Hospitals and obliged the reluctant Commissary to issue good Wine, instead of bad Rum, Bread instead of Biscuit, and Two ounces of Rice per man each day to put in their soup.... I have been reaping the benefit of these regulations for ten days at least—150 men have been restored to the ranks, and no more new cases have occurred.... This will prove to you, that good feeding has been all wanting—The Commissary of my Brigade made many objections, all of which were easily overruled, and I see no reason why the whole division ... should not have been fed from their first coming into quarters—Wine is so plentiful that you can get the very best for 50 Dollars a Pipe—and Bread is so plenty, and excellent, that the whole country for Twenty miles around is supplied from hence—and yet our men have been eating hard ship biscuit with jaws scarcely able to crack the live stock in them.[158]

Unfortunately, Robinson does not record Wellington's response. In the end, nothing changed, however, and the soldiers' diets and rates of sickness returned to the norm. Nevertheless, his efforts on behalf of the men were unusually humane and would have made at least some difference over the long haul. As always, it was a matter of economics, and nothing was done to improve the quality of the ranker's life. Most officers were financially capable of ensuring that they did not suffer the same deprivations as their men, which may have played a role in inhibiting Parliament's perception that the matter required immediate attention.

For the British soldier, usually existing on a subsistence diet far from home, with little hope of returning and few compelling reasons to do so, life was often difficult. The redcoat was poorly fed and constantly exposed to the elements; he was treated as a beast of burden, beaten savagely for his mistakes, and expected to march and fight in a long series of battles and sieges. The ranker's existence was dependent not only on his comrades but on his officers as well. It was the officer's leadership capacity that made campaign life either barely tolerable or insufferable and survival on the battlefield possible. While the redcoats' immediate superiors, the NCOs, were from the same general strata of society as themselves, their officers were most likely from an echelon above.

It was these men who trained, judged, and administered punishment to the rank and file, who stole to eat and drank to forget. The officers, meanwhile, with different perceptions, needs, and expectations, attempted to control the men, often resorting to harsh discipline to do so. The British regular, despite having little in the way of commonly accepted sustaining motivations, learned his trade, persevered, and became a more than competent, and often outstanding, combat soldier.[159] That his officers saw life differently and sometimes viewed the ranker with varying degrees of disdain was not always the fault of the common soldier and rarely his immediate concern.

4

A STICK WITHOUT A CARROT

Leadership and the Soldiery

The officers who led Wellington's soldiers were for the most part from a different socioeconomic class than the common soldiers. The vast majority of officers, however, were not from the aristocracy or from extremely wealthy backgrounds, as is sometimes assumed. Michael Glover has shown that less than 140 out of the 10,000 officers on full pay during Wellington's time were peers or sons of peers. This amounts to less than 2 percent. Using educational background as an indicator of wealth, Glover also contends that only 283 officers or 3 percent attended one of the major public schools (Eton, Westminster, Harrow, Rugby, and Winchester).[1] The majority of officers were sons of professional men, such as lawyers, doctors, bankers, and clerics.[2] What these officers needed, and often had, was supplemental income provided by their families.

Access to money beyond army wages was truly the distinguishing factor that separated the campaign experiences of the rank and file from those of upper-echelon officers. A man could not purchase his captaincy, majority, or lieutenant-colonelcy and participate in the officers's mess without a source of revenue in addition to his army pay. When uniforms, horses, baggage, food, and personal accouterments were considered (all of which came from the officer's own purse), an officer could expect annual expenses in the £400 to £500 range. In contrast, a subaltern made only £129 a year in 1804. The cost to maintain the lifestyle required of a gentleman officer was so oner-ous that in 1815 the colonel of the Scots Greys laid down the edict that in order to be eligible for a cornetcy in his regiment a young man must have at least £200 per annum (in addition to his army salary) at his disposal.[3]

Such outside income allowed officers of means to do what the common soldier could not: buy food on campaign. While prices var-ied, of course, according to location and supply considerations, over-all costs do not appear to have been a major concern for many of Wellington's officers during the Peninsular War. In 1814 two pounds of bread and one pound each of sugar and soap together cost almost 7 shillings,[4] which would have constituted a week's wages for a ranker, before deductions. Larpent willingly purchased a turkey at 25 shill-ings, tea at 22 to 25 shillings a pound, butter and cheeses at 4 shillings a pound, and brandy at 7 shillings a bottle.[5] Similarly, Captain George Woodbury of the 18th Hussars did not hesitate to purchase a seven-pound wheel of cheese for 73 shillings and two cow tongues for 27 more.[6] George Hennell, an infantry officer of means, writes of paying 3 to 4 shillings each for hares, 2 for partridges, and 1 shilling a pound for mutton. Purchasing this type of food was beyond the means of every common soldier. Hennell's biggest complaint was about the quality of the local Spanish dinner service. "Their cutlery," he grum-bled, "is infamous & most of their earthenware is very clumsy."[7] Such niceties were hardly the concern of the British ranker, who was naturally more intent on supplementing his sparse diet than he was on the condition of the eating utensils, cups, and plates.

We have no way of knowing the percentages of officers with inde-pendent means and those who were financially insolvent and forced to rely on the men for food. A good many accounts, though, present a view of army life that was markedly different from that experienced by the common soldier. Edward Fitzgerald, who rarely recorded any mention of the men in his care, wrote home pleased to have found a French servant to act as valet, cook, shoemaker, and tailor. He paid 30 guineas a year for the man's service.[8] This was almost twice the yearly wages of a British regular before deductions; using For-tescue's calculation of available funds after stoppages (about six shillings monthly), the salary of Fitzgerald's servant was roughly equivalent to nearly nine year's wages for a private in the king's service.

Obviously, a definite divide (more financial than anything else, but also social and cultural) separated the ranker from the officers who led him. One constant in the majority of firsthand accounts left by British officers is how infrequently they voice concerns related to the care of the soldiers. Complaints about the cost of supplemental food and wine for the officer's mess, colorful descriptions of the countryside and occasionally of local women, requests for money from home, and similar personal considerations abound. They generally express little interest, though, in the failures of the commissariat to feed the men, clothing inadequacies, sickness rates, or the general welfare of the soldiers. Perhaps this was because the logistical problems were of such a magnitude that they exceeded the authority and skill of individual officers.

Nonetheless, the attitudes expressed by a great many officers who left accounts convey a certain disinterest in common soldiers. The British soldier was expected to obey, regardless of his circumstances and attitude, and that was perhaps all that most officers thought they needed to know. The British army operated on the basis of coercive compliance, as officers seemed to consider their men to be of an inferior nature.[9] Many officers appear to have believed that the common soldier could only be controlled through strict discipline and the fear of punishment. This expectation was very much in line with civilian attitudes toward the lower socioeconomic classes. Instead, the ranker was compelled by normative compliance generated by loyalty to his primary group, which helps explain why the majority of officers, including Wellington, failed to have a good understanding of the motivations that underlay the behaviors of the rank and file. This supposition might also help account for the incompatibility of the negative stories and appraisals of the British regular supplied by select officers and the historical record of the redcoat's actions and accomplishments.

It was the officer corps, however, that provided two essential motivations that helped the rankers face the difficulties of campaign and battle: a belief in their leaders' tactical competence and the army's insistence on battlefield drill and practice. The combination of Sir John Moore's training and later Wellington's operational and tactical capabilities meshed with the strong group bonds between the British regular and his comrades to create an army that knew its business on the battlefield. It was the officers and subordinate NCOs who trained the rankers and taught them drill, formations, fire discipline, and how to respond to orders without hesitation.

The victories that resulted gave the men tremendous confidence in themselves, their officers, and the army as a whole, particularly under Wellington's command. The ranker might not understand the nuance of Wellington's strategic retreats after battlefield victories, but he learned that the British army would not be defeated in combat. This was more than a simple matter of pride: combat success increased survival probability. If drill and repetition translated to tactical competence, then the redcoat was more than willing to learn the infantryman's craft. The men were also well aware of the role that Wellington played in their survival. Although he might spend their lives in siege assaults, Wellington normally husbanded them in battle; his tactical doctrine and battlefield management offered the greatest chance of success at the lowest possible cost.

A comment by Kincaid, a long-time veteran of the 95th, epitomizes how the common soldier viewed Wellington: "The sight of his long nose among us was worth ten thousand men any day of the week. I will venture to say that there was not a heart in the army which did not beat more lightly when we heard the joyful news of his arrival."[10] A soldier expressed similar feelings to Wheeler upon hearing that Wellington was given command of the Allied force during the Hundred Days campaign: "Glorious news. Nosey has got the command, won't we give them a drubbing now."[11]

When Wellington was not in command, the men missed him. At the battle of Albuera in May 1811, Marshal Beresford commanded the British force that was assaulted by the French under General Soult. This brutal, close-up infantry battle, resolved by the courage of the British regular, cost the British almost 6,000 casualties out of the 32,000 men who participated; though the British outnumbered the French three to two, the French inflicted almost as many casualties as they received and only the stalwart nature of the British infantry enabled Beresford eventually to claim the field. After the battle Cooper recalled a conversation between himself and a comrade. "Whore's ar [sic] Arthur?" the soldier asked. Cooper responded that he had not seen him but had heard that Wellington had just arrived. His friend replied, "Aw wish he wor [sic] here." Cooper commented, "So do I," noting: "Had he come sooner we should have had more confidence of victory."[12]

As Oman has pointed out, Wellington did "everything that would win confidence, but little that could attract affection."[13] Quick to punish and reluctant to praise, Wellington said little to the men's credit or their liking. His lack of sympathy ensured that he would never be popular; his aloofness and flinty hardness distanced him from the soldiers he commanded. Yet, as John Cooke, a sergeant in the Light Division, observed: "I know that it has been said that Wellington was unpopular with the army. . . . Now I can assert with respect to the Light Division that the troops rather liked him than otherwise . . . the troops possessed great confidence in him, nor did I ever hear a single individual express an opinion to the contrary."[14]

Kincaid further praised Wellington for teaching his subordinate officers warcraft, arguing that Wellington never left anything to chance and that "his energy and unswerving perseverance" turned the officers and men into "the most renowned army that Europe ever saw."[15] Kincaid also commented that Wellington's efforts made the ranker feel confident; it was this belief in self—melded with tactical proficiency, competent leadership, and primary group cohesion—that supported the soldier on campaign and on the battlefield.

Competent officers added to this confidence. Those who displayed skill, led by example, and treated the men fairly were respected. Costello wrote that "our men divided the officers into two classes, the 'come on' and the 'go on' types." He expressed great admiration for Captain Uniacke, who was one of the former. "None were seen so often in the van as Uniacke," Costello reported with pride; "his affability and personal courage had rendered him the idol of the men of his company."[16] For similar reasons, Harris had great respect for Generals Rowland Hill and Robert Craufurd. Harris especially admired Craufurd, despite his hard ways, because he toiled with the men, shared their troubles, and made them successful.[17]

This faith in themselves, in Wellington, and in select officers was of crucial importance, given the grave difficulties of campaign life. Success and trust helped establish the standards on which group mores were based. Military virtues such as unhesitatingly following orders to the letter, performing tactical maneuvers with skill, maintaining their place in a formation to ensure its integrity, keeping their weapons in fighting condition, and not straggling during marches all begin as external demands, forced on the men by officers representing military authority. Initially, the expectations of command were often enforced with coercive discipline. Gradually, however, the British soldier developed self-pride in his capacity to meet the demands placed upon him. This satisfaction and belief in his own worth soon extended to the redcoat's group, company, and battalion and to the army as a whole.

The ranker's willingness to adhere to a code of conduct based on military values established the basis of discipline and *esprit de corps*,[18] the foundation of British military success. This transition was successfully accomplished because the demands of the army aligned with the norms of the soldier's primary social group. The army demanded discipline, boldness, and steadiness under fire in order to ensure victory in battle, while the group required them because they enhanced its chances for survival. The British regular's personal identification with and loyalties to the group combined with a set of behavioral expectations to provide his fundamental motivation to endure the tribulations of army life.

The self-confidence and pride that the men derived from their personal and collective ability to adhere to British standards of discipline is evident in the tribute paid by the 95th Rifles to their recently deceased divisional officer, Major-General Robert Craufurd. Killed during the storming of Ciudad Rodrigo in 1812, Craufurd was a formidable disciplinarian who had trained the Light Division never to break ranks to find the easiest march route, as he considered any diversion that caused a march delay to be unacceptable and a potential threat to unit integrity. He was known to flog men who straggled or stopped to fill canteens in a stream. On the return march from his funeral, the Light Division came upon a water-filled excavation that was part of the siege works at Ciudad Rodrigo. The trench lay directly across the division's advance route. The Light Division trod straight through the obstacle, emerging wet and muddy on the other side but proud at having displayed the same discipline and ardor that Craufurd had instilled in them.[19] Self-discipline and group pride are the cornerstones of unit cohesion.

This alignment of army and group purposes sometimes failed, mostly on campaign, when two aspects of the soldiers' day-to-day existence created a conflict of interest between the army and the soldiers' primary groups. The arbitrary and harsh nature of army discipline and the constant failure of the army to supply adequate rations often interacted to create frictions between the rank and file and the officers who governed them.

To his credit, Wellington did his best to ensure that the men were fed. The largest share of his dispatches deal with either trying to convince the Spanish to fulfill their stated obligation to provide the British troops with food and funds or requesting additional money from a rather parsimonious Parliament in order to feed and pay the army. Portugal and Spain had difficulties providing food for their own people, let alone their British allies, especially after the depredations of French armies. Wellington's strategy therefore involved supplying his army by sea and with whatever provisions could be purchased by the commissariat from locals. Lack of available funds proved to be the greatest obstacle, as war costs by 1810 had risen to over £9 million, of which £6 million was in bullion or bills of exchange. Provisions from America cost an additional £300,000, and debt for upkeep of the Portuguese army not met by the Portuguese government totaled another £1 million.[20] In the Peninsula the specie that was needed to meet expenditures was always in short supply. Wellington was so cash strapped in 1810 that he had repeated exchanges with the secretary for war, Lord Liverpool, concerning the possibility of withdrawing the army.[21] The army remained; but when the money and supply failed, the burden naturally fell on the common soldiers, as rations and pay were cut or stopped altogether.

Equally troubling was the inability of the commissariat to fulfill its duties even when funds were available. All the armies of the Napoleonic periods experienced logistical difficulties; in this the British army was no different and the commissariat probably no worse than those of other armies of the period. The organization of the British supply system, however, coupled with Wellington's necessary decrees against plundering, placed a huge burden on the common British regular when supplies could not be furnished through army channels.

The logistical branch of the British army was a chaotic arrangement of overlapping jurisdictions and responsibilities. The commissariat was a subdepartment of the Treasury under the command of a commissary-general, who was not directly subordinate to Wellington.[22] Commissariat officers, who were technically civilians, no doubt coordinated their duties with Wellington's needs in the field, but he had no authority to discipline them. The commissariat's assignment entailed the procurement, storage, and transport of food, which included the purchasing or hiring of all mules, carts, and teamsters (who were civilians).

Arms and ammunition, in contrast, came from the Board of Ordnance, while pay fell to the paymaster-general and clothing and equipment to the adjutant-general. These supporting services funneled their requests through the quartermaster general, Sir George Murray, who held the post from 1808 to 1811 and, according to S.G.P. Ward, acted as the "intermediary link in the chain between the demands of the army and the response of the supplying departments."[23] Murray was responsible for overseeing and managing all the supplying departments to Wellington's satisfaction and had the authority to require these departments to issue equipment to the soldiers of other branches (say, distributing blankets from the commissariat to artillerymen, who under normal circumstances should have been looked after by the Ordnance Department).[24] The colossal numbers of such problems related to keeping an army supplied while on campaign ensured that many, if not most, logistical predicaments were never rectified.

The ad hoc nature of this essential bureau did not align well with Wellington's penchant for order. As Ward notes, departmental allegiance and subordination created command problems for Wellington and hindered his ability to make certain that his army was properly supplied in the field.[25] Wellington assigned an assistant, and later deputy assistants, from the adjutant-general and quartermaster-general's departments to each division in an effort to expedite requests and improve efficiency; the arrangement allowed him to exercise some control over these branches. With the commissariat, it was usually a question of having available funds to buy provisions. This persistent problem hampered Wellington even more than not having direct authority over the branch. Assistant-commissaries and their deputies were also assigned to brigades and regiments, but, according to historian Philip Haythornthwaite, "many were little more than half-trained clerks, totally unprepared for campaigning."[26]

Even with Wellington's more centralized command structure, the separate supply arms found fulfilling their responsibilities nearly impossible. Given their enormous tasks, the lack of money, and the difficulties inherent in campaigning in foreign lands where food, supplies, and shelter were dear and native suspicion high, it is easy to see how the supply branches became overwhelmed.

The commissariat, in particular, had an extraordinarily difficult job. The work of the commissariat men began before the troops were awakened and ended well after the day's march. In the morning the supply officers fanned out in front of the army in search of deliverable foodstuffs, forage, road networks, and available transport; in the evening they distributed the rations and fodder and made preparation for the next day's march. In addition to enduring the hardships of the road, these men were required to exert themselves almost continually, snatching rest only after scouring nearby areas and villages.[27] No amount of work or planning, however, could compensate for not having the necessary cash in hand to purchase food for the men or animals or hire men and wagons to convey it. Incompetence and sometimes outright fraud also worked to lessen the effectiveness of the commissariat.[28]

While any judgment of the supporting services should be tempered by the knowledge of these ongoing supply obstacles, it is fair to evaluate the effects of logistical failures, which had terrible consequences for the men. The soldiers certainly blamed the commissariat. John Aitchison, an officer in the Scots Guards, wrote with evident anger at the incompetence of Colonel James Gordon, Wellington's quartermaster-general (appointed after Murray's promotion in 1811), who found his responsibilities and logistical challenges to be crushing. On the retreat to Salamanca in 1812, Gordon—lacking transport and a solid understanding of the Spanish road network—sent supplies along the wrong route; the food eventually arrived not at the destination point but closer to where the day's march began. As a result the men were reduced to eating acorns and searching the woods for pigs. Aitchison recorded that two men were shot for being successful in the latter endeavor.[29]

Rifleman Kincaid succinctly summarized how the soldiers felt about repeated supply failures: "Had he [Wellington] hanged every commissary . . . who failed to issue regular rations to the troops dependent on them, unless they proved that they themselves were starved, it would only have been a just sacrifice to the offended stomachs of many thousands of gallant fellows."[30] Larpent adds further corroboration regarding the miserable state of the men, writing about their condition upon reaching Ciudad Rodrigo in 1812: "The truth was, the troops, poor fellows, came through the town quite starving; during the retreat supplies and been mismanaged—regiments went three and four days without rations, and numbers died of absolute starvation, besides the sick. Lord Wellington is I hear very angry."[31]

Wellington's patience with commissariat incompetence quickly wore thin; by 1809 he was already well aware of the various supply problems and their effects on the men and horses of the army. In a letter to Lord Castlereagh dated 21 August, Wellington expressed his exasperation: "Since the 22nd of last month . . . the troops have not received ten days bread; on some days they have received nothing, and for many days together only meat. . . . The cavalry . . . have not received, in the same time, three regular deliveries of forage. . . . The consequence of these privations . . . has been the loss of many horses. . . . The sickness of the army, from the same cause, has increased considerably."[32]

Wellington wrote to his brother Henry in 1812, complaining about the cyclical nature of the logistical problems as they related to the Spanish army. He could just as well been describing his own men: "I consider troops that are neither paid, fed nor disciplined (and they cannot be disciplined, and there can be no subordination amongst them unless they are paid and fed) to be dangerous."[33]

Yet despite Wellington's efforts on behalf of the men and his displeasure with the performance of the commissariat, the army remained perpetually short of supplies and often months in arrears in pay, which historians sometimes overlook.[34] Wellington's awareness that the men were going hungry did not prevent him from railing against their scavenging practices. His anger, piqued by what he considered the misbehavior of the soldiers on the retreat from Burgos, where they pillaged for food and drink with a desperate need, led to his infamous Memorandum of 28 November 1812 to all officers commanding divisions and brigades. In the memorandum he accused his officers and NCOs of losing all control over the soldiers in their charge. Stating that "irregularities and outrages of all descriptions were committed with impunity," Wellington assigned blame "for these existing evils to the habitual inattention of the Officers of the regiments to their duty."[35]

Frustrated by the inability of the commissariat to feed the men properly and the soldiers' refusal to curtail their pillaging, Wellington stated what he knew to be a falsehood: "Yet this army has met with no disaster; it has suffered no privations which but trifling attention on the part of the officers could not have been prevented . . . nor has it suffered any hardship excepting those resulting from the necessity of being exposed to the inclemencies of the weather." He then openly derided his officers' efforts to bring their men to the battlefield in any state of efficiency. He accused the officers of neglecting their duty and failing to follow orders, especially in disciplining the men. Wellington brusquely informed the officers that better use of the chain of command and attention to orders of the army regarding acts of plunder would greatly reduce the work of the provosts and regimental courts. In addition, more thorough inspections would prevent the men from selling their equipment, presumably for food and drink.[36] He even went so far as to outline camp arrangements and assignment of mess duties.

Although never meant for publication, this scathing document nevertheless made its way into the papers. The memorandum infuriated Wellington's officers, who felt that he had ignored the circumstances of the retreat and their efforts on behalf of their men. To be publicly shamed for what they felt were situations beyond their control did not sit well with the officers. John Mills, an officer of the Coldstream Guards, considered Wellington's accusations unjust: "And now, after a most severe campaign, successful as far as the courage of soldiers could make it, the army, naked, without hay, and reduced by sickness, is told that they have conducted themselves so ill, that they have brought all the evils upon themselves. Is this fair? What encouragement has a man to do his duty?"[37]

Ensign Aitchison was also offended by Wellington's memorandum. His fury over the duplicity of Wellington's remarks is evident in a letter written shortly after the memorandum was issued:

> Lord W. says that "the army met with no disaster, it suffered no privation . . . that the marches were short, the halts long and frequent"!!! Is it then no disaster to be obliged to fight for existence and then to leave on the field to die or be eaten by birds of prey those who were wounded? Yet this happened on the retreat at Duenas!! . . . Is it then no privation to be without food—absolutely for 24 to 36 hours? Yet this was the case. . . . It often happened that the men had no bread, as it was issued 3, 4 or 5 days in advance which they could not

keep so long. . . . Is it no hardship to march fourteen hours
without food, on the worst of roads in bad weather? . . . I do
not know what are long marches but I do know we marched
eight Spanish leagues—that it was nearly 3 hours after dark
before we arrived on our ground—it was then a wine country
surrounded by cellars—the men broke into them and irregularities were the consequence of the drunkenness. Nor do I
consider the crime so great when the system of destroying
everything to prevent falling into the hands of the enemy had
been enforced *by these same soldiers by order* when retreating in Portugal who now *for the first time since* were retreating into Spain.[38]

Aitchison then offered his view of Wellington's inspiration to
issue the general order criticizing his officers: "The letter of Ld. Wellington to the army, in my opinion, ought not to have been published . . . the picture is overdrawn, and what I admit to be correct I
think may in great part be ascribed to other causes than what his
Lordship does. As you would alarm a man with a belief of great danger, to make him provide the *better* for his security, so Ld. W. seems to
have overstated the want of discipline in his army to encourage it
being increased."[39]

Aitchison's assessment seems closer to the mark regarding the
reasons behind the recent spate of pillaging than does Wellington's
memorandum. In addition, he seems to see through Wellington's motivation for issuing it. Aitchison also provides evidence that counters
Wellington's claims, pointing out that there had been only one complaint against the men of his regiment and only one general court-
martial convened for the entire army.[40]

The officers resented being made scapegoats for what was obviously a persistent problem; the soldiers would continue to loot until
Wellington found a way to feed them regularly and adequately. With
no improvement in funding, staff administration, or logistics, the
men's motivation and penchant for stealing food and drink remained.

Wellington, however, was not mollified by circumstances. He
complained angrily to Larpent, the judge advocate general of the British army in the Peninsula, about the problems of disciplining officers
for failing to control their men: "How can you expect a Court to find

an officer guilty . . . when it is comprised of members who are all guilty of more or less the same?"[41]

As for the plundering habits of his men, Wellington was exasperated again after the British victory at Vitoria in June of 1813, when British soldiers found and stripped clean most of King Joseph Bonaparte's royal baggage train.[42] The men looted and kept the lion's share of the more than 5 million francs' worth of treasure, money that Wellington was counting on to feed and pay the army. Determined to secure some of the French funds, he went to great lengths to locate the missing gold. Green recalled, with more than a little pride and resentment, that the members of his battalion had acquitted themselves well during the ransacking but had been forced to surrender their ill-gotten swag. In the search after his regiment was ordered to strip, money equaling more than £32 per man was confiscated.[43] Most of the money, however, was never recovered by authorities. Livid, Wellington was forced to settle for what he could squeeze from the men; this included Marshal Jean-Baptiste Jourdan's baton, which was presented to Wellington sans its gold end-pieces. Eventually the gold pieces were found and forwarded to Wellington, who asked that ten Spanish dollars be given to the corporal of the 18th Hussars who "found" them.[44]

The sudden availability of gold brought out previously hidden stores of Spanish food.[45] Demand soon sent prices skyrocketing, however, and the soldiers found themselves paying exorbitant amounts for food and drink. In a short time most men found their pockets and stomachs empty again.

The dangers of life in the British military were not restricted to the commissary or the enemy. Breaches in discipline, from minor offenses related to appearance to major violations such as insubordination, often brought swift justice to the offender. Lawrence was no exception. He once absented himself without leave from guard duty for twenty-four hours and upon his return was drum-head court-martialed. Even though this was his first offense and he was barely in his teens, Lawrence received a sentence of 400 lashes. He had no problem remembering his feelings when the sentence was handed down: "I felt ten times worse on hearing this sentence than I ever did on any battle-field."[46] After receiving 175 lashes meted out in increments of 25, Lawrence, enraged by pain, managed to push over the spontoons to which he was strapped.[47] The colonel relented at this point, calling Lawrence a "sulky rascal," and ordered him cut down and conveyed to the hospital.

Lawrence then provided an after-the-fact, shamefaced declaration on the positive merits of such punishment. "Perhaps it was a good thing for me as could then have occurred," he reflected, "as it prevented me from committing any greater crimes which might have gained me other severer punishments and at last brought me to ruin."[48]

This is one of the few such proclamations extant in firsthand accounts from enlisted men,[49] and it is unfailingly quoted by writers seeking to corroborate Wellington's assessment of the men as being of a type that needed savage corporal punishment and accepted it without question.[50] What is usually overlooked, however, is Lawrence's accompanying statement: "But for all that it was a great trial for me, and I think that a good deal of that kind of punishment might have been abandoned with great credit to those who ruled our army; for it is amazing to think of four hundred lashes being ordered on a man as young as I was, undergoing all the privations of a most sanguinary war, just for an offense, and that the first, which might have been overlooked, or at any rate treated with less punishment and a severe reprimand."[51]

Such harsh discipline was the norm in the British army. Patterned in large part on civilian law (the infamous Bloody Code, which included over two hundred capital offenses), army discipline was brutal and punitive by nature; its aim was total obedience. Richard Holmes reminds us that "flogging [in the military] does not stand alone. It must be judged by the standards of civilian penology of the age."[52] Lashing was but one of many punishments applied to soldier and civilian alike, and its use reflects more on the society that approved it than on those who suffered its torments.

Flogging was actually a late addition to a series of corporal punishments dating back to Richard I's Charter of Chinon (1189), in which the first regulations for military punishment were stipulated.[53] Death, branding (actually a kind of tattooing), disfiguring, riding the wooden horse, running the "gautelop" (gauntlet), isolation in confined quarters, reduction in rations, and forfeiture of pay or rank remained standard administrative tools through the eighteenth century, when they slowly gave way to flogging as the most expedient type of reprimand.[54] In an article on the evolution of military punishment in the British army, Glenn Steppler offers evidence confirming that by the eighteenth century punishments had become far less brutal and arbitrary than they had been in previous centuries.[55] A series of graduated punishments was called for, with flogging being a last resort. The lesser penalties included verbal reprimands, additional guard duty or drill, public humiliation, menial work, fines, pay stoppages, and reduction of rations to bread and water. The types of transgressions and appropriate penalties were listed in the Articles of War, supplemented by the unwritten British "Customs of War," which dealt with conduct on a practical, day-to-day level, addressing appearance, kit repair, and general company expectations. Theoretically this was intended to make the disciplinary code consistent across all regiments.

Minor transgressions were handled on the spot, informally and immediately by NCOs and officers, who meted out blows with fist and cane or punished soldiers with extra drill. More egregious but noncapital offenses were tried by regimental courts-martial; proceedings were recorded solely at the discretion of the company officers and were not subject to review. Thus, the majority of the crimes and outcomes were never officially acknowledged, and most of the accounts for those that were have been lost.

The records of the 44th Foot (1778–84) are one of the very few surviving examples (see table 6). While they predate the period of the war against the French, they still provide insight into the functioning of regimental courts-martial. Men who faced regimental courts-martial had little hope of acquittal and not much more for either pardon or sentence reduction. Robbery and theft, usually of food, were the most common crimes.

Capital crimes, such as desertion, murder, rape, assault, gross insubordination, and striking an officer, were handled by general courts-martial. These events were required by law to be officially transcribed.[56] At this level acquittals were rare: the amount of evidence was usually substantial, or the event would never have progressed past company or battalion-level justice. Moreover, the accused often acknowledged his guilt in hopes of leniency, meaning that the principal responsibility of the courts was to mete out punishment.

This officially sanctioned justice was for the most part accepted by the men. The system of British military justice, however, was

Table 6. Regimental courts-martial records, 44th Foot, 1778–1784

Disposition of case	Number of cases	Percent of cases
Brought to court-martial	323	100
Acquitted	39	12
Found guilty	284	88
Sentenced to corporal punishment	280	87 (99% of guilty)
Pardoned	78	24 (27% of sentenced)
Part of sentence remitted	68	21 (24% of sentenced)

Type of charge	Percent of cases
Robbery and theft	36.2
Misbehavior on duty	26.8
Absent without leave	14.4
Misconduct toward military superiors	12.4
General misconduct	6.0
Misconduct while in hospital	4.0

Source: Steppler, "British Military Law," 882.

based primarily on minor punishments, administered at the level of the regimental courts. It is here that the "devil's clause" came in. This catch-all gave the regimental commander the ability to have regimental courts try soldiers for offenses not prescribed in the Articles of War.[57] Offenses could be small, such as a dirty kit, being tardy for roll call, losing army equipment, being slow to respond to a command, or any number of similar mistakes. The clause allowed penalties on "all crimes not capital" to be decided as the court saw fit.[58] Flogging became the punishment of choice, with the number of lashes to be administered left to the court's discretion. It was this sometimes arbitrary system of discipline and retribution to which most soldiers objected. They viewed it as a source of abuse and suffering, having little to do with fairness or justice.

Some officers abhorred flogging and used it only for the most serious transgressions. Others openly advocated its weekly use, to punish even the pettiest offenses. Major Hudson, of the 51st, for example, spoke in 1809 about what he saw as the positive effects that such treatment would have on one particular soldier: "It will do him good, make him grow and make him know better for the future."[59]

Flogging was certainly not an insignificant experience from the viewpoint of the punished soldier. It was a harrowing, tortuous ordeal, mixing overwhelming pain with the humiliation of having the lashes inflicted in front of the men with whom the soldier coexisted day-to-day. O'Neil of the 8th Regiment of Foot recalled with a chilling detachment his memory of the implement that was used to administer punishment: "The cat is composed of nine small cords, twisted very hard, and having three knots on each cord; sometimes the ends are bound with wire. The whip is usually about eighteen inches long, and the handle fifteen." O'Neil, a Catholic, was all too familiar with the cat, having received 300 lashes for refusing an order to attend a Sunday Church of England service.[60]

Floggings were handled with ceremonial precision.[61] The battalion was usually called to attention at sunrise and then told to form a hollow square with an open side. Richard Blanco, in his study of punishment in the British army, provides an excellent description of events: "The soldiers were required to be the passive audience of the ordeal. The charges were read aloud, the victim stripped to the waist and his hands tied to a post.[62] As a husky sergeant applied the lash, a muffled drum-beat solemnly kept a count. Often a comrade in arms would faint at the sight of the victim's blood or at the sound of his terrifying shrieks. The 'cat' . . . was in every respect a relic of a barbaric age."[63]

The physiological and psychological shock to both the victim and the soldiers observing was extensive. Each stroke was preceded by ten drum beats, heightening the anxiety for the soldier suffering the punishment and the men who were forced to watch. The damage could be substantial: sometimes flogging laid bare the bones of the spine and scapula. An officer who observed a number of lashings commented on their severity: "I have seen men suffer five hundred and even seven hundred lashes . . . the blood running down into their shoes and their backs flayed like raw, red, chopped sausage meat."[64] Green admitted that he almost fainted upon seeing his first flogging and that several of his comrades did, even though the soldier was pardoned after receiving only 50 lashes of the 150 to which he had been sentenced.[65]

Cooper recalled that the worst cases usually involved men who were flogged but fainted after receiving only a portion of the sentence. They were allowed to heal and then had the remaining lashes administered. He wrote: "It may be imagined that the second lashing was worse than the first," which is something of an understatement. Cooper also recorded the effects of flogging on a man whose back failed to heal: "A man of ours was flogged for breaking into a church and steal-ing some silver candlesticks. By some neglect his back festered. Being in the hospital one morning, I saw the poor fellow brought in to have his back dressed. He was laid upon the floor, and a large poultice taken off the wound. O! what a sickening sight! The wound was per-haps eight inches by six, full of matter, in which were a number of black-headed maggots striving to hide themselves. At this scene those who looked on were horrified."[66]

The demoralizing effect of such punishment on the men can well be imagined. When it came their turn to face the cat, an almost inevi-table event given its common use in the army, some men found they could not confront its horrors. Thomas Morris, a soldier in the 73rd, wrote of a comrade in his battalion who chose to commit suicide, using a musket and a string attached to his trigger and big toe, rather than receive 300 lashes for a minor offense. Morris described the man prior to his suicide as being "remarkably clean and well conducted."[67] Larpent, the judge advocate general, made a notation in his journal in April 1813 of a similar incident regarding a commissariat clerk found guilty of fraud; the man shot himself to avoid the pain and disgrace of a flogging.[68] The journal entry is almost administrative in nature, perhaps indicating that such drastic measures were not all that un-usual for men sentenced to the lash. Haythornthwaite mentions a soldier who poisoned himself and another who chopped off his own hand to escape punishment.[69]

While the men abhorred flogging, their real objection lay in the capricious manner in which many officers resorted to it as a means of control. Morris states that his ardor to be a soldier cooled when he joined the 73rd and found its commanding officer to be a man who lashed anyone for the slightest error, which he calls "disgraceful" and a "gross inhumanity."[70] Tales concerning the officer's propensity to abuse his men somehow made their way into an English newspaper, and he was removed shortly thereafter. His conduct, which was only a bit beyond the norm, was no doubt judged unsatisfactory less be-cause of the lashings than because his zealous use of the cat caused army command at Horse Guards in London to deal with potentially embarrassing publicity.

With few exceptions, the personal accounts of British regulars are filled with impassioned statements decrying the use of flogging as a standard punishment. It did not sit well with the rank and file that innocent men or men with clean records could be made to suffer the same as the hardened types who were repeat offenders. Donaldson relates the stories of one man with 12 years of unblemished service receiving 500 lashes for his first trifling offense of eating while on sentry duty and another soldier suffering 400 strokes for being 10 minutes late for roll call.[71] William Surtees of the 95th tells the story of a soldier who, during the retreat to Vigo as part of the epic evacuation in 1809, was lashed for calling out to General Robert Craufurd that "he had more need to give us some bread." Surtees, noting the extreme conditions of the march, adds: "It was a severe, but perhaps necessary discipline, in order to check in the bud the seeds of murmuring and insubordination, although I own it appeared harsh."[72]

Rifleman Thomas Plunkett fared no better. He had distinguished himself in a rearguard action as part of the Corunna retreat by racing toward an oncoming French cavalry contingent and shooting the French officer leading the reconnaissance and an officer who came to his assistance. Plunkett's actions disrupted the enemy cavalry advance. Six months later he was sentenced to 700 lashes for threatening to shoot his captain while intoxicated. Costello, who witnessed the punishment, commented that "flogging is at all times a disgusting subject of contemplation."[73] Fortunately for Plunkett, his lieutenant-colonel stopped the proceedings after Plunkett had received 35 lashes, citing his previous good conduct.[74]

O'Neil states that it took between six weeks and three months to heal from floggings, depending on the number of lashes administered.[75] Flogging not only temporarily removed a man from the line but also affected his self-esteem and made him question his place with his messmates and regimental comrades. Each man's bonds with these primary and secondary groups and his attachments to the regiment with its history, traditions, and colors acted as sustaining motivations that allowed him to identify himself proudly first with his primary social group then with his parent unit. The lash worked to sever these important connections.

Donaldson wrote on the effects of flogging with a simmering resentment. He despised a temporary captain who flogged daily and made the men wear yellow and black patches with holes cut in them, signaling how many times they had been lashed. Donaldson made note that the badges and corporal punishment broke the spirit of the men in his unit; some of them openly turned to crime, while others became reckless during encounters with the French. "Honour and character were lost," he commented in explaining the change in the behavior of the men.[76] He was much relieved when the lieutenant-colonel returned, stopped the abuse, and had the men remove their badges of shame.

According to Donaldson, a "debasement of feeling and character" was the natural result of such harsh treatment. The beatings had the "effect of making a man so little in his own eyes that he feels he cannot sink lower. . . . But let soldiers be taught that they have character to uphold . . . that they are made of the same materials as those who command them and there will soon be a change for the better in the army."[77]

Donaldson, however, saw little hope of salvation coming from the officer corps. "I have seen an officer," he remembered, "quietly eating when one of his men was flogged for procuring, without making any effort to save him." He also commented: "I have known an officer shed tears when his favourite horse broke his leg, and the next day exult in seeing a poor wretch severely flogged for being late of delivering an order." Donaldson had little doubt that the lash was the worst type of external coercion. "Terror," he sadly reflected, "seems to be the only engine of rule in the army; but I am fully persuaded . . . that if a more rational method were taken, the character of the soldiers in quarters would be as exemplary as in the field." Contemplating what happened to soldiers who were flogged relentlessly by a particular officer, he offered the following judgment: "Good men were liable to be punished for the slightest fault, the barrier between them and the ill-doers was broken down, and as they had lost respect in their own eyes, they either become broken-hearted and inefficient soldiers, or grew reckless of everything and launched into crime; those who were hardened and unprincipled before . . . seemed to glory in misconduct. In fact, all ideas of honour and character were lost."[78]

Morris used almost these same words to describe his perceptions of the negative outcomes related to such treatment of men: "It is an extraordinary fact, that, horrible as this form of punishment [flogging] is, it seems to have no effect whatever in reforming the character; it inevitably makes a tolerably good man bad, and a bad man infinitely worse. Once you flog a man, you degrade him forever."[79]

Bell, an officer in the 34th Regiment of Foot, also viewed the use of the lash with disgust, calling the process "inhuman." When he came to command a regiment he abolished flogging. "It does not tend to reform a man by bullying and abusing him before his comrades."[80]

Nevertheless, flogging remained the norm.[81] Roger Buckley, in his study of British soldiers in the West Indies, contends that the intent of military courts was to make examples of the condemned. He describes floggings as "prolonged and emotionally rich rituals of barbaric retribution and salutary terror. Flogging . . . was not merely the beating of the convicted soldier, but a solemn, measured, and calculated ritual."[82] Executions were handled in the same way, apparently for the same reasons.[83]

It is evident that flogging was used excessively: King George III's royal warrant of 1807 pronounced 1,000 lashes the maximum allowable, declaring that it was "a sufficient example for any branch of military discipline short of a capital offense."[84] The king felt compelled to intercede after hearing that a private of the 54th had suffered 1,500 strokes. In 1812 regimental courts were limited to sentences of 300 lashes; the Duke of York admonished officers that when they were "earnest and zealous in the discharge of their duty, and competent to their respective stations, a frequent recurrence to punishment will not be necessary."[85] This edict, however, seems to have been largely ignored. Larpent noted in his journal three exceptions over a two-month period. On 27 March 1813 a man convicted of two separate courts-martial offenses was sentenced to 2,000 lashes. Larpent observed: "This is absurd, he will bear six or seven hundred, and then it will end." He also mentioned that on 17 April of the same year he tried and convicted two soldiers for sheep stealing and gave them each 1,200 lashes.[86] Over the next six decades the number of lashes allowed decreased incrementally, to 25 strokes by 1879.[87]

Other punishments were available, as outlined above.[88] But flogging remained the default choice; it was easily administered on the march and army leaders, taking their cues in part from Wellington, shortsightedly viewed it as essential for preserving discipline. Wellington was an advocate of the lash and resented civilian attempts to limit its use. In a speech to the 93rd Highlanders at the presentation of the king's colors in 1834, he rightly spoke of the need for discipline: "It is . . . by the enforcement of rules of discipline, subordination, and good order, that such bodies [of soldiers] can render efficient service to their King and Country; and can be otherwise than a terror to their friends, contemptible to their enemies, and a burden to the

State. . . . They teach the soldiers to respect their superiors the non-commissioned Officers and the Officers."[89]

While Wellington was referring to the whole range of available sanctions, his later conversations with the Earl of Stanhope make it clear that he viewed discipline as being largely punitive in native, with flogging being a key component.[90] Wellington was known for his impatience with courts-martial that he believed were unnecessarily lenient. In his mind, the courts had but one responsibility: to inflict the proscribed punishment. Larpent recalled how Wellington "fell into a passion about the Courts martial for not doing their duty by acquitting and recommending mercy."[91]

Fifty years later the sentiment of the army's commanding officer regarding flogging had changed very little. Field-Marshal Viscount Garnet Wolseley commented blithely that it remained the best tool for upholding discipline: "It was cheap [and] simple and withdrew the soldier from his duty for the shortest period of time."[92] Only after the issue of flogging was brought before the public in the 1860s by *Lancet*, the British medical journal, and the *Times* were army and navy policies (as outlined in the Mutiny Act, the Articles of War, and courts-martial procedures) significantly altered.[93] The *Examiner* acknowledged that it was public opinion, not the goodwill of the Horse Guards, that brought about the change: otherwise "Brown Bess, pigtails, leather stocks, and the Cat-o'-nine tails would have been honoured institutions to this day."[94] The subject would be debated for almost a quarter-century, with the press coming down on the side of the common soldier and those in positions of authority almost uniformly demanding that flogging be retained as a disciplinary tool.[95] The commanding officers saw it as a question of obedience and unfailingly believed that fear of punishment always superseded any question of justice or alternative methods of soldier motivation.[96] Flogging was not outlawed altogether until 1881.

Given the reliance of the officer corps on corporal punishment as a motivating force, it is not surprising that British officers collectively failed to reflect or act on more abstract considerations, such as the development and sustainability of soldier morale. Perhaps the social difference between the rank and file and officers, reinforced by tradition and the expected social standards that guided officer-soldier interaction, made such endeavors to improve individual morale difficult in the tradition-bound environs of the British officer corps. Or perhaps it was just the way business was always done. Regardless of the cause, flogging and the related failure to address soldier motivation with other methods worked to loosen the ties between the rankers and the army; at the same time, it forced the men to rely more on each other.

The battlefield successes of the British army are even more unusual because of the lack of an established systems of rewards and the absence of supporting patriotic and ideological measures such as those that worked to inspire American Civil War soldiers, as described by James McPherson in his work on the motivations of Union and Confederate fighting men.[97] Unlike the soldiers on both sides of the Civil War, the British soldier could expect no appreciation from civilians back home. Perhaps because the army was generally disliked, service therein was openly disparaged, if not scorned. When a husband, son, or brother joined the army he was probably never seen again. Awareness of the kind of degraded life that soldiers lived often elicited more derision than pity. The people back home might celebrate victories, but they did not cheer the soldiers whose actions made the victories possible. The adulation of Great Britain would instead be showered on individual commanders, like Wellington; a select few were fêted, turned into heroes, and christened peers of the realm. Meanwhile the individual soldier was largely ignored, his deeds going unrecognized. The British ranker did not even enjoy regular mail service or expectations that he might have any sort of continual contact with home and family. In short, he received little support from the people he safeguarded.

In addition, the army made no ongoing efforts to bring nationalistic concerns or even political indoctrination to the troops in any written form (army journals, Orders of the Day, bulletins), such as those regularly distributed to the French armies during the Revolution and by Napoleon to his soldiers.[98] Napoleon was especially adept at using such written material to improve morale. Issued at crucial times during campaigns, his Orders of the Day were forceful exhortations to his soldiers to do their best to honor their emperor, France, their regiments, and themselves. Ringing with cries of glory, honor, and *patrie*, these orders were reminders of the abstract ideals that Napoleon knew appealed to the men, as John Elting notes. His bulletins were "after-action reports, directed as much at civilians as at the Grand Armée." These bulletins inevitably downplayed French losses, exaggerated enemy casualties, and dramatically described the exploits of the individual French regiments. Understandably, they were well received by the French soldiery, who enjoyed seeing their exploits made larger than life. The effects of such masterfully contrived propaganda as a motivational force should not be overlooked. Adding a touch of humor regarding the veracity of these bulletins, Elting reminds us that any soldier who played fast and loose with the truth was said to "lie like a Bulletin."[99]

These written appeals were but a small part of Napoleon's ongoing strategy to increase soldier morale and encourage martial virtues. French military songs that characterized the soldier as a "lover of glory" and indomitable on campaign and on the battlefield served the same purpose.[100] Napoleon's awareness that the morale of the men was the basis for his continued campaign and battlefield success is evident in one of his best-known maxims: "In war, the moral is to the physical as three is to one."[101] Even as a captive at St. Helena, he reiterated this conviction: "Moral force, rather than numbers, decides victory."[102] Napoleon's intent was to instill *le Feu Sacré* (Sacred Fire) in the hearts of his soldiers, in order to inspire them to face the hardships of war willingly.[103] David Chandler best describes Napoleon's rationale and method:

> In order to obtain the unquestioning obedience of his rank and file, Napoleon unhesitatingly set out to gain their affection as well as their respect. He wished to develop two main qualities in his officers and men: "If courage is the first characteristic, perseverance is the second." Bravery was needed in the field and at the moment of crisis; perseverance and endurance at all other times. Napoleon was aware that "Bravery cannot be bought with money" and deliberately aimed to create the illusion of *La Gloire* by playing on the vanity and underlying credulity of his men. "A man does not have himself killed for a few half-pence a day for a petty distinction." A carefully graded system of military awards— ranging from the coveted Cross of the *Légion d'Honneur*, swords of honor, monetary grants and nomination to a vacancy in the Imperial Guard for the rank and file, to the ward of duchies, princedoms and even thrones to the elect among the leaders—was one aspect of this policy; the rewarding of

talent and proven ability by accelerated promotion another; the creation of an air of general *bonhomie* with the ordinary soldiers, yet a third.[104]

Napoleon's machinations at the individual level were best exemplified by his sometimes contrived gesture of asking an officer to point out which of his men served in a particular battle. In a seeming moment of spontaneity, Napoleon would then single out such soldiers in formation or around a campfire for personal recognition. These deliberate efforts were intended to foster a personal connection between himself and his men; in a commensurate way, Napoleon hoped that such a bond would motivate the soldiers to endure his marches and carry out his attacks. He knew how to bind men to his service and was openly frank about his methods: "If I want a man I am prepared to kiss his a——."[105]

To this end, Napoleon instituted a number of awards, ranging from "arms of honor" (standard issue weapons engraved to commemorate acts of bravery) to the highly valued Légion d'Honneur, whose recipients numbered over 25,000 living members by 1814.[106] In between, Napoleon handed out to his soldiers the purely military Trois Toisons d'Or (Order of the Three Fleeces), the Order of the Iron Crown, numerous smaller awards, pensions, and monetary gifts. In addition, his marshals merited duchies, marriage to the daughters of the rich and noble, and sometimes crowns. Like Louis XIV, Napoleon kept them squabbling over such rewards, ensuring that his marshals were ever vigilant of their place and eager to rise in his favor. Thus, he retained their loyalty as he spurred them to greater endeavors.

Moreover, Napoleon understood the value of ceremony and went to great lengths to award battle honors to regiments and eagles to new units. Each event was a celebration, as were the various military fêtes such as New Year's Day, which included the pardoning of all military offenses and toasts to everyone's health. Perhaps the biggest event was Napoleon's birthday, which, as Elting points out, meant "double rations, wine, contests of all sorts with prizes, music, dancing, and fireworks" for the men.[107] Military masses, *Te Deum*s, and even wage bonuses were also common on this day.

In addition to these celebratory events, Napoleon's soldiers understood that promotion for steadfastness and valor on the battlefield was always possible. Merit, not title or financial status, was the means by which men rose in the French army. While it was an exaggeration that every French soldier "carried a marshal's baton in his knapsack," it can safely be said that the opportunity for promotion through the ranks was real enough to make the soldiers want to adhere to the written and unwritten rules of conduct pertaining to campaign and battlefield behavior. Winning a place in a regimental guard or light company was also a possibility;[108] such promotion brought not only extra pay but the enormous pride of wearing the company's colors and plumes and being recognized as an elite soldier. Eventual promotion to an Imperial Guard company stood as one of the greatest achievements of any French soldier.

Napoleon also addressed one of his soldiers' greatest fears and concerns: what would happen to them should they become seriously injured? To this end he kept up the Hôtel des Invalides, created for the care of soldiers unfit for service by Louis XIV in 1674, as well as branch establishments in other locales. As an extension of this care, Napoleon established veteran's colonies on public land in the Rhineland and the Piedmont, where wounded soldiers could farm and live out their lives. He even went so far as to adopt all the abandoned children of French soldiers killed at Austerlitz in 1805, having the boys brought up in one imperial palace and the girls in another and allowing all of the children to add "Napoleon" to their names.[109] How much of this was heartfelt and personal and how much was a carefully considered ploy is not as important as the effect of his gesture. We can imagine the reactions of the veterans of Austerlitz when they learned that their emperor cared enough about their dead comrades to adopt and care for their children.

In contrast, the British had only two old soldiers' homes, at Chelsea and Kilmainham. These refuges had limited beds and served only a few hundred men in all. As for pensions, the common soldier usually needed to prove a service-related disability. Enlisted men applying for such a disability pension had to appear before a board at the Horse Guards. The soldiers often found that their requests were delayed three months or more, while the board combed over service records, checking for monies owed or notations of lost equipment. Even Wellington acknowledged the cruelty of such treatment: "While this is going on, many die who might be saved."[110]

The men who eventually did come before the board received a pittance, if anything, for their years of service to the king. A few examples will suffice to represent how the wounded soldiers were mostly abandoned to their fates by the board when their usefulness was at an end. Macfarlane of the 71st was invalided home after Corunna. Upon examination, the board declared that he was £5 in debt for necessities and then paid him this same amount for his wound and pension, clearing Macfarlane's debt but leaving him nothing on which to live.[111] For five years' service and a wound at Waterloo, which almost necessitated amputation of this arm, O'Neil received one shilling a day for life, which he felt lucky to get.[112] Lawrence went before the board and was granted seven pence a day for his ten years in the ranks. This was increased to nine pence when one of the examining board members brought attention to the knee wound that Lawrence had received at Badajoz. Later recalled to duty, from 1819 to 1821, Lawrence petitioned the authorities at Chelsea and was granted an additional three pence a day.[113]

Plunkett, the Rifleman who won battlefield honors, received a severe head wound at Waterloo. Invalided out of the army, he was granted six pence a day; when he complained to the board, telling them "to keep it [the small pension] for young soldiers, as it wasn't enough for the old, who had seen all the tough work out," his pension was stopped altogether.[114] Plunkett's comrade Costello would likewise be shortchanged. After the better part of a decade in the army, he was retired due to wounds. His pension of six pence a day left him, his wife, and his daughter starving. Having little choice, his wife took the child back to France. Costello never saw either of them again.[115] Harris of the 95th was cast aside in a similar fashion. After Napoleon was sent to Elba, Harris was released from duty. For his eleven years of service he was granted a pension of six pence a day. But before he received even one day's payment, he was called up to serve again when Napoleon escaped to France. Still sick with fever contracted on campaign, he was unable to answer roll call and was informed that his pension was forfeit.[116]

Harris's descriptions of hobbled and maimed discharged soldiers lining the streets and public houses are a poignant reminder of how Britain cared for its soldiers when they were no longer needed; such treatment of the British soldier at the hands of the government did little to improve morale or convince civilians to serve.[117] French efforts orchestrated by Napoleon to care for injured and discharged soldiers, in contrast, at least reassured enlisted men that their martial efforts were appreciated and that life after the army need not include penury.[118]

British officers injured in the line of duty were not so ill-treated, as Michael Glover has shown. Officers without limbs and even some who were totally blind were allowed to continue serving on full pay. If men of rank were unable to endure campaigning, they could count on substantial pensions: a lieutenant who lost an eye or limb was entitled to £70 a year, a far cry from the ranker's top rate of one shilling a day.[119]

Finally, in regard to French campaign motivations, the French soldier in the field always had the enticement of plunder. Contrary to common belief, the French army had rules regarding such conduct. Rape and outright assault of civilians as a means of procuring valuables were considered crimes and punishable at the regimental level. Circumstances in Portugal and Spain, however, reduced the chances that such crimes would be considered offenses, at least by the French officers in charge. The rape of local women, in any case, was usually acceptable to French tastes, though not to the women themselves. Sex as a reward for service was part of the French soldier's expectations.[120] As for looting opportunities, plundering towns after assaults, stripping valuables from downed enemy soldiers on the battlefield, and taking anything of worth from local inhabitants all were standard behavior for the men of Napoleon's armies.

Thus, Napoleon was well aware of the needs of his men and worked to address them on many levels in order to ensure the soldiers' combat readiness.[121] His manipulation of these motivations to achieve his own means does not lessen their inspirational effectiveness on his soldiers.

The British army, however, made little effort to see to the psychological needs of the men. Regularly supplying daily rations or other necessities proved beyond the capability of the army commissariat, just as it was for most Napoleonic armies. Little regard was paid to the redcoats' well-being, other than efforts to make certain they were at least marginally fit for marching and battle. No attempt was made to cater to the ideological considerations of the men or to ensure that the soldiers' personal identities and ideas about why they were fighting were aligned with the values and concerns espoused by army leadership. Moreover, the British did not engage in the ideological indoctrination based on racial superiority and hatred for the enemy that Omer Bartov alleges helped keep Wehrmacht cohesion from disintegrating in World War II when Eastern Front casualty rates threatened unit integrity.[122] The British viewed the French as professionals and, with the exception of French conduct regarding civilians in Spain and Portugal, had no contempt for them.[123]

Unlike the attention given to their French counterparts regarding ideological and internal motivations, the British regular was virtually ignored in this regard. This is best illustrated by the absence of medals or awards of any kind for meritorious service in the British army. Other than the Army Gold Medal and Gold Cross, both rare and restricted to officers, the British military did not award medals for bravery or exceptional service. A very small number of regiments had their own medal, such as the "Order of Merit" in the 5th Regiment of Foot and the long-service medal for 71st Highland Light Infantry, established in 1767 and 1808, respectively.[124] A few units had unofficial rewards whose requirements were vague at best. Only the "VS" badge, indicating "Valiant Stormer" for survivors of Forlorn Hope, was awarded at the army level.

It was not until the Waterloo Medal, instituted in 1815, that a campaign medal of any type was issued. Available to all ranks, the Waterloo Medal credited its wearer with an extra two years of service. The medal was also the first British medal to have the recipient's name impressed around its edge and was the first campaign award to be posthumously awarded to a soldier's next-of-kin. This medal was greatly resented by campaign veterans who had never been officially recognized for their service in Spain and Portugal. They felt that the Peninsula effort was a much longer and more arduous campaign and certainly merited some decoration. It was not until 1848, when the Military General Service Award was issued, that such service was acknowledged by the government. By that time most of the Peninsula veterans were dead.[125] No decorations for gallantry by enlisted men existed until 1854, when first the Distinguished Service Cross and then the Victoria Cross were created.[126]

The best a British soldier could hope for was promotion for exceptional conduct under fire. Such promotions were rare, however. Costello, the sergeant in the 95th Rifles, vividly remembered such an event, in part because the man performed his deed in front of the battalion and because of the salubrious effect that both the deed and its recognition had on the men of the 95th. During Sir John Moore's epic retreat to Corunna, a bold French general, August Colbert, was aggressively leading the cavalry pursuit. The British commanding officer in charge of the rearguard action at Cacabellos, General Sir Edward Paget, challenged any of the Riflemen to earn his acclaim and his purse by shooting the officer in order to slow the pursuit. A Private Plunkett volunteered: the very same Plunkett whose government later flogged him then cheated him of his pension. He ran 100 yards toward the approaching cavalry, lay down on his back on the road (the standard Rifleman's posture for long shots), took aim, and shot Colbert from his saddle. Then Plunkett shot the general's orderly when he charged to avenge his commander.[127]

For his efforts, Plunkett—already known for his bravery, skill, and daring—was awarded Paget's purse, some kind of unofficial medal, promotion, and high words of praise from Colonel Beckwith, the regimental commander.[128] The ceremony was conducted in a hollow square, usually reserved for battalion punishment. Costello remembered with pride the effect the presentation had on the men: "I am convinced that it was attended with the happiest effects upon many of the men, and perhaps, indeed, induced much of that spirit of personal gallantry for which our corps afterwards became celebrated."[129] This example, a singular find among all the firsthand accounts, demonstrates the effectiveness of recognition and reward for exemplary service.

The inequities of the ranker's treatment by his government highlight the difficulties that continually worked to lower his morale. The lack of sustaining campaign motivations shaped the men's behaviors and attitudes, making most soldiers fatalistic about their lives. They lived day-to-day, with little in the way of hope or expectation that the next day would be any better; basic survival became the accepted level of aspiration. Soldiers could dance like children at Christmas when the ration wagons arrived and plunder with an extraordinary thoroughness when the supplies did not.[130] Exposing men to privation of the type experienced by the redcoat is not the ideal way to create cohesive fighting units. A certain amount of shared hardship is necessary to bond men together, for it is such experience that engenders trust and mutual dependence. But the extremes endured by British regulars pushed the bounds of human tolerance. Thousands of them succumbed to disease and exhaustion when these limits were exceeded. Men can only be hardened to a point; after that they simply wear out by degrees.

The mess group of six to eight men provided the physical and psychological support that allowed the ranker to face the hardships of life with the army in the Peninsula. The ties between these men evolved into the paramount force in their lives. As he shared what victuals were available, huddled under the night sky, stole and parceled out illicit food and drink, suffered long marches and draconian discipline, and faced the French in battle, the British soldier learned to rely on a small cadre of men who made the difference between life and death. These bonds between comrades, combined with leadership, drill, and aggressive tactical methods, became their inspiration and the source of their resolve.[131]

5

ORDEAL BY FIRE

The British Soldier in Combat

British strategic, operational, and tactical successes in the Peninsular War can be attributed in large part to the Duke of Wellington. His grasp of the various command challenges that faced him in Spain and Portugal allowed him to maintain a functional army and to use it where and when it gave him the best chance of victory. He shaped the operating and combat environments to his advantage, and his decision-making has been lauded (then and now); Wellington's recognition as one of the premier military commanders in history is well merited.

Wellington took command of the British army of the Peninsular War in 1809, after Sir John Moore's death during the Battle of Corunna. The army that Wellington led over the next six years included not only men from the British Isles but also Portuguese, foreign (notably the King's German Legion), and sometimes Spanish troops. He merged these contingents into a fighting force that bested the French army in every major engagement, a remarkable achievement by any standard.

As Charles Esdaile has pointed out, though, Wellington's army was not a balanced, combined-arms force.[1] Often short of artillery (at least until 1813) and hampered by a cavalry arm that was not only small in number but equally capable of glory and misadventure, Wellington's army was infantry-centric.[2]

Limitations in numbers of guns, ordnance size, and ammunition supply diminished the artillery's effectiveness and caused the British to use their guns differently than the French did. On the battlefield British artillery was maneuvered and fired in battery-sized elements; they had no grand batteries of the style utilized so well by the French. Moreover, fire was almost always reserved for fairly close-range attacks against massing French infantry formations; counter battery fire was rarely attempted.[3] Thus, British artillery, while playing an important role in combat, was not a dominant battlefield force. Rather, it was a supporting arm that protected the infantry and worked to attrite enemy ground troops in preparation for assault by British infantry.

As for the battlefield efficacy of the British cavalry, the shock value of this branch, so well exemplified by the attacks at Sahagun (1808), Salamanca (1812), and against d'Erlon's corps at Waterloo, was sometimes overshadowed by the cavalry's unpredictable nature. Occasional mounted charges went out of control, the formations disintegrating as the horses raced or stumbled through and sometimes past targets until fatigue, unexpected terrain features, or the French cavalry put an end to the attacks.[4]

Command inexperience, regulations, training limitations, and leadership expectations resulted in officers with limited familiarity and skill attempting to control the lines of attacking cavalry. Relying more on leadership by example than on actual command influence, these officers were, by regulations, placed one horse-length in front of the troops they were expected to manage.[5] There all the officer could do was direct the cavalry toward a target. Supervising the charge by governing attack speed or maintaining formational integrity was a difficult proposition, as was recalling an assault at any point or rallying enough troopers afterward to be of continued battlefield use. Ian Fletcher, however, rightly notes that the cavalry excelled at "patrols, intelligence gathering, escort work, and foraging."[6] These efforts, while reflecting the skill and value of the cavalry, took place away from the battlefield; it was in combat that the cavalry sometimes exhibited its flaws. In a dining room conversation with Colonel Felton Hervey after Waterloo, Wellington stated his dissatisfaction with his cavalry branch: "but this I will say, the cavalry of other European armies have won battles for their generals, but mine have invariably got me into scrapes."[7]

Wellington, naturally, preferred to rely on the infantry as the ascendant combat arm. It was their resoluteness and fierceness in battle that won him victories in India; these same traits allowed the branch to lead Wellington's army to an unbroken string of tactical successes throughout the Peninsular War. Time and time again—from the battle of Vimerio in 1808, through Talavera (1809), Salamanca (1812) and Vitoria (1813), and all the fights in between—the infantry formed the rock upon which Wellington orchestrated the crash and destruction of French forces.[8] The French general Maximilien Foy, who matched-off against the British in Portugal and Spain, openly acknowledged the redcoat infantry as being the heart of Wellington's fighting force: "The infantry is the best portion of the British army. It is the *robur peditum*, the expression applied by the Roman army to the *triarii* of their legions. . . . [They] are more silent, more quiet and more obedient [than the French], and for that very reason their fire is more destructive. You will not find them resigned under the bullets like the Russians, but they draw together with less confusion and preserve their original formations better."[9]

On the tactical level, Wellington's ability to array his army—placing his experienced infantry in key positions and taking full advantage of topographical features to protect his troops, guard flanks, and channel enemy attacks—was a critical factor in these triumphs.[10] Esdaile has also noted that the British capacity to maintain and change formation during the chaos of battle was a prominent characteristic of the infantry that enhanced the army's chances of victory in battle.[11]

Wellington's capacity to maneuver his army, deploying it correctly at the right time and place, would have meant nothing, however, if the combat effectiveness of the British infantry had not been exceptional. This fundamental characteristic was a key component of the British tactical methodology that disrupted and defeated the French system of arms. The British came to dominate the French on the battlefield because they adopted a close-range fire-and-charge technique that depended heavily on lower-level leadership and the British soldier's strongest attribute: his willingness to endure risks in order to preserve the group and maintain his place in it.

A summary of French tactical doctrine helps elucidate the interplay between British and French forces and clarifies the reasons behind British tactical success. Napoleon's combined arms approach dictated that a heavy artillery bombardment of the enemy's position at the point of attack was to precede an advance. As this fire commenced, swarms of skirmishers (*voltigeurs*) moved to within musket range of the enemy in order to mask the infantry advance and to snipe at officers and NCOs. Under the cover of the skirmish screen, French infantry (formed in columns) would close the distance to enemy positions, preceded by cavalry charges whose purpose was to defeat enemy cavalry and force the enemy's infantry into a square. This protected the French columns from attack and reduced the amount of fire they would have to endure as they crossed the battlefield.

Tactical doctrine under Napoleon continued to rely in large part on the threat of the bayonet; the infantry was intended to engage and penetrate enemy formations as part of a combined arms attack. This concept never changed over the long years of war, although the method of execution did. The preferred French formation was *l'ordre mixte,* consisting of two battalion columns in open order flanking one battalion in line.[12] This evolution from Revolutionary assault columns added the element of firepower to the French attacks. Over time, though, campaign and battlefield attrition led to deterioration in the quality of French infantry; this began in 1805–1806 and became a critical factor from 1809 on. The loss of experienced troops, NCOs, and officers forced the French to abandon *l'ordre mixte* and resort to columnar attacks, which demanded less training to employ and placed less emphasis on coordination between units. By the time of the Peninsular War, the mixed order was no longer a French option.

Exactly what the French did next or how they adapted tactically is uncertain. The preponderance of evidence makes it appear likely that the French adopted the practice of changing from column into line before making contact with enemy formations. If the French were able to mix units in line with some in column, an ad hoc version of *l'ordre mixte* may have provided the French with the benefits of both shock and fire combat.[13] It is also possible that French columns that stalled during attacks in the Peninsular War attempted to change formation into lines as a last resort in order to respond to the threat of incoming British fire and the bayonet assault that was sure to follow.

James Arnold provides an excellent summation of how Revolutionary ideas were altered and integrated into French army doctrine.[14] He makes note of the French focus on tactical flexibility and the requirement that columns expeditiously make the transition from column to line while under fire, citing Marshal Michel Ney's codified instructions (presented in 1805) for his soldiers as evidence. Each of Ney's regulations regarding bayonet charges specifies that all close-action assaults should be delivered in line formation.[15] At least nine additional contemporary sources refer to French columns deploying into line, four from French sources and five from British.[16] All involve eyewitnesses to the events, leaving little doubt that at least some French columns were intended to deploy into line formation as part of the French combined arms attack. As Chandler writes, "This evidence is reasonably conclusive on the issue."[17]

The British tactical response was based on Wellington's use of the two-rank line. Preceded by a skirmisher screen, the British infantry posed a number of tactical dilemmas for the French. The redcoats refused to give ground and could be expected to fire only at ranges that would prove lethal to the front and side ranks of French columns. Moreover, the British penchant and enthusiasm for following fusillades with bayonet charges was a frightening and disconcerting component of their method. Wellington's occasional use of reverse slopes only exacerbated the difficulties of dealing with the British on the battlefields of Spain and Portugal; by concealing the position of British infantry on the field, he not only protected the soldiers from French artillery and small arms fire but upset the timing of French attacks.[18]

Generally speaking, French commanders needed to see the approximate locations of enemy units in order to deploy skirmishers to protect columns and to maneuver the columns into attack position. French officers also required time and space to guide the columns toward weak points in the British line or to deploy from column into line, all the while maintaining formational integrity.

Properly executed, Wellington's preferred methodology frequently caused a tactical systems failure for the French, disrupting their ability to observe, orient, decide, and act.[19] Unseen behind slight terrain elevations, British units could rise up unexpectedly and volley and charge the advancing French columns before French officers could orchestrate a tactical countermove. Getting men to rise from the prone position and advance while under fire was a difficult maneuver that depended heavily on unit discipline and *esprit de corps.* Marshal Ney advised against even having men kneel to fire, as they were often reluctant to rise and continue forward movement toward the enemy.[20] Nevertheless, the British regular did so time and time again.

Even when in plain sight, British infantrymen were capable of rapid tactical transitions, moving from static, defensive positions into all-out assaults; the redcoats could cover the ground to the oncoming French units in a rapid and silent fashion and then deliver the standard British close-range fusillade topped off by a rush with steel.

The suddenness of the British attacks caused the French soldier to experience a succession of shocks. The fleeting recognition of relative positions was quickly replaced by an understanding that the British were about to deliver a close-range volley, which the French soldier knew could not be answered in kind. Flintlock muskets could be quite deadly within a range of 50 yards or so, as numerous accounts confirm. At Auerstadt in 1806, for example, Charles Etienne Gudin's division suffered 70 percent casualties at this distance, losing 3,500 of out of approximately 5,000 combatants.[21] If the French were still in column, this fire could be coming from the front and both flanks as the British line wrapped around the French formation. If the French were in line, the British two-rank formation would extend beyond the ends of the French line, which, because it was three ranks deep, occupied a third less frontage.

The impact on surviving individuals can only be imagined. French cohesion would begin to disintegrate as comrades fell by the score; the bonds between men that held them in combat would be severely tested as each man took stock of the situation, the losses, and his options. The French soldiers would slow their advance or begin edging back away from the source of fire. The remaining men, some wounded and others reeling from psychological stress and fear, were given little time to react or regroup. Exacerbating the effects of this already distressing series of events, British troops would then charge, sometimes with cheers and at other times with eerie silence, and move to close quarters with bayonets leveled. This is the real meaning of the term "shock combat," as the threat of grievous injury or death is delivered in a face-to-face clash. To French soldiers unfamiliar with such tactics and faced with the threat of steel delivered by highly motivated soldiers, retreat became a viable and preferred option.

British initiative in dictating the tactical tempo allowed red-coat battalions to control time and space on the battlefield; musket fire at optimal ranges and bayonet assaults were the culminating actions that worked to disorder French formations. Thus, a combination of leadership, training, group cohesion, and discipline permitted the British to create a set of tactics that preserved soldiers' lives and greatly increased the probability of defeating the French in combat.

A great deal of historical misinterpretation, however, stemming from Charles Oman's misunderstanding of events at Maida in Italy during 1806, has sometimes presented the British tactical method as being predicated on British firepower alone. In his 1907 lecture to cadets at the Royal Artillery Institution at Woolwich, later published in the *Journal of the Royal Artillery Institution*, Oman (relying on the testimony of one British witness) argued that the French tactic of attacking in columns was purposeful and flawed.[22] Oman summarized that "5,000 infantry in line received the shock of 6,000 in column, and inflicted on them one of the most crushing defeats on a small scale that took place during the whole war."[23] For Oman, it was strictly a massed fire issue: every soldier in a British line was able to discharge his weapon at the enemy, while only men in the front few ranks and the side files of a French column could fire their muskets in response. John Fortescue incorporated Oman's assessment into his *History of the British Army*, as Chandler has noted, further perpetuating the column-versus-line firepower misconception.[24]

Oman's contention that the French somehow failed to fathom the tactical nuances of column versus line interaction is refuted by a passage written by French military theorist Comte Jacque Antoine Hippolyte de Guibert, three decades before the French experience in the Peninsular War. He accurately envisioned the outcome of an attack in column formation: "One approaches the enemy . . . the ranks are soon mingled . . . the column forms no more than a tumultuous mass. . . . If the head and flanks of the column are struck by a lively fire, the soldier dazed begins to fire in the air, the mass whirls, disperses, and can only rally at a very great distance."[25]

The French understood that a column by itself against a line suffered a grave firepower and frontage deficiency. In such a situation, the column was susceptible to both musket fire and bayonet. Pressed too hard, the column would begin to collapse in the manner that

Guibert described. The French method, which included cavalry attacks, preparatory artillery bombardment, and light troops for screen-
ing, was more sophisticated than Oman implied. Battalions were
never intended to fight strictly in column formation.

From the British perspective, the practical consideration of maintaining the fire rates required by Oman's scenario was also an issue.
While a slightly more reliable musket than its French Charleville
"1777" counterpart, the British Brown Bess still experienced fouling
problems, due to black powder residue and misfires caused by broken
or worn-out flints.[26] Chandler estimates that the French musket mis-
fired perhaps one time in six;[27] the rates for the British flintlock
would have been similar. With barrels requiring washing every forty
rounds or so and flints needing replacement every ten to twelve shots,
the ranker would have been hard pressed to keep his musket service-
able over the course of a battle. Rates of fire rapidly declined to approximately one or two rounds a minute at most; this was substantially lower than the three to five rounds that have sometimes been
suggested. The number of rounds available per soldier was another
consideration. Most nations provided sixty rounds per man, which
were intended to be enough for an entire battle. The three rounds a
minute ideal, even setting aside all the problems of fouling and broken flints, would have consumed the soldier's entire allotment in 20
minutes. While fire was not, of course, continuous, such high rates of
fire could only have been sustained for short periods.

Theoretically, even relatively low fire rates might have put
enough lead into the air over the 100 yards or so that constituted the
effective range of smoothbore muskets to inflict enough casualties to
have a serious impact on the cohesion of an advancing French column
or line. An 800-man battalion firing only one round a minute could, in
ideal conditions, expect about 60 percent of its rounds to strike the
approaching formation at a range of about 80 yards.[28] This translates
to perhaps as many as 480 casualties. But tests conducted with carefully loaded weapons and in the best possible circumstances do not
come close to approximating the realities of combat.[29]

Needless to say, casualty rates never approached the level just
described, as battlefield conditions worked to lower fire rates and
accuracy significantly. Inclement weather turned powder into a con-
gealed mass, making firing impossible. Clouds of gunpowder smoke
also obscured vision, and the cacophony of battle disconcerted sol-

diers; the din of thousands of firearms and scores of artillery pieces, all firing in succession, and the emotional strain of combat led to accidental discharges, spilled powder and ball, fired ramrods, and double-loading.[30] Moreover, continuous firing for just eight minutes could leave the barrel too hot to touch. Of equal importance was the effect of "flintlock flinch" on accuracy.[31] This phenomenon involved the natural human reaction to the delay between pulling the trigger and actual weapon discharge. During the fleeting moments after the flint struck the frizzen cover, causing the gunpowder in the pan to fire and igniting the rammed charge when the gunpowder trail burned down the touchhole into the barrel, soldiers tended to shy away from the expected explosion for a moment in anticipation of musket-butt recoil. If the musket was not properly seated between the pectoral and deltoid muscles, the recoil could turn a man's shoulder black-and-blue.[32] The flinch caused the men to elevate the end of their musket barrels a bit, causing their rounds to go high.[33] None of these unintended outcomes would have worked to the advantage of a British unit relying on firepower alone to stop an attacking French formation. Nosworthy, in fact, estimates that during combat a musket was at least 40 times less effective than during tests.[34]

As General B. P. Hughes points out in his study of weapon effectiveness during this period, the ballistic performance of muskets had only marginally improved since the eighteenth century. He calculated that only 0.2 to 0.5 percent of bullets fired hit their targets.[35] Using the battle of Albuera (1811) as an example, Hughes estimated that perhaps 3 to 5 percent of infantry rounds might find their targets if the firing distances were under 200 yards and the attacking and enemy formations were stationary over an extended period, about half an hour in this case.[36] After analyzing all the studies on the subject, Rory Muir concluded that it took between 200 and 500 smoothbore rounds to inflict one casualty during Napoleonic battles.[37] This explains Colonel Hanger's remark in 1814 that "a soldier must be very unfortunate indeed who shall be wounded by a common musket at 150 yards provided his antagonist aims at him; as to firing at a man at 200 . . . you may as well fire at the moon."[38] The contention that British success on the battlefield was directly related to infantry firepower alone appears to be a questionable conclusion at best. Instead, it becomes apparent that the most effective tactic incorporated close-range fire and the immediate use of the bayonet.

The British regular's ability to function in a two-rank line was one of the keys to British tactical superiority over the French. While providing the redcoat an edge in combat, the two-rank line demanded more of the soldier than did the French three-rank line or assault column. The principal difficulty involved the formation's linear nature. The openness of the two-rank line provided the soldier less psychological support than did denser formations. Such emotional sustenance was normally generated by the close proximity of comrades. In a column, most soldiers had men to their front, flank, rear, and each of the four diagonals; the number of ranks offered a certain perceived insularity against harm, even if such a perception was more illusion than reality. Such support was not available in a two-rank line.

The benefits of the proximity of comrades in the French three-rank line acted to support the individual soldier to a greater degree than did the British formation. The removal of the third rank had a greater effect than the fractional shortfall (one-third) implies. The loss of the back rank made the two-rank line a lonely formation in which to fight. Spacing shifted each man in the second row to occupy the gap between the soldiers in the front rank. The men in the second rank also tended to crowd together with the front line for emotional assistance and to ensure that the muskets of the soldiers in the back row extended well beyond the heads of the men in the first row, effectively reducing the formation to one compacted rank. With a turn of his head, each soldier was fully aware that he had no one directly behind him. This increased the stress on the soldier, making him feel exposed, even though he had comrades on each side.

The spacing of a line formation, with approximately 18 inches between men, put a greater demand on each soldier to stand his ground. The flight of but a few men in a two-rank line could have catastrophic consequences, as their absence opened complete gaps in the formation. For soldiers still in the ranks, the absence of a man in the files to their left or right made them feel isolated and vulnerable. This greatly increased their inclination to flee, as heightened threat potential and the loss of psychological support began chipping away at group allegiance. The loss of men from wounds or flight also caused the line to constrict, because without the third rank no replacements were available to step into the openings.[39]

Thus, lower-level leadership (company commanders, lieutenants, and NCOs) was greatly needed to control and guide British formations. Leaders were called upon to close the ranks, compress formations in order to fill holes, coordinate movement with other British units, direct advances, and attempt to manage the men's emotions. Both zeal and terror could lead to unit disintegration; the emotionality of the soldier required close observation and skillful management in order to maintain unit cohesion and keep the soldiers focused on the tasks at hand. Lawrence remembered the active participation of his officers at Waterloo as the men formed and reformed against a succession of French cavalry charges: "The men in their tired state were beginning to despair, but the officers cheered them on continually throughout the day with the cry of 'Keep your ground, my men!' It is a mystery to me how it was accomplished for at last so few were left that there was scarcely enough to form square. . . . Few as we were . . . we poured volley after volley into them [French cuirassiers], doing fearful execution."[40]

During the battle, Lawrence's company commander was decapitated by a cannon shot. One private in the company whose last name was Marten cried out, "Hullo, there goes my best friend." A lieutenant unhesitatingly stepped forward and assumed command, remarking loudly: "Never mind, I will be as good a friend to you as the captain." Although Marten was being sarcastic, that does not diminish the leadership abilities exemplified by the young officer. Lawrence, who was splattered with the captain's blood, explained that Marten was continually unable to keep his person clean and that the captain had repeatedly punished him for his failures. Marten's personal hygiene deficiencies did not keep him from being "an excellent soldier in the field," which was all that mattered to Lawrence, if not to the men who shared Marten's tent.[41]

Mobility was also an issue when it came to linear formations. Moving a line, especially the two-rank variety, across open ground was a difficult and potentially dangerous maneuver. Ground undulations, natural obstacles, battlefield debris, and the bodies of the dead and wounded worked to distend the formation as the files and ranks separated; keeping the line contiguous with adjacent units was also taxing. These complications made the officers' and NCOs' tasks of maintaining formational integrity and directing the line along a preferred route a demanding undertaking. Moreover, the loss of men during campaign would shrink the frontage of the line, potentially reducing its linear advantage over a column. These problems explain why no national European army other than the British, or the national contingents they trained,[42] fought in a two-rank line.[43]

The French three-rank line had its flaws too, principally the reduction in firepower and the increased risk to the soldiers in the front rows from shots fired by the third rank. One of Napoleon's marshals, Gouvion St. Cyr, estimated that approximately one-quarter of all infantry casualties were related to accidents involving men in the front ranks being shot by those in the rear.[44] Men moving laterally and hurrying to reload were quite vulnerable to rear-rank fire, as the length of the musket and the spacing needed for three ranks combined to form a potentially deadly combination. St. Cyr may have exaggerated the casualties inflicted by the third line, but the danger was real enough. The morale benefits of the third row, however, convinced all armies except the British that the two-rank line was too risky, especially for inexperienced troops.

Napoleon was well aware of the strengths and limitations of the three-rank line and attempted to intercede, making his one contribution to French infantry tactics. In 1813, after years of complaints by his officers regarding the hazards of the three-rank line, Napoleon decided that "the formation of infantry should be always in two ranks, because of the length of the musket. . . . The discharge of the third rank is not only uncertain but frequently dangerous to the ranks in the front."[45] He then ordered French infantry to adopt the British method of fighting in two ranks.[46] Napoleon's order to adopt the two-rank line also may have been initiated by the declining numbers of available French soldiers. Unit frontage for a French line could be maintained with a third less men using the two-rank line approach. Lack of training time, coupled with the continued influx of raw recruits, however, prevented French line officers from incorporating the change.

The British method required drill and training, which at least until 1788 was generally left to the preferences of regimental commanders, although regulations were issued.[47] In that year Sir David Dundas published what became officially sanctioned in 1792 as the first manual outlining tactical doctrine. His *Rules and Regulations for the Movements of His Majesty's Infantry,* or the "Eighteen Manoeuvres" as they came to be called, were a bit on the convoluted side and sometimes more theoretical than practical. Nevertheless, they did, to a large extent, standardize infantry maneuver and drill. In

regard to line depth, Dundas agreed with the tacticians of other nations: he declared that the only viable line formation was three ranks
deep. The impracticalities of some of his ideas and British fondness
for the two-rank line led to the official approval of this formation in
1801. Philip Haythornthwaite suggests that the three-rank line had
been abandoned by units in the field well before this date.[48]

Training, leadership, and a high level of mutual trust among the
rankers were needed to coordinate tactical movement and make the
two-rank line an effective combat formation. Daily drill and ceremony provided the basis for muster and parade, battlefield maneuver
and formation change, and unit identification. This helped turn inexperienced soldiers into steady, competent professionals. According to
Roger Buckley, the men learned "manual exercise, platoon exercise,
the evolutions, the firings, and the maneuvers."[49] The required movements were assimilated through slow repetition at first, then executed more rapidly as the soldiers became proficient. Basic training
encompassed drill and more drill, just as it does today. William Bell,
an ensign in the 88th Foot, remembered how he learned his trade: "I
have been out at six o'clock in the morning for some time past—since
I joined the regiment. We are drilled with the men exactly the same as
the privates. We begin with facings and went through all the different
steps and evolutions of the marching squads. We then executed it
with the firelock."[50]

Soldier accounts (including Lawrence's) do not often mention
close order drill, however, perhaps because it was such a standard part
of daily life that it did not merit highlighting. Drill must have been
fairly frequent, though, for only through practice could the British
soldier master march and fire procedures, become familiar with verbal commands and drum signals, learn the types of formations and
how to execute formation changes, and recognize how individual soldier behavior affected unit performance. The leadership provided
by NCOs, company, and battalion commanders who taught drill
and made formational decisions in battle was a key to tactical proficiency. Skilled officers who knew their craft, treated the soldiers
fairly, and led by example (men like Costello's Captain Uniacke) were
esteemed by the rankers, who understood that officer competence
increased the chances of tactical success, which usually translated to
improved survival rates. The British also had an organizational advantage: they had more officers and sergeants per battalion than the

French.[51] The British had more companies per battalion as well as more officers per company. This augmented their ability to deal with command and control challenges.

As we might expect, Lawrence provides a vivid, though remarkably unruffled, description of how the British utilized the two-rank line to employ close range fire-and-charge tactics. This encounter at the Villebar heights near Pampeluna (Pamplona), Spain, in 1813 found the British with a terrain advantage and the French determined to dislodge them:

> Our regiment was soon on the scene, and hastening in that direction, we managed to get there [the heights] before the enemy had gained the summit of this important ridge. Orders had been given by our officers not to fire till we could do good work; but this soon came to pass, for the French quickly sallied up and fired first, and we returned it in less than a minute. I never saw a single volley do so much execution in all my days of campaigning, almost every man of their first two ranks falling; and then we instantly charged and chased them down the mountain, doing still further and more fearful havoc.[52]

Lawrence's continued narrative has the 40th Foot withstanding a series of assaults that day; the 40th was required to wheel in a timely fashion and repeatedly counterattack the French infantry. Each time, Lawrence writes proudly, "we reloaded and were ready to meet them, again pouring another of our deadly volleys into their ranks and then going at them again with our bayonets like enraged bulldogs."[53]

Lawrence's example is not anomalous; in fact, this dynamic appears to be the standard British tactical sequence employed against the French. The British used a number of variations on this theme in order to unbalance their French counterparts. All the versions required the redcoat to hold his fire, even when the enemy did not, and then summon up the courage to close rapidly with French units and make use of the bayonet. Knowledge that such methods usually led to victory instilled a high level of confidence, as the men realized that their abilities allowed them to take care of themselves given the contingencies of battle.[54] These assault tactics worked to minimize fear for the British regular by making use of his group ties and normative pressures in concert with the natural adrenal rushes that are experienced by every soldier in combat. James Anton, a sergeant in the 42nd, describes the British soldier's perspective, effectively capturing the physical and emotional effects of a charge: "No movement in the field is made with greater confidence of success than that of the charge; it affords little time for thinking, while it creates a fearless excitement, and tends to give a fresh impulse to the blood of the advancing soldier, rouses his courage, strengthens every nerve, and drowns every fear of danger or of death; thus emboldened amidst cheers that anticipate victory, he rushes on and mingles with the fleeing foe."[55]

John Macfarlane of the 71st provides one battlefield example of the many British techniques. Like all the versions, it was based on fondness for close assault work. Writing about the battle of Vimerio in 1808, he very nonchalantly describes the British method and the results. "We got orders to prime and load, and lie down," Macfarlane comments. As the French approached, the British stood up and the French fired immediately. The British then advanced. "At last we got nearer, we fired on them . . . [and then] they turned and made off. We cheered and went on . . . they went over the hill, and left three guns and wagons behind."[56] This sequence exactly matches Wellington's instructions to Rowland Hill at Busaco in 1810. "If they attempt this point again, Hill," he advised, "you will give them a volley and charge [with] bayonets; but don't let your people follow them too far down the hill."[57]

Lieutenant-Colonel William Gomm relates the same chain of events in a letter regarding a skirmish near the Duero River in 1812. The French were in the process of changing formation when "the spirit of our people rose . . . and when [after advancing] they reached the enemy's solid columns . . . a general shout of exaltation [came from our men]. . . . The enemy wavered . . . till at length it was impossible to withstand the ardour of our soldiers . . . and complete rout ensued."[58]

Costello offered yet another variation, this time describing the advance of the 88th during a British attack. British élan again was the crucial ingredient. The ability of the Connaught Rangers to accept fire from the French while moving into closer range (in this case perhaps 250 yards) is typical, as is the denouement of the final bayonet attack. Costello recalled:

The 88th deployed into line, advancing all the time towards their opponents, who seemed to wait very coolly for them. When they [the 88th] had approached to within three or four hundred yards, the French poured in a volley or I should say a running fire. . . . As soon as the British regiment had recovered the first shock, and closed their files on the gap it had made, they commenced advancing at the double until within fifty yards nearer to the enemy, when they halted and in turn gave a running fire from their whole line, and without a moment's pause cheered and charged up the hill against them. The French meanwhile were attempting to reload. But being hard pressed by the British, who allowed them no time to give a second volley, they came immediately to the right about, making the best of their way to the village.[59]

This sequence also illustrates the difficulty of maintaining fire rates during battle as well as the British capacity to manipulate battlefield space to their advantage. It would have taken the 88th at least 60 seconds or so to cover the uphill distance from the point at which they fired on the French line. Yet, as Costello comments, the pressure of the British assault harried the French so that they were unable to get off a second volley.

John Aitchison of the Scots Guards, William Grattan of the 88th, and John Carss, an officer in the 53rd, furnished three additional examples, this time of the British on the defensive. In Aitchison's account, the British relied on the bayonet alone to repulse a French attack at Talavera: "On their [the French] approaching within 200 yards, we were ordered to advance without firing a shot and afterwards to charge. This we did. . . . The enemy did not wait for us, [and] we carried everything before us."[60]

In a letter home, Carss described his regiment exhibiting this same steadiness at Talavera. The 53rd, in plain sight, stood in line awaiting the advance of a French column. Carss remembered: "We never fired a shot until they cleared the wood and got over a small bank which was about 60 yards from our line, then we gave a volley, then rushed on with the bayonet. They ran instantly when we charged."[61]

Grattan's account echoed the stories of Aitchison and Carss: the 88th also resorted to the bayonet, this time at Busaco in 1810. Grattan heard Alexander Wallace, the lieutenant-colonel of the 88th, remind the men not to fire early: "Now Connaught Rangers. . . . Pay attention to what I have said so often—don't give the false touch, but push home to the muzzle!"[62] His advice worked: the French broke before the oncoming Irishmen and their mates and were pursued down the hill.

An anonymous soldier in the 71st Highland Light Infantry provided an anecdote that gives a clear impression of British tenacity against a French column at the battle of Vimerio in 1808. In this instance, the unsettling silence of the British rankers and a late charge stopped the French advance: "[After forming into line] we gave them one volley and three cheers—three distinct cheers. Then all was as still as death. They came upon us crying and shouting, to the very point of our bayonets. Our awful silence and determined advance they could not stand. They put about and fled without much resistance. At this charge we took thirteen guns and one general."[63] (General Antoine-François Brenier was captured by Corporal Mackey of the 71st.)

An officer in the 85th wrote of this contrast between the French method of attack and the silent British defense. He recalled that the French would "raise a loud but discordant yell," while the British remained absolutely quiet. At close range, the redcoats "poured in but one volley, and then rushed on with the bayonet."[64] The unknown private of the 71st captured the psychological effects of group cohesion on his willingness to press forward with such an attack. His commentary also highlights the British method of silently and grimly closing to close quarters: "In our first charge I felt my mind waver; a breathless sensation came over me. The silence was appalling. I looked alongst the line. It was enough to assure me. The steady, determined scowl of my companions assured my heart and gave me determination. How unlike the noisy advance of the French."[65]

In a letter written two months after Talavera, Aitchison vividly describes yet another such encounter. His recollection emphasizes two key aspects of British tactics: unit integrity under fire and the benefits of reverse slope tactics. Marveling that such behavior was standard for British soldiers, Aitchison credited the men for making such tactics work:

> From the numerous instances recorded, even in my own
> time, of the intrepidity of the British troops, I have formed an

idea of the coolness with which they ... oppose the impetuos-
ity of a French attack and their bravery in advancing to the
charge. ... I am persuaded but few persons who have not seen
it, will credit. ... I have seen men killed in the ranks by
cannon shots—those immediately round the spot would remove the mutilated corpses to the rear, they would then lie
down as if nothing had occurred and remain in the ranks,
steady as before. That common men could be brought to face
the greatest danger, there is a spirit within which tells me it is
possible, but I could not believe they could be brought to
remain without emotion, when attacked, not knowing from
whence. Such, however, was the conduct of our men on 28
July, and from this steadiness so few suffered as by remaining
quiet the shots bounced over their heads.[66]

The same general tactics that worked in Spain and Portugal served
the British well at the battle of Quatre Bras, two days before Waterloo.
Frederick Patterson, a lieutenant in the 33rd, recorded the outcome of
the advance by some of Marshal Ney's infantry. "We gave them a
beautiful volley," writes Patterson, "and charged, but they ran faster
than our troops (already fatigued) could do and we consequently did
not touch them with the bayonet."[67]

Perhaps the most compelling depiction of a clash between a British line and a French column comes from Major Thomas Bugeaud,
who experienced the episode firsthand from within the attacking
French column. The effect of British resoluteness on the morale of
the French soldiers in the column is striking:

> The English generally occupied well-chosen defensive
> positions having a certain command, and they showed only a
> portion of their forces. The usual artillery action first took
> place. Soon, in great haste, without studying the position,
> without taking time to examine whether there were means
> to make a flank attack, we marched straight on, taking the
> bull by the horns. About 1,000 yards from the English line
> the men became excited, called out to one another, and has-
> tened their march; the column began to become a little con-
> fused. The English remained quite silent with ordered arms,
> and from their steadiness appeared to be a long red wall.
> This steadiness invariably produced an effect on our young

soldiers. Very soon we got nearer, crying *"Vive l'Empereur!*
En avant! A la Baionnette!" Shakos were raised on the muzzles of muskets; the column began to double, the ranks got
into confusion, the agitation produced a tumult; shots were
fired as we advanced. The English line remained silent, still
and immovable, with ordered arms, even when we were only
300 yards distant, and it appeared to ignore the storm about to
break. The contrast was striking; in our innermost thoughts
we all felt the enemy was a long time in firing, and that
this fire, reserved so long, would be very unpleasant when
it came. Our ardor cooled. The moral power of steadiness,
which nothing can shake (even if it be only appearance),
over disorder which stupefies itself with noise, overcame
our minds. At this moment of intense excitement, the English wall shouldered arms; an indescribable feeling would
root many of our men to the spot; they began to fire. The
enemy's steady, concentrated volleys swept our ranks; deci-
mated, we turned round seeking to recover our equilibrium;
then three deafening cheers broke the silence of our opponents; at the third they were on us, pushing our disorganized
flight.[68]

The British ability to withhold fire until the French formation
moved to close range is evident in this account, as is redcoat enthusiasm for pressing home the assault. Most of these incidents did not
involve the use of reverse slopes; the British were usually in full view
of the French column from the beginning of the attack, as Bugeaud's
account confirms. Protected by light troops, British lines stood their
ground until their officers called for a fusillade and a charge. These
light troops, dispersed in teams of two (one soldier firing while the
other loaded), made a difference on the battlefield. Acting not only
as screens but as NCO and officer-hunters, British skirmishers attempted to disrupt command and control and diminish the collective
morale of the unit they faced, while preventing their French counterparts from doing the same. As Esdaile has indicated, such troops
did not exist in the British army until 1800, when the precursors of
the 95th Rifles came into being. Sir John Moore ensured that seven
regiments were trained to fight as skirmishers.[69] Coupled with units
from the King's German Legion, the Brunswick-Oels Jägers, and 12

Portuguese battalions, the British army under Wellington was able to field a sizable number of light troops.[70]

The British used a number of tactical variants, and most involved skirmish screens. At times the British were visible to the French and awaited their approach before firing and charging. In other cases, British units advanced toward the French and fired at close range before charging. Paddy Griffith's study of 19 British firefights during the Peninsular War reveals that in only 4 instances did the British open fire at a distance of greater than 100 yards. In 9 cases the distance was 20 yards or less. Griffith calculated that the average range of British fire was about 64 yards, with an average opening range of 75.5 yards and a closing fire distance of 30.4 yards.[71] As Rory Muir points out, however, the precision of remembered distances calculated by officers during the heat of combat is questionable.[72] Nevertheless, even as vague approximations, such numbers help explain how British combat methods combined fire ranges that overcame flintlock limitations with leadership, discipline, and group cohesion to create a winning tactical system.[73]

In some cases, though, the British closed with the French without firing at all; they relied instead on the ominous silence of their advance and the implied threat of cold steel to unbalance their Gallic counterparts.[74] Fear of the bayonet was real, despite the relatively few such wounds that were inflicted on either side. Dominique-Jean Larrey, Napoleon's surgeon general, discovered only 5 bayonet wounds compared to 119 bullet wounds in two hand-to-hand encounters between French and Austrian units.[75] Christopher Duffy, using admissions from Invalides from 1762, concluded that only 2.4 percent of all wounds were caused by bayonets.[76] Although Duffy's numbers refer to a different era, the data confirm that soldiers were extremely reluctant to come into actual contact with men wielding musket bayonets, despite Frederick the Great's reliance on close assault tactics. Like Larrey's results, however, Duffy's totals only include those who survived their experience with cold steel. The number of men who perished after being run through remains unknown. The long triangular blades caused gaping wounds, which were often impossible to suture, due to the shape of the bayonet.[77] This made the puncture wound prone to suppuration, often leading to gangrene, amputation, and death. Thus, one side or the other in a melee tended to choose flight rather than face such injuries.

James Arnold has suggested that "British linear infantry tactics in 1809–1815 paralleled Ney's instructions to the Grand Armée in 1805."[78] Yet, as Nosworthy has argued, the level of British aggressiveness was entirely new and "should not be viewed simply as some sort of mechanical and wholesale duplication of the pre-existing continental system."[79] The capacity to hold fire and the fondness for finishing a clash with a swift bayonet charge created a tactical dynamic that was, if not uniquely British, at least unusual for the period. It was a tactic against which the French never fully adapted. The Austrians, Spanish, Prussians, and Russians often found such a tactical sequence to be beyond the everyday capabilities of their soldiers.[80] Individual units were capable of replicating this approach, of course, but cohesion limitations, tactical restrictions, and differing group norms among each country's soldiery prevented nations from universally adopting this series of tactics. The British dependence on soldier *esprit* and the bayonet most closely resembles the doctrine settled on by French Revolutionary armies.[81] In fact, the combat methods of the British army under Wellington bring to mind the eighteenth-century close-quarter tactics of Jacobite highland regiments, such as those that fought with broadsword and the bayonet at Culloden in 1745, and the infantry of Frederick II during the early stages of the Seven Years War.[82] This method was still in use and reaping benefits for the British as late as the Sikh Wars in the 1840s.[83]

Wellington's method of safeguarding his men behind gentle contours in terrain whenever possible further enhanced the tactical value of the technique. He chose his battlegrounds carefully, picking those that afforded him defensible positions. This often allowed Wellington to place his soldiers on reverse slopes and protect them from incoming fire until he needed to deploy them. He did not invent reverse slope tactics, but he used them to a greater extent than any other commanders before or during the Napoleonic period.

The silent, grim battlefield determination of the British rank and file, born of the relentless physical and psychological pressures that were an inherent part of British military life, has often been misinterpreted as an expression of national characteristics. The words "pluck," "mettle," and "phlegmatic" have been used to describe the British regular's strength under fire. British battlefield success over the French (from Egypt in 1801 through the Peninsular War and finally at Waterloo in 1815) cannot be attributed, as Chandler has so eloquently acknowledged, to the "cool, typically modest, inborn, insular, even racially-blue-blooded British superiority in such matters."[84] Collective portraits misrepresent the underlying mechanism that allows soldiers to function in combat. Such characterizations are applied after the fact; they are adjectival descriptors that have been transformed into causal factors.

It was not genetic or cultural superiority that made the redcoat into a good soldier. And it was not external, coercive discipline that beat him into submission either. The ranker's steadiness was based on an acquired self-confidence and the knowledge that, as part of a squad, he was not alone. Time on campaign and in battle allowed the redcoat to grasp the degree to which his life depended on the actions of others. Circumstances usually led the British regular to lean on his comrades, believe in his officers, and trust the effectiveness of the standard volley-and-charge combat tactic. On campaign the ranker discovered that his mess group, the men with whom he lived and next to whom he stood in combat, played a significant role in determining his survival. When rations were short, the group scrounged, stole, and shared, distributing an equal portion to each member of band. This collaborative foraging and the ritual sharing of provisions, issued and stolen, had a positive consequence: group unity. In a very real sense, the immediacy of the hardship, the demands of combat, and the realization that death was an ever-present part of the equation drove the men together and forced them to function as a collective.

William McNeill has suggested that the most basic military drill, marching together in unison, works to strengthen the psychological bonds between soldiers; he argues that walking in step as part of a group increases a man's confidence and identification with the unit.[85] Thus, while no longer a battlefield necessity, drill remains a small but important component of modern military training. When it is done smartly and correctly, drill creates cohesion, discipline, confidence in leadership, and pride. If something as subtle and as nonthreatening as learning to march together can have a unifying effect on soldiers, then the extended campaign experiences of daily training, shared privation, and combat must have worked as a blast furnace in comparison, forging relationships of unusual strength among the British soldiers of the Peninsular War.

This ongoing mutual support on campaign and the close relationships among the men had a collateral effect: enhanced cohesion during combat.[86] Those veterans who persevered provided the core foundation of each unit; the ties among them created a group ethos based on mutual dependence and trust developed over years of hard campaigning. By adhering to certain standards—such as maintaining his place in the line during combat, firing on command, and advancing ardently with the bayonet when so ordered—the soldier improved the group's chances of survival as well as his own. The conduct of each group member was measured according to these established group norms.[87] Esteem or disapprobation was meted out by the group according to whether or not men conformed to these values.[88] The ranker, once adopted into the group, attempted to behave according to these mores in order to gain the respect of his peers. In this way, the soldier's behavioral patterns were defined by social interaction.[89] General Sir Henry Lawrence, killed at Lucknow in 1857, summed up the effects of group norms on the conduct of men under fire: "Courage goes much by opinion, and many a man behaves as a hero or coward according to how he is expected to behave."[90]

It was group affiliation that made redcoats loath to give into their fears and act in natural and seemingly sensible ways (such as fleeing during an intense French artillery bombardment) that violated group requirements. In most combat circumstances such behavior portrayed the soldier as interested only in his own welfare. From a group-survival perspective, the comrades of a soldier exhibiting this characteristic judged him to be selfish, unreliable, potentially dangerous, and unworthy of further support. For the vast majority of soldiers seeking entry into and acceptance by these small cadres, ego, personal pride, and social pressure became intertwined as each man learned to align his interests with those of the group. The outcome was a type of emotional connection among soldiers that cannot be equaled in civilian life except under exposure to the threat of death.[91]

A life-sized figure of a Worcestershire soldier of the 29th Regiment of Foot in the Peninsular War: tired, hungry, and with aching feet. (Worcester City Art Gallery and Museum)

A watercolor portrait of a soldier of the 40th Regiment of Foot, William Lawrence's unit (*Grenadier—in Marching Order—40th Foot, 1815 Campaign* by J.D. Shakespeare, 1950). (Brown University Digital Library)

Arthur Wellesley, the 1st Duke of Wellington (*Field Marshal. His Grace Duke of Wellington, K.G. & G.C.B.* by Sir W. Beechey, 1817; Henry Meyer, engraver). (Brown University Digital Library)

The 5th Fusiliers in Spain attacking French units on the high ground (*Fifth Fusiliers* by Richard Simkin, 1885). An officer leads, and a sergeant (with his spontoon) helps guide the formation. (Brown University Digital Library)

The 94th Foot defending Matagorda (*The 94th Regiment—Scots Brigade—at the Defense of Matagorda, March 21st 1810* by Richard Simkin, n.d.). (Brown University Digital Library)

The assault on Ciudad Rodrigo (*The Storming of Ciudad Rodrigo, by the Light Division on the Night of the 19th of January 1812* by Edward Orme, 1813). (Brown University Digital Library)

The site of the great breach at Ciudad Rodrigo, with the cathedral tower in the background. (Richard Tennant)

The ditch and ramparts of Ciudad Rodrigo, through and over which the British soldiers were required to attack. (Richard Tennant)

The terrain and walls of Ciudad Rodrigo. Negotiating and successfully assaulting such a bastion came at a heavy price in human lives. (Richard Tennant)

The narrow streets of the inner town of Ciudad Rodrigo. It was in these tight confines that the Spanish townsfolk were confronted by British rankers hell bent on plunder. (Richard Tennant)

A watercolor showing the obstacles to be overcome in a siege assault (British Troops Storming Citadel in Peninsular Campaign by Charles Mitchell, 1810). Taking such positions required a great deal from the British soldiers, even when they somehow survived intact. (Brown University Digital Library)

A close-up of the harrowing, face-to-face combat involved in taking bastions by assault (*British Troops Storming Citadel in Peninsular Campaign* by Charles Mitchell, 1810) (Brown University Digital Library)

The officers and rank and file making their way through the breach at Badajoz in the spring of 1812 (*Badajoz, Taken by Storm on the 6th of April 1812 by the Allied Army under Lord Wellington by Atkinson, from Stationers Almanack, 1813*). (Brown University Digital Library)

The fortress wall of Badajoz. The size of the woman at the base provides scale, illustrating the daunting challenge of taking Badajoz by storm. (Richard Tennant)

A tower of Badajoz, still showing damage caused by the assault. It was a key attack point in the storming of the citadel. (Richard Tennant)

Another perspective revealing the size and scope of the
Badajoz fortifications. (Richard Tennant)

6

BANDED BROTHERS

Combat Motivation and the British Ranker

The series of British army victories in Peninsula battles and at Waterloo is best understood not at the macro level but at the micro level, starting at the smallest primary group: the mess contingent of approximately six men. It is the strength of the bonds between these men, multiplied over companies, battalions, brigades, and finally the army itself, that helped make the difference during battle.[1] The vast majority of the literature analyzing the behavior of soldiers in battle identifies the primary social group, a term coined by sociologist Charles Cooley in the first decade of the twentieth century,[2] as the essential force that determines how they will act under fire.[3] In the seminal work on the subject, founded on post-action responses from over 12,000 combat soldiers who saw action in both the European and Pacific theaters during World War II, Samuel Stouffer et al. confirmed the premise that group ties are the underlying force that allows men to function in combat: "The group in its informal character, with its close interpersonal ties, served two principal functions in combat motivation: it *set and enforced group standards* of behavior, and it *supported and sustained the individual* in stresses he would otherwise not have been able to withstand."[4]

According to Stouffer, the exchange of trust and support was the "one way in which the resources of the individual were maintained at a level at which he remained capable of coping with the stresses of combat."[5] Stouffer also captures the essence of group interaction and why soldiers come to care so deeply about the men of their group:

> The combat situation was one of mutual dependence. A man's life depended literally and immediately upon the actions of others; he in turn was responsible in his own actions for the safety of others. This vital interdependence was closer and more crucial in combat than in the average run of human affairs. Any individual's action which had conceivable bearing on the safety of others in the group became a matter of proper concern for the group as a whole. Mutual dependence, however, was more than a matter of mere survival. Isolated as he was from contact with the rest of the world, the combat man was thrown back on his outfit to meet the various affectional needs for recognition, approval, and in general for appreciation as a significant person.[6]

Edward Shils (in his article explaining the primary group underpinnings of the Stouffer study) describes how the group allows the individual soldier to function day-to-day: "Primary group relations help the individual soldier to bear threatened injuries and even death by increasing his self-esteem and his conception of his own potency. They help particularly to raise his estimate of his capacity to survive deprivations."[7]

At the same time when S.L.A. Marshall was conducting his postaction interviews that would eventually be the source of his groundbreaking but later controversial work *Men against Fire*,[8] Shils and Morris Janowitz were undertaking the field research that would result in their essay "Cohesion and Disintegration in the Wehrmacht in World War II." Very much in agreement with the conceptualization of group processes first put forth by Cooley, Shils and Janowitz believed that the group was "fundamental in forming the social nature and ideals of the individual. The result of intimate association . . . is a certain fusion of individualities into a common whole, so that one's very self, for many purposes at least, is the common life and purpose of the group."[9]

Combat is about many things, but at its essence it involves peril, groups of men, the individual soldier's willingness to face danger and death, and the sometimes slow but inevitable destruction of the primary group. If, as Richard Holmes has observed, "fear is the common bond between fighting men,"[10] then one of the primary purposes of the group is to share risk among all members; the seemingly equal distribution of danger reduces the apprehension of individual soldiers and allows the unit to function with a higher degree of effectiveness than would otherwise be the case.[11]

Marshall concluded that "one of the simplest truths of war . . . the thing that enables an infantry soldier to keep going with his weapon is the presence or presumed presence of a comrade."[12] Exchanging words or gestures with a buddy, watching and copying an action during a firefight, or sometimes just the mere proximity of trusted pals allows soldiers to believe that they have some control over what occurs on the battlefield. The chaos and apparent randomness of combat is thus ostensibly minimized to some extent. This assumption enables soldiers to take actions that otherwise would be beyond the capacities of isolated individuals.[13] Ardant du Picq, one of the first writer-soldiers to produce a general theory of battlefield behavior, simply but powerfully captured the dynamic of how this played out in combat: "Four brave men who do not know each other will not dare attack a lion. Four less brave, but knowing each other well, sure of their reliability and consequently of mutual aid, will attack resolutely. There is the science of the organization of armies in a nutshell."[14]

This perception of control has important biological consequences. As noted, Stephen Rosen provides evidence that the presence of stressors in an environment will cause the body to release adrenaline if the soldier experiencing the stress believes that his or her actions make a difference. This creates feelings of excitement and arousal. Conversely, perceptions of helplessness lead to reduced levels of testosterone and elevated levels of cortisol, which is biochemically related to depression.[15] Thus, it would appear that group connections have the capacity to have a positive affect on the way in which soldiers discern the combat environment and the efficacy of their actions. The impetus derived from proactive behaviors, in turn, causes physiological responses that further drive them to take action. At the same time, the likelihood of helplessness-based lethargy and distress-induced depression is reduced.

Interestingly, Rosen also suggests that decision-making in war is not strictly a cognitive process. He argues that strong emotional experiences, such as those encountered during the stress of combat, may greatly influence the choices that soldiers make in battle. "Memories of perceived external patterns that are formed at times of emotional arousal are preferentially stored and retrieved by the brain. These memories form the basis of emotion-based pattern recognition. They are persistent and slower to change than unemotional lessons learned. . . . When activated, these memories strongly predispose the person having the memories toward certain broad categories of action, such as like/accept/trust or dislike/resist/distrust, but do not select detailed courses of action." In short, the result is faster reaction times, as the brain "does not have to work through each facet of its environment in sequence before becoming aroused, and it did not have to review all of its memories of patterns before reacting, but only those associated with emotional arousal."[16] Rosen's emotion-based "like/accept/trust or dislike/resist/distrust" motivations suggest that soldiers in a combat environment may make choices that give precedent to comrades and the continued existence of the group —memories that carry great affective significance, while at the same time opting against alternative actions that have emotional associations of lesser value.

These biochemical responses help soldiers take actions that preserve each other. The group cohesion that results is a complex phenomenon. Rather than being an absolute, all-or-nothing concept, group unity is a fluid and emotionally sensitive construct predicated on perception. Hierarchical adjustments occur almost continually; individual and collective experiences and observations—and the evolving awareness of individual members regarding threat level, group status, norms, leadership, group effectiveness, and the value of membership—continually cause fluctuations in unity and performance. Thus, as Marshall concluded over forty years ago, "morale is not a steady current . . . but an oscillating wave."[17]

External, environmental stressors (such as the death of comrades or leaders, fatigue, and malnutrition) and interactive frictions also work on the individual soldier and affect his internal struggle with self-concept, his assessment regarding the significance of the group and its various group members, and the value of his efforts on their behalf. The more lethal the environment is perceived to be, the more each member of the group reaches out to give and receive support from comrades. The immediacy of risk and need makes each soldier sensitive to the group's code of conduct and averse to behaving in ways that might jeopardize the group or cost him the support of his mates at the very time when he most desires their assistance.

On the continuum that constitutes battlefield behavior, individual soldiers participate to different degrees. Some actively fire their weapons, others do so halfheartedly, while still others are immobilized with fear. Some soldiers, overwhelmed by events, choose flight.[18] The extent to which an individual soldier is expected to fight is usually determined by leadership effectiveness, training, the soldier's experience, his confidence in himself and fellow soldiers, and, primarily, the standards and unity of his particular small group. The degree to which a man actively meets group norms determines how he will be treated by his comrades. Forsaking comrades usually brings immediate sanctions: exclusion from the group and loss of all respect and cooperation. In his work on group influence on combat behavior, Roger Little learned that men who "bugged out" (using the phrase popularized during the Korean War) were never able to live down the incident and were never again viewed as significant members of the group. Little did observe that such ostracized soldiers still served a group purpose: they were used as examples in teaching new men the consequences of *not* doing their share and endangering the group.[19]

Shils has posited that the soldier's "sensitivity to the opinion of his comrades with its clear implication of the need for comradely approval [works] as an incentive to exertion in battle."[20] In his work analyzing the actions of men in combat, Elmar Dinter has reached the same conclusion: while each man in a small band of soldiers is interested in satisfying his own personal needs, "the strongest emotional force in this socially constituted group is the desire of each of its members for love, friendship, sympathy, recognition, respect, and power."[21] Dinter identified group integration as the determining factor that allows some units to fight better than others.[22] As Stouffer et al. discovered during their surveys of World War II combat veterans, soldiers queried about what kept them going in combat "when the going was tough" responded that prayer and fear of letting the other men down were the dominating motivations.[23] This same concern was expressed by American soldiers fighting in Iraq during 2003.[24] One American enlisted man remembered that "everybody did what they had to do. It was just looking out for one another. We weren't fighting for anyone else but ourselves. We weren't fighting for some higher-up who is somebody; we were fighting for each other."[25] Thus, it is reasonably safe to say that social cohesion and group relationships play an essential role in determining combat effectiveness.

In comparing the British regular with other fighting men of the period, one crucial factor may have tipped the scale of unit cohesion in favor of the redcoat: how much the men needed the group. The ranker certainly valued his place within it. The importance of the primary group to the individual redcoat becomes evident when his experiences as a whole are considered. The British soldier probably joined the army out of economic need; his decision to take the drastic step of enlisting involved little in the way of ideological motivation. The bounty and the promise of employment, regular food, and a living wage were the primary incentives. As for these enticements, the army would disappoint him repeatedly over time. He was forced to plunder food, for even when delivered his rations were nutritionally deficient. When the redcoat was caught pilfering food and drink, he was harshly punished. While on campaign, he received little in the way of sustaining motivations: he garnered no medals or awards recognizing his courage and competence; no efforts were made to address his patriotic ideals or personal concerns. The ranker had limited opportunities for professional advancement and even fewer still for improving his economic status. His medical care was also marginal at best.[26] Moreover, he had no expectations of going home: service was usually for life or for as long as the army needed him. The redcoat's only hope was to survive and qualify for a pension, an aspiration that most soldiers never attained.

Marginalized to an extraordinary extent, the British soldier withstood these conditions because his mess group became a surrogate, albeit demanding, family unit. In the army the British soldier found a permanent home and forged new primary group affiliations; for a man separated, possibly forever, from home and family and sent to suffer hardship and experience battle in foreign lands, these groups were of paramount importance. Continual privation created a cycle of want and requisite aid. As individuals broke down physically and psychologically over time, their messmates were there to provide succor. As

Charles Moskos has noted, it is this process of mutual support and shared experience that ties men together and enables them to face the demands of combat: "In ground warfare an individual's survival is directly related to the support—moral, physical, technical—he can expect from his fellow soldiers. He gets such support largely to the degree that he reciprocates it—to the others in his group in general and to his buddies in particular."[27]

Firsthand accounts provide repeated examples of the extremes to which the British regular, motivated by such close loyalties, went to protect the group and his place in it. The need for the social reinforcements offered by the group and the fear of losing status among his messmates challenged the ranker to weigh his needs against those of his closest companions. Unflinching behavior during combat was required because it helped protect the group and because the behavior was a direct indication of how much the individual valued his comrades. To react otherwise brought forth the possibility of condemnation and rejection by the men that the soldier cared about most.

Once during battle Rifleman Harris came across a former sergeant named Mayberry, who had been stunned by a cannon blast. Mayberry had previously stolen money while working for a commissary officer and had received 700 lashes as punishment in addition to demotion. He was subsequently shunned by his fellow soldiers. At Badajoz he stormed the breach and behaved so bravely that Captain John Hart told him that he had obliterated his disgrace and would be restored to his previous rank. Told to retire to the rear, Mayberry refused, even though he had been wounded numerous times. Harris offered to assist him to the rear, but Mayberry dismissed him, saying, "No going to the rear for me. I'll restore myself to my comrades' opinion, or make a finish of myself altogether."[28]

Harris voiced similar sentiments regarding his own battlefield conduct before the battle of Vimiero in 1808. His comments, though self-reported, seem credible. He stated to a fellow soldier, Rifleman John Lowe:

> If you see any symptoms of my wishing to flinch in this business I hope you will shoot me with your own hand. Lowe as well as myself, survived the battle, and after it was over, whilst we sat down with our comrades and rested . . . Lowe told them of our conversation during the heat of the day . . .

and the Rifles from that time on had a great respect for me. It is, indeed, singular, how a man loses or gains caste with his comrades from his behavior, and how closely he is observed in the field.[29]

Edward Costello of the 95th Rifles provides one further example of how rankers feared losing status. A Sergeant Fairfoot of his company was robbed of £31 of the company's money the first time he was entrusted with funds as pay-sergeant. Being inebriated at the time of the robbery, Fairfoot felt he had let down the men of his battalion. He confided to Costello that he was going to desert out of despair, for he felt he had lost and would never regain the esteem and confidence of his comrades. To cover his losses, Costello gave him £31, his share of the Vitoria spoils and looting of Joseph Bonaparte's baggage. Costello proudly notes that the sergeant later won a commission in the regiment.[30]

Two of the most striking representations of primary group identification and allegiance come from Rifleman Harris. He related two separate incidents wherein soldiers in the process of receiving 200 and 700 lashes (one being Mayberry), respectively, were offered the option of "banishment," which entailed transfer to another regiment. If the men accepted, their remaining strokes would be remitted. Both declined, apparently with little hesitation.[31] That men in such a predicament valued their place among their friends in the battalion more than they wanted to escape the dreadful punishment of the lash reveals much about the depth of feeling connecting British soldiers to their units.

Group bonds unquestionably cemented the relationship between Lawrence and his mates, such as "Pig" Harding and George Bowden. These connections compelled Lawrence to join Harding and Bowden voluntarily in one of the first storming parties at Badajoz in 1812. Even the strongest ties between soldiers, however, do not guarantee their safety. As was expected for men leading the first wave of assaults, Lawrence, Harding, and Bowden did not make it through the breach. Harding received seven wounds, and Bowden had his legs blown off. Both were killed instantly. Lawrence received four wounds during the attack, the most serious being to his knee; his injuries required a six-week hospital stay.

Like many soldiers under similar circumstances, Lawrence missed the men of his unit. Though his wounds were not fully healed, he returned to his company. Still weak, Lawrence fell ill due to fever and was sent back to the hospital, where he would stay for an additional seven months before he was fit to rejoin his battalion.[32]

This compelling need to belong to a self-sustaining collective is the dynamic underlying primary group cohesion. Ironically, emotional ties to comrades and the related self-identity as part of a proxy family often evolve to have such intrinsic value that concern for group members may override the most basic human instinct: survival. In this set of circumstances a soldier who joined the group partly out of fear (with the expectation that this small cluster of men might help him survive) and partly out of hoped-for companionship will willingly sacrifice his life to save group members. Such mutual reliance and devotion become possible because the individual soldier's natural drive for self-preservation is gradually overridden and replaced with social incentives that act to link the soldier's esteem and world view to the continued existence of the group.[33]

Like Lawrence, John Green, a veteran of the 68th Regiment of Foot, experienced the same longing to be with his company mates, even though it almost cost him his life. Green fell sick after the attack on Ciudad Rodrigo in January 1812. Despite severe illness, he tried to keep up with his battalion; when he could not, he fell out and collapsed; he was carted off to the general hospital at Castel Branco. There Green recovered, relapsed, and recovered again. He returned to light duty at the depot, "shoveling the dirty Portuguese streets." Displaying the same stubbornness and need to be with his mates that Lawrence exhibited, Green left the depot and the hospital before he was well in order to return to his unit. On the journey back to the army, he found that he could not keep up with the convalescent party. A fellow soldier and longtime friend, James Mann, dropped out and stayed with Green, who was incapacitated for days on end. Mann eventually escorted him to a hospital in Abrantes, where he was nursed back to health. Green, who credited Mann with saving his life, recovered in time to join the 68th for the siege of Badajoz.[34] There Green again faced the awful necessities of siege assault work, alongside the men he most admired.

Costello wrote about how rivalries between regiments arose during exhausting forced marches, each element of the brigade attempting to maintain the pace without losing men. Costello, who at one point fainted, recalled with admiration the remarks and conduct of a friend named Burke, who refused to allow illness to separate him from his company during the march. Advised by Colonel Thomas Beckwith to fall out, Burke declined to do so. Casting a look of contempt back at the men who littered the sides of the road, he commented, "No sir. I certainly am not well, but I still have the heart of a man, and will keep up with my comrades as long as my legs will carry me."[35] Burke never shirked doing his share and more: he volunteered for the Forlorn Hope at Ciudad Rodrigo, Badajoz, and San Sebastian. Miraculously, he survived all three assaults, no doubt earning the awe and admiration of all who knew him.[36]

Grattan of the 88th articulated these same sentiments under almost exactly the same conditions. During the siege of Badajoz, Grattan was severely wounded: a musket round hit him in the side and carried a part of his tunic through his torso, the remnants protruding from his back. He remembered that his thoughts went first to his closest friends in the company, half of whom had been killed during the attack. Unable to march, Grattan was forced to watch the 88th move on without him. In remembering the incident many years later, Grattan's anguish at being separated from his comrades is palpable in his writings. It is significant that he wrote more about being left behind than he did about his terrible wound.[37]

Major-General George Bell provides a comparable tale of a soldier of the 43rd who was shot through the thigh at Salamanca. The man refused to leave the field and struggled on with his mates, bleeding heavily from the wound and losing his shoes in the process.[38] Costello well understood such devotion to the men with whom he served. When asked about his family, he replied, "I have no such ties, save my comrades."[39]

William Wheeler of the 51st Regiment of Foot behaved in the same fashion upon suffering the concussive effects of a cannon shot that nearly decapitated him during the siege of Badajoz. He succinctly sums up why absenting himself from the battlefield was not an option: "One of the round shot must have passed pretty near my cranium, I thought I was wounded, my head ached violently. I felt the pain a long time and it was with difficulty I could perform my duty.

Had I been working in a place where there was no danger I certainly should have given up, but here I was ashamed to complain, lest any of my comrades laugh at me."[40]

Another veteran, John Douglas of the Royal Scots, was wounded in the foot near Calirico. The regimental surgeon suggested that Douglas stay and assist with the other patients, telling him that he would draw no rations if he did not. Like Lawrence, Green, Burke, and the soldier of the 43rd described by Bell, Douglas was undeterred. He told the surgeon: "I would beg my way to the Regiment rather than be left behind." A captain who overheard the conversation gave Douglas some money to assist him on the road. "[Nearly] penniless, without a biscuit in my old haversack," Douglas remembered, "in a country partly desecrated . . . in the depth of winter I plodded my way and joined the regiment at a village called Burtegrande."[41]

Joseph Donaldson, a veteran in the 94th Regiment of Foot, offered a woeful story of group loyalty on campaign by a soldier who was forced to abandon his wife on a retreat from Madrid in November 1813. She was unable to go on and begged him to stay with her. Anguished over her possible fate of being left to the mercy of the French or dying of exposure, the soldier faced a daunting choice: allegiance to his comrades and abandoning his wife or falling out and safeguarding her. Fearing being labeled a shirker or deserter by his mates, the ranker left his wife by the side of the road and trudged on with his company.[42]

Men not in extremis were equally attached to their units. Wheeler wrote of the great reluctance with which he accepted a transfer to another company. Even though the move to a position as an officer's batman ensured an easier life, Wheeler quickly came to miss his comrades and longed to return to them. "I had frequently applied to join my company," he recalled, "but was always refused." Wheeler then schemed and misbehaved his way back to his company, almost receiving 300 lashes in the process. He later offered his perspective on the possibility of being invalided home to Britain, reflecting that as much as he desired to see home he would "much rather rejoin my regiment again and take my chance with it. . . . Then, when this protracted war is over . . . I should have the proud satisfaction of landing on my native shores with many a brave and gallant comrade, with whom I braved the dangers of many a hard fought battle."[43]

Lawrence experienced the same emotional need to be with the men of his unit. After recovering from the injuries received during the storming of Badajoz, he was notified that he had been promoted to corporal and transferred to another company. Although he relished the slight increase in pay, Lawrence soon became miserable. He wrote mournfully: "I was far from feeling at home in this company, as I lost all my old companions; and not only that, but I then stood six feet one inch high, whilst not one man in that company stood more than five feet seven inches. I made my complaint to the captain who promised that as soon as there was a vacancy, I should go back to my old company, and that cheered me up a little, but made me look with intense anxiety for the change back again." Although Lawrence was a hardened veteran by 1812, his writings express a high degree of emotion; such sentiments would be surprising had they not been directed at his old comrades. After three months the company commander found an opportunity to place him back with his old company, to Lawrence's "great satisfaction."[44]

Historian William Manchester expressed the personal reasons behind such extraordinary efforts and sentiments. Writing about his experiences as a marine in the Pacific in World War II, he captured the essence of the relationship among men who live through combat together:

> You're dealing with excesses of love and hate, and among men who fight together there is an intense love. You are closer to those men than to anyone except your immediate family when you were young. . . . I was not a brave young man [but after I was wounded] I went back because I learned that my regiment was going to . . . land behind the Japanese lines, and I felt that if I were there I might save men who had saved my life many times, and the thought of not being there was just intolerable. I missed them, I yearned for them—it was, as I say, a variety of love, and I was joyful to be reunited with them.[45]

Like most soldiers who experience battle, the British regular felt the same way about his comrades. Grattan, who amazingly recovered from the musket wound that carried part of his coat through his body, eventually managed to rejoin his battalion. He learned in 1814 that he was being shipped home to join the second battalion. Thinking back about how he felt when he realized that army life as he knew it was at an end, Grattan remembered with evident admiration how the men of the 88th had persevered; he had no trouble pinpointing the connection between comrades as the mechanism that made it all worthwhile: "The 'boys of Connaught' were not much put out of their way by the want of shoes, a good coat on their back, or a full allowance of rations: they took all these wants *aisy!* [easy]. . . . Years of hard fighting, fatigues and privations that we now wonder at, had, nevertheless, a charm that, in one way or another, bound us together. . . . I am of the opinion that our days in the Peninsula were the happiest of our lives."[46]

These bonds between a soldier and the men he respected most were enduring, as long as group standards were met. Norms that dictated behavior when lives were at stake (such as when soldiers were without provisions for days on end and especially when they went into battle) were sacrosanct. These norms carried the most weight and the severest consequences for failure. Grievous missteps under fire threatened the safety of the group and often brought instant and permanent loss of status. Rifleman Harris provides us with a prime example. He once "encouraged" a soldier in the front rank who had turned and tried to flee past Harris by telling him that "if he did not keep his ground, I would shoot him dead on the spot; so that he found it would be quite as dangerous for him to return as to go on."[47] Harris stated that this was the only instance he could remember of someone within his battalion attempting to run away under such circumstances. Because of his failure to support his comrades, the man was viewed with such derision and contempt that the battalion commander eventually involuntarily transferred him from the 95th to another regiment.

Such a removal from a home unit was perhaps the most feared punishment, for the regiment and the small mess group were home; the behavior of British soldiers shows that they feared ostracism nearly as much as they did death. Bell recalled the conduct of Kit Wallace, a private in the 34th Foot. Wallace, a simple fellow, had become an outcast because he had gained a reputation as a malingerer who failed to stand his ground in battle. In a skirmish with the French, Wallace rushed to the front of the attack and shot off all 60 of his rounds. He then turned to the men of his company and cried out, "Now am I a coward?"[48]

Rifleman Costello remembered the fate of another man named "Long Tom," who violated group mores by leaving his comrades during a skirmish at Redinha in 1811, supposedly to help the wounded. When the soldiers broke up into their mess groups that evening, Tom was refused entry into any of the clusters; his efforts to avoid combat caused him to be "marked with indignation by the brave men." Costello went on to comment that "no good soldier would venture, under so frivolous a pretense, so to expose himself to the indignation of his comrades." Tom, hungry and desperate, worked his way through the picket lines and shot a French soldier, whom he attempted to carry back to the British camp in order to see what food the man possessed in his knapsack.[49] His efforts were probably also intended to show the men of his regiment that he was not wanting in courage.

Anton corroborates Costello's warning about engaging in behaviors (such as lagging behind or dropping out during combat) that could cause a group member to lose face among his comrades. He describes the consequences of violating group norms:

> A man may drop behind in the field, but this is a dreadful risk to his reputation, and even attended with immediate personal danger, while within the range of shot and shells: and woe to the man that does it, whether through fatigue, sudden sickness, or fear; let him seek death and welcome it from the hand of a foe, rather than give room for any surmise respecting his courage; for when others are boasting of what they have seen, suffered, or performed, he must remain in silent mortification. If he chances to speak, some boaster cuts him short; and even when he is not alluded to, he becomes so sensitively alive to those merited or unmerited insults that he considers every word, sign, or gesture, pointed at him, and he is miserable among his comrades.[50]

Lawrence offers an example of what happens to men who fail to live up to group expectations. He writes about the sudden appearance in camp of stragglers, including seven sergeants, who had rejoined the company upon hearing that Napoleon had surrendered in 1814. Figuring that the danger of battle was at an end, the men hoped to be accepted back into their previous affiliations. They were rejected to a man. The soldiers turned their backs completely on these men who had shirked their duty, refusing even to acknowledge their existence. Forlorn and rejected, the soldiers had no one for company but each other. The sergeants were immediately transferred and told by the colonel that the regiment "would not be disgraced by them any longer than he could help."[51] When the battalion was refitting in Ireland shortly thereafter, the remaining stragglers were all sent to the second battalion.

Lawrence also provides details regarding a telling incident that illustrates how a soldier's ties to his group can be severed irrevocably by violating group standards during combat. His recollection also demonstrates the difficulty of surviving in the field without the help of comrades. During the initial stages of the battle of Waterloo, on 18 June 1815, a new recruit asked to leave the ranks because he was sick, the illness brought on by a just-discovered fear of French artillery fire. Lawrence chided him, but the soldier fell to the ground and refused to move. Angered, Lawrence considered shooting him on the spot. He did not do so but let the man know that he would "not forget him for this affair of cowardice." The man disappeared that day, only to return six months later. While Lawrence does not say what type of reception the man received from his fellow soldiers, it can easily be imagined. The man's troubles were only beginning, however, as Lawrence reported him to the company commander. The deserter was found guilty of absenting himself from the battle without leave and received 300 lashes for his actions. Lawrence felt the sentence was well deserved. As always, he provides a pragmatic assessment: "This may seem to some a hard case, three hundred lashes for absenting himself, but it must be remembered that had there been many like this man, for I cannot call him a soldier, that day would decidedly have ended in favor of the French."[52]

After recovering from the flogging, the man was spurned by all his comrades, who "would scarcely speak to him at all."[53] The man's wages were stopped to pay for lost equipment, and he found himself in dire straits without the help of his comrades. As Bell observed, men who lost the respect of their mates were also likely to suffer from want of food. When meat was served out to each company, the men subdivided it. Those who were out of favor received the stringier pieces, if they were given anything at all.[54]

Having no one to aid him, Lawrence's recalcitrant private deserted again, slipping off to Paris, where he sold his kit for food and shelter. He was discovered, apprehended, and flogged again, receiving another 300 strokes. Lawrence notes that "it may be . . . taken for granted that the drummers did not fail in their duty [laying on the strokes] towards such a man as this, for there is no one they feel more strongly against than a coward." Within a short time he was lashed again and drummed out of the service. Summing up the attitudes of the men of the company, Lawrence adds: "And I never saw him again, which I was not sorry for."[55]

Costello characterized the men of his unit as being composed of three types: those who were "zealous and brave to absolute devotion"; men who did their duty, like Long Tom, when under the watchful eye of a superior or a comrade; and soldiers who "were seldom seen until after a battle had been fought." He labeled men in the last category "skulkers and poltroons" and was pleased that the number of them in his regiment was very small.[56]

British regulars, like most soldiers who have seen combat and suffered as a result, took pride in their minor wounds. Anton wrote about rankers who boasted of their battlefield injuries because they considered them confirming evidence that they had done their duty in battle (and had followed the behavioral expectations of the group). He also noted, though, that it was not deemed necessary to attempt "feats of extraordinary daring . . . [as] individual daring is lost in orderly movements."[57] Such sentiments were also expressed by U.S. infantrymen in Korea. Men who aspired to be heroes were disdained. They were viewed as being interested in personal glory rather than the survival of the group and thus were considered dangerous.[58]

Replacement soldiers only added to the redcoat's concerns and further complicated group interaction. There is a stark contrast between the connections of men who have shared combat and campaign experiences for months or years and the relationship between a veteran and a replacement. The lack of trust in the latter case is natural and often acts to separate a man from the group. While this may slightly diminish the fighting potential of a unit, veterans of combat are unlikely to put their lives in the hands of men who, for them, are unproven commodities. As Peter Kindsvatter explains in his book on the experiences of the twentieth-century American soldier, "Veterans were slow to accept replacements, and even pitied or despised them for their lack of combat prowess."[59] Men kept their distance from new soldiers until it could be determined whether they were "shooters or shakers."[60]

Private Wheeler fully grasped the practicalities of such an assessment. Probably understanding that the new men recently added to his unit were unproven and, with no ties to the group, were apt to be flight risks during combat, Wheeler made a sensible decision. When the replacements were distributed throughout his regiment, he ensured his safety by making it a point to trade places in the line, in order to be adjacent to "a man who had stood next to me in many fights."[61]

This lack of faith in new men was based partly on emotional resentment, as the replacements were taking the places of killed or wounded soldiers who were trusted members of the group. This reaction to new soldiers also had a practical side. The actions of each soldier in battle affected the fate of the group; thus, men who had not established their bona fides represented a real risk to members of the established squad.[62] Given time and the right circumstances, replacements were assimilated into the group; cohesion, meanwhile, remained in a greater state of flux than usual when new soldiers were introduced into units.

One key component affecting group cohesion merits mentioning, in part because it is essential to combat effectiveness and in part because it can potentially destroy unity between army elements and between subgroups and the army itself. If small group norms are not aligned with army standards and expectations, group cohesion may foster behavior that defies the wishes of leadership and possibly endangers the mission as well as other units.[63] An order or a mission that seems unreasonable or too dangerous may unite a cadre of soldiers against participation or cause them to use force preemptively and to a greater degree than the army command requires.[64] When group norms, particularly those related to survival, come into conflict with military requirements imposed by higher echelons, potential mutiny and army disintegration become a real possibility.

When on campaign in Spain and Portugal, the ranker and his comrades often found themselves at odds with British military authority, mostly over the quantity and frequency of rations. Many soldiers, driven by hunger, regularly defied army regulations and Wellington's orders against plundering because the army's inability to feed the men regularly endangered the individual and the group. This remained a constant problem for British army authorities during the Peninsular War.

Sometimes redcoats became desperate and deserted, often in large numbers, feeling that the army had broken its contract with them.

Using annual percentages, desertion constituted approximately 37 percent of all tried offenses from 1800 to 1815.[65] The degree of misery must have been overwhelming for so many men to abandon their mates and the groups that normally sustained them. The British army's reliance on external coercive discipline, which ran counter to the normative influence at work within the soldiers' primary groups, may also have played a role in convincing men to abandon their units.[66]

In combat, though, the military leadership's demand for full and aggressive participation in battle aligned perfectly with the needs of the individual soldier and his goal to preserve his life and the lives of group members. The redcoat willingly learned to hold fire, even when his instincts screamed for him to squeeze the trigger, and to move with alacrity toward French columns, bayonet leveled, because he understood that such a maneuver sequence usually led to victory and an improved chance that he and his mates might escape death.

At the point of the bayonet, the slightest edge in cohesion and intent made a difference in combat. As opposing formations came together, and the likelihood of lethality increased, one side or another gave way as the instinct for self-preservation increased and eventually overrode group loyalty. The strong bonds among redcoats helped the British infantry to weather the stress of battle just fractionally better than did the French and hence win the field.

Combat effectiveness, of course, is not based solely on group cohesion.[67] Leadership and discipline all played a crucial role in guiding the efforts of the British regulars during battle, for soldiers under stress revert to the nearly automatic actions learned through repetitive training.[68] Experience, fatigue, logistics, personnel losses, and the effects of extended time in combat also affected how the redcoat behaved when bullets flew.[69] Any of these variables, alone or in combination, might provide an advantage in battle or lower the general effectiveness of a unit on any given day. Yet all these factors worked on the individual ranker as a member of a soldier cadre, making group dynamics the fundamental influence on his behavior in battle.[70]

Unlike Napoleon's army, which attempted to augment this interactive process with rhetoric, songs, oaths, and letters, the British army was predominately coercive; its nature precluded such appeals to the soldiery. It was left to the interaction of group members, isolated from civilian society and outside influences, to reinforce standards of behavior that promoted combat aggressiveness.[71]

Although Wellington may not have understood the working mechanism of group cohesion, he recognized its product: an effective army that knew its worth and proved it repeatedly in battle. Wellington disparaged the men's reputations, but he never doubted the courage of the soldiers under his command or their conduct under fire. Even when veteran battalions suffered significant attrition over the course of the Peninsula campaign, he attempted to keep them intact. In a letter from Cadiz on 26 December 1812, Wellington requested permission from the Duke of York, commander-in-chief of the army, to do so. "I should prefer," he explained, "to keep as many of the old regiments as I can with the army."[72]

Wellington may have unintentionally enhanced the ties among his soldiers in March 1813 when tents were first issued.[73] The tents were large: three could house a company of 100 men. Their size required that they be transported on mules, which previously had carried the soldiers' cooking kettles. The kettles, which were substantial enough to serve ten soldiers, were too large for an individual soldier to port. This threatened to limit march-rates, so Wellington had lighter tin kettles made.[74] The new version served six men,[75] which, by coincidence, is the approximate size of the smallest functional combat unit. From the *contubernium* of the Roman legion to the fire-teams of twentieth- and twenty-first-century armies,[76] the smallest functional battle group appears to be about this size.[77] Not all the men appreciated the change to the smaller kettle: it was but one more item the men had to carry, the load being shared every six days.[78] But Wellington never asked their opinion, so tote it they did. The serendipitous benefits of having soldiers daily share their meals with the same group of men, undoubtedly the same comrades who stood in line together during battle, may have strengthened the bonds among British regulars.[79]

F.M. Richardson, writing about the spirit of soldiers in battle, contends that loyalty to comrades is the "cardinal military virtue."[80] The redcoat, cast off by society and with little future outside the boundaries of the army, came to depend heavily upon such allegiance. If the more soldiers share privation and confide in each other, the more likely they are to depend on one another, as Roger Little asserts,[81] then the redcoat almost certainly clung to the group and its standards of behavior with both urgency and deep-seated need. He expected no medals, promotions, or rewards for his combat behavior.

Stated simply, the British soldier fought to live one more day among the adopted members of his military family.

The ranker believed in his officers, his training, and the British volley-and-charge tactical specialty almost as much as he trusted the men with whom he fought. This faith gave the redcoat a perceptible advantage on the battlefield; as Marshall has observed, "Fear is contagious but courage is not less so."[82] Wellington harnessed this unity and competence and turned common men bound together by hardship into some of the most proficient combat soldiers of the Napoleonic era.[83] As Major-General Bell remembered: "We had the bravest, the best . . . army in the world; fighting was their daily bread—it gave them an appetite. No other soldier on earth had a chance against them on fair and open ground; the Duke knew it."[84]

7

INTO HELL BEFORE
DAYLIGHT

Peninsular War Sieges

Often outnumbered and strategically pressed during the Peninsula campaign, the British army under Wellington was faced with significant challenges posed by French fortresses that threatened British maneuver as well as supply and communication lines. With little time to reduce the bastions using regular siege techniques, Wellington chose instead to assault the French strongholds directly, spending his men's lives to achieve his ends, which required a rapid occupation of each fortress. A collateral need was the purchasing of time for strategic movement; Wellington hoped that even more time could be bought if the defenders of other citadels knew of the ferocious consequences of defending against British attacks.

The behavior of the British soldier after the successful siege assaults of 1812 and 1813 merits special attention, because much of the collective memory of the redcoat as a drunken thug bent on rape and violence originates from this period. Siege assaults were dreadful, deadly nighttime affairs in which soldiers attacked breaches in bastion walls, using zeal and numbers to overpower the defenders. Such an attack required a number of preparatory efforts. The soldier's first task was to dig a series of zigzagging trenches, allowing the placement of siege artillery close enough to be effective in bringing down a portion of the bastion's wall. For half-starved men, the manual labor involved must have been extraordinarily difficult.[1]

This trench work was open, dangerous duty. The garrison often fired at the work teams, as Lawrence quickly discovered. He caught a spent six-pound roundshot in the chest during the preparatory work at Ciudad Rodrigo. He writes almost cheerfully about the episode, which bruised his chest and made him ill for a week, but it must have terrified him at the time. Lawrence also relates a story about a French shell falling among the soldiers laboring in the trenches just before the attack on Badajoz. The round killed or wounded about 30 men, severing a number of limbs in the process. He commented that "I never saw a worst sight of its kind." Lawrence's mate, Pig Harding, pointed to the gruesome pile of human debris and jokingly said, "Lawrence, if any one is in want of an arm or a leg he can have a good choice there."[2] Such were the ghastly reminders of the butcher's bill regarding siege preparation. This cost, however, paled in comparison to the actual expenditure of human life during assaults.

Once the artillery was in place, a bombardment began. The effectiveness of the artillery salvos was dependent on time, the caliber and numbers of available cannons, ammunition supplies, weather, and the degree to which the enemy put up an active defense. This could include lively small arms and counterbattery fire against the besieging artillery, defensive sorties, and relieving forces. Adding to Wellington's challenges was having a proper siege train in hand when he needed it. He lacked this fundamental resource at the first siege of Badajoz in 1811 and at Burgos in 1812, being short of large-caliber artillery.[3] To compound the difficulties, Wellington was also without a fully functional corps of engineers. This meant that it often took longer to create a breach than he preferred. In addition, when it was made, the opening was often smaller than desired by Wellington and the soldiers leading the assault. It may have been the quality of the breaches that caused the governors in charge of Christoval, Ciudad Rodrigo, Badajoz, Burgos, and San Sebastian to hesitate when making their decisions regarding surrender after the initial breaches were made. Napoleon's threat to execute any governor who surrendered a citadel before withstanding at least one assault, however, probably played a greater role in the defender's decision-making process.[4]

Knowing the price for such assaults, attackers and defenders were supposed to adhere to an unwritten rule of siege warfare that had existed since the Middle Ages. When a practical breach was made, it became incumbent upon the defenders to make a crucial choice: surrender and live or defend the breach and suffer the uncontrolled wrath of the attackers should the assaulting force be victorious. If they chose to surrender, the citadel's defenders and townspeople would usually be entitled to military honors, meaning that they would be allowed to leave unmolested, carrying both valuables and weapons. If, however, they decided to defend the bastion despite the breach, all standard rules of conduct would be suspended, with no mercy being shown to the defenders or the civilians inside the fortress.

It is against the backdrop of this understood agreement between besieger and besieged that the conduct of the British infantry during and after sieges must be considered, as the French steadfastly refused to surrender at any point during the Peninsular War sieges of 1811–13. In every case, the slaughter of the assault cost the British attackers dearly; and in the three instances in which the assaults succeeded, the British troops truly "let slip the dogs of war" once inside the walls, unleashing their anger and satisfying their long-neglected physical needs in every manner imaginable.

When the French defenders refused to yield after the British succeeded in destroying a wall section, Wellington launched the infantry to take the fortress by storm. Just to reach the openings in the bastion walls was a difficult task, as the barriers of glacis and ditch had to be negotiated. The redcoats first had to climb the slanting glacis and then jump into the ditch that surrounded the fortress. The men in front lugged ladders that would be lowered into the ditch. When sufficient ladders were unavailable, the men threw down bundles of grass or straw to form a cushion of sorts that allowed them to hazard the drop, which could be ten feet or more. After crossing the trench, the attacking soldiers faced the daunting task of fighting up and through the breached wall. Heavily defended by artillery and infantry, the opening in the fortress wall was most likely well above ground level; the rubble from the collapsed section formed a perilous staircase up which the British soldiers were expected to climb while enduring a withering fire from the French defenders.

Braving the breach meant running a gauntlet of canister and musket fire, hidden explosives, and hurled objects, all the while trying to climb the broken stones of the destroyed wall. For such assaults the British made use of the Forlorn Hope, a designated company of volunteers led by a single officer, whose task was to be first into and, with luck, through the breach. Promotion and uniform patches (to mark the courage of the wearer forever) were offered for those brave or foolish enough to volunteer as a member of the company.[5] Such limited recognition did not satisfy every soldier, though. Edward Costello of the 95th notes that the only real distinction designating a Forlorn Hope survivor was his "empty sleeves or wooden stump."[6]

Despite the terrible casualties among storming parties, most soldiers seemed to feel a great degree of pride when their battalions were designated to follow the Forlorn Hope into the breach. Surtees describes the way soldiers viewed being in the Forlorn Hope or the battalions that came in its wake: "Among the men also the same noble enthusiasm prevailed, for he who was selected for this dangerous service . . . was envied by his comrades. . . . In fact, it required a character for good conduct to entitle a man to this honorable employment."[7]

Enlisted man Charles O'Neil of the 28th Foot offers a similar viewpoint. While acknowledging the perils of such an assault, he uses the phrase "thrilled at the honor" to describe the distinction of having his unit designated for the assault on Badajoz. These words were written well after the attack, of course, which O'Neil somehow survived unscathed. At the time of the storming, he was no doubt also deeply afraid, far more than his account relates.[8]

The redcoats were well aware of the dangers of storming citadels. That they did so in five different sieges says much about the courage of the men and the strength of the bonds that kept them at their comrades' sides even when death seemed inevitable. One factor making such a risky endeavor acceptable to soldiers may have been the realization that the first units through the breach would have the best choice of plunder. Thus, pride, mixed with the anticipation of loot, may have motivated the British regular to face the terrors of the breach. Lawrence certainly saw the practical side to this dangerous endeavor, having been quartered at Badajoz after the battle of Talavera in 1809. Knowing the most valuable shops and understanding that "if we succeeded in taking the place, there was to be three hours' plunder," he plotted with his mates, George Bowden and Pig Harding, how to make the most of the opportunity.[9] Although Lawrence does not write about it directly, he would probably not have allowed Bowden and Harding to risk the assault without him by their sides.

Once the attacking forces traversed the ditch, the soldiers were funneled to the opening in the fortress wall; this meant that they were crowded together into a mass, making them easy targets for the intense artillery and musket fire by the defenders. Repeated forays by fresh units were required to take a breach; at Badajoz it took nearly 40 attacks to break through into the town. Three accounts suffice to describe the journey that historian Ian Fletcher has aptly called "in hell before daylight."[10] John Cooper of the 7th Regiment of Fusiliers provides a frightening summary of an aborted attack on the breached portion of Badajoz:

> When our men had approached within 300 yards of the ditch, up went a fireball. This showed the crowded state of the ramparts, and the bright arms of our approaching columns. Those men who carried grass bags to fill up the ditch, and ladders for escalading the walls, were now hurried forward. Instantly the whole rampart was in a blaze, mortars, cannon, and muskets, roared and rattled unceasingly. Mines ever and anon blew up with horrid noise. To add to this horrible din, there were the sounds of bugles, the rattling of drums, and the shouting of combatants. Through a tremendous fire our men rushed to the top of the glacis, down the ladders, and up the breach. But entrance was impossible, for across the horrid gap the enemy had placed, in spite of our fire, a strong beam full of sword blades, etc., forming a cheveaux-de-frise, behind which, entrenched, stood many ranks of soldiers, whose fire swept the breach from end to end. Besides, the top of the parapet was covered with shells, stones, sand bags, and logs of wood, etc., ready to be thrown into the ditch. As the breaches could not be forced, and as our men kept pouring down the ladders, the whole ditch was soon filled with a dense mass which could neither advance nor retreat. Upon these the enemy threw down missiles from the parapet, with a continuous fire of musketry and round shot. My comrade was killed descending a ladder. Some men went further to the right, and jumped that part of the ditch that was filled with water, and were drowned.[11]

Harry Smith, a young officer who survived the siege unscathed, offers a similar perspective on the Badajoz assault:

We flew down the ladders and rushed at the breach, but we were broken and carried no weight with us, although every soldier was a hero. The breach was covered by a breastwork from behind and ably defended on the top by chevaux-de-frise of sword blades, sharp as razors, chained to the ground; while the ascent to the top of the breach was covered with planks with sharp nails in them. However, devil a one did I feel at this moment. One of the officers of the Forlorn Hope, Lieutenant Taggert, of the 43rd, was hanging on my arm—a mode we adopted to help each other up; for the ascent was most difficult and steep. A Rifleman stood among the sword blades at the top of one of the chevaux-de-frise. We made a glorious rush to follow, but, alas! in vain. He was knocked over. . . . I had been some seconds at the revetment of the bastion near the breach, and my red coat pockets were literally filled with chips of stones splintered by musket balls. Those not knocked down were driven back by this hail of mortality to the ladders.[12]

Finally, Lawrence recounts his experience as a member of the assault troops at Badajoz. Like many other British soldiers, he was a skilled plunderer who also willingly shouldered his share of hazardous duty. His journey across the glacis, down into the ditch, and into the breach should have ended his life, as it did for so many of the men around him, including Harding and Bowden:

I was one of the ladder party. . . . On our arriving at the breach . . . a shower of shot, canister and grape, together with fireballs, was hurled . . . amongst us. Poor Pig [Harding] received his death wound immediately, and my other accomplice, Bowden, became missing, while I myself received two small shots in my left knee, and a musket shot in my side, which would have been mortal had it not been for my canteen. . . . Still, I stuck to my ladder and got into the entrenchment. Numbers had by this time fallen, but . . . we hastened to the breach; but there, to our great . . . discouragement, we found a *chevaux de frise* had been fixed. . . . Vain attempts were made to remove this fearful obstacle, during which my left hand was dreadfully cut by one of the blades . . . but finding no success in that quarter, we were forced to retire for a time. . . . My wounds were still bleeding, and I began to feel very weak. My comrades persuaded me to go to the rear, but this proved a task of great difficulty, for on arriving at the ladders, I found them filled with the dead and wounded, hanging . . . just as they had fallen . . . so I crawled on my hands and knees till I got out of the reach of the enemy's musketry.[13]

An accounting of Wellington's siege assault casualties illustrates the human cost of taking fortresses by storm. The British lost 400 officers and men during the two unsuccessful assaults at Christoval (the first of Wellington's four sieges in 1812), with the siege evolving into just a cordon. Wellington and the British army next besieged Ciudad Rodrigo, with over 700 men falling during the assault; this offered only a hint of what was to follow. Badajoz, the most formidable of the French bastions that Wellington felt forced to take by direct assault, claimed the lives of an additional 3,500 men, with 700 men slain just in the ditches and the breach.[14] In his next siege endeavor at Burgos (the fourth of his targeted forts), Wellington sent five assaults forward; each failed as badly as its predecessor, forcing him to raise the siege after the loss of 2,000 men. The first storming of San Sebastian in July 1813 also failed, resulting in almost 600 casualties. The last of Wellington's Peninsula sieges succeeded after another series of assaults and, for the British, the fortuitous accidental explosion of a French magazine, but not before 2,500 fell during the final attack.[15]

Soldiers who succeeded in taking a breach after repeated assaults were naturally bent on taking revenge for their dead comrades. Surtees writes of such retribution, commenting: "All [the men] thought of what they owed their wounded comrades, and of the probability that ere long a similar fate might be their own." He adds that this motive was soon "swallowed up in their abominable rage for drink and plunder."[16] O'Neil of the 28th Foot wrote about his experience at Badajoz, using the words "revenge for those who had fallen" as his opening statement. His summation of the aftermath from the participant's perspective is representative of many such accounts. Calling the rampages a horror and a "feature of war more repulsive than [any] other," O'Neil explains the cause: "Men's passion, wound up almost to a frenzy by the exciting and maddening scenes through which they had passed, will have a vent. . . . All the dreadful passions of human nature were excited."[17]

Costello voices similar sentiments regarding the human carnage. His description of the British dead piled in the breach at Ciudad Rodrigo captures the feeling of loss and hints at barely restrained anger: "I now proceeded to the breach, which had been carried by the 3rd Division, where the mine had been sprung. The sight exhibited was heart-rendering in the extreme. The dead lay in heaps, numbers of them half-stripped, and displaying the most ghastly wounds. Here and there, half-buried under the blackened fragments of the wall, or reeking on the surface of the ruin, lay those who had been blown up in the explosion, their remains dreadfully mangled and discoloured, and strewed about amongst dissevered arms and legs."[18]

Under such circumstances, the release of strain that accompanies close brushes with death, the desire to avenge lost compatriots, and the availability of the spoils of war combined to supersede normal group mores. For a brief time, much of the moral restraint that guided the soldiers' conduct was set aside, allowing the men to sate their anger and physical needs for food, drink, and sometimes women. Alcohol, once found, added fuel to the men's licentiousness; it accelerated the rate at which the soldiers abandoned the social constraints that ordinarily prevented them from committing acts like rape or violent robbery.

Captain John Harley was once confronted by a Spanish woman after the storming of San Sebastian. She asked him to explain the actions of his men; his reply conveys the difficulty of pinpointing the exact causes, but he manages to identify the primary underlying motivation: "[A lady commented:] 'You have come from England to assist them [the Spanish]; you take a Spanish town from the French, a brave and meritorious act; but why have you plundered it?' I must confess I could make her no reply, but that it was impossible to restrain an enraged army, who had lost so many men."[19]

Costello again offers his insight, commenting on how saddened and disturbed he still felt years after the rampages. His explanation for the men's behavior substantiates Harley's statement. His words are perhaps the best summary of the forces that drove many British regulars to act as they normally would not: "It is to be considered that the men who besiege a town in the face of such dangers generally become desperate from their own privations and sufferings; and when once they get a foothold within its walls—flushed by victory, hurried on by the desire for alcohol, and maddened by drink, they stop at nothing: they are literally mad, and hardly conscious of what they do in such a state of excitement. I do not state this in justification; I only remark what I have observed human nature to be on these occasions."[20]

Historian Roger Buckley voices his agreement, concluding that the same upsurge of emotions that allowed the British soldiers to surmount the citadel walls also pushed the men to seek vengeance and release once inside the fortresses. As in his work on British soldiers in the West Indies, he touches on the human experience as his key to deciphering the motivations and limitations of the British ranker: "This undeserved criticism [of the men's behavior after Badajoz] suggests that human beings have an inexhaustible capacity for self-restraint in the face of horror. It also infers that the extraordinary human emotions and powers which miraculously drove British troops to mount no less than forty assaults into the breach were suddenly to be turned off like an electric switch."[21]

The psychological shock experienced by soldiers who survived the uncertainty, immediacy, lethality, and revulsion of hand-to-hand combat was significant. The rankers often felt deep regret for the violent acts that they had been forced to commit during the attack. Lawrence describes an experience just prior to the assault on Badajoz that helps illustrate the impact of such face-to-face life and death decisions. He recalls vividly that during the Badajoz trench work soldiers of the French garrison sortied out to assail the redcoats who were preparing British positions. Lawrence quickly found himself exchanging bayonet thrusts with a large French soldier. When the man stumbled, Lawrence stuck his bayonet through him, pinning him to the ground; the Frenchman soon expired.[22] Lawrence writes that it troubled him that he had not taken the Frenchman captive, but circumstances did not allow it. The situation bothered Lawrence enough to cause him to reflect on and record the event many years after it occurred, which speaks against the portrayal of British regulars as men who killed without compunction or reason. And, it must be remembered, this incident was a more-or-less spontaneous response to a surprise encounter. Thus, Lawrence's actions were not driven by rage as they might have been had he seen his comrades struck down in great number, as would soon be the case during the storming of the breach. Nevertheless, the event became one of the war memories that he carried with him forever.[23]

The men's wrath toward fortress inhabitants could be tempered, as it was at Ciudad Rodrigo, where the Spanish had defended themselves gallantly against the French. The unleashed anger could also be heightened by knowledge that the locals actively supported the French in their siege defense. This was the case at Badajoz and San Sebastian.[24] Wellington shared this causal factor with his brother. In a letter referring to San Sebastian and its aftermath, he writes that "in the course of the inquiry upon this subject, a fact has come out, which I acknowledge that I had not heard before, and as little suspected . . . viz. that the inhabitants . . . cooperated with the enemy in the defense of the town, and actually fired upon the allies."[25] The outcome was a nightmare of violence for the fortress defenders and inhabitants.

John Aitchison of the Scots Guards puts the violence in perspective, explaining how the British viewed the rules of war regarding siege assaults:

> The behavior of the British troops must be judged against contemporary customs of war. Because of the great casualties which an assailant must expect if forced to carry a place by assault, it had become practice to summons a place before making an assault. If the summons was accepted, terms of surrender were negotiated, which probably included the garrison marching out "with the honours of war." If the summons was rejected and the place carried by assault, the garrison was considered to have lost the right to quarter and the place would be sacked unless the inhabitants were considered friendly.[26]

Lest Aitchison's perception be misconstrued as the singular viewpoint of a soldier seeking to justify the actions of his comrades, it must be remembered that Wellington also blamed Napoleon's order to fortress governors forbidding surrender before the assault phase began as the cause of British casualties and the resulting vengeance-inspired bloodshed. His sanguinary words, written nearly a decade after the sieges, seem more appropriate for a medieval lord facing internal rebellion than for a British army commander of the nineteenth century: "The consequence of this regulation of Bonaparte's was the loss of the flower of my army, in the assault on Ciudad Rodrigo and Badajoz. I should have thought myself justified in putting both garrisons to the sword and if I had done so at the first, it is probable I should have saved

5,000 men at the second . . . the practice which refuses quarter to a garrison that stands an assault is not a *useless* effusion of blood."[27]

Regarding depredations against French soldiers, we have creditable testimony that the British soldier did not seek unending retribution on fortress defenders. Major F.P. Robinson, for example, writes in amazement at the control exhibited by the British regulars after the assault on San Sebastian in 1813. He also mentions the men's thoroughness while looting: "Although our people were destroyed by the Enemy in such numbers before they entered the town—yet once in, all the Frenchmen they overtook were made Prisoners—hardly a man being killed—What other Troops in the whole World can act thus?...[as for valuables] what the fire spared, our men took, the plunder was immense."[28]

Costello tells a tale that reflects both the anger of the redcoats toward the French garrison and the degree to which mercy was extended. In pain from a slight head wound received during the assault on Badajoz, Costello came across a small group of French soldiers near a street corner. All but one ran away upon noticing Costello and his comrade, O'Brien. The remaining soldier ran at them with his musket held high. Before Costello could fire, O'Brien wrested the rifle from the Frenchman's hands. Unsatisfied, Costello moved to shoot the French soldier. "A feeling of revenge," he recalls, "prompted by the suffering I endured from my wounds, actuated my feelings, and I exclaimed, 'O'Brien, let me have the pleasure of shooting this rascal, for he may be the man who has brought me to the state I am now in!'" Costello then pressed his rifle close to the man's chest, intending to kill him. "But as my finger was about to pull the trigger," he writes with much contrition, "he fell upon his knees and implored mercy. The next moment the rifle dropped from my hands and I felt a degree of shame that a feeling of irritation should have betrayed me into a commission of a crime for which I could never have forgiven myself."[29]

Lawrence recounts a further example of British restraint toward wounded French soldiers following the taking of one of the forts at Badajoz. Upon entering the fort, Lawrence and a few mates found a number of French defenders, mostly suffering from serious though not mortal wounds. He and his men attempted to relieve the suffering of their French counterparts by giving them rum and water and then conveying them to the rear.[30]

After quickly venting their initial anger on French or Spanish defenders immediately after the breach was taken, the thoughts of the rankers usually turned to plunder. Rifleman John Kincaid recalled the result: "Wherever there was anything to eat or drink (the only saleable commodities), the soldiers turned the shopkeepers out, and placed themselves behind the counter, selling off the contents of the shop."[31]

Grattan of the 88th Foot marveled at the "rapidity and accuracy" exhibited by the men as they traversed and looted Ciudad Rodrigo. He later learned that the more enterprising soldiers had employed Spanish guides, with whom they shared the spoils. The outcome was inebriated soldiers dressed in priests' robes, nuns' habits, and women's dresses. Other soldiers were nearly naked.[32] Joseph Donaldson of the 94th wrote of the aftermath of Ciudad Rodrigo: "The camp . . . for some days afterward was like a masquerade, the men going about intoxicated and dressed in the various dresses they had found in the town; [the clothes of] French and Spanish officers, priests, friars, and nuns were promiscuously mixed, [the men] cutting as many antics as a mountebank."[33]

The attitudes of the British regulars and their women (who brazenly followed their men into the fortresses as soon as it was marginally safe to do so) toward plundering and pernicious vandalism were captured by Charles Von Hodenburg, an officer in the King's German Legion. Although his motivations to enter the town are suspect (he was probably there to see what loot he could find for himself), his account of the incident provides insight regarding the nature of post-assault behavior:

> In less than an hour after it fell into our possession it
> [Badajoz] looked as if centuries had gradually completed its
> destruction. The surviving soldier, after storming a town,
> considers it as his indisputable property, and thinks himself
> at liberty to commit any enormity by way of indemnifying
> himself for the risking of his life. The bloody strife has made
> him insensible to every better feeling; his lips are parched by
> the extraordinary exertions that he has made, and from the
> necessity, as well as the inclination, his first search is for
> liquor. This once obtained, every trace of human nature vanishes, and no brutal outrage can be named that he does not

commit. The town was not only plundered of every article which the soldiers carry off, but whatever was useless to them or could not be removed was wantonly destroyed. . . . A couple hundred of their women from the camp poured into the place, when it was barely taken, to have their share of plunder. They were worse, if possible than the men. . . . But no more of these scenes of horror. I went deliberately into the town to harden myself to the sight of human misery—but I have had enough of it: my blood has been frozen with the images I have witnessed.[34]

John Harley, a British officer, recalled these same images of destruction wrought by the soldiers and their women on the fortress town of Badajoz. His account echoes much of what Grattan described concerning the aftermath of Ciudad Rodrigo, particularly the men's fondness for clerical attire:

> The town had now become a scene of plunder and devastation; our soldiers and our women, in a state of intoxication, had lost all control of themselves. There, together with numbers of Spanish and Portuguese, who had come into the city . . . in search of plunder, filled every street. Many were dispossessed of their booty by others; and these exchanges of plunder in many cases were not effected without bloodshed, when the party about to be deprived of his spoils was sufficiently sober to offer resistance. . . . Hundreds of both sexes were lying in a state of helpless intoxication in various costumes. . . . Churches and convents, shops and stores . . . private houses and palaces, had all been plundered. The actors of these excesses were attired in the habits of priests with broad-brimmed hats of monks and nuns, and in the dresses of grandees and ladies of rank.[35]

These drunken escapades went on for days. Wellington found that the most expedient method to regain control of his soldiers was to allow them time to satisfy their urges, eventually drinking themselves into near-unconsciousness states. Then he would send in the provost marshals to herd the redcoats slowly back to their regiments. For most soldiers, conquered towns provided immediate if temporary escape from their lives of hardship. Once their alcohol-induced stupors wore off, after having had their fill of food and especially drink and perhaps unwilling females, the soldiers' licentious behavior ended. Carrying whatever goods they had acquired, they made their way back to their companies stationed outside the bastion walls. Not until they were once again asked to take a fortress by assault, with similar circumstances driving them to emotional extremes while simultaneously providing them the means to satisfy their neglected needs, would British regulars conduct themselves in a like manner.

Wellington may have complained vociferously about the conduct of his soldiers, but he well understood the unwritten rules related to siege assaults. Years after the war he remarked: "I believe it has always been understood that the defenders of a fortress stormed have no claim to quarter."[36] Wellington used the lure of plunder to entice his men to brave the incredible dangers of breach assaults. Surtees acknowledged the arrangement: after long exposure to fatigue, deprivation, and death, the men thought it only fair that they should reward themselves for their success.[37] According to Captain Thomas Browne, one drunken soldier, "heavily laden with plunder," actually had the temerity to address Wellington during the plundering of Badajoz. "We poor fellows," the soldier exclaimed, "fights hard and gets nothing." Wellington, in the process of addressing an equally inebriated woman weighed down with loot, said nothing in reply.[38] He may not have agreed, but he knew that fair was fair: the men had done his bidding and were allowed to claim their recompense in accordance with the customs of war.

Wellington used the post-assault behavior of the men to send a message to the defenders of all citadels still in French hands, so it is reasonable to surmise that he was loath to bring men up on charges for what was considered acceptable siege behavior. His real anger emerged because he had difficulty bringing the men back under his control after they stormed the towns. The day after Badajoz, for example, he sent in Power's Portuguese Brigade to protect the inhabitants and relieve the units that made the final attack. Wellington later complained that Power's men, succumbing to the allure of available food, drink, and valuables, plundered more extensively than did the men who took the citadel.[39] It took another day, and much work by the provost marshals, to restore order.

Here Wellington's patience was sorely tried. His dissatisfaction and wrath, which have sometimes been misinterpreted, were not directed entirely at the men's excesses, which he knew would be great. They were instead focused on the soldiers' recalcitrance in rejoining their units in a timely fashion and their rebellion against military authority. According to Lawrence, some redcoats, in their drunken madness, attacked fellow soldiers and even killed two or three officers who were trying to reestablish discipline after the Badajoz assault.[40] When he heard this, Wellington's disgust with the men probably reached new depths. But even then Lawrence claims that Wellington only punished the suspected offenders by stopping their grog rations.[41] Browne offers a conflicting account, stating that "gallows were erected in several streets, & Soldiers were hung on them, but all in vain."[42] It is unclear how many soldiers were actually hanged after Badajoz. Costello adds a telling recollection that may corroborate Lawrence's depiction of Wellington's momentary tolerance for soldiers' misdeeds after the stormings of fortresses. Johnny Castles, a quiet little man of his company with a fondness for drink, was arrested, presumably by the provost marshals for some alcohol-induced offense, and dragged off to the newly erected gallows in the center of town. A rope was placed about his neck, but he was not hanged. Costello comments that "the circumstance had such an effect on him that he took ill, and was a little deranged for some time after."[43]

The degree to which individuals strayed from their normal patterns of behavior varied greatly; their reactions were as diverse as their backgrounds. Some soldiers became the personification of evil, at least to the townspeople on whom they preyed. Others had internal gauges that even alcohol could not affect. In a number of recorded incidents soldiers relate that individuals or small groups of regulars protected inhabitants and sought to reestablish order, if only within the limited confines of their presence.[44] Perhaps the most famous incident involved Harry Smith, an officer of the 95th, who rescued 14-year-old Juana María de Los Dolores after the siege of Badajoz. Smith protected the girl, whose ears were bleeding after soldiers tore out her earrings, until the marauding soldiers had thoroughly sacked the town and were shepherded back to their battalions. Smith and María later married, and she became the darling of the Light Division. Years afterward, when Smith was governor of the Cape of South Africa, he named a town after her, calling it Ladysmith.[45]

Such incidents of gallantry by both officers and enlisted men did little to offset the general misconduct of the rampaging soldiers. The chaotic state of the environs within the fortresses also provided the few psychopaths within British ranks with the perfect environment in which to seek their own perverse entertainments; they no doubt found ransacking the towns and terrorizing civilians much to their liking.[46] Such men were few in number, however, and the evidence suggests that most of these individuals already existed on the periphery of or outside a primary group, beyond and immune to its limiting effects.

The greatest difficulty lies in deciphering the degree to which the soldiers mistreated French defenders and Spanish civilians after winning their way into the fortresses of Ciudad Rodrigo, Badajoz, and San Sebastian. Separating the frequency of looting acts and drunken excesses from occurrences of more egregious misdeeds is a confounding process. Many observers (usually officers) generalized when writing about the conduct of their men: all behaviors not strictly adhering to regulations were perceived as crimes and described as such. This is especially true regarding drunkenness and pillaging. Thus, the lines separating acts of plunder and inebriation from physical assaults are blurred almost beyond recognition.

Adding to the Gordian complexity, few formal charges were ever brought against the soldiers, in large part because Wellington allowed them free rein to satisfy themselves after the ordeal of the assault and because the sacking of cities that resisted after the opening of a practicable breach was a universally accepted military practice. Without formal records, it is impossible to ascertain positively the number and types of crimes committed. While civilian criminal proceedings, of course, would have been impossible, some regimental charges should have surfaced had the men's behavior been as widespread and injurious as has been asserted. The chaos and the duration of the drunken rampages did work against rapid apprehension and proceedings against soldiers who committed heinous acts, but the situation does not preclude charges later being filed against miscreant soldiers by officers and NCOs who observed serious offenses such as rape and murder. It is as injudicious to assume that the lack of evidence in the cases of post-siege assaults indicates collective guilt as it is to posit that the missing proof absolves the men of all crimes.

The lack of court proceedings forces us to rely on first-person accounts, which have inherent limitations. Primary sources such as letters, journals, and diaries are unlikely to list specifics regarding behaviors that the men knew would bring them shame and the disapproval of their readers.[47] We have no way of knowing the extent to which the soldiers were being decorous and self-protecting when they omitted details regarding their behavioral transgressions or those of their comrades. The lack of detailed evidence neither proves nor disproves the accusations against the redcoats, although it is impossible to ignore the numerous accounts that hint at acts of violence and rape.

In order to come to any tentative conclusion, the existing primary source information must be carefully weighed and considered, as in evaluating the testimony of witnesses in criminal proceedings. The burden of proof falls on each witness; the veracity of each account can be measured through a comparative analysis of the details offered, consideration of possible witness bias, and the corroborating testimony of others.

Two opposing types of firsthand accounts surface: those that openly accuse the soldiers of untold numbers of rapes, violent assaults, and murders and those that contend that such acts were quite limited. The chronicles are mostly divided along class lines, with the accounts by officers falling into the former category, although some enlisted men also wrote about the excesses of the soldiers after they successfully stormed the three citadels. Like hearsay testimony, both types tend to be vague regarding details. Generally, though, historians have believed the officers, perhaps because their descriptions of the British soldiers' offenses align with Wellington's "scum of the earth" portrayal.

One such officer, Robert Blakeney, offers a graphic account. Often disdainful of the men and inured to their misery,[48] Blakeney provides one of the most scathing indictments of their behavior after siege assaults. Writing after Badajoz, he exclaimed:

> There was no safety for women even in churches, and any who interfered or offered resistance were sure to get shot. Every house presented a scene of plunder, debauchery and bloodshed committed and wanton cruelty . . . and in many instances I saw the savages [the soldiers] tear the rings from the ears of beautiful women. . . . Men, women, and children

were shot . . . for no other . . . reason than pastime; every
species of outrage was publicly committed . . . and in a manner so brutal that a faithful recital would be . . . shocking to
humanity.[49]

Surgeon Walter Henry sometimes saw the men in the worst light,
often misunderstanding their actions and motivations. He offers a
similar appraisal of the rampage within the citadel: "I beheld a scene
of the most dreadful drunkenness, violence and confusion. Parties
of intoxicated men, loosed from all discipline and restraint and im-
pelled by their own evil passages, were roaming and reeling about,
firing into the windows, bursting open doors . . . plundering, shooting
any person who opposed them, violating and committing every horrid excess and sometimes destroying each other."[50]

Private William Browne of the 45th adds further evidence in his
description of the aftermath of the assault at Badajoz. His passage
ranks with Blakeney's in scope and overall condemnation of the men:

When the garrison surrendered, leave for two hours was
given to us to go to the town, camp, or wherever we pleased,
but the town was universally preferred. All rushed to the gate
which . . . the enemy had built up . . . as a means of defence leaving a narrow passage through which but one man
could pass at a time. They all, however, got to the town soon
enough for the inhabitants, who were by many of our men
shamefully and barbarously treated. There was not, I believe,
a house in the whole town that was not ransacked from top to
bottom—murder, rape, and robbery were committed with the
greatest impunity.[51]

Other primary source evidence, however, does not fully support
the perceptions of Blakeney, Henry, and Browne. Writing about the
siege of Ciudad Rodrigo, William Swabey offers contradictory testimony, stating that the men never intentionally resorted to bloodshed while looting the town: "Our troops, as soon as the breach was
gained, more eager for plunder than their duty, broke and ran in de-
fiance of their officers . . . and committed shameful excesses disgraceful to the whole army. [There was] not a soul that was not rifled. . . .
No intentional murders were committed, though some of the men

were so drunk that they fired promiscuously in the streets and killed many of their comrades."[52]

Lawrence writes openly of the extended plunder that took place. He also observes that many soldiers resisted the temptation to engage in wanton destruction and that murder, even during the pillaging of cities, was rare: "But while all this debauchery [at Badajoz] was going on amongst some of our soldiers, I will give a word of credit to a great many of the more respectable, who were trying as much as lay in their power to stop the ferociousness of the same. . . . Things that could not be taken were often destroyed, and the men threatened if they did not produce their money, and the women sometimes the same. Comparatively few murders were, I believe, committed, but some no doubt occurred."[53]

Rifleman Costello relates a story that illustrates the difficulty of ciphering degrees of truth in first-person recollections. Coming to the aid of a civilian, he restrained a soldier intent on shooting an old man for not disclosing the whereabouts of money allegedly hidden somewhere in his house. Costello, using his command of Spanish, convinced the man to surrender his valuables in order to keep his life. His account is remarkably honest, for he admits that he then received a share of the cash. Although Costello's motives for stopping the shooting seem sincere, the apparent willingness of the soldiers to shoot the Spaniard is a mark against them.[54] It might be conjectured, of course, that Costello was in on the robbery from the beginning and that the threatened act of violence was a sham. Such is the nature of the evidence for and against the British ranker.

An incident recalled by subaltern George Gleig conveys the chaos and resulting civilian terror of the British entry into San Sebastian. His narrative is an example of most such accounts. It makes references to looting, property destruction, the men's intoxication, and mass rape, but it lacks details concerning the actual fate of the female inhabitants that he mentions. Nevertheless, his account leaves the reader with distinct impressions: "As soon as the fighting began to wax faint, the horrors of plunder and rapine succeeded. Fortunately, there were few females in the place, but of the fate of the few which were there, I cannot even now think without a shudder. The houses were everywhere ransacked, the furniture wantonly broken, the church profaned, the images dashed to pieces; wine and spirit cellars were broken open, and the troops, heated already with angry passions, became absolutely mad by intoxication."[55]

Grattan's chronicle of post-siege incidents provides insight into the role that semantics plays in the depiction of the men's behavior. Such texts perhaps have been interpreted too severely by historians looking to assign blame to the redcoat's conduct. Grattan refers to "scenes of the greatest outrage" but then describes only the effects of plunder and alcohol on the soldiers and the townspeople of Ciudad Rodrigo: "Scenes of the greatest outrage now took place, and it was pitiable to see groups of the inhabitants half-naked in the streets . . . while their houses were undergoing the strictest scrutiny. Some of the soldiers turned to the wine and spirit houses, where having drunk sufficiently, sallied out in quest of more plunder; others got so intoxicated that they lay in a helpless state."[56]

Grattan also details the sequence of events once the men entered the captured fortress. As in all the other accounts, drink plays an important role. He writes that for the soldiers it was simply about the enterprise of looting, with the majority of the men seeking alcohol first. Grattan observes that the soldiers, once adequately drunk, turned to pillaging, some for valuables and others for more liquor. Many men became helplessly intoxicated, while others broke into shops and stores of all types. Grattan makes no mention, however, of soldiers committing acts of rape or murder.

John Cooper of the 7th Foot offers a comparable picture of men intoxicated and out of control after the storming of Ciudad Rodrigo. Like Grattan, Cooper does not refer to physical assaults on the inhabitants; his use of the phrase "horrible scenes commenced" seems to be describing theft, property destruction, and drunkenness. Given the fairly descriptive language of the passage, we might expect at least a hint of violent outrages against the inhabitants had they been common: "Our maddened fellows rushed into the town by the thousands. Wine stores were broken open, and horrible scenes commenced. All order ceased. Plunder was the order of the night. Some got loaded with plate, etc.; then beastly drunk; and lastly were robbed by others. This lasted two days."[57]

Lawrence furnishes additional substantiation. Writing of the "horrors of soldiery," he describes examples of miscreant conduct that do not include any mention of physical assaults on civilians. Lawrence's summation of the men's behavior in the aftermath of the

Ciudad Rodrigo and Badajoz assaults aligns closely with the testimony of Grattan and Cooper, although his definition of "debauchery" remains unclear: "[I saw in Ciudad Rodrigo] all the horrors of the soldiery, excesses, riot, and drunkenness taking place on every side. Houses were plundered of their contents, cellars broken open and emptied, and many houses were even set on fire, amid the yells of the dissipated soldiers and screams of the wounded. . . . [After taking Badajoz, the men] began all the horrors that generally attended a capture by assault—plunder, waste, destruction of property, drunkenness and debauchery."[58]

Grattan does admit that the men, intoxicated and heated by angry passions against citadel inhabitants, stripped women of their property and often of their clothes. This is one of the most specific accounts of crimes against persons rather than property. He expresses his shock and shame at the behavior of the soldiers: "[I saw them] turn upon the already deeply injured females, and tear from them the trinkets that adorned their necks, fingers, and ears! And finally, they would strip them of their apparel . . . many men were flogged, but although the contrary has been said, none were hanged—yet hundreds deserved it."[59]

The phrases "already deeply injured" and "none were hanged—yet hundreds deserved it" clearly intimate that personal assaults occurred, although Grattan never provides specifics regarding the extent of the violations. The testimony certainly supports a charge of robbery, and possibly of rape, but not of murder. Costello adds confirmation that the latter two offenses must have been limited, noting the lack of official action by Wellington and his provosts. Referring to Badajoz, he states: "I am not aware that a single execution took place, notwithstanding the known severity of the Duke toward plunder and outrage."[60]

It would be naive, however, to think that drunken men would strip defenseless women and not attempt to press their advantage further. This no doubt occurred in more than a few instances. Captain Harley provides the best eyewitness testimony with his description of the aftermath of the San Sebastian assault. Harley writes that the raping of women after the siege was so prevalent that officers could not stop it. He details the experience of Lieutenant Powers, who defended a house with two female occupants. Powers disarmed one soldier who had tried to force his way in. Called away to duty in the trenches, he returned to the same house later that evening to find both women beaten and raped.[61] Costello also hints at a similar outcome for the two daughters and the wife of an old *patrón* who tried to conceal them on the second floor of his ransacked home.[62]

Such accounts help confirm the assertion that some women were grossly mistreated by British soldiers after siege attacks. Many chronicles, however, lack the corroborating details supplied by Harley and Costello. Grattan, Cooper, and Lawrence could have described such scenes at no cost to themselves or their immediate comrades, but they failed to do so. This cannot be attributed to the sensitivities of the time, since Henry, Browne, and Gleig were not shy about using the words "rape," "rapine," and "violating." The first-person chronicles, though, tend to be more accusatorial than substantive in nature, perhaps in part because they were based on rumor rather than empirical evidence. Thus, while it cannot be argued that no attacks against women occurred, the absence of unassailable substantiating records leaves some doubt about the frequency of these assaults.

Donaldson indirectly offers a possible explanation, as he attributes most "outrages" to regimental bullies whose actions were isolated and beyond accepted group mores. His description of these men hints at their sociopathic nature: "I never knew one of them that displayed even ordinary courage in the field; and it was invariably by fellows of this description that outrages, such as those perpetrated at Badajoz, were committed." Donaldson freely mentions drinking, "mischief," and wanton destruction. He also comments on the role that alcohol played in the men's misdeeds, again making reference to the small numbers of "villains" that he accuses of committing the worst of the offenses. The profile of soldiers considered both skulkers and deviants adds credence to the idea that a good share of the most egregious siege assault crimes may have been committed by a relatively small number of soldiers who were the very worst of their units. As Donaldson recalls: "The effect of the liquor now began to show itself, and some of the scenes which ensued are too dreadful and disgusting to relate; where two or three thousand armed men, many of them mad drunk, others depraved and unprincipled, were freed from all restraint, running up and down the town, the atrocities which took place may be readily imagined—but in justice to the army, I must say they were not general, and in most cases perpetrated by cold-blooded villains who were backward enough in the attack."[63]

Perhaps the "irreclaimables" (the approximately 50 men in each regiment identified by Sir John Colborne), as Sir Charles Oman puts it, perpetrated a disproportionate share of the serious offenses.[64] These individuals were already held in contempt by the soldiers in their units. As a result, soldiers whose allegiance and pride centered on group values and an agreed-upon code of conduct in all probability considered the acts of cruelty and self-gratification perpetrated by primary group outcasts to be aberrations. The small number of troublemakers, whose failings represent their own shortcomings more than those of the rank and file, in general, may be largely responsible for the negative opinions formed by Wellington and some of his officers regarding the men's characters.

It is likely, though, that common soldiers did in fact commit a limited number of rapes and murders, especially under the influence of alcohol. The men who recorded their impressions of post-siege rampages may have failed to mention many such acts because the transgressions were relatively few in number or the writers were too ashamed or too considerate to inflict such indelicate images upon their readers. Excessive drinking may have lowered inhibitions and allowed men to act as they otherwise would not. The evidence is too sparse to ascertain with any certainty the actual types and frequency of crimes, beyond robbery, that were carried out by common redcoats.

Charles Esdaile, however, argues that British soldier misconduct was willful and widespread. A scholar with a justifiable sympathy for the Spanish inhabitants who suffered at the hands of the largely drunken rankers, Esdaile refers to the "sacking" of San Sebastian; he posits that the redcoats wrought indiscriminate havoc with sword and flame. Murders were so common, he asserts, that "what took place was quite simply a disgrace—a war crime, indeed."[65] But the vehemence of his language does not appear justified by the evidence.

Given the conflicting accounts and the lack of direct documentation, some doubt arises about the degree of guilt that should be assigned to the British soldiers for their conduct regarding civilians. That the men ran wild after siege assaults is established; the many eyewitness accounts of drinking, pillaging, acts of folly, and even some of rape and a few references to murder confirm this premise. It is nearly impossible, however, to determine absolutely the number of heinous acts committed by British regulars after siege assaults, given the extant sources. We can at best conjecture about the extent of the men's injudicious behavior and hazard a guess at the frequency of personal assaults, rapes, and use of lethal force. Judgment must be tempered by the knowledge that the evidence against the soldiers for these crimes is uneven and often contradictory. This is not meant to excuse the transgressions of the ranker against fortress inhabitants. Rather, it is a cautionary note proposing that the evidence is not as injurious to the British soldier's reputation as has been presumed.

These siege incidents of gross misconduct were the exceptions to the redcoats' accepted rules of conduct; they were limited in duration and tied directly to the dynamics of siege assaults and their aftermath. The British regular's life of privation made him especially susceptible to the temptation of having immediate access to the things he desired most: drink, food, potential wealth, and, quite likely, women. The soldiers, freed from group values, beyond the control of military law, and perhaps encouraged by situational dynamics, sated themselves, committing the kinds of acts (in whatever number) that would permanently tarnish their reputations. Much of the condemnation of the British ranker is based on this special situation of siege warfare. This does not eliminate the image of the honorable pillager; it is another set of circumstances altogether. But as surgeon Charles Boutflower commented after the siege and subsequent looting of Ciudad Rodrigo: "Gallant as our soldiers are when opposed to an Enemy, I fear they yield to no people on earth in their thirst for plunder."[66]

Conclusion

In his work on the influence of culture on the traits and combat capabilities of soldiers, John Lynn has advanced the argument that only through cultural interpretation and social analysis can the motivations and conduct of soldiers of any historical era be properly understood. The special, separate nature of British military society during the Peninsula campaign molded the ideals and behaviors of the redcoat in a manner different from that experienced by soldiers of other periods and even other combatants of the Napoleonic Wars. It is through an examination of the internal and external forces at work on the British soldier—and the gulf between civilian and military life, far greater in the British case than in the French—that the ranker's decisions in the field and in battle come into clearer focus. Referring to his work on the subject of combat and culture, Lynn playfully writes, "This volume has come to bury the universal soldier, not to praise him."[1] Perhaps *All for the King's Shilling* can add a shovel or two of dirt onto the carcass of the generalized portrayal of fighting men.

British Peninsular War veterans have suffered more than most from the kinds of assumptions that Lynn argues against. For nearly two hundred years they have borne Wellington's "scum of the earth" assessment, which casts aspersions on their character and their conduct on and off the battlefield. The British regular's remarkable capacity for survival on campaign and his unequaled combat success against the French have become lost amid misperceptions attributing his behavior to antisocial characteristics and the innate toughness that is somehow considered to be an inherent trait of all men from the lower economic classes.

In discourse concerning the composition of armies, the implication that common soldiers throughout history were scum (possessing unsavory characters and predisposed toward criminal activities) arises all too frequently. The capacity of such men to function under extreme circumstances is chalked up to their hardy and savage natures. This suggests that low economic status somehow prepares men to wage and endure war; the everyday soldier is imagined to be more skilled at using violence than a man born to affluence and more suited to withstand the physical and emotional stresses of campaign and battle. It is an assumption that ignores the role that culture, group norms, shared hardship, bonding, primary group dynamics, circumstances, leadership, logistical failures, and human limitations play in shaping the behavior of soldiers. In many ways, this supposition is as demeaning to soldiers of today as it was to the British redcoat.

The British soldier was not, as has often been presumed, a brute forced to choose between the army and incarceration. The man who enlisted in the British army during the war against Napoleon most likely did so out of economic necessity. He was usually young; the vast majority of recruits were between 15 and 24 years of age. The recruit was an unemployed agricultural or manual laborer, textile worker, shoemaker, or tradesman from any of a hundred occupations. He chose the army because it offered the promise of regular food and pay. It was not his fault that the army failed miserably to fulfill its end of the bargain. Left without means to survive in Portugal, Spain, France, and Belgium, the ranker did what anyone would do: he learned to forage and plunder food, valuables, and, when he could find it, drink. Commissariat failure and army neglect, not character flaws, caused the redcoat to steal in order to clothe and feed himself.

While on campaign the British soldier quickly bonded with the men with whom he shared the hardships of British army life. Unlike the soldiers under Napoleon, the ranker received few public statements of appreciation, which Lynn argues are so important to sustaining motivation. (This is in sharp contrast to the praise heaped on officers.) The British regular was tendered no tangible rewards such as medals or personal honors. His rations and pay were grossly inadequate and irregularly supplied. Physical comforts were negligible; ideological concerns were rarely considered or addressed. Letters from home were uncommon, their frequency likely diminishing as the years passed. The redcoat could not even count on a pension should he be wounded. Physically and psychologically neglected, the British soldier lived a dreary, frequently dangerous, and debilitating daily life governed by harsh discipline. Many of his officers, constrained by societal views, considered him worthy of being motivated only through coercive measures, which added little but misery to an already difficult existence.

Because the ranker was enlisted for life, his messmates became his family, and group norms dictated his behavior. Group mores regarding the sharing of food, treatment of civilians and captured French soldiers, and conduct during combat molded the soldier's actions to a remarkable degree. The strength of the bonds between British regulars allowed Wellington to formulate battlefield tactics that made optimal use of his soldiers' willingness to risk death to preserve the group. He combined tactical variations, based on close-range fire and bayonet assaults, with the use of reverse slopes to create a combat methodology unique to the British army. In applying Westbrook's model of compliance theory,[2] it becomes clear that the British rank and file were motivated primarily by the normative influence of group interaction and its related incentives. The threat of external, coercive force or the hope of financial remuneration had very limited effects on the soldiers' conduct. Group allegiance, not sociopathic tendencies, the allure of money, or fear of punishment, allowed the British redcoat to become one of the most reliable combat soldiers of the period.

For far too long Wellington's derogatory appraisal of the British rank and file has prevented a fair analysis of their battlefield and campaign behavior. Perhaps, as C. T. Atkinson has suggested, "famous sayings, especially those of great and prominent persons, are often quoted inaccurately . . . while the tendency of historians to copy each other's mistakes often causes those celebrated phrases . . . to be taken out of context."[3]

Distilling the accomplishments and the motivations of the rankers under Wellington amid the difficulties of campaigning and the chaos of the battlefield requires a more detailed process than has been applied to understanding their behavior. The army was anything but kind to these men, treating them as expendable commodities. British redcoats were accorded neither honor nor respect by the citizenry and the government they served; fate treated them no better, as this paragraph from the 18 November 1822 edition of the *London Observer* illustrates:

> It is estimated that more than a million bushels of human and inhuman bones were imported last year from the continent of Europe in the port of Hull. The neighborhoods of Leipzig, Austerlitz, Waterloo, and of all the places where, during the late bloody war, the principal battles were fought, have been swept alike of the bones of the hero and the horse which he rode. Thus collected from every quarter, they have been shipped to the port of Hull and thence forwarded to the York- shire bone grinders who have erected steam-engines and powerful machinery for the purpose of reducing them to a granularly state. In this condition they are sold to the farmers to manure their lands.[4]

While many of the British soldiers shared the same final destiny as did their French opponents, their reputations have suffered much in comparison. It is time to disregard the accepted but inaccurate portrait of British regulars as rogues and perpetrators of misdeeds and consider them for what they were: common men who bonded to- gether to endure frightful circumstances. The battlefield victories they attained should rightly be credited to competent leadership and the redcoats' collective will to preserve their primary social groups. Comrades, rather than violent natures and criminal tendencies, were the soldiers' driving motivation. The British rank and file may have earned their daily shilling from the king, but they fought for each other.

Epilogue

William Lawrence survived the Peninsular War and eventually made his way home. After Napoleon was sent to Elba in 1814, Lawrence's regiment, the 40th Foot, was dispatched to Ireland. There the men finally received the wages they were owed for their long years of service. Lawrence wrote that many men had received advances but never their full pay during all their years on the continent. He received £40, which constituted six years of accumulated pay; this included the higher rates for his service as a corporal and sergeant. The soldiers also were given a week's furlough, during which, according to Lawrence, "most of the money melted away in that period—at least, I know mine did, for not having been to the British Isles in so long, we were all resolved to have a spree."[1]

From Ireland, Lawrence was sent first to Jamaica and then to New Orleans, during the last stages of the War of 1812.[2] The British contingent that he accompanied skirmished near the city and captured a battery of artillery. The guns were protected primarily with barrels of brown sugar; their contents, once discovered, soon filled the men's stomachs and haversacks.[3]

Lawrence's regiment then sailed back to Britain. Before landing in Portsmouth, they received word that Napoleon had escaped Elba.

New orders directed the 40th Foot to Flanders, where they landed at Ghent. Lawrence and his regiment marched nearly 50 miles from Ghent to meet up with the main army south of Brussels, arriving in time for the Battle of Waterloo on 18 June 1815.

Lawrence and the 40th Foot were part of Sir John Lambert's brigade of the British 6th Division and functioned as Wellington's tactical reserve. They were initially stationed in the rear of the Allied force, behind the farmhouse at Mont.-St.-Jean, just to the east of the road that bisected the battlefield. The 40th Foot later helped repulse the Imperial Guard and assisted in the recapturing of La Haye Sainte.[4] Lawrence's writings capture the chaos and uncertainty of that famous battle, particularly the frenzy of the repeated French cavalry charges and the British haste in forming square. Lawrence acknowledged that the soldiers around him were exhausted and "beginning to despair." But despite thinning ranks and the combined effects of the charges and French fire, he wrote proudly: "We did not lose a single inch of ground the whole day. . . . It was a mystery to me how it was accomplished, for at last so few were left that there were scarcely enough to form square."[5] The regiment suffered the loss of its commander, Major Arthur Heyland, 12 other officers, and about 180 rank and file casualties that day.[6]

During the battle, Lawrence survived two incidents in which cannon shots killed the men beside him. The second near-miss occurred after he was ordered to join a detachment guarding the regimental colors. Of this honor, he recalled: "This, although I was used to warfare as much as any, was a job I did not at all like; but still I went as boldly to work as I could. There had been before me that day fourteen sergeants already killed and wounded while in charge of those colours, with officers in proportion, and the staff and colours were almost cut to pieces. This job will never be blotted from my mind."[7]

Miraculously, Lawrence survived the battle with only a small facial gash. The wound's severity was slight, but the pain was exacerbated when the soldier standing next to Lawrence overprimed his musket. The discharge blew the excess powder into his wound, making him "dance for a time without a fiddle."[8]

After the Allied victory, Lawrence recalled that "if there ever was a hungry and tired tribe of men, we were that after that memorable day of the 18th of June." The men's first thought was to find dry timber in order to cook a meal.[9] Discovering some abandoned French provisions, which included corn, a ham, and two fowls, they quickly made and enjoyed a fine dinner. Lawrence, showing no hard feelings toward the French, offered a portion of the feast to a French soldier he discovered lying under a cannon.[10]

The next day Lawrence and the army began the march to Paris; they met little resistance on the way. As he recounted: "We saw no more of Napoleon's army, nor did we want to much, for most of us had had quite enough of it at Waterloo."[11] During his long stay in Paris as part of the occupation force, Lawrence met a French woman, Marie Louise Claire, who ran a small produce stand near his barrack gate. He became a frequent visitor to her produce stall and endeared himself to her by pursuing a soldier from a different regiment who had stolen some tobacco from her stand. Lawrence returned with the tobacco and thus began his courtship. The language barrier proved no obstacle to Lawrence; he soon beguiled Marie, who called herself Clotilde.[12] She agreed to marry him.[13]

Lawrence was equally persuasive with his colonel, who was against his soldiers marrying French women. The colonel eventually consented to the marriage, and Lawrence and Clotilde were soon wed. She marched with him and his regiment to Calais, even though it meant leaving her family. Again proving his resourcefulness, Lawrence found her official transport to Scotland. This was no easy task, as French women were not allowed to be company wives, meaning that no transport was supposed to be available to them. Costello's sad tale of being forced to abandon his French wife at the docks (previously related) confirms the difficulties that Lawrence found a way to overcome. On the way to Calais, Clotilde was introduced to the harshness of British military discipline. She and Lawrence saw two men of the 27th Foot hanged for robbing a farmer.[14]

Lawrence's regiment was sent to Glasgow, where he arrived sometime in the fall of 1817. In the winter of that year he received word of his father's terminal illness; after obtaining his furlough, he and Clotilde found transport to London to see his ailing *père*. The return trip proved anything but easy, as Lawrence's plan to travel to Glasgow by ship was thwarted by low funds and the lack of available transports. Undeterred, and noting that his wife was an "excellent walker," he hiked back with her to Glasgow by stages, a journey of slightly more than 400 miles. Lawrence considered the endeavor so commonplace that he devoted only a portion of a paragraph to its description, merely mentioning that they arrived with "twopence-halfpenny" in his pockets and one day before his leave expired. His wife might have disagreed about the journey's ease, but she apparently communicated no discontent to Lawrence and faithfully walked at his side all the way to Glasgow. He mentions later, however, that Clotilde was ill for almost a week afterward due to the effects of frostbite.[15]

Not long after, the army was reduced. Those soldiers chosen by lot like Lawrence and the other "old and disabled" soldiers in his regiment traveled by boat and road march to the Tower of London.[16] From there, with Clotilde ever-present by his side, Lawrence walked to Chelsea Hospital, where he was examined and discharged with a pension of nine pence a day, due to the wound in his knee.

From London the couple journeyed to Lawrence's home parish in Studland, which is in the county of Dorset, a trek of a little more than 100 miles. He barely mentions the trip, only commenting that they "walked every step of the way."[17] After getting settled, Lawrence found employment as a farm laborer, earning 10 shillings a week. He was called to service again in 1819, being deployed in Ireland to suppress smuggling. Clotilde, naturally, went with him. After his regiment was ordered home, Lawrence was discharged for good at Plymouth in 1821. He and Clotilde marched from Plymouth back to Studland, another hike of over 100 miles. There he returned to work on the farm, being accepted back by his former master.

After drifting from trade to trade, Lawrence eventually saved enough money to open a small public house. With his meager pension and the money from the pub he lived "pretty prosperously" with his French wife until she died. Lawrence writes that soon thereafter he began feeling ill and decided to give up his tavern. We might conjecture that the loss of Clotilde had a great deal to do with his condition and that her absence may have caused him to slip into depression. He eventually recovered some of his spirit, though. Again seizing the initiative, he boldly "wrote the authorities at Chelsea, and obtained through the influence of a kind gentleman an addition of threepence a day to my pension, making a shilling in all, and with that I am now living in a house bequeathed to me for so long as I live by my late master, as comfortably as these circumstances and the interposition of a few friends can make me."[18]

Lawrence died in 1867, at the approximate age of 76. His tale is one of the few from the chronicles of British enlisted men with anything close to a happy ending. He certainly deserved it.

Appendix A

THE BRITISH SOLDIER COMPENDIUM

SOURCES AND DISTRIBUTION OF THE SAMPLE

The BSC is a compilation of demographic data from 14 British infantry regiments, 4 cavalry regiments, and 3 sources representing a pool for "unspecified artillery battalions." The War Office citations are listed by regiment in table 7. The returns for each regiment were compiled by randomly selecting pages from regimental description books. Two of the artillery enlistment books were done in exactly the same format and handwriting; these records are listed in the BSC as being from Artillery 1, while records from the other book (which were done in a different format) are given as Artillery 2 to differentiate the two groups.

The regiments included in the BSC are the only units for which information could be found. Data concerning casualty returns, officers, and even detailed descriptions of cavalry mounts were much more easily uncovered, but such records did not contain demographic information relevant to this study. The variation in regimental totals is for the most part related to the number of men listed on each page. Some regiments had 90 or more men per page, while others had as few as 10. In addition, some pages were incomplete. It should also be noted that the vast majority of regimental description books were not paginated; thus, it is impossible to include the page numbers used for each regiment. In addition, the varied nature of regimental record-keeping ensured that information contained in the description books was anything but uniform.[1]

All of the records in the BSC represent single individuals. Each entry includes the year of enlistment, country of origin, age and height at enlistment, and previous occupation of the enlistee. It should be noted that all references to men of English nationality include Welshmen. The regiment and branch of service (artillery, cavalry, or infantry) into which the men enlisted was also recorded. Most of the records (82.3 percent) gave the month of enlistment as well as the year. The BSC was restricted to records showing an enlistment date between January 1790 and June 1815. The disposition of the enlistee (for example, killed, deserted, or held prisoner) is in the BSC if it was recorded in the description book, but only 11.5 percent of the records provided such information.

Table 7. Nationality of enlistees by regiment in the BSC sample and sources

Regiment	English	Irish	Scottish	Foreign	Total	Source
1st Foot	317	507	225	26	1,075	WO 25-308
6th Foot	224	65	6	6	301	WO 25-329
8th Foot	47	112	5	0	164	WO 67-7
25th Foot	238	46	4	6	294	WO 25-352
28th Foot	67	71	20	5	163	WO 25-357
32nd Foot	141	34	5	4	184	WO 25-368
34th Foot	93	23	2	3	121	WO 67-14
42nd Foot	21	30	343	0	394	WO 25-382
53rd Foot	892	295	93	12	1,292	WO 25-412/413
58th Foot	54	242	11	1	308	WO 25-435/436
79th Foot	9	5	97	5	116	WO 25-477
88th Foot	30	348	9	0	387	WO 25-516
Grenadier Guards	261	7	13	0	281	WO 25-874
Scots Guards	196	36	90	3	325	WO 67-1/3
Artillery 1	566	116	131	1	814	WO 54-303/305
Artillery 2	118	5	51	0	174	WO 54-307
3rd Lt. Dragoons	128	20	5	2	155	WO 25-276
18th Lt. Dragoons	86	82	10	0	178	WO 25-292
19th Lt. Dragoons	117	58	14	1	190	WO 25-283
20th Lt. Dragoons	222	43	11	63	339	WO 25-285
Total	3,827	2,145	1,145	138	7,250	

Table 8. Nationalities of enlistees by regiment (%)

Regiment	English	Irish	Scottish	Foreign	Total
1st Foot	29	47	21	2	100
6th Foot	74	22	2	2	100
8th Foot	29	68	3	0	100
25th Foot	81	16	1	2	100
28th Foot	41	44	12	3	100
32nd Foot	77	18	3	2	100
34th Foot	77	19	2	2	100
42nd Foot	5	8	87	0	100
53rd Foot	69	23	7	1	100
58th Foot	18	79	4	0	100
79th Foot	8	4	84	4	100
88th Foot	8	90	2	0	100
Grenadier Guards	93	2	5	0	100
Scots Guards	60	11	28	1	100
Artillery 1	70	14	16	0	100
Artillery 2	68	3	29	0	100
3rd Lt. Dragoons	83	13	3	1	100
18th Lt. Dragoons	48	46	6	0	100
19th Lt. Dragoons	62	31	7	1	100
20th Lt. Dragoons	65	13	3	19	100

Note: All table values are rounded to one decimal place, which may result in occasional rounding errors.

Table 9. Nationalities of enlistees by branch

Branch	English	Irish	Scottish	Foreign	Total
Artillery	684	121	182	1	988
Cavalry	553	203	40	66	862
Infantry	2,590	1,821	923	66	5,400
Total	3,827	2,145	1,145	133	7,250

Table 10. Nationalities of enlistees by branch (%)

Branch	English	Irish	Scottish	Foreign	Total
Artillery	9.4	1.7	2.5	negligible	13.6
Cavalry	7.6	2.8	0.5	1	11.9
Infantry	35.7	25.1	12.7	1	74.5
Total	52.7	29.6	15.7	2	100

Table 11. Percent of each nationality's enlistees in each branch

Branch	English	Irish	Scottish	Foreign
Artillery	17.9	5.6	15.9	0.8
Cavalry	14.4	9.5	3.5	49.6
Infantry	67.7	84.9	80.6	49.6
Total	100	100	100	100

Table 12. Nationality of each branch's enlistees (%)

Branch	English	Irish	Scottish	Foreign	Total
Artillery	69.2	12.2	18.4	0.1	100
Cavalry	64.2	23.5	4.6	7.7	100
Infantry	48.0	33.7	17.1	1.2	100

Table 13. Disposition of soldiers (when listed)

Disposition	Number	Percent (of those listing disposition)
Dead	542	65.0
Prisoner	124	14.9
Deserted	164	19.7
Executed	1	negligible
Transferred	1	negligible
Invalided	1	negligible
Total	833	100

Table 14. Percent of each nationality's enlistees with each disposition

Disposition	English	Irish	Scottish	Foreign
Dead	60.6	69.6	76.6	66.6
Prisoner	22.7	5.2	3.1	13.3
Deserted	16.0	24.8	20.3	20.0
Executed	0.2	0	0	0
Transferred	0.2	0	0	0
Invalided	0	0.3	0	0
Total	100	100	100	100

Age and Height

A small problem arises regarding the inclusion of young boys in the totals. Most boys were identified as drummers and were therefore not included. The BSC sample contains 75 cases of boys under age 15 who were listed in the description books and were at least five feet tall and thus appear to have been accepted as full-status recruits. They were not identified as drummers and were of sufficient height that recruiting officers may have been willing to accept them for full duty.

Table 15. Age distribution of 1806 enlistees

Minimum	Mean	Maximum	Standard Deviation
14	23.1	55	6.71

Table 16. Age distribution of all enlistees

Minimum	Mean	Maximum	Standard Deviation
11	22.44	55	6.12

Table 17. Age distribution by nationality

Nationality	Minimum	Mean	Maximum	Standard Deviation
English	12	21.71	51	5.75
Irish	11	22.89	53	6.06
Scottish	12	23.68	54	6.92
Foreign	14	25.35	55	6.96

Table 18. Age distribution by branch

Branch	Minimum	Mean	Maximum	Standard Deviation
Artillery	11	18.89	40	2.68
Cavalry	12	20.48	42	4.20
Infantry	11	23.40	55	6.51

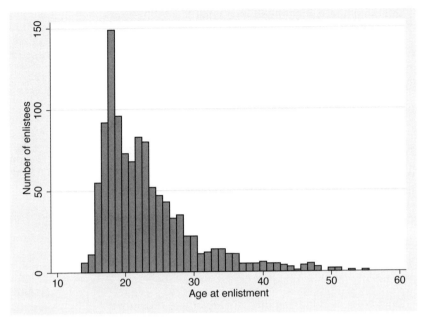

Figure 4. Age distribution of 1806 enlistees.

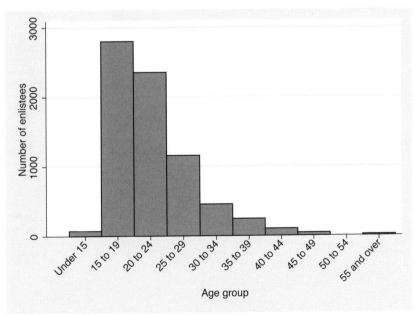

Figure 5. Age-group distribution of 1806 enlistees.

Table 19. Height distribution of all enlistees (inches)

Minimum	Mean	Maximum	Standard Deviation
60	66.32	79	2.36

Table 20. Height distribution by nationality (inches)

Nationality	Minimum	Mean	Maximum	Standard Deviation
English	60	66.30	79	2.30
Irish	60	66.18	77	2.50
Scottish	60	66.60	75	2.23
Foreign	60	66.74	73	2.39

Table 21. Height distribution by branch (inches)

Branch	Minimum	Mean	Maximum	Standard Deviation
Artillery	60	66.52	73	2.31
Cavalry	61	66.76	73	1.83
Infantry	60	66.22	79	2.43

Table 22. Height distribution of enlistees aged 18 and older (inches)

Minimum	Mean	Maximum	Standard Deviation
60	66.6	79	2.26

Table 23. Number and percentage of enlistees not meeting recruiting standards

Qualification	Number	Percent
Recruits less than 15 years old	75	1.0
Recruits more than 25 years old	1,690	23.3
Recruits less than 65 inches tall	1,507	20.8

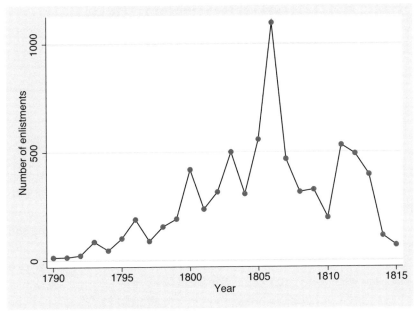

Figure 6. Enlistment per year.

ENLISTMENT PATTERNS

While a portion of the increased 1806 enlistment can be explained, the reasons behind this increase remain unclear. A comparison of the BSC sample to general returns (see Trades and Seasonal Enlistment Patterns below) appears to confirm the validity of the BSC. A sampling anomaly, however, may possibly account for part of the 1806 enlistment jump. According to army records, 1807 had the single highest recruiting totals (ordinary recruiting) with 19,114 men.[2]

Table 24. Enlistment per year as reflected in the BSC sample

Year	Enlistments	Year	Enlistments	Year	Enlistments
1790	14	1799	191	1808	315
1791	15	1800	419	1809	326
1792	23	1801	236	1810	197
1793	87	1802	315	1811	532
1794	46	1803	500	1812	492
1795	102	1804	306	1813	396
1796	189	1805	558	1814	113
1797	89	1806	1,097	1815	69
1798	155	1807	468	TOTAL	7,250

Table 25. Regression comparing enlistment and bread prices

R^2	0.29
Coefficient of bread prices	38.7
Confidence level	greater than 99%
Standard error of estimate	210

TRADES AND SEASONAL ENLISTMENT PATTERNS

Possibly the most challenging part of the data collection was organizing the list of previous trades provided by enlistees. Trades were entered into the database exactly as recorded by the sergeant in charge of the regimental books. Before the data were analyzed, however, I examined the list of trades and corrected many repetitions and spelling errors. Variant spellings included "brasier" for "brazier" and "callier" for "collier." Many trades were listed in some records with a space between two parts of a compound word and without a space in others, such as "needle maker" and "needlemaker." I revised the dataset so that all such occupations were written without a space. Other trades that were obviously the same (such as cooper and barrel maker, tinsmith and whitesmith, and shoemaker and cordwainer) were combined under one of the two variants.

For the aggregate information about the trades prior to enlistment, the types of employment are broken down into laborers, textile workers, and other trades. Men were classified as textile workers if they listed an occupation that was explicitly involved with any part of the textile industry, such as woolcombers, weavers, drapers, and tailors. The term "other trades," although somewhat imprecise, applies to all men who listed a definable job that was not "laborer" and was not related to textile work. In all, the BSC lists 230 occupations. These run the gamut from true craftsmen, such as watchmakers and cabinetmakers, to less skilled trades such as colliers and chimney sweeps.

Table 26. Enlistees with no trade by nationality

Trade	English	Irish	Scottish	Foreign	Total
No trade	54	98	34	9	195
Definable trade	3,773	2,047	1,111	124	7,055
Total	3,827	2,145	1,145	133	7,250

Table 27. Enlistees with no trade as percent of nationality

Trade	English	Irish	Scottish	Foreign
No trade	1.4	4.6	3.0	6.8
Definable trade	98.6	95.4	97.0	93.2
Total	100	100	100	100

Table 28. Enlistees with no trade by nationality as percent of whole sample

Trade	English	Irish	Scottish	Foreign	Total
No trade	0.7	1.4	0.5	0.1	2.7
Definable trade	52.0	28.2	15.3	1.7	97.3
Total	52.7	29.6	15.8	1.8	100

Table 29. Trades by nationality

Type of Trade	English	Irish	Scottish	Foreign	Total
Laborers	1,480	983	412	68	2,943
Textile workers	1,044	593	402	12	2,051
Other trades	1,249	471	297	44	2,061
Total	3,773	2,047	1,111	124	7,055

Table 30. Trades by nationality as percent of each nationality's enlistees

Type of Trade	English	Irish	Scottish	Foreign
Laborers	39.2	48.0	37.0	54.8
Textile workers	27.6	29.0	36.2	9.7
Other trades	33.1	23.0	26.7	35.4
Total	99.9	100.0	99.9	99.9

Table 31. Trades by nationality as percent of whole sample

Type of trade	English	Irish	Scottish	Foreign	Total
Laborers	21.0	13.9	5.8	1.0	41.7
Textile workers	14.8	8.4	5.7	0.2	29.1
Other trades	17.7	6.7	4.2	0.6	29.2
Total	53.5	29.0	15.7	1.8	100.0

Table 32. Enlistees with no trade by branch

Trade	Artillery	Cavalry	Infantry	Total
No trade	15	4	176	195
Definable trade	973	858	5,224	7,055
Total	988	862	5,400	7,250

Table 33. Enlistees with no trade by branch as percent of branch

Trade	Artillery	Cavalry	Infantry
No trade	1.5	0.5	3.3
Definable trade	98.5	99.5	96.7
Total	100	100	100

Table 34. Enlistees with no trade by branch as percent of whole sample

Trade	Artillery	Cavalry	Infantry	Total
No trade	0.2	0.1	2.4	2.7
Definable trade	13.4	11.8	72.1	97.3
Total	13.6	11.9	74.5	100

Table 35. Trades by branch

Type of trade	Artillery	Cavalry	Infantry	Total
Laborers	371	401	2,171	2,943
Textile workers	327	314	1,420	2,061
Other trades	275	143	1,633	2,051
Total	973	858	5,224	7,055

Table 36. Trades by branch as percent of each branch's enlistees

Type of trade	Artillery	Cavalry	Infantry
Laborers	38.1	46.7	41.6
Textile workers	33.6	36.6	27.1
Other trades	28.2	16.7	31.2
Total	99.9	100.0	99.9

Table 37. Trades by branch as percent of whole sample

Type of trade	Artillery	Cavalry	Infantry	Total
Laborers	5.3	5.7	30.7	41.7
Textile workers	4.6	4.5	20.1	29.2
Other trades	3.9	2.0	23.1	29.0
Total	13.8	12.2	73.9	99.9

Table 38. Distribution of trades in 1806 sample

Type of trade	Number	Percent
None	12	1.1
Laborers	418	38.1
Textile workers	363	33.1
Other trades	304	27.7
Total	1,097	100

Table 39. Trades by type reported in the BSC

Trade	Number	Trade	Number	Trade	Number
laborer	2,943	clothdresser	29	potter	12
weaver	1,307	cutter	29	skinner	12
shoemaker	377	wheelwright	29	bookbinder	8
tailor	234	hosier	24	brazier	8
none	195	hairdresses	23	ropemaker	8
smith	145	joiner	23	watchmaker	8
carpenter	123	farmer	21	basketmaker	7
servant	76	woolcomber	21	collarmaker	7
spinner	76	founder	19	cordwinder	7
baker	63	plasterer	19	silversmith	7
mason	62	stocking maker	19	tobacconist	7
bricklayer	59	cabinetmaker	18	brushmaker	6
miner	58	cotton spinner	18	bucklemaker	6
clothier	49	farrier	18	combmaker	6
butcher	46	flaxdresser	18	glover	6
nailer	46	slater	18	jeweler	6
cutler	45	groom	17	presser	6
hatter	44	miller	17	shearman	6
sawyer	39	collier	16	turner	6
framework/wool knitter	35	glazier	16	breecher maker	5
gardener	34	knitter	16	chandler	5
tinsmith	34	locksmith	14	leather dresser	5
grinder	31	saddler	14	papermaker	5
painter	31	tanner	14	plaiter	5
clerk	30	bleacher	12	schoolmaster	5
cooper	30	buttonmaker	12	tinker	5
dyer	30	gunsmith	12	tinman	5
printer	30	musician	12	wagoneer	5

Trade	Number	Trade	Number	Trade	Number
wheeler	5	glassmaker	2	drover	1
wire worker	5	lawyer	2	fender maker	1
bellowsmaker	4	machinemaker	2	filer	1
brickmaker	4	manufacturer	2	forger	1
broguemaker	4	millwright	2	frame setter	1
confectioner	4	nailmaker	2	frame smith	1
cork cutter	4	patternmaker	2	gun molder	1
cotton carder	4	pinmaker	2	gunstocker	1
currier	4	plateworker	2	hair dyer	1
file smith	4	pumpmaker	2	hammersmith	1
harnessmaker	4	sailmaker	2	hempmaker	1
ironfounder	4	sawmaker	2	hostler	1
ladler	4	scrivener	2	husbandman	1
needlemaker	4	shipwright	2	ironmonger	1
pipemaker	4	silverplate	2	keymaker	1
plumber	4	sinkermaker	2	Lt. Cleaver	1
porter	4	stamper	2	mariner	1
stone mason	4	storer of cloth	2	musical instrument maker	1
woolcarder	4	thatcher	2	muslin dresser	1
cardmaker	3	wireworker	2	noustino	1
coachmaker	3	wright	2	ostler	1
dresser	3	yeoman	2	packer	1
engineer	3	actor	1	postcutter	1
engraver	3	barber	1	potmaker	1
glassblower	3	bitmaker	1	razor grinder	1
grocer	3	blockcutter	1	razor smith	1
gunmaker	3	book closer	1	sailor	1
lapper	3	buckle caster	1	scribbler	1
moulder	3	button burnisher	1	setter upper	1
reedmaker	3	carpetmaker	1	silk dresser	1
saddlemaker	3	carter	1	soldier	1
stonecutter	3	cartwright	1	spindlemaker	1
surgeon	3	chainmaker	1	springmaker	1
toymaker	3	chairmaker	1	stationer	1
victualer	3	chaise driver	1	steelmaker	1
whipmaker	3	cigar shaper	1	stone polisher	1
wire drawer	3	clockmaster	1	tappener	1
apothecary	2	coachman	1	tile cutter	1
armorer	2	coachsmith	1	timber dresser	1
blockmaker	2	colbmaker	1	tin plate worker	1
boatman	2	copper miner	1	tobacco spiker	1
bookkeeper	2	copperman	1	toolmaker	1
bootmaker	2	coppersmith	1	twinemaker	1
brewer	2	cotton strainer	1	twiner	1
carver	2	cotton worker	1	upholsterer	1
chimney sweep	2	courier	1	warehouse man	1
cloth draper	2	cratemaker	1	wine merchant	1
clothmaker	2	cymbal maker	1	wood carver	1
forgeman	2	die tinker	1	woolstapler	1

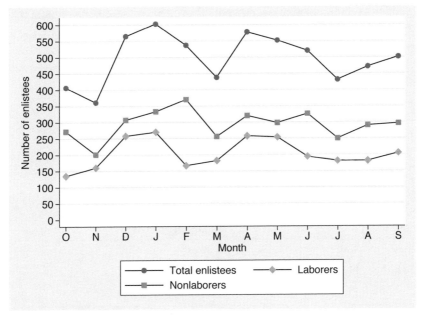

Figure 7. Enlistment per month.

Comparisons to General Returns

In order to confirm the randomness and reliability of the sample in the British Soldier Compendium, information drawn from it was compared to general returns from four separate regiments. General returns gave a summary of the state of the regiment on a given date, including information on the nationalities, heights, and ages of all men in the regiment at that time. Out of all the regimental description books examined, general returns were found for only four regiments. For the two regiments that had more than one general return available, I examined the general return with the latest date.

The regimental general returns were compared to the same regiments in the BSC sample up to the time the returns were compiled. For the height data, the general returns listed how many men were each height only for men 65 inches and taller. Therefore only the corresponding data from the BSC were used to calculate comparable means and standard deviations. For ages, the general returns listed how many men were in each age bracket; this was directly compared to the BSC data.

The overall comparison reveals that the BSC sample is consistent with the general returns. Thus, it is fairly safe to say that the BSC data can be used to represent the British army of the period as a whole.

COMPARISON OF THE BSC SAMPLE TO THE GENERAL RETURN
FOR THE 88TH FOOT (1815)

Table 40. Nationality (%): 88th Foot (1815) and BSC sample

Nationality	88th Foot (1815)	BSC sample
English	7.3	7.8
Irish	90.2	89.9
Scottish	2.4	2.3
Foreign	negligible	0

Table 41. Height (inches): 88th Foot (1815) and BSC sample

Height	88th Foot (1815)	BSC sample
Mean	66.7	66.6
Maximum	74	72
Standard deviation	1.57	1.69

Table 42. Age (%): 88th Foot (1815) and BSC sample

Age bracket	88th Foot (1815)	BSC sample
Under 20	3.6	1.3
20–24	34.0	27.6
25–29	33.4	34.9
30–34	16.7	27.9
35–39	7.3	5.4
40–44	2.9	1.0
45–49	1.5	1.0
50–54	0.4	0.5
55 and over	0.2	0.3

COMPARISON OF THE BSC SAMPLE TO THE GENERAL RETURN
FOR THE 6TH FOOT (1811)

Table 43. Nationality (%): 6th Foot (1811) and BSC sample

Nationality	6th Foot (1811)	BSC sample
English	75.7	74.4
Irish	20.5	21.6
Scottish	2.3	2.0
Foreign	1.4	2.0

Table 44. Height (inches): 6th Foot (1811) and BSC sample

Height	6th Foot (1811)	BSC sample
Mean	67.1	67.1
Maximum	74	77
Standard deviation	1.73	1.87

Table 45. Age (%): 6th Foot (1811) and BSC sample

RCAge bracket	6th Foot (1811)	BSC sample
Under 20	3.7	1.3
20–24	30.1	35.9
25–29	37.5	26.9
30–34	17.2	21.6
35–39	5.8	8.6
40–44	3.7	5.0
45–49	1.3	0.7
50–54	0.6	0
55 and over	0	0

COMPARISON OF THE BSC SAMPLE TO THE GENERAL RETURN
FOR THE 58TH FOOT (1803)

Table 46. Nationality (%): 58th Foot (1803) and BSC sample

Nationality	58th Foot (1803)	BSC sample
English	38.5	30.1
Irish	55.0	64.1
Scottish	6.0	5.1
Foreign	0.5	0.6

Table 47. Height (inches): 58th Foot (1803) and BSC sample

Height	58th Foot (1803)	BSC sample
Mean	67.8	67.2
Maximum	73	74
Standard deviation	1.69	1.73

Table 48. Age (%): 58th Foot (1803) and BSC sample

Age bracket	58th Foot (1803)	BSC sample
Under 20	12.2	32.7
20–24	33.7	37.2
25–29	30.5	25.0
30–34	9.2	2.6
35–39	6.0	1.9
40–44	7.3	0.6
45–49	0.4	0
50–54	0.5	0
55 and over	0.2	0

Table 49. Distribution of trade types (%): 58th Foot (1803) and BSC sample

Type of trade	58th Foot (1803)	BSC sample
No trade	0	0
Laborers	47.6	44.9
Textile workers	31.6	30.1
Other trades	20.8	25.0

Table 50. Distribution of the most frequently listed trades (%): 58th Foot (1803) and BSC sample

Trade	58th Foot (1803)	BSC sample
Laborer	47.6	44.9
Weaver	21.3	17.3
Tailor	5.7	5.8
Shoemaker	5.0	3.9

Comparison of the BSC Sample to the General Return for the 20th Light Dragoons (May 1810)

Table 51. Nationality (%): 20th Lt. Dragoons (1810) and BSC sample

Nationality	20th Lt. Dragoons (1810)	BSC sample
English	77.5	65.5
Irish	19.1	12.7
Scottish	2.4	3.2
Foreign	1.0	18.6

Table 52. Height (inches): 20th Lt. Dragoons (1810) and BSC sample

Height	20th Lt. Dragoons (1810)	BSC sample
Mean	66.7	67.0
Maximum	72	71
Standard deviation	1.62	1.46

Table 53. Age (%): 20th Lt. Dragoons (1810) and BSC sample

Age bracket	20th Lt. Dragoons (1810)	BSC sample
Under 20	11.4	0.9
20–24	27.7	41.0
25–29	33.4	34.5
30–34	19.9	15.9
35–39	5.3	5.3
40–44	1.7	1.8
45–49	0.5	0.6
50–54	0	0
55 and over	0	0

Characteristics of Enlistees in 1806

As discussed in chapter 3, 1806 was a banner year for recruiting. The spike in enlistment for that year merits closer examination of that year's enlistees.

Table 54. Nationality of the 1806 sample by branch

Branch	English	Irish	Scottish	Foreign	Total
Artillery	27	23	9	0	59
Cavalry	62	6	1	5	74
Infantry	760	121	76	7	964
Total	849	150	86	12	1,097

Table 55. Nationality of the 1806 sample by branch (%)

Branch	English	Irish	Scottish	Foreign	Total
Artillery	2.5	2.1	0.8	0	5.4
Cavalry	5.7	0.6	0.1	0.4	6.8
Infantry	69.3	11.0	6.9	0.6	87.8
Total	77.5	13.7	7.8	1.0	100

Table 56. Percent of each branch's enlistees of each nationality in 1806

Branch	English	Irish	Scottish	Foreign	Total
Artillery	45.8	39.0	15.3	0	100
Cavalry	83.8	8.1	1.4	6.8	100
Infantry	78.8	12.6	7.9	0.7	100

Table 57. Percent of each nationality's enlistees in each branch in 1806

Branch/Country	English	Irish	Scottish	Foreign
Artillery	3.2	15.3	10.5	0.0
Cavalry	7.3	4.0	1.1	41.7
Infantry	89.5	80.7	88.4	58.3
Total	100	100	100	100

Table 58. Trades in 1806 sample

Type of trade	Number	Percent
None	12	1.1
Laborers	418	38.1
Textile workers	363	33.1
Other trades	304	27.7
Total	1,097	100

Table 59. Age distribution of 1806 enlistees

Minimum	Mean	Maximum	Standard Deviation
14	23.1	55	6.71

Appendix B

REGRESSION ANALYSIS USING THE BRITISH SOLDIER COMPENDIUM

The British Soldier Compendium allows for a quantitative examination of the backgrounds and possible motivations of the men in Wellington's army. The records of fluctuating enlistment rates show clear correlation with the economic factors of the time: when the economy worsened, enlistment rose; and when the economy recovered, enlistment plummeted. When the economy was in contraction, older men were forced to enlist, raising the maximum age of enlistees.

To assess these correlations systematically, I undertook a series of analyses using ordinary least squares linear regression. The dependent (explained) variable in all of these regressions is the number of enlistees per year in the BSC sample. The independent (explanatory) variables are meant to represent the economic dislocations that would have caused men to consider the army a viable alternative to mendicancy or starvation.

Bread prices were initially used in this analysis as a measure of changes in the economy at the level of the individual consumer. Since the major fluctuations in prices during this period can be traced to recurring harvest failures that raised the price of grain to extraordinary levels, this approach is a good first approximation of the eco-

nomic pressures on working-class men.[1] Data on average annual
bread prices (in pence) for the city of London were drawn from B.R.
Mitchell and Phyllis Deane's *Abstract of British Historical Statistics*.[2] While these prices are specifically for the London market, they
may be assumed to represent the general trend throughout Great Britain, since prices in major Scottish markets tended to move in concert
with London prices.[3]

Table 60. Regression comparing enlistment and bread prices

R^2	0.29
Coefficient of bread prices	38.7
Confidence level	greater than 99%
Standard error of estimate	210

The results of this regression show that 29 percent of the change
in enlistment from year to year can be explained by changes in bread
prices. The coefficient of bread prices was 38.7, meaning that when
prices rose by one penny this model predicts that 39 more men would
enlist in the BSC sample in that year. This result may not seem significant when compared to the whole of the British army, but it must
be considered in the context of the BSC sample. Since that sample of
7,250 men is taken to represent an army that may have numbered
more than 230,000, the predictions of this model must be scaled up
proportionally to get a sense of their meaning with respect to the
whole army. In other words, 39 more men enlisting in the BSC sample
would be equivalent to 1,237 more men joining the army as a whole
in that year. This gives a much better appreciation of the correlation
between bread prices and enlistment. We can predict with greater
than 99 percent confidence that if bread prices had not risen by one
penny in any given year over a thousand men would not have chosen
to enlist. The true scale of the economic impact on recruiting becomes clear if we consider that when bread prices peaked in 1812 they
were 11.1 pence higher than at their low point in 1792. That difference may have caused an additional 13,731 men to enlist by 1812
compared to 1792. It is apparent in figure 8 that 1806 is an outlier
year; this anomaly is addressed below.

Bread prices only reflect information about a very small portion
of the economy, so it is logical to compare enlistment rates to a wider

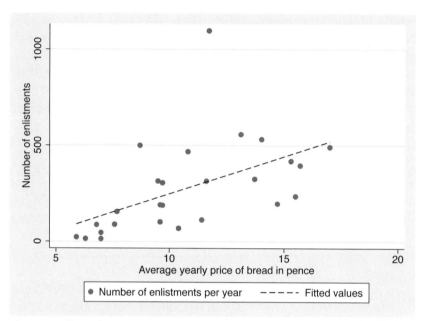

Figure 8. Effect of bread prices on enlistment.

range of economic data. A separate regression was performed that incorporated information on wages, prices, trade, and other social factors in multiple independent variables.

Clearly, the strongest possible proxy for the direct impact of total economic conditions on the working classes in the United Kingdom would be a measurement of purchasing power fluctuations during this time. For this information, Tucker's data on real wages were used.[4] His data form the only complete series found for this period that attempts to measure fluctuations in real wages on a year-to-year scale. Other complete series list data in five- or ten-year increments, which make them too broad to be of use in this analysis. In addition, many series that reflect yearly changes are extremely limited in scope and have multiple gaps where no original source data are available. Tucker's series is constructed from data on a limited area and portion of the population (because of the difficulty of finding complete and consistent source data) but is still the best series found for this period. Therefore, for the purposes of this study, it has been assumed that Tucker's index is at least representative of general fluctuations in real wages for some of the population. I hypothesize that as purchasing power decreases, as represented by real wages, enlistments will rise, all else being equal.

One note of caution applies here. In Tucker's original estimate of real wages, he attempted to include rents in his cost of living estimate by assuming that rents "tended to equal one-sixth of [London artisans'] weekly wage" and proceeded to calculate real wages on this assumption.[5] In the words of Elizabeth Gilboy, another economic historian studying this period, "deflation of a given wage series by means of a cost of living index in which the same wage series is a significant element appears to be a questionable statistical procedure."[6] Tucker published his estimates of money wages and his cost of living index without including wages separately from his estimate of real wages, perhaps because he anticipated such critiques. Tucker's study used the series for money wages and cost of living to generate an estimate of real wages excluding rents. Given the argument that rents tended to change only slowly,[7] it is unlikely that rents had a significant impact on the fluctuations of purchasing power over the comparatively short time (in economic terms) involved in this study.

This estimate of real wages is not adjusted to take into account the changes in unemployment, both seasonal and long-term, that occurred during this period. Data on unemployment are unavailable because little to no social relief was provided in an organized way at that time.[8] Given this, the fluctuations in army enlistment may actually represent more information about changing employment rates in the private sector than has been available to date.

Napoleon's blockade caused a significant shock to the economy of the United Kingdom during this period. The Continental System was enforced from 1806 through the end of the war with fluctuating effectiveness.[9] Problems with America surrounding the War of 1812 (but beginning years earlier) also limited foreign markets until the end of 1814.[10] In order to represent the impact of the Continental System and the War of 1812 on British trade, data on the yearly volume of imports were drawn from Gayer et al.[11] When the blockade was enforced more carefully and the War of 1812 had an effect on trade, imports presumably fell, and the effects of limited trade spread through the economy in many forms, including fewer jobs. Therefore it is hypothesized that, all else being equal, as imports fall, enlistments will rise.

Even though the continental blockade and the War of 1812 affected both imports and exports, imports alone were used to measure the disruption of the United Kingdom's international commerce. Much historical analysis has gone into demonstrating how the blockade caused exports from the United Kingdom to be shifted from their previous continental destinations to markets in other areas of the world, including especially areas such as Spain and South America that previously had not received much British trade, if any at all.[12] While the United Kingdom's merchants may have been somewhat successful in finding new outlets for their goods, it was not as easy to replace the volume of imports usually drawn from the continent by looking to less developed areas such as South America. Therefore imports alone represent a better approximation of how deeply the blockade may have affected economic conditions in the United Kingdom.

The final piece of data used in analyzing enlistment changes from year to year is a binary variable that is zero before 1806 and one during and after 1806. This variable represents a collection of qualitative factors that influenced recruiting and that all came into existence circa 1806. Most prominent is the initiation of Napoleon's continental blockade in that year; while the explicit effects of the blockade on trade may be measured in the volume of imports, it is also possible that fear of the blockade and anticipation of its economic effects may have led to increased enlistment regardless of whether such economic consequences actually occurred.[13] Concurrently, the mechanization of the spinning, carding, and weaving took hold in Great Britain, throwing thousands out of work.[14] One final variable occurring in the period 1805–1807 is the beginning of the end of the volunteer system, no longer required after Nelson's victory at Trafalgar. This resulted in 100,000 men, many of them poor, being released from service and the supplemental pay that it provided;[15] if even a portion of such men turned to the army for employment, then at least some of the 1806 enlistment increase can be explained. All of these factors may have increased recruiting in 1806 and following years, so it is hypothesized that this variable will have a positive coefficient.

Table 61. Regression comparing enlistment and multiple economic factors

R^2	0.63
$F(3, 22)$	12.6
Confidence level for F-test	greater than 99%
Standard error of estimate	156

The model as a whole is statistically significant based on the F-test. The R^2 value indicates that 63 percent of the change in enlistment can be explained fully by these combined economic factors. On a human level, this means that the enlistment of almost two-thirds of the men in Wellington's army can be explained solely in terms of economic factors. Given different economic circumstances, these men would not have chosen to enlist. This belies the collective myth of the British regular as a vagabond or psychopath with no home, no occupation, and no redeeming value. Providing more details on this new image of the rank and file, the effects of the various economic factors can be analyzed separately.

Table 62. Effects of independent economic factors on enlistment

Variable	Coefficient	Absolute value of t-statistic	Confidence level for one-tailed t-test
Real wages	−59.9	5.05	greater than 99%
Imports	−26.2	2.76	greater than 99%
Qualitative factors	231	2.93	greater than 99%

An analysis of the coefficients from the regression shows the following:

- When real wages fell by one-hundredth of what they were in 1900, all else being equal, this model estimates that 60 more men would have enlisted that year. This translates to approximately 1,920 more enlistees in the army as a whole (data from Tucker).[16]
- When imports fell by £1 million per year, all else being equal, this model estimates that 26 more men would have enlisted that year or approximately 832 more across the entire army (data from Gayer et al.).[17]
- When the continental blockade was initiated, the mechanization of the textile industry took hold, and the volunteer system began disbanding (all in 1806), this model estimates that 231 more

men would have enlisted that year or approximately 7,392 more recruits in the whole army (binary variable).

A one-tailed *t*-test was used for the confidence levels shown in the table because there were directional hypotheses about all three variables based on qualitative information. All three independent variables are statistically significant and show coefficients that confirm the hypotheses.

The variable that has the largest single effect is the qualitative factors that take hold in 1806. This is unsurprising, because that variable represents a combination of events and influences, including the growing effects of Napoleon's blockade, the Industrial Revolution, and the dissolution of the volunteer system. The year 1806 still appears as an outlier, based on internally studentized residuals and leverages, but the size of the residual has been significantly reduced from the previous model. There is always the possibility of sampling error causing that outlier, but it is much more likely that the confluence of unusual events in that year cannot be fully captured quantitatively. Aside from showing 1806 as an outlier, all other statistical tests showed that this model is valid and reliable.[18]

If any of the men in the army were driven to enlist because they were forced out of work by economic circumstances, it is expected that some of these men would be older (possibly aged 25, 30, or more). Comparing some features of the groups of enlistees from good economic years and bad economic years substantiates this argument. In bad economic years, it appears that there are more enlistees with a previous occupation other than laborer and that the enlistees are, on the whole, older.

Table 63. Characteristics of enlistees in poor economic years

Year	Number of enlistees	Enlistees with a trade other than laborer (%)	Maximum age of enlistees	Enlistees age 30 and older (%)
1800	419	67.8	48	7.4
1806	1,097	60.8	55	13.9
1812	492	59.1	50	12.4

Table 64. Characteristics of enlistees in good economic years

Year	Number of enlistees	Enlistees with a trade other than laborer (%)	Maximum age of enlistees	Enlistees age 30 and older (%)
1803	500	39.8	50	13.0
1810	197	41.6	37	3.6
1813	396	56.8	50	4.0

Appendix C

NUTRITIONAL ANALYSIS
USING THE BRITISH SOLDIER
COMPENDIUM

METHODS

To clarify and put into perspective the impact of diet on the ordinary British soldier of the Napoleonic Wars, I have examined
dietary data from a wide range of sources. In order to evaluate the
diets of various armies across time, historical examples of military
rations from the late Roman army, fourteenth- and sixteenth-century
Mediterranean oarsmen and galley slaves, sixteenth-century Spanish
soldiers and sailors, and soldiers in the English Civil War were gathered and compared to the standard rations of the British soldier in the
Napoleonic period. I analyzed these diets in terms of macronutrients
(energy, carbohydrates, fat, and protein) and micronutrients (necessary vitamins and minerals). This appendix explains in detail the
sources and methods used to analyze the components of each diet.

All the food items described in historical sources were matched
with the closest equivalent in the *USDA National Nutrient Database for Standard Reference, Release 20.*[1] Bread was the single most
difficult food to analyze because of the inaccuracy of comparison
to modern equivalents. The *National Nutrient Database* entries for
modern bread assume the use of modern flour, which is enriched with

substances such as folate,[2] and modern milk, which is supplemented with Vitamin A and other essential nutrients. This supplementation would misrepresent the historical diets as being much more valuable in terms of some essential nutrients than they actually were. Descriptions of bakers' methods indicated that a one-pound baked loaf would have been made from some 20 ounces of unbaked dough, which contained only flour, water, and small amounts of yeast and salt. The dough would have required varying amounts of water based on the precise quality of the flour as well as a myriad of environmental factors, but the flour would have absorbed at least half its weight in water or more.[3] This would result in a dough composed of two-thirds flour and one-third water, by weight. By this reasoning, 20 ounces of dough would contain 13⅓ ounces of flour or just under 400 g. Thus, one pound (454 g) of baked bread or biscuit was counted in the nutritional analysis as 400 g unenriched flour, with the assumption that the remaining weight consisted of water and negligible amounts of yeast and salt. Figures for unenriched flour were drawn from the database entry for "wheat flour, white, all-purpose, unenriched."

Meat formed a staple of many armies' rations, particularly as a protein source. One pound of meat ration was evaluated as the edible portion of one pound of meat, excluding refuse, as defined in the *National Nutrient Database* for "beef, composite of trimmed retail cuts, separable lean and fat, trimmed to ⅛" fat, all grades, cooked" (with 13 percent bone weight). For the British soldier, who often complained of small portions and questionable meat quality, these values were scaled down to allow for 20 percent bone weight. Since this analysis assumes trimming of fat and restricts itself to modern retail cuts, it probably overestimates the nutritional value of the rations in terms of protein and slightly underestimates the value in terms of fat.

Other major sources of protein included cheese and beans, depending on the culture involved. Cheese was analyzed as "cheese, cheddar." Cheddar was deemed a reasonable choice because any cheese purchased and transported for long periods by an army must have been a hard cheese and various choices in this category led to highly similar results. Individuals on board Spanish and Venetian galleys are reported to have consumed garbanzo beans as part of their daily rations; these are evaluated as "chickpeas, mature seeds, cooked, boiled, with salt." The bacon that officers, sailors, and soldiers aboard Spanish galleys also consumed as part of their diets was treated as "pork, cured, bacon, cooked, broiled, pan-fried or roasted," while the salt pork supplied to Venetian oarsmen was analyzed as "pork, cured, salt pork, raw." The other component of the diets of nonslaves aboard Spanish galleys was fish; this was taken to be sea-trout or a similar fish.

Armies' daily rations frequently included alcohol of some type. Wine was analyzed as "alcoholic beverage, wine, table, all," and rum was evaluated as "alcoholic beverage, distilled, rum, 80 proof." Beer was assumed to be equivalent to "alcoholic beverage, beer, regular." Other additions to military diets included oil, analyzed as "oil, olive, salad or cooking," and vinegar, taken to be "vinegar, cider."

For some soldiers, such as the officers, soldiers, and sailors aboard Spanish galleys, the diet included a regular rotation of various components. In this case, the typical diet for a week was averaged in order to approximate the daily intake. For the common soldier in the English Civil War, the rations were expressed with alternatives: one pound of meat or one pound of cheese, one bottle of wine or two bottles of beer. These analyses averaged the results over all possibilities, since no information on the frequency of each alternative was available. For the British soldier in the Napoleonic period, the values for wine, which was occasionally supplied in place of rum, are given separately, but the summary information assumes the use of rum, which was far more common. Thus, the totals include rum for six days, with wine substituted on the seventh day.

After describing the rations in terms of energy, carbohydrates, fat, and protein, I compared the total values for all the armies in terms of both raw units and the percent of calories coming from each type of nutrient. These caloric amounts were calculated using the standard Atwater factors for amount of digestible calories available per gram of nutrient.[4] This calculation allowed the distribution of calories in the diet to be compared to modern recommendations. In addition, a more detailed analysis used the same *USDA National Nutrient Database* entries (except for bread, as mentioned above) to assess the amount of vitamins and minerals available in each type of food. These values were summarized in terms of percent of Dietary Reference Intakes for individuals, as determined by the Institute of Medicine.[5] The percentages of Dietary Reference Intakes translate the raw content of the historical diets into terms that can be compared to modern recommendations to determine the possible ill-effects of their diet on the men.

DIET ANALYSIS: CALORIES, CARBOHYDRATES, FAT, AND PROTEIN

Table 65. Nutritional breakdown of standard rations for the Roman soldier

Daily allowance	3 lb bread	1 lb meat*	33.8 fl oz wine	1.6 fl oz oil	Totals
Calories	4,368	829	828	382	6,407
Carbohydrates (grams)	915	0	0	0	915
Fat (grams)	12	56	0	43	111
Protein (grams)	123	75	0	0	198

Source: Goldsworthy, Roman Army at War, 291. Goldsworthy states that this was the smallest daily ration recorded.
* This includes 13 percent bone.

Table 66. Nutritional breakdown of standard rations for the common soldier serving in the English Civil War

Daily allowance	2 lb bread	1 lb meat	1 lb cheese in place of meat	1 bottle of wine*	2 bottles of beer in place of wine	Totals, averaged over different possibilities
Calories	2,912	829	1,828	294	307	4,541
Carbohydrates (grams)	610	0	6	0	22	624
Fat (grams)	8	56	150	0	0	111
Protein (grams)	82	75	113	0	2	177

Source: Ration details provided by Sir James Turner, who fought with the Swedish, Scots, and later Royalist armies. Young and Holmes, English Civil War, 50.
* A bottle of beer today is 12 ounces, which is the volume used in determining these values.

Table 67. Nutritional breakdown of rations for 16th-century Spanish officers, soldiers, and sailors aboard galleys

Weekly allowance	26 oz biscuit (seven days)	34 fl oz wine (seven days)	8 oz beef (three days)	6 oz bacon (one day)	6 oz cheese (one day)	6 oz fish (one day)	Daily average*
Calories	2,366	832	415	920	686	323	3,654
Carbohydrates (grams)	496	0	0	2	2	0	496
Fat (grams)	7	0	28	71	56	14	39
Protein (grams)	67	0	37.65	63	42	45	105

Colección Navarrete, vol. 12, fol. 313, dto. 84. Corroborating examples may be found in *Colección Navarrete*, vol. 12, fol. 371, dto. 100, and vol. 8, fol. 114, dto. 14, and in *Colección Sanz de Barutell (Simancas), Artículo 5*, dto. 2, fols. 5–14, dto. 12, fols. 45–47, dto. 17, fols. 59–62, and *Artículo 4*, dto. 322, fols. 420–22, cited in Guilmartin, *Gunpowder and Galleys*, 223.
* This daily average includes totals for the seventh day, which was meatless.

Table 68. Nutritional breakdown of standard rations for 14th-century Venetian oarsmen

Daily allowance	25.2 oz biscuit	1.1 pt wine	1.41 oz cheese	1.83 oz salt pork	0.6 cup garbanzo beans	Totals with wine
Calories	2,293	431	161	388	161	3,434
Carbohydrates (grams)	481	0	0	0	27	508
Fat (grams)	6	0	13	42	3	64
Protein (grams)	65	0	10	3	9	87

Lane, "Venetian Merchant Galleys," 179–203. Compiled nutritional data from this work and notations identifying the primary sources that follow were generously provided by Dr. John Guilmartin.

Table 69. Nutritional breakdown of minimal standard rations for
16th-century Spanish galley slaves

Daily allowance	26 oz biscuit	0.6 cup garbanzo beans	0.21 fl oz oil	0.6 fl oz vinegar	Totals
Calories	2,366	161	50	4	2,581
Carbohydrates (grams)	496	27	0	0	523
Fat (grams)	7	3	6	0	16
Protein (grams)	67	9	0	0	76

Colección Navarrete, vol. 12, fol. 371, dto. 100. Corroborating examples may be found in *Colección Navarrete*, vol. 12, fol. 313, dto. 84, vol. 8, fol. 114, dto. 14, and in *Colección Sanz de Barutell (Simancas)*, *Artículo 5*, dto. 2, fols. 5–14, dto. 12, fols. 45–47, dto. 17, fols. 59–62, and *Artículo 4*, dto. 322, fols. 420–22, cited in Guilmartin, *Gunpowder and Galleys*, 223.

Table 70. Nutritional breakdown of standard rations for the British
common soldier during the Napoleonic Wars

Daily allowance	1 lb biscuit	1 lb meat*	5.3 fl oz rum	15.9 fl oz wine in place of rum	Totals with rum**	Totals with wine
Calories	1,456	663	340	389	2,459	2,508
Carbohydrates (grams)	305	0	0	0	305	305
Fat (grams)	4	44	0	0	48	48
Protein (grams)	41	60	0	0	101	101

* Includes 20 percent bone.
** The rum allocation was usually a part of the standard ration, with wine being used as a substitute only in rare cases. The men much preferred the rum, with its higher alcohol content.

Diet Analysis: Essential Micronutrients

Table 71. Vitamin and mineral analysis of Roman soldier's diet

Nutrient	1 lb meat	33.8 fl oz wine	3 lb bread*	3.2 tbsp olive oil	Totals	DRI**	Percent DRI consumed
Calcium (mg)	26	80	180	0	286	1,000	29
Copper (mg)	0.32	0.07	1.73	0	2.12	900	0
Iron (mg)	7.64	3.69	14.04	0.24	25.61	8	320
Magnesium (mg)	66	110	264	0	440	400	110
Manganese (mg)	0.04	1.24	8.18	0	9.46	2.3	411
Phosphorus (mg)	593	199	1,296	0	2,088	700	298
Potassium (mg)	909	987	1,284	0	3,180	4,700	68
Selenium (μg)	56.4	2.0	406.8	0	465.2	55	846
Sodium (mg)	180	50	24	1	255	1,500	17
Zinc (mg)	17.1	1.30	8.4	0	26.8	11	243
Folate (μg)	20	10	312	0	342	400	86
Niacin (mg)	10.6	1.66	15	0	27.26	16	170
Pantothenic acid (mg)	1.02	0.37	5.26	0	6.65	5	133
Riboflavin (mg)	0.63	0.23	0.48	0	1.34	1.3	103
Thiamin (mg)	0.26	0.05	1.44	0	1.75	1.2	146
Vitamin A (IU)	0	0	0	0	0	900	0
Vitamin B-6 (mg)	0.97	0.54	0.53	0	2.04	1.3	157
Vitamin B-12 (μg)	7.04	0	0	0	7.04	90	8
Vitamin C (mg)	0	0	0	0	0	90	0
Vitamin D (IU)	0	0	0	0	0	200	0
Vitamin E (mg)	0.51	0	0.72	6.20	7.43	15	50
Vitamin K (μg)	5.1	0	3.6	26	34.7	120	29

Note: μg = micrograms; IU = International Units.
* 1,200 g unenriched flour.
** DRI = Dietary Reference Intakes.

Table 72. Vitamin and mineral analysis of common soldier's diet in the English Civil War

Nutrient	2 lb bread*	1 lb beef	1 lb cheese**	2 bottles beer	1 bottle wine	Totals, average	DRI	Percent DRI consumed
Calcium (mg)	120	26	3,270	29	28	1,796.5	1,000	180
Copper (mg)	1.15	0.32	0.14	0.04	0.03	1.42	900	0
Iron (mg)	9.36	7.64	3.08	0.14	1.31	15.7	8	196
Magnesium (mg)	176	66	127	43	39	313.5	400	78
Manganese (mg)	5.5	0.04	0.05	0.06	0.44	5.8	2.3	252
Phosphorus (mg)	864	593	2,322	100	71	2,399.5	700	343
Potassium (mg)	856	909	445	192	350	1,804	4,700	38
Selenium (µg)	271.2	56.4	63.1	4.3	0.7	333.45	55	606
Sodium (mg)	16	180	28.2	29	18	143.6	1,500	10
Zinc (mg)	5.6	17.10	14.1	0.07	0.46	21.47	11	195
Folate (µg)	208	20	82	43	4	282.5	400	71
Niacin (mg)	10	10.6	0.36	3.66	0.59	17.6	16	110
Pantothenic acid (mg)	3.5	1.03	1.87	0.29	0.13	5.16	5	103
Riboflavin (mg)	0.32	0.63	1.7	0.18	0.08	1.61	1.3	124
Thiamin (mg)	0.96	0.26	0.12	0.04	0.02	1.18	1.2	98
Vitamin A (IU)	0	0	4,545	0	0	2,272.5	900	252
Vitamin B-6 (mg)	0.35	0.97	0.33	0.33	0.19	1.09	1.3	84
Vitamin B-12 (µg)	0	7.04	3.76	0.14	0	5.47	90	6
Vitamin C (mg)	0	0	0	0	0	0	90	0
Vitamin D (IU)	0	0	54	0	0	27	200	14
Vitamin E (mg)	0.48	0.51	1.32	0	0	1.40	15	9
Vitamin K (µg)	2.4	5.1	12.7	0	0	11.3	120	9

Note: µg = micrograms; "IU = International Units.
* 800 g unenriched flour.
** Instead of meat

Table 73. Vitamin and mineral analysis of 16th-century Spanish soldier, sailor, or officer's diet aboard a galley

Nutrient	26 oz biscuit*	34 fl oz wine (seven days)	8 oz beef (three days)	6 oz bacon (one day)	6 oz fish (one day)	6 oz cheese (one day)	Totals, average	DRI	Percent DRI consumed
Calcium (mg)	98	80	13	19	94	1226	374.86	1,000	37
Copper (mg)	0.94	0.07	0.16	0.28	0.41	0.05	1.18	900	0.1
Iron (mg)	7.60	3.71	3.82	2.45	3.26	1.16	13.93	8	174
Magnesium (mg)	143	110	33	56	48	48	288.86	400	72
Manganese (mg)	4.43	1.24	0.02	0.04	1.86	0.02	5.95	2.3	259
Phosphorus (mg)	702	201	296	906	534	871	1360	700	194
Potassium (mg)	696	993	455	960	787	167	2157.42	4,700	46
Selenium (μg)	220.3	2	28.2	105.4	27.5	23.6	256.74	55	467
Sodium (mg)	13	50	90	3,927	114	1056	829.71	1,500	55
Zinc (mg)	4.55	1.3	8.55	5.95	1.44	5.29	11.33	11	103
Folate (μg)	169	10	10	3	26	31	191.86	400	48
Niacin (mg)	8.13	1.67	5.3	18.9	9.8	0.14	13.39	16	84
Pantothenic acid (mg)	2.85	0.37	0.51	1.99	3.80	0.70	4.37	5	87
Riboflavin (mg)	0.26	0.23	0.31	0.45	0.72	0.64	0.88	1.3	68
Thiamin (mg)	0.78	0.05	0.13	0.69	0.72	0.05	1.09	1.2	91
Vitamin A (IU)	0	0	0	63	107	1704	267.71	900	30
Vitamin B-6 (mg)	0.29	0.54	0.49	0.59	0.39	0.13	1.2	1.3	92
Vitamin B-12 (μg)	0	0	3.52	2.09	12.73	1.41	3.83	90	4
Vitamin C (mg)	0	0	0	0	0	0	0	90	0
Vitamin D (IU)	0	0	0	0	0	20	2.86	200	1.4
Vitamin E (mg)	0.39	0	0.26	0.53	0	0.49	0.65	15	4
Vitamin K (μg)	1.9	0	2.6	0.2	0	4.8	3.73	120	3

Note: μg = micrograms; IU = International Units.
* 650 g unenriched flour.

Table 74. Vitamin and mineral analysis of 14th-century Venetian oarsman's diet

Nutrient	25.2 oz biscuit*	0.6 cup garbanzo beans	1.1 pt wine	1.41 oz cheddar cheese	1.83 oz salt pork	Totals	DRI	Percent DRI consumed
Calcium (mg)	94	48	42	288	3	475	1,000	48
Copper (mg)	0.91	0.35	0.04	0.01	0.03	1.34	900	0.1
Iron (mg)	7.37	2.84	1.92	0.27	0.23	12.63	8	158
Magnesium (mg)	139	47	57	11	4	258	400	65
Manganese (mg)	4.3	1.01	0.64	0.004	0.003	5.96	2.3	259
Phosphorus (mg)	680	165	104	205	27	1,181	700	169
Potassium (mg)	674	286	514	39	34	1,547	4,700	33
Selenium (μg)	213.6	3.6	1	5.6	3	226.8	55	412
Sodium (mg)	13	239	26	248	739	1,265	1,500	84
Zinc (mg)	4.41	1.51	0.67	1.24	0.47	8.3	11	75
Folate (μg)	164	169	5	7	1	346	400	87
Niacin (mg)	7.88	0.52	0.86	0.03	0.84	10.13	16	63
Pantothenic acid (mg)	2.76	0.28	0.19	0.17	0.11	3.51	5	70
Riboflavin (mg)	0.25	0.06	0.12	0.15	0.03	0.61	1.3	47
Thiamin (mg)	0.76	0.11	0.26	0.01	0.11	1.25	1.2	104
Vitamin A (IU)	0	27	0	401	0	428	900	48
Vitamin B-6 (mg)	0.28	0.14	0.28	0.03	0.04	0.77	1.3	59
Vitamin B-12 (μg)	0	0	0	0.33	0.15	0.48	90	1
Vitamin C (mg)	0	0	0	0	0	0	90	0
Vitamin D (IU)	0	0	0	5	0	5	200	2.5
Vitamin E (mg)	0.38	0.34	0	0.12	0	0.84	15	6
Vitamin K (μg)	1.9	3.9	0	1.1	0	6.9	120	6

Note: μg = micrograms; IU = International Units.
* 630 g unenriched flour.

Table 75. Vitamin and mineral analysis of 16th-century Spanish galley slave's diet

Nutrient	26 oz biscuit*	0.6 cup garbanzo beans	0.21 fl oz oil	0.6 fl oz vinegar	Totals	DRI	Percent DRI consumed
Calcium (mg)	98	48	0	1	147	1,000	15
Copper (mg)	0.94	0.35	0	0.001	1.29	900	0.1
Iron (mg)	7.60	2.84	0.03	0.04	10.51	8	131
Magnesium (mg)	143	47	0	1	191	400	48
Manganese (mg)	4.43	1.01	0	0.05	5.49	2.3	239
Phosphorus (mg)	702	165	0	1	868	700	124
Potassium (mg)	696	286	0	13	995	4,700	21
Selenium (μg)	220.3	3.6	0	0	223.9	55	407
Sodium (mg)	13	239	0	1	253	1,500	17
Zinc (mg)	4.55	1.51	0	0.01	6.07	11	55
Folate (μg)	169	169	0	0	338	400	85
Niacin (mg)	8.13	0.52	0	0	8.65	16	54
Pantothenic acid (mg)	2.85	0.28	0	0	3.13	5	63
Riboflavin (mg)	0.26	0.06	0	0	0.32	1.3	25
Thiamin (mg)	0.78	0.11	0	0	0.89	1.2	74
Vitamin A (IU)	0	27	0	0	27	900	3
Vitamin B-6 (mg)	0.29	0	0	0	0.29	1.3	22
Vitamin B-12 (μg)	0	0	0	0	0	90	0
Vitamin C (mg)	0	0	0	0	0	90	0
Vitamin D (IU)	0	0	0	0	0	200	0
Vitamin E (mg)	0.39	0	0.81	0	1.2	15	8
Vitamin K (μg)	1.9	3.9	3.4	0	9.2	120	8

Note: μg = micrograms; IU = International Units.
* 650 g unenriched flour.

Table 76. Vitamin and mineral analysis of British common soldier's diet during the Napoleonic Wars

Nutrient	1 lb biscuit*	1 lb meat**	5.3 fl oz rum	15.9 fl oz wine	Totals with rum	Totals with wine	DRI	Percent DRI consumed***
Calcium (mg)	60	21	0	38	81	119	1,000	9
Copper (mg)	0.58	0.26	0.07	0.03	0.91	0.87	900	0
Iron (mg)	4.68	6.12	0.18	1.74	10.98	12.54	8	140
Magnesium (mg)	88	53	0	52	141	193	400	37
Manganese (mg)	2.73	0.03	0.03	0.6	2.79	3.36	2.3	125
Phosphorus (mg)	432	474	7	94	913	1,000	700	132
Potassium (mg)	428	727	3	464	1,158	1,619	4.700	26
Selenium (µg)	135.6	45.1	0	0.9	180.7	181.6	55	329
Sodium (mg)	8	144	1	23	153	175	1,500	10
Zinc (mg)	2.8	13.7	0.1	0.61	16.6	17.11	11	151
Folate (µg)	104	16	0	5	120	125	400	30
Niacin (mg)	5	8.48	0	0.78	13.48	14.26	16	85
Pantothenic acid (mg)	1.75	0.82	0	0.17	2.57	2.74	5	52
Riboflavin (mg)	0.16	0.5	0	0.11	0.66	0.77	1.3	52
Thiamin (mg)	0.48	0.21	0.01	0.02	0.7	0.71	1.2	58
Vitamin A (IU)	0	0	0	0	0	0	900	0
Vitamin B-6 (mg)	0.18	0.78	0	0.25	0.96	1.21	1.3	77
Vitamin B-12 (µg)	0	5.63	0	0	5.63	5.63	90	6
Vitamin C (mg)	0	0	0	0	0	0	90	0
Vitamin D (IU)	0	0	0	0	0	0	200	0
Vitamin E (mg)	0.24	0.41	0	0	0.65	0.65	15	4
Vitamin K (µg)	1.2	4.08	0	0	5.28	5.28	120	4

Note: µg = micrograms; IU = International Units.
* 400 g unenriched flour.
** Including the bone. Calculated as 0.8 lbs to allow for the weight of the bone, problems involving portion sizes, and meat quality (stringy/grizzled/spoiled).
*** Calculated using the rum ration for six days and wine for one.

ESTIMATION OF CALORIC NEEDS OF THE BRITISH RANKER

Estimates based on population studies show that the average BMI for men in 1800 to 1819 was about 20.7.[6] I used two different approaches to approximate the average caloric needs of the British common soldier. Both methods depended on calculating the total energy expended (TEE) in a day, using a current formula that represents the TEE of modern adults with a not particularly active lifestyle.[7] This calculation should be a reasonable estimate of the British ranker's needs, if something of an underestimate. In one approach, I found the TEE for several different combinations of typical heights, ages, and BMIs and then averaged it across the entire set; in the other approach,

I found the TEE for a British soldier possessing the average height and average age based on the BSC and the estimated BMI. Both methods agreed closely on the average caloric needs of men in this part of the population.

Table 77. Total energy expenditure for an average British ranker

Age*	Height (inches)*	BMI	Weight (lbs)	TEE (calories)
22.5	66.3	20.7	130	3,044

* For the age and height distribution of men in the BSC, see appendix A.

All possible combinations of typical ages, heights, and BMIs included ages in five-year increments from 15 to 40, the average height plus and minus one and two standard deviations, and a BMI of 20, 20.5, 21, 21.5, or 22. This resulted in 150 different possibilities for analysis. The first six lines of table 78 are an example of how the full calculations were done; the rest of the calculations are collapsed, with all age groups for given physical characteristics represented on one line and the corresponding range of caloric needs given on the right. Note that caloric needs decrease with age, so the maximum amount listed on each line is for 15-year-olds, while the minimum is for 40-year-olds (and other age groups would be in between).

Table 78. Total energy expenditure for all plausible body types and ages

Age(s)	Height (inches)	BMI	Weight (lbs)	TEE (calories)
15	61.5	20	107	2,945
20	61.5	20	107	2,858
25	61.5	20	107	2,771
30	61.5	20	107	2,683
35	61.5	20	107	2,596
40	61.5	20	107	2,509
15–40	63.9	20	116	2,603–3,039
15–40	66.3	20	125	2,701–3,137
15–40	68.7	20	134	2,801–3,237
15–40	70.7	20	142	2,887–3,323
15–40	61.5	20.5	110	2,532–2,969
15–40	63.9	20.5	118	2,629–3,065
15–40	66.3	20.5	128	2,728–3,164
15–40	68.7	20.5	137	2,830–3,266
15–40	70.7	20.5	145	2,918–3,354
15–40	61.5	21	113	2,556–2,992
15–40	63.9	21	122	2,654–3,090
15–40	66.3	21	131	2,755–3,191
15–40	68.7	21	141	2,860–3,296
15–40	70.7	21	149	2,949–3,385
15–40	61.5	21.5	115	2,579–3,016
15–40	63.9	21.5	125	2,679–3,116
15–40	66.3	21.5	134	2,783–3,219
15–40	68.7	21.5	144	2,889–3,325
15–40	70.7	21.5	153	2,980–3,416
15–40	61.5	22	118	2,603–3,039
15–40	63.9	22	128	2,705–3,141
15–40	66.3	22	137	2,810–3,246
15–40	68.7	22	147	2,918–3,354
15–40	70.7	22	156	3,011–3,447

The results for extraordinary caloric expenditures compiled in table 79 were derived by using the same methods and nutritional data described throughout this appendix. Weight loss was calculated using 3,600 calories per pound as the standard.[8] The calculations of energy expended rely on METS (metabolic equivalents for each activity), defined as one calorie per kilogram bodyweight per hour.[9] A march rate of 20 miles a day is assumed.[10]

Table 79. Examples of extraordinary caloric expenditure

Campaign experience	Total energy expenditure (calories)	Rations	Calories provided	Approximate caloric deficit	Potential weight loss (lbs)
Marching 25 miles then running 4 miles into battle[a]	2,438 marching and 384 running plus about 3,000 normal daily expenditure[b]	Standard	2,466	3,356	0.9
One day without rations[c]	3,000	1 quart roasted chestnuts	1,401	1,599[d]	0.4, plus effects of protein-deficiency
Marching four and a half days[e]	9,750 marching plus about 12,000 normal daily expenditure	A half allowance of biscuit	728	21,022	5.8, plus effects of protein deficiency
Two days without rations[f]	6,000	None	None	6,000	1.7, plus effects of protein deficiency
Marching 16 miles[g]	1,560 plus about 3,000 normal daily expenditure	Standard with 2 oz. rice	2,466 plus 65 for rice[h]	2,029	0.6
One day without rations[i]	3,000	Ground bark	None[j]	3,000	0.8, plus effects of protein deficiency
Two days without bread or rum while pursuing French[k]	3,900 marching plus about 6,000 normal daily expenditure[l]	2 lbs meat (with bone)	1,326	8,574	2.4
A 42-mile march over one day[m]	4,095 marching plus about 3,000 normal daily expenditure	Standard	2,466	4,629	1.3
A 30-mile march in a day and a half[n]	2,925 plus about 6,000 normal daily expenditure	Standard	2,466	6,459	1.8
Three days on minimum rations[o]	9,000, if at rest; 5,850 additional if marching	2 oz. bread and 2 oz. flour	415	14,435	4.0, plus effects of protein-deficiency
Marching 32 miles in two days over the mountains[p]	3,120 marching plus about 6,000 normal daily expenditure	Standard but with little or no water	4,932	4,188	1.2, plus effects of dehydration

Table 79. *Continued*

Campaign experience	Total energy expenditure (calories)	Rations	Calories provided	Approximate caloric deficit	Potential weight loss (lbs)
Two-day march[q]	3,900 marching plus about 6,000 normal daily expenditure	2 lbs biscuit and half rum ration	3,082	6,818	1.9, plus effects of protein deficiency
A routine of 18 miles in one day[r]	5,070 marching plus about 3,000 normal daily expenditure	Standard	2,466	5,604	1.6
Three-day march[s]	5,850 marching plus about 9,000 normal daily expenditure	1 lb bread and meat, barley acorns, and small beans	2,119 for bread and meat, 110 per oz of acorns, 254 per cup of beans[t]	12,257 with 2 oz acorns and 1 cup beans	3.4, plus effects of protein-deficiency

[a]Cooper, *Rough Notes*, 8.
[b]Calculated assuming that the men marched about 4 mph and ran about 5 mph.
[c]Costello, *Peninsular and Waterloo Campaigns*, 72.
[d]Calculated as four cups of roasted European chestnuts, "nuts, chestnuts, European, roasted," from the *USDA National Nutrient Database*.
[e]Wheeler, *Letters*, 49–50.
[f]Donaldson, *Recollections*, 111.
[g]Green, *Vicissitudes of a Soldier's Life*, 63, 71.
[h]Value for "white, unenriched, long-grain rice, cooked," from the *USDA National Nutrient Database*.
[i]O'Neil, *Military Adventures*, 156.
[j]It is highly unlikely that the British soldier could absorb any substantial nutritive value out of ground bark because of its extreme fiber content, which made it hard to digest. See *Energy and Protein Requirements*, 118–20, 139.
[k]Donaldson, *Recollections*, 111. The British were chasing the French through the Pyrenees. Donaldson also mentions receiving half-rations of biscuit on other days.
[l]Includes marching approximately 40 miles.
[m]Harris, *Recollections* (1970 ed.), 71–72. This march distance may seem an exaggeration, but Hibbert points out that General John Hope's division slogged over 47 miles in just over 36 hours in December 1808. Ibid., 48.
[n]Douglas, *Douglas's Tale*, 55. Douglas lamented, "There was no use grumbling and to the road we went, hungry, wet, and weary."
[o]Hennell, *Gentleman Volunteer*, 79. This occurred near Vitoria.
[p]Surtees, *Twenty-five Years in the Rifle Brigade*, 238.
[q]*Soldier of the Seventy-first*, 71. This was on route to Badajoz. The double ration of bread was served in lieu of meat and an alternative day's rations was half a pound of rice per man. "Hunger made little cooking necessary." Ibid., 68.
[r]Ibid., 63. Captain William Stothert corroborates that marches of such a distance, even up very hilly terrain, were not unusual. The men accomplished the 18-mile march in 13 hours. Stothert, *Narrative of the Principle Events of 1809, 1810, and 1811*, 75.
[s]Harley, *Veteran*, 2:62.
[t]Values for "acorns, raw," and "small white beans, mature, cooked," from the *USDA National Nutrient Database*.

Notes

1. Stouffer et al., *American Soldier.*

INTRODUCTION

1. Wellesley became the Duke of Wellington in 1814. For uniformity and clarity, he is referred to as Wellington throughout this book, even though many of the references contained herein predate his elevation to the title.

2. Wellington, *Dispatches*, 10:473; Henry, *Notes of Conversations with the Duke of Wellington*, 10, 13. Wellington did add "but you can hardly conceive such a set brought together, and it really is wonderful that we should have made them the fine fellows they are." He also made other, equally derisive, comments about the soldiers right up to his death that more than offset this qualifier.

3. Oman, *Wellington's Army, 1809–1814*, 211–12; Davies, *Wellington's Army*, 83; Barnett, *Britain and Her Army, 1509–1970*, 170; Bryant, *Years of Victory*, cited in Strawson, *Beggars in Red*, 222; Glover, *Wellington as Military Commander*, 20–21; and *Wellington's Army*, 24; Glover, *Peninsular Preparation*, 176–77; Steppler, "Common Soldier in the Reign of King George III," 121–24; Frey, *British Soldier in America*, 6–7; and Gates, "Transformation of the Army," 143.

4. See Hanson, *Western Way of War*; Goldsworthy, *Roman Army at War*; Lynn, *Bayonets of the Republic*, and *Battle*; McPherson, *For Cause*

and Comrades; Hess, *Union Soldier in Combat;* Linderman, *Embattled Courage;* Bartov, *Hitler's Army;* and Rush, *Hell in Hürtgen Forest.* The social-psychology studies of men in combat are cited below.

5. Shils and Janowitz, "Cohesion and Disintegration," 285. Shils conducted a similar study in 1977, looking at 20,000 young American men who were affected by President Gerald Ford's 1974 clemency program. Shils found the same pattern that he uncovered with Janowitz: "The deserter turned out to be the soldier who has not been integrated into society at large, into his family, or into his military unit." Shils, "Profile of the Military Deserter," 429.

6. Cooley, *Social Organization,* 23, 24, 26.

7. Ibid., 23; Shils and Janowitz, "Cohesion and Disintegration," 283.

8. The British soldier signed on for a life term until 1806, when a limited term of seven years was introduced for the infantry, ten years for the cavalry, and twelve for the artillery. In actuality, the soldier's life term was often less than that, as the government discharged soldiers *en masse* at the conclusion of conflicts. Even after 1806 the great majority of volunteers enlisted for life service.

9. American combat veterans in World War II listed (in descending order) prayer, not letting the other men down, and finishing the job in order to return home as the three most common answers to the query "When the going was tough, which thoughts helped a lot?" Stouffer et al., *American Soldier,* 177–79.

10. I have had the pleasure of discussing this topic with numerous American captains, majors, and lieutenant colonels in military history classes at the U.S. Army Command and General Staff College. They uniformly identify the group and the soldier next to them as the primary catalysts for taking action in combat.

11. Furet and Ozouf found the correlation to be +0.91. Furet and Ozouf, *Reading and Writing,* 16–19.

12. Forest, *Napoleon's Men,* 38.

13. Such a number is consistent with similar studies on literacy rates for the British population in general, which registered in the 58 to 63 percent range for this period and the decade after Waterloo. Nicholas and Steckel quote an average literacy rate of about 58 percent for England (1824–27) using the registrar-general's records, while R. Schofield estimates a rate of about 63 percent utilizing a random sample of slightly less than 300 parish registers from the period 1790–1820. Nicholas and Steckel, "Heights and Living Standards of English Workers," 943; and Schofield, "Dimensions of Literacy."

14. William Lawrence and John Harris are the exceptions. See Lawrence, *Autobiography;* and Harris, *Recollections.*

15. We might conjecture that illiterate men like Lawrence and Harris were more susceptible to economic fluctuations, given their limited educations, and thus more willing (in need) to take the enlistment bounty and army's daily shilling.

16. Forest, *Napoleon's Men,* 23.

17. Concurring with Forest's contention, Hynes (in his work on how and why men preserve their memories of war) describes memoirs as "com-

plex . . . reflective, selective, more consciously constructed." Hynes, "Prologue: The Actual Killing," in *The Soldiers' Tale,* xiv.

18. Ibid.

19. Forest, *Napoleon's Men,* 51–52.

20. It is impossible to say for certain which men in the BSC sample fought in the Peninsular War and which did not. Some regiments never saw service in Portugal or Spain; for these units, such as the 8th and 25th Regiments of Foot and 19th Light Dragoons in the BSC, making a judgment is fairly clear cut. For other regiments, one battalion may have fought in the Iberian campaign while the other did not. In the BSC sample, this was true for the 32nd and 53rd Regiments of Foot. (The two battalions in the BSC did not serve in the Peninsula.) Yet soldiers certainly transferred between battalions and, more rarely, between regiments. Unfortunately, these data were rarely recorded in the battalion description books, which vary in their completeness. Because much of the enlistment information has been lost, I decided that all the available data should be included in the BSC, which is meant to represent the army under Wellington and the army as a whole. In a comparison of the data for men who may not have served in the Peninsula (perhaps 1,830) and those who apparently did (5,420), some minor statistical variation was observed. The numbers for those men who may have participated in the Peninsular War are as follows: mean age 22; height 66.5 inches; about 40 percent listed laborer as their trade. For the men who may not have seen the Peninsula, the numbers are: average age 24; height 65.9 inches; 43 percent laborers. One interesting difference is noteworthy: only 48.5 percent of the men who probably saw Spain and Portugal were English, while 65.4 percent of those who did not were English. This might be because most of the sample of men who may not have been sent to the Iberian Peninsula were from three regiments: the 25th, 53rd, and 32nd Regiments of Foot, who were 81, 69, and 77 percent English, respectively. The problem is determining the nature of a representative sample, given the nationalistic flavor of British regiments and the limited availability of records. Thus, I assume that the information drawn from the BSC is a fairly accurate representation of the Peninsular War army, given the limits of available data. For a guide to which British units fought in Spain and Portugal, see Park and Nafziger, *British Military,* 89–109.

21. See appendix A for specific details and the War Office records used.

22. Steppler, "Common Soldier in the Reign of King George III," iii.

23. Lawrence, *Autobiography.*

24. Lynn, *Bayonets of the Republic,* 61–63.

25. The similarities between the chapter presentations in this book and Lynn's model of soldier motivation (initial, sustaining, and combat) are purposeful.

26. Westbrook, "Potential for Military Disintegration," 247.

27. See chapter 2 and tables 60–64 in appendix B.

28. See the work of Michael Hughes on the honors and recompense accorded to the French soldiers under Napoleon. I would like to thank Dr. Hughes for sharing his dissertation (" 'Vive la république! Vive l'empereur!' ").

29. Westbrook, "Potential for Military Disintegration," 247.

30. Rosen, *War and Human Nature,* 99, 100, 105, 113.

31. Ibid., 124.

32. Bell, *Rough Notes*, 1:42.

33. Grattan, *Adventures with the Connaught Rangers*, 44–45. Captain Thomas Browne wrote of the soldiers' thoroughness when searching for loot. He recalled men using bayonets to thrust through floorboards: when that did not produce satisfaction, they would "water the floor, when, any spot that that had been lately disturbed, would absorb the water first, which led to the detection of many a hidden store of eatables, drinkables, or linen." Browne, *Napoleonic War Journal*, 139.

34. Surtees, *Twenty-five Years in the Rifle Brigade*, 38. Surtees is describing his experiences in Ireland in 1800. Such sufferings and related thefts were common occurrences for the British ranker in the Peninsular War as well. Surtees was raised to the rank of quartermaster-sergeant in the 2nd Battalion of the 95th in 1806 and to officer status as quartermaster of the 3rd Battalion in 1810. That such a man would condone food theft speaks volumes about the soldiers' needs, the widespread frequency of their applied remedies, and the resignation of many officers to the fact that such actions, while regrettable, were necessary for the soldiers' survival.

35. Anton, *Retrospect of a Military Life*, 115.

36. See Grattan, *Adventures with the Connaught Rangers*, 71; Harris, *Recollections* (1970 ed.), 154; and Lawrence, *Autobiography*, 34, 83, 137, 163–64, for a few examples.

37. Macfarlane, "Peninsula Private," 7 (Macfarlane states that someone stole his beef ration); *Soldier of the Seventy-first*, 31–32; and Cooper, *Rough Notes*, 29. Cooper's story of theft involved a sheep's head that he had begged from the cook and that was somehow taken from him without him noticing. It is presumed that alcohol may have played a part in the sequence of events.

38. *Soldier of the Seventy-first*, 37.

39. Anton, *Retrospect of a Military Life*, 63.

40. In the British system, the regiment and battalion were essentially the same organizations. According to Park and Nafzinger in their work on the structure of the British military, the regiment was "an administrative unit which never took the field." Park and Nafzinger, *British Military*, 25. The number of battalions per regiment varied, but most had only two. The second battalion of each regiment, in a greatly reduced form, was stationed in Great Britain and functioned as a recruiting depot of sorts.

41. Lawrence, *Autobiography*, 98.

42. Larpent, *Private Journal*, 2:228. Charles Oman contends that 200 of the 500 courts-martial cases he examined (40 percent) were for desertion. He found that 78 men were shot for that crime during the six years of the war (52 British and 26 foreigners). Oman, "Courts Martial of the Peninsular War," 1710.

43. For the period from January 1811 to May 1814 the British army in the Peninsula averaged 66,772 soldiers. Cantlie, *History of the Army Medical Department*, 1:373.

44. Oman found only a total of 80 cases related to plundering during the war. Oman, "Courts Martial of the Peninsular War," 1711.

45. Wellington, *Dispatches*, 5:549–50, 9:225, 10:106–107, 200.

46. Wellington does mention a specific case of murder at Cascaes involving an artilleryman. In the letter he advocates trying soldiers by the law of the country; if the government preferred such cases to be tried according to the Articles of War, Wellington asked for assistance "in obliging witnesses to come forward and give their testimony on oath." Ibid., 5:502.

47. Esdaile, *Peninsular Eyewitnesses*, 66–67.

48. Esdaile, *Fighting Napoleon*, 11.

49. Esdaile refers to this process of generating French atrocity stories to rouse the Spanish citizenry as the "Spanish 'great fear.'" Ibid., 63. His chapter "The Guerrillas in Context" deals with this problem in detail.

50. Donaldson, *Recollections*, 108–109, 115–16.

51. Esdaile, *Peninsular Eyewitnesses*, 158.

52. Carss, "2nd/53rd in the Peninsula," 3.

53. Esdaile, *Peninsular Eyewitnesses*, 19–20. Baste goes on to describe "some sensible and generous [French] souls" who saved Spanish families from the soldiers.

54. Ibid., 51. This comes from André Miot de Melito, a senior French official.

55 Ibid., 89.

56. Vallée and Pariset, *Carnet d'étapes du dragon Marquant*, 231, cited in Forest, *Napoleon's Men*, 147.

57. Buckley argues that at least 50,000 of the 200,000 casualties suffered by the French army in the Peninsular War can be attributed to guerrillas. Browne, *Napoleonic War Journal*, 344.

58. Esdaile, *Peninsular Eyewitnesses*, 88. The governor of Avila, Abel Hugo, wrote of the French methods of repression, describing "undesirables from the village of Las Vegas de Matute" being executed and mutilated, with their heads and bodies being displayed above a church door and along a main road.

59. Ibid., 21, 88, 125.

60. Esdaile, *Peninsular War*, 195, and *Peninsular Eyewitnesses*, 86.

61. For details on the origins and effectiveness of guerrilla warfare in Spain, see Esdaile, *Fighting Napoleon*. Also useful is Alexander, *Rod of Iron*.

62. Hunt, *Charging against Napoleon*, 183.

63. Heeley, "Journal," 106.

64. Hughes, "'Vive la république! Vive l'empereur!'" 232. His chapter on the possible effects of such values on the behavior of the French soldier is revealing and convincing.

65. Esdaile, *Peninsular War*, 318.

66. Blakeney, *Boy in the Peninsular War*, 274.

1. AN UNJUST REPUTATION

1. Jay Winter and Emmanuel Sivan have compiled some interesting essays on the phenomenon of collective memory. For specifics, see Winter and Sivan, *War and Remembrance in the 20th Century*, 6.

2. Contrary to Wellington apologists, who try to mitigate his derisive words, Wellington's letters and comments lead us to believe that he did in-

deed consider the character of the British soldier to be of questionable nature at best and most unsavory in the majority of cases. The excuses offered to soften his words rarely agree. C. T. Atkinson writes that Wellington's "scum" commentary "was spoken in reference to corporal punishment . . . and in opposition to flogging." Atkinson, " 'Infamous Army,' " 48. Eileen Hathaway argues that Wellington's pejorative words were the result of British soldiers stripping a French treasure convoy before he could confiscate the funds for army use. Hathaway, "Introduction," 9. Michael Glover claims that the comment referred "not to the soldiers but to the men who enlisted." Glover, *Wellington's Army*, 24. Philip Haythornthwaite, however, contends that Wellington "was not adopting a superior attitude by way of condemnation— He . . . used the term to indicate the social background from which they came." Haythornthwaite, *Armies of Wellington*, 44. These contradictions should cause us to question why Wellington made so many disparaging remarks about his soldiers and why historians have interpreted his words so differently in their quest to take the edge off his statements.

3. In psychological terms, the tendency to attribute the behaviors of other people to internal causes and character faults, while underestimating situational factors, is called the fundamental attribution error. Its companion error is the actor-observer bias, which is the personal tendency to attribute one's own behaviors to outside causes rather than to personality traits.

4. Wellington, *Dispatches*, 10:495–96.

5. Wellington, *Supplementary Despatches and Memoranda*, 5:594.

6. Ibid., 5:594, 8:235.

7. Henry, *Notes of Conversations with the Duke of Wellington*, 10. Realizing that his conversations with Wellington were of historical import, Stanhope moved quickly to his writing table each time Wellington left in order to record for posterity the words of the man he so admired.

8. Ibid., 13. This comment seems to typify Wellington's attitude toward the men: he saw them as unsavory characters who somehow managed to win battles for him. The implication is that Wellington's victories were in spite of, not because of, his men. It is doubtful that he intended to garner a greater share of glory by such statements, but that has been the result. His comment about the soldiers being made into "fine fellows" is at odds with the vast majority of his writings on the subject. Perhaps, as has sometimes been suggested, he did not totally despise the rankers. More likely, Wellington was referring to their combat effectiveness, which made him more than appreciative of how the men behaved under fire.

9. Wellington, *Dispatches*, 4:560.

10. Ibid., 5:54.

11. Ibid., 4:567.

12. The letters cited are offered as a representative sample of many such letters in Wellington's dispatches.

13. Ibid., 5:549–50.

14. Ibid., 6:133, 494.

15. Ibid., 7:333.

16. Ibid., 639.

17. Ibid., 1:323; see also 1:31, 36, 37, 44–45, 60, 64–65, 70–71, 76, 188, 194–96, 387–88, 450, 551–52. 18. The commander-in-chief at this time was Sir David Dundas, who replaced the Duke of York after the latter's resignation during a parliamentary investigation into "perceived abuses in purchasing commissions revolving around the Duke's mistress." Linch, "Recruitment of the British Army," 31.

19. Wellington, *Dispatches*, 7:195–96.

20. Ibid., 9:225. He brings up this idea of improving the character and situation of noncommissioned officers again in a letter to Bathurst in February 1813, indicating that the situation had not changed. Ibid., 10:106–107.

21. Ibid., 6:33–34, 16.

22. Ibid., 16.

23. Wellington acknowledged that pay was often one month later than required by regulation. He also added that the men committed other crimes (such as murder and highway robbery) all too frequently, while noting that British logistical convoys were often plundered by those in charge of them, which denied the men necessities. Ibid.

24. Ibid., 9:221–22.

25. Ibid., 9:582.

26. Thomas Carlyle's history of the French Revolution reflects many of these notions regarding the lower classes and the threat they represent. Writing with a passionate intensity, he decries the actions of the French Third Estate, calling them "mobs" and making it a point to emphasize their propensity for violence while downplaying the reasons that drove them to act. Thomas Carlyle, *French Revolution*.

27. In regard to the notion that most officers came from an aristocratic or extremely wealthy background, Michael Glover has shown that less than 2 percent of Wellington's active duty officers were peers or sons of peers. Glover, *Wellington's Army*, 36–37.

28. Scott, *Response of the Royal Army to the French Revolution*, 19.

29. Leach, *Rough Sketches*, 155, 188.

30. Sherer, *Recollections of the Peninsula*, 98, 101. For more examples of the difference between the recollections and experiences of officers and the rank and file, see chapter 3.

31. See the introduction.

32. Not surprisingly, Wellington's words have even percolated into historical fiction. Bernard Cornwell, creator of the popular Richard Sharpe books and television shows, presents a typical depiction. His largely sympathetic series recounts the exploits of a line NCO raised from the ranks to become an officer and the hero of assorted British regiments (notably the 95th Rifles). He writes: "The Light Company were no different to the rest of the army. They were failures, almost to a man, whose failings had led them to courtrooms and jails. They were thieves, drunks, debtors, and murderers, the men Britain wanted out of sight and mind." Cornwell, *Sharpe's Company*, 121.

33. Roger Buckley, however, takes a counterposition and examines evidence other than the testimonial. In his work on the British army in the West Indies, he found no evidence to support the much-repeated perception that

recruits were gathered in jails. Buckley, *British Army in the West Indies*, 105. Silvia Frey, writing on the British soldier in America during the American Revolution, also questions the accuracy of the assessment of British soldiers as the dregs of society. Although she falls back on this position, she does offer some of the first demographic work in an attempt to identify the backgrounds of these men. Her data on the employment backgrounds of recruits from Middlesex, drawn from a small sample, show that over 80 percent listed definable trades. In the BSC sample, 97 percent of volunteers avowed having a previous occupation. Frey, *British Soldier in America*, 13.

34. Glover, *Peninsular Preparation*, 176–77.

35. Bryant, *Years of Victory*, 222.

36. Atkinson, " 'Infamous Army,' " 48.

37. Carss, "2nd/53rd in the Peninsula," 6.

38. Wellington, *Dispatches*, 7:591. Wellington's dissatisfaction with Marshal Beresford's handling of the troops at Albuera and Beresford's dispatch afterward, which Wellington had rewritten by his military secretary, is well known. His esteem for the rank and file's performance, though, seems authentic. For more on Wellington and his dispatches, see Woolgar, "Writing the Dispatch."

39. Sanger, *Englishmen at War*, 252–53.

40. Wellington, *Dispatches*, 10:539.

41. Hunt, *Charging against Napoleon*, 141.

42. Creevey, *Creevey Papers*, 136. While we should not make too much of Wellington's semantic choice in referring to the British redcoat as an "article," the language does seem to reinforce the idea that he may have seen the men more as instruments or commodities rather than as human beings.

43. Longford, *Wellington*, 404.

44. Richardson, *Fighting Spirit*, 27.

45. Longford, *Wellington*, 547.

46. Richardson, *Fighting Spirit*, 27. Like all of Napoleon's writings after Waterloo, most of which were written to minimize his own culpability in his downfall, this assessment may have been more of an excuse than it appears at first blush. Nevertheless, it is noteworthy that Napoleon singled out the British army as meriting inclusion in his wishful reminiscences.

47. Napier, *War in the Peninsula*, 3:271–72. Napier's political views were fairly radical for the time, which may explain why he viewed the common soldier with far greater respect than many men of his social position and rank did.

48. Kincaid, *Adventures in the Rifle Brigade*, 258.

49. Sherer, *Recollections of the Peninsula*, 132.

50. Ibid., 241.

51. Holmes, *Redcoat*, 151.

52. See chapters 3 and 4 for multiple examples of such behavior and the reasons behind it.

53. Porter, *Letters from Portugal and Spain*, 232.

54. McGuffie, "Recruiting the Ranks of the Regular British Army," 123–24.

55. Richardson, *Fighting Spirit*, 59.

56. Esdaile, *Duke of Wellington,* 7. Esdaile's work has been chosen for critical analysis because, unlike most historians who provide summative evaluations of the British soldier based solely on Wellington's various denigrating remarks, he takes the time to furnish evidence to back his conclusions.

57. Porter, *Letters from Portugal and Spain,* 238, 244. It is also worth noting that British soldiers were not immune from attacks by Portuguese civilians. In a letter dated 26 January 1813, Wellington requests Marshal Beresford to notify the governor of Alemtejo about the murder of a British sergeant and private of the 9th Light Dragoons "by banditti which infest the road from Abrantes to Alter do Chao." Wellington, *Dispatches,* 10:35.

58. Gordon, *Journal of a Cavalry Officer,* 150, 158.

59. Harris, *Recollections* (1929 ed.), 127.

60. Colley, "Reach of the State," 166.

2. GONE FOR A SOLDIER

1. Lynn, "Preface," in *Battle,* xiv.

2. Ibid., xv. Eminent historian Russell Weigley acknowledges the importance of this very issue. Praising John Keegan's insight into the social history of the British soldier as one of the key elements in Keegan's groundbreaking *The Face of Battle,* Weigley contends that it would be impossible to understand the British ranker's behavior under fire without first knowing about the social backgrounds of the men. Weigley, "Foreword," viii.

3. See appendices A and B.

4. Lawrence, *Autobiography,* 2.

5. On this foray into the world, Lawrence met two other boys on the run. Portending his future experiences in the army, hunger forced Lawrence to share food with them. Ibid., 7.

6. Ibid., 14.

7. Tables 54–59 in appendix A.

8. Ibid., tables 9–11. Kevin Linch shows that about 3 percent of the army was made up of foreigners. Linch, "Recruitment of the British Army," 172.

9. Table 12 in appendix A. The Irish represented 25 percent of the population and the Scots 10 percent. Linch, "Recruitment of the British Army," 173. The BSC sample does not include data for every regiment. The 7,250-man sample has its limitations. Regiments were not homogeneous when it came to nationality; thus, because description books were available only for certain regiments, some deviation from actual totals is expected and acknowledged. The 42nd, 78th, 79th, 91st, and 92nd Regiments of Foot were predominately Scottish, while the 18th, 27th, 87th, 88th, and 101st Foot were Irish. The remaining infantry regiments were English, with 70 percent being the threshold. Ibid., 176. I found enlistment records for only the 1st, 6th, 8th, 25th, 28th, 32nd, 34th, 42nd, 53rd, 58th, 79th, and 88th Foot. The BSC is based on this unintentionally select sample.

10. Mokyr, "Has the Industrial Revolution Been Crowded Out?" 302. Cited in Bowen, *War and British Society,* 13. Arthur Gilbert provides sup-

porting data for the BSC numbers, showing that the representation of Irish and Scottish soldiers in the British army in Ireland during the American Revolution ranged from 27.6 percent and 15.3 percent, respectively, to 50.3 percent and 19.4 percent in the three years of his sample. Gilbert, "Ethnicity and the British Army in Ireland," 477.

11. Table 11 in appendix A.

12. Tables 15 and 16 in appendix A. For 1806 the average age was slightly older, at 23.1 years.

13. Ibid. Glenn Steppler offers limited confirmation of age ranges and mean age, showing that in samples of 128, 832, and 906 men (14th, 58th, and 96th Regiments of Foot, 1779 to 1792) the ages of soldiers ran from 12 to 64, with the mean age averaging 20.5, 18.4, and 23.6 years, respectively. Steppler, "Common Soldier in the Reign of King George III," 228. Samuel Scott, dealing with men already in the French army during the French Revolution, found similar numbers reflecting the young age of soldiers. Excluding NCOs, Scott shows that half of the men were between 18 and 25 years of age, with another 5 percent being younger than 18; 90 percent of the soldiers were 35 years of age or less. Scott, *Response of the Royal Army to the French Revolution,* 7–8.

14. Table 17 in appendix A. Looking at just a small sample of recruits, Steppler admits that the youthful age of so many recruits makes it doubtful that most were hardened vagabonds or miscreants. Steppler, "Common Soldier in the Reign of King George III," 40.

15. Scott, "Les soldats de l'armée de ligne," 511.

16. Bertaud, *La révolution armée,* 37, 70–71.

17. Corvisier, *L'armée française,* 2:618.

18. Ibid., 1:393. Corvisier's figures for 1763 reveal that the numbers of soldiers from rural settings increased from 1716. Ibid., 406–408. Scott, "Les soldats de l'armée de ligne," 504. Bertaud, *La révolution armée,* 103.

19. Cockerill, *Sons of the Brave,* 74. Cockerill points out that the Royal Military Asylum, a home for orphans and the destitute families of soldiers killed on active duty, was established by Royal Charter in 1800. The asylum proved a constant source of boy volunteers, perhaps as many as 250 annually. Ibid., 78.

20. Fortescue, *County Lieutenancies and the Army,* 292. Fortescue's category of "boys," however, is never clearly defined. His numbers refer to ordinary recruiting only, not to men or boys entering from the militia. Linch provides data showing that the number of regiments allowed to recruit boys more than doubled from 1811 to 1812 (from 19 regiments to 45), with a limitation of 50 boys per regiment and 5 per company. Linch, "Recruitment of the British Army," 125.

21. Cockerill, *Sons of the Brave,* 80.

22. See appendix A.

23. Numbers drawn from BSC data.

24. When comparing service branches, the average cavalry recruits were slightly taller, at 66.76 inches. Infantry volunteers were about 66.22 inches tall, while artillery enlistees were 66.52 inches. Table 21 in appendix A.

25. See Crafts, "Some Dimensions of the 'Quality of Life,'" 618–22, for a discussion of using height as a proxy for living standards. Stephen Nicholas

and Richard Steckel argue that varying years of food consumption and lower per capita food expenditures resulted in "retarded growth during this period." Nicholas and Steckel, "Heights and Living Standards of English Workers," 937 (on Irish and English convicts transported to Australia between 1770 and 1815).

26. Floud, "Height, Weight and Body Mass," 33, 39.

27. Corvisier, *L'armée française*, 2:649. For a concise overview of Corvisier's findings, see Lynn, *Giant of the Grand Siècle*, 321–36. Corvisier's numbers are for veteran soldiers, not recruits.

28. Bertaud, *La révolution armée*, 36, 83, 138.

29. Scott, "Les soldats de l'armée de ligne," 497.

30. Roth, *Logistics of the Roman Army at War*, 9.

31. Steckel, "New Light on the 'Dark Ages,' " 216.

32. The warming period in medieval Europe that preceded the Little Ice Age played a significant role in crop yields and thus in average height. For details regarding this climatic shift, see Fagan, *Little Ice Age*.

33. Ibid., 218–19.

34. The colder periods often extended well into the growing seasons of spring and summer. Among the plants most susceptible to shifts toward colder weather were cereal grain crops, the dietary staple of the masses.

35. Ibid., 216. The coldest period ended in the second decade of the eighteenth century.

36. Ibid., 222.

37. As further support for Steckel's hypothesis, see Margo and Steckel, "Heights of Native-Born Whites," 168, which provides evidence showing that by the American Civil War the average height of a soldier was 68 inches.

38. Seton, "Infantry Recruiting Instructions in England in 1767," 86, 88. Instructions to Captain Sir Henry Seton, 17th Regiment of Foot, while on recruiting duty in Edinburgh.

39. Ibid., 87.

40. WO 3/17, cited in Cockerill, *Sons of the Brave*, 72. In addition, Cockerill cites an order of 17 January 1811 that allowed colonels to enlist boys under 16 years of age at the rate of 10 boys per company. Ibid., 73.

41. Ibid., 87.

42. Table 23 in appendix A. Linch provides evidence that in the first four months of 1811 only 242 out of 4,975 recruits were rejected for any reason. He shows that almost 19 percent of infantry recruits from 1807 to 1815 were under the minimum height requirement. Linch, "Recruitment of the British Army," 117, 119.

43. Holmes, *Redcoat*, 140.

44. WO 3/584, 408. For more details on recruiting, see Linch, "Recruitment of the British Army," 98–133.

45. Haythornthwaite, *Armies of Wellington*, 49. Similarly, Napoleon was forced to fill the ranks of his army with undersized men. After 1812 the minimum height for conscripts was reduced to 4 feet 8 inches. Forest, *Conscripts and Deserters*, 44.

46. Gayer et al., *Growth and Fluctuation of the British Economy*, 1:72.

47. Bailey, *Luddite Rebellion,* 34. Also Darvall, *Popular Disturbances and Public Order,* 61.

48. Lyons, *Napoleon Bonaparte,* 218.

49. The blockade was initiated on 21 November 1806 with the Berlin decree. Theodore Ropp points out that some historians believe that the blockade could have starved the British into submission had Napoleon not preferred to sell French wheat for British gold. He goes on to argue that Napoleon considered British credit to be the British weak point and that the blockade was still effective, given that focus. As a final note, Ropp brings up one important positive side effect of the blockade for the British: it drove them to find alternative overseas markets. Ropp, *War in the Modern World,* 122–23.

50. Gayer et al., *Growth and Fluctuation of the British Economy,* 1:81. John Komlos shows a real wage decline of 20 percent from 1750 to 1820. Komlos, "Shrinking in a Growing Economy?" 780. Also see Crafts and Mills, "Trends in Real Wages."

51. Tucker, "Real Wages of Artisans in London," 29.

52. Ibid., 53. Tucker was using data provided by William Rowbottom from an unpublished manuscript, "The Chronology or Annals of Oldham."

53. Best, *War and Society in Revolutionary Europe,* 140–41.

54. Haythornthwaite, *Armies of Wellington,* 47. These parties produced over 19,000 recruits in 1807. Linch, "Recruitment of the British Army," 108. Haythornthwaite makes the point that the "number of recruiting parties operational at any one time varied with the demand for recruits." Given the disruptive economic forces extant at the time and the army's difficulties in procuring the amount of soldiers needed for Britain's worldwide endeavors, it seems likely that the decision to nearly triple the number of recruiting parties was based to a great degree on both need and the sudden availability of masses of unemployed workers.

55. Western, "Volunteer Movement," 605.

56. Bowen, *War and British Society,* 14.

57. Cookson, "English Volunteer Movement," 867.

58. Ibid., 886. Cookson argues that for these reasons "volunteering most suited the poor."

59. Western, "Volunteer Movement," 609.

60. Cookson, "English Volunteer Movement," 886.

61. Wells, *Wretched Faces,* 1.

62. Ibid., 51. Also Chambers and Mingay, *Agricultural Revolution,* 112–13.

63. Bowen, *War and British Society,* 37.

64. Flinn, "Trends in Real Wages," 397.

65. Fortescue, *County Lieutenancies and the Army,* 292. The BSC showed 1806 as being the best year for recruitment. A sampling anomaly, however, may possibly account for part of this discrepancy. A comparison of the BSC sample to general returns (see Trades and Seasonal Enlistment Patterns in appendix A) appears to confirm the validity of the BSC in general.

66. Wells, *Wretched Faces,* 69, 64.

67. For a look at the effects of the continental blockade on Europe, see Crouzet, "Wars, Blockades, and Economic Change in Europe." Jon Latimer

writes that "one of the defining themes of the Revolutionary and Napoleonic Wars was economic warfare." Latimer, *1812*, 18. For a more detailed analysis of how America, Britain, and France waged economic warfare during the period that led to the War of 1812, see Latimer's first chapter in ibid., 13–34.

68. *Journal of the House of Commons* 64 (1809): 640–48, cited in Frankel, "1807–1809 Embargo," 295.

69. Frankel, "1807–1809 Embargo," 295.

70. Ibid., 296. As a further example, the number of bags of cotton imported into Liverpool fell from over 100,000 in 1806 to slightly more than 25,000 within a two-year span. Heckschler, *Continental System*, 147.

71. Frankel, "1807–1809 Embargo," 296, 302.

72. Ibid., 305. Frankel's charts showing the concurrent effects of the embargo on Great Britain and America are especially informative (305–306).

73. Landes, *Unbound Prometheus*, 85, 87.

74. For an economic overview of how technology acted as a catalyst for industrial change, see Brown, *Society and Economy in Modern Britain*, 73–105.

75. By 1813 there were about 100 large-scale power looms in use in England. In 1820 that number rose to over 12,000, and by 1829 it would exceed 45,000. Baines, *History of the Cotton Manufacture*, 235.

76. See Mantoux, *Industrial Revolution*, 422–28, for a telling depiction of factory life as experienced by children. The commensurate effect on adults is easily imagined from his descriptions.

77. George Wood labels 1803 the "golden age of hand-looming." From that point on, machines increasingly encroached upon the domain of the hand-loom trades. Wood, "Statistics of Wages (Part XVIII)," 426.

78. Bailey, *Luddite Rebellion*, 13.

79. Ned Ludham, a Leicester stockinger's apprentice, supposedly initiated machine breaking. After being reprimanded by his father-employer about better aligning his frames, Ludham allegedly took up a hammer and smashed them instead. Thus, those who followed his example became "Luddites."

80. Cited in Bailey, *Luddite Rebellion*, 24.

81. Ibid., 33.

82. Darvall, *Popular Disturbances and Public Order*, 2.

83. This act was repealed by the British government on 16 June 1812, just two days before America declared war. The word of the repeal did not reach American shores until August 1812.

84. See Caffrey, *Twilight's Last Gleaming*, 62, 92, 120–21, 299–300.

85. Darvall, *Popular Disturbances and Public Order*, 19.

86. Best, *War and Society in Revolutionary Europe*, 140.

87. Holderness, "Prices, Productivity, and Output," 174, cited in Clark et al., "British Food Puzzle," 216.

88. Hay, "War, Dearth, and Theft," 131.

89. Darvall, *Popular Disturbances and Public Order*, 19–20.

90. Ibid., 46. Also Peel, *Rising of the Luddites*, 27.

91. Darvall, *Popular Disturbances and Public Order*, 54.

92. Peel, *Rising of the Luddites*, 27.

93. Flinn, "Trends in Real Wages," 410.

94. O'Brien, "Impact of the Revolutionary and Napoleonic Wars," 354.

95. The same sorts of economic forces are presently at work in America. As jobs disappear, more and more young people are enlisting. See the article "More Americans Joining Military as Jobs Dwindle," *New York Times*, 18 January 2009.

96. Table 60 in appendix B.

97. Corvisier, *L'armée française*, 1:317. I am indebted to John Lynn for pointing out this connection.

98. This is also an ordinary least squares linear regression. See table 60 in appendix B. Tucker, "Real Wages of Artisans in London," 21–35.

99. Tables 61–62 in appendix B. Gayer et al., *Growth and Fluctuation of the British Economy*, 1:11, 32, 66–67, 87, 89–90, 119.

100. For a more detailed explanation of the regressions, see appendix B. Limited service was also introduced in 1806. This option, however, proved unpopular and should not be considered a factor in 1806 enlistment. As an example, J.M. Brereton shows that in 1814 approximately 75 percent of recruits signed on for life. Brereton, *British Soldier*, 47. Linch's data also provide corroboration. Linch, "Recruitment of the British Army," 122. C. Dupin presents similar evidence in a small sample from 1814: only one Irishman took the limited service option, while 565 opted for life service. Similarly, 84 Scots signed on for limited service, with 226 enlisting for life. Dupin, *View of History of the Actual State of the Military Forces*, 305, cited by McGuffie, "Recruiting the Ranks of the Regular British Army," 54–55. Limited service was abolished in 1829 and not reestablished until 1847. See appendix B for regression details.

101. O'Brien, "Impact of the Revolutionary and Napoleonic Wars," 361.

102. Darvall, *Popular Disturbances and Public Order*, 54–55. Darvall shows that hand-weaver wages recovered by 1814, only to plummet to nine shillings a week by 1818 due to the influx of surplus labor caused by the mass release of soldiers back into the civilian population in 1815–16.

103. Ibid., 55.

104. Wood, "Statistics of Wages (Part XVIII)," 428.

105. Darvall, *Popular Disturbances and Public Order*, 54. In his recent book on the history of the 95th, Mark Urban argues that the "fickle dictates of fashion" led to unemployment in the textile industry and were the causal factor behind much of the enlistment. As has been shown, the economic stressors at work were far more complex than he contends. Urban, *Wellington's Rifles*, 7.

106. Table 39 in appendix A.

107. Table 31 in appendix A. For all the occupation data, see tables 27–39 in appendix A.

108. Asa Briggs, addressing the combined impact of war and technological progress on the working masses, argues that the latter may have been the predominant factor behind the discontent of the working class. He suggests that "changes in the industrial structure of the country and fluctuations in the means of livelihood were more important than the war itself in stirring both hand and machine workers." Briggs, *Age of Improvement*, 182.

109. Flinn, "Trends in Real Wages," 397.

110. Tables 63–64 in appendix B. About 63 percent of volunteers held positions other than "laborer" during the poor economic years versus about 46 percent during good economic years.

111. Ibid.

112. BSC analysis confirms that the men who swelled the ranks of Wellington's army during the Peninsula campaign were not just young men with a taste for adventure and nothing else to do; they were men as old as 50 and 55 who were driven to enlist merely to feed and clothe themselves. From 1790 to 1815 only one year (1791) in the BSC shows a group of enlistees with a maximum age under 30. In other years, the proportion of men over 30 ranges from less than 5 percent to more than 40 percent, with the years of highest proportion also being difficult economic years. These older men, who were probably more aware of the hardships that army life entailed, are unlikely to have enlisted in the army given any other choice.

113. Anderson, *People's Army*, 27.

114. Tables 26–28 in appendix A. In comparison, about 76 percent of the soldiers entering the French army between 1737 and 1763 listed a former occupation. Corvisier, *L'armée française*, 1:543–51.

115. Tables 27–28 in appendix A.

116. Table 29 in appendix A.

117. Ibid. The compilation of foreigners, who represent only 124 of the more than 7,000 recruits in the BSC sample, actually has the highest percentage of laborers: 54.8 percent.

118. Patrick O'Brien estimates that approximately 38 percent of the workforce was made up of laborers, a number very much in line with the BSC total. O'Brien, "Impact of the Revolutionary and Napoleonic Wars," 338.

119. See table 39 in appendix A. Steppler, using a small sample, found that 12.5 percent of men in the 96th Regiment of Foot (1779–1883) and 37.8 percent of the 58th Foot (1784–92) were weavers. The proportions of laborers in these regiments were 50 percent and 35.8 percent, respectively. Steppler, "Common Soldier in the Reign of King George III," 34. Gilbert found that 19.25 percent of 161 men enlisting from London and Middlesex during the later eighteenth century were weavers, with 80 percent listing definable trades. Gilbert, "Analysis of Some Eighteenth-Century Army Recruiting Records," 41, 46.

120. Using a sample of 300 men from 1809 to 1816, McGuffie arrived at three conclusions, two of which support the BSC sample: he concluded that the ranks contained (1) a "preponderance of laboring classes"; (2) a "considerable percentage of weavers and frame knitters"; and (3) an absence of men "from the middle and trading classes." The limited size of his sample prevented him from observing the breadth and number of such occupations. McGuffie, "Recruiting the Ranks of the Regular British Army," 126.

121. Gilbert, "Analysis of Some Eighteenth-Century Army Recruiting Records," 41.

122. See the cautions in Frey, *British Soldier in America*, 9.

123. Lawrence, *Autobiography*, 14.

124. Crafts, citing Peter Lindert and Jeffrey Williamson's social tables for England and Wales in 1688, 1759, and 1801/1803, estimates that in the latter years 14.6 percent of men worked in the agricultural occupations and 15.5 percent were laborers, noting that "laborer" is a term "without any clear demarcation and includes 'both agricultural and non-agricultural labourers.'" Crafts, *British Economic Growth*, 13. Without real employment and unemployment data, these summations are just estimates and perhaps no more reliable than the BSC.

125. Corvisier, *L'armée française*, 1:319–322. For the BSC results, see appendix A.

126. Interestingly, Linch offers data showing that the best recruiting months were actually in the summer. He argues that "this suggests that recruiting was concentrated in urban areas where the annual agrarian cycle was less of an influence on employment." Linch, "Recruitment of the British Army," 110–11.

127. See table 39 in appendix A.

128. Darvall, *Popular Disturbances and Public Order*, 15.

129. Corvisier, *L'armée française*, 1:393. Corvisier's figures for 1763 reveal that the number of soldiers from rural settings increased from 1716. Ibid., 406–408.

130. Scott, "Les soldats de l'armée de ligne," 504.

131. Bertaud, *La révolution armée*, 103. Also, Crafts cites Phyllis Deane and W.A. Cole's calculations that 35.9 percent of the workforce in 1801 was employed in agriculture, forestry, and fishing. Crafts, *British Economic Growth*, 15.

132. The New Settlement Act of 1622.

133. The Poor Act of 1697. This was not officially abolished until 1948.

134. Sir Edward Knatchbull's Act of 1722–33, "For Amending the Laws Relating to the Settlement, Employment and Relief of the Poor." This act created informal workhouses.

135. The Gilbert Act of 1782, also called the Poor Relief Act of 1782, "An Act for the Better Relief and Employment of the Poor."

136. Ibid. The much-hated formal workhouse system would not come into existence until 1834.

137. For a more in-depth look at the evolution and efficacy of English Poor Laws, see Lees, *Solidarities of Strangers*; Brundage, *English Poor Laws*; and Rose, *English Poor Laws*. While treatment of the poor varied by locale, it is safe to say that most of the unfortunates felt the system to be degrading. Poor Law administration was absolute and often harsh and arbitrary. The poor had to take what was offered and acquiesce to local officials. See Wells, *Wretched Faces*, for a good accounting of how the process worked and how the poor endured the various stipulations forced upon them.

138. A standing police force would not be established until 1829, when Wellington's government passed home secretary Sir Robert Peel's Metropolitan Police Act. This act raised a force only in the City of London, however. It was not until the Municipal Corporations Act of 1835, which mandated that all incorporated boroughs set up their own police forces, that a regular constabulary was instituted.

139. These incidents were usually spontaneous gatherings and varied by locale and circumstances. Almost all had one thing in common, though: the demand for affordable bread.

140. Darvall, *Popular Disturbances and Public Order*, 260.

141. Originally the Riot Act required a formal warning by a justice of the peace and a waiting period of an hour before action was taken. The policy, however, devolved into calling out the troops and using them at the commander's discretion, even against passive demonstrators.

142. Army pay had been raised in 1797 from eight pence to one shilling a day, where it would remain for the next 70 years.

143. Haythornthwaite, *Armies of Wellington*, 47. This amount was for life service. Limited service merited a bounty of £18 12 shillings 6 pence. When Napoleon first fell from power in 1813, the bounty dropped to £3 14 shillings.

144. O'Neil, *Military Adventures*, 27.

145. Emsley, *British Society and the French Wars*, 112.

146. Cited in ibid., 37.

147. Cited in ibid., 111.

148. Macfarlane, "Peninsula Private," 54–55.

149. Watteville, *British Soldier*, 97.

150. McGuffie, *Rank and File*, 14–15.

151. Ibid., 96. The man received 279 lashes and died eight days later.

152. Donaldson, *Recollections*, 91.

153. Ibid., 89–91.

154. Haythornthwaite, *Armies of Wellington*, 46.

155. Linch, "Recruitment of the British Army," 22.

156. Holmes, *Redcoat*, 135.

157. Haythornthwaite, *Armies of Wellington*, 43. Losses do not include men who perished in the West Indies. Using data provided by Fortescue, it can be calculated that the British army lost, on average, 20,526 men annually for the years 1803 to 1813. Fortescue, *County Lieutenancies and the Army*, 291.

158. Rory Muir has compiled slightly different numbers than Haythornthwaite and Fortescue. Muir states that the army reached 260,000 men near the end of 1813. Deaths, or "wastage" as he calls the losses, rose from 17,000 men a year (1803 to 1807) to more than 24,000 annual deaths (1809, 1812, 1813). He lists total losses from 1803 to 1813 as 225,000 men. Muir, *Britain and the Defeat of Napoleon*, 14. When men in the navy are included, the armed services held roughly between 11 and 14 percent of all male workers aged 15 to 40. O'Brien, "Impact of the Revolutionary and Napoleonic Wars," 336.

159. Bowen, *War and British Society*, 16. Bowen cites Emsley, *British Society and the French Wars*, 169.

160. Fortescue lists 1807 as the most successful recruiting year, with 19,114 men enlisting. Fortescue, *County Lieutenancies and the Army*, 292.

161. Best, *War and Society in Revolutionary Europe*, 42.

162. Robert Burnham, "Filling the Ranks: How Wellington Kept His Units up to Strength," cited in Muir et al., *Inside Wellington's Peninsular*, 210–15.

163. For an excellent analysis of this topic, see Linch, "Recruitment of the British Army," 67–90.

164. The militia existed until 1908, when its units were transferred to the Special Reserve.

165. Burnham, "Filling the Ranks," 221.

166. Linch, "Recruitment of the British Army," 134.

167. Philip Coates-Wright, University of London, in a session discussion on the British soldier in the Iberian Peninsula, Conference on the Iberian Peninsula, Lisbon, Portugal, 1991. I presented the paper that initiated this discourse and am grateful to Professor Coates-Wright for his line of questioning during the session and at dinner.

168. Fortescue, *History of the British Army*, 5:211.

169. McGuffie acknowledges this: "For only if a balloted man were too poor to pay for a substitute would he enlist; the substitutes belonged to the same class, for who else would take money to enter the army, and sell his liberty for ten or twelve guineas cash?" McGuffie, "Recruiting the Ranks of the Regular British Army," 50.

170. Fortescue, *County Lieutenancies and the Army*, 47–48.

171. Ibid., 196, 4.

172. Rodger, *Wooden World*, 109, 184.

173. Gilbert, "Analysis of Some Eighteenth-Century Army Recruiting Records," 44. Counties were responsible for raising their own bounty fees and for bringing the men before justices for official confirmation of their enlistments.

174. Ibid., 42.

175. Buckley, *British Army in the West Indies*, 100–101, 94, 58.

176. Fortescue, *History of the British Army*, 2:276. Michael Duffy, using embarkation returns and regimental musters, comes up with similar numbers: 45,000 deaths out of 89,000 men sent. Duffy, "British Army and the Caribbean Expeditions," 65.

177. Buckley, "Destruction of the British Army in the West Indies," 81. Buckley's data reveal that soldiers had about one chance in four of dying each year in the West Indies. Ibid., 90.

178. Buckley, *British Army in the West Indies*, 105. I have found no recent studies on the criminal backgrounds of the British soldiers since Buckley made his assertion. This is not to assert that no criminals enlisted or that no men learned criminal skills in the army. Charles Oman reminds us that when Wellington needed to create 5-franc coins after Waterloo he had no trouble finding 40 coiners in the ranks to accomplish the task. Oman, *Wellington's Army*, 274. The supposition is that the numbers of such men were far fewer than has been surmised. Rodger, writing about the British navy in the eighteenth century, confirms the reluctance of the armed services to accept criminals as recruits. He argues that with the exception of smugglers and a small number of men released from debtor's prison, "criminals were never accepted" into the navy. Rodger, *Wooden World*, 158, 171.

179. Buckley, *British Army in the West Indies*, 105, citing Frey, *British Soldier in America*, 5–6.

180. Gilbert, "Analysis of Some Eighteenth-Century Army Recruiting Records," 47.

181. The number of capital crimes rose from 50 in 1688 to 225 by 1815. It bears mentioning that the number of executions did not rise commensurately due to royal pardons. Executions averaged a high of 53 annually for 1788–89 and a low of 21 a year during the last decade of the eighteenth century. Hay et al., *Albion's Fatal Tree*, 23–24. Peter King provides further evidence that the percentage of persons actually executed for capital crimes in Essex (1740–1805) was relatively low, ranging from no executions for petty larceny and 1.3 percent for grand and aggravated larceny to 20.6 percent for horse theft and to a high of 45.2 percent for highway robbery. His data reveal that less than 8 percent of convicted criminals sentenced to the death penalty in Essex were actually executed. Numbers for various capital property crimes on the Home Circuit (1755–1815) were higher, ranging from no executions for larceny from a person to 65 percent for coining and 68.3 percent for forgery. King, *Crime, Justice, and Discretion in England*, 262, 274.

182. Hay et al., *Albion's Fatal Tree*, 13–25.

183. King, *Crime, Justice, and Discretion in England*, 146, 150, 167, 195. King shows a distinct correlation between property crime and wheat prices, among other economic indices.

184. Hay et al., *Albion's Fatal Tree*, 121, 124, 135, 134.

185. Beattie, *Crime and the Courts in England*, charts on 202–203, 206, 214–15, 205.

186. Cited in Radzinowicz, *History of English Criminal Law*, 1:530–31.

187. King, *Crime, Justice, and Discretion in England*, 194–95. Beattie, however, cautions that "indictments are a fragile guide to criminality. Prosecutions arose from a complex of interacting forces." Beattie, *Crime and the Courts in England*, 263. Hay confirms the difficulty of distinguishing between "changes in the frequency with which the poor stole ('appropriation') from changes in the enforcement ('control') of criminal law." Hay, "War, Dearth, and Theft," 120. But despite these qualifiers, both Beattie and Hay conclude that crime rates were directly tied to fluctuations in the economy.

188. One basis of the underground myth originates with Patrick Colquhoun's treatise on wealth and crime written during the Napoleonic Wars. He correctly concluded that poverty was at the root of crime. His estimate of the numbers of criminals or *potential* criminals in Britain, however, included indigent people; thus, his oft-quoted guesstimate that one-eighth of the British people were criminals is inherently flawed. Colquhoun, *Treatise on the Wealth of the British Empire*, 111–12.

189. Rudé, *Criminal and Victim*; and Jones, *Crime, Report, Community, and Police in Nineteenth-Century Britain*.

190. Nicholas and Steckel, "Heights and Living Standards," 944. They compare offenders in Warwickshire with a convict sample of over 100,000 men and come up with similar results: 48.8 and 53.4 percent were unskilled, respectively, leaving 51.2 and 46.6 percent skilled.

191. Rudé, *Criminal and Victim*, 11. Food constituted 23.3 percent of stolen items, while clothing made up 21.2 percent of the sample.

192. Ibid., 18. Money or valuables made up 19.9 percent of the total, with clothing coming in a close second at 19.8 percent. Food was third at 13.9 percent.

193. Beattie, *Crime and the Courts in England*, 187. For Sussex (1660–1800), the numbers were clothes 23.7 percent and food 14.0 percent. In Southwark clothes were first at 27.1 percent, with food coming in fourth at 11.4 percent. The numbers for the rural parishes of Surrey were food first at 26.5 percent and clothes second at 21.4 percent.

194. Rudé, *Criminal and Victim*, 11, 79, 118.

195. Ibid., 117. Haythornthwaite provides similar data showing that in 1803 about 4,600 persons in England and Wales were bound over for trial. Of those, 3,555 were charged with larceny. Haythornthwaite, *Armies of Wellington*, 67.

196. Rudé, *Criminal and Victim*, 41. Of these, 88.9 percent were males.

197. Ibid., 42, 48, 51.

198. Bowen, *War and British Society*, 35.

199. To add to the tribulations of the people of Britain, as well as all the populace of the northern hemisphere, Mount Tambora erupted in April 1815. The eruption ejected massive amounts of volcanic dust into the upper atmosphere. The result was a cataclysmic climatic shift by the summer of 1816, during which temperatures plummeted to record levels; frost and summer snowfalls killed crops, triggering food shortages, famine, and epidemics. In this "year without summer," the British soldiers released from the army attempted to make a go of it in a land already unable to cope with the combined impact of industrialization, population surges, unemployment, increased urbanization, and growing social instability.

200. Bowen, *War and British Society*, 35.

201. Cockerill, *Sons of the Brave*, 80.

3. OVER THE HILLS AND FAR AWAY

1. Donaldson, *Recollections*, 44–45.

2. Ibid., 45.

3. Edward Costello of the 95th mentions £4, while John Macfarlane wrote of paying £2 2 shillings for just a knapsack. Costello, *Peninsular and Waterloo Campaigns*, 2; and Macfarlane, "Peninsula Private," 4. T.H. McGuffie also estimates that the recruit's kit came to £4. McGuffie, "Recruiting the Ranks of the Regular British Army," 57.

4. Glover, *Wellington's Army*, 29. Charles O'Neil said his kit consisted of two shirts, two pairs of stockings, a plate, knife, and fork, and a few other small articles. O'Neil, *Military Adventures*, 18. According to infantry recruiting instructions to Captain Sir Henry Seton (17th Regiment of Foot) while on recruiting duty in Edinburgh in 1767, "Every soldier was to be completed constantly with the following necessaries: 1 knapsack, 4 good white shirts, 2 good white stocks, 1 black hair stock, 3 pr. strong thread stockings, 2 pr. of strong shoes, 1 pair regimental gaiters, 1 pair half gaiters, a pair of white breeches, a set of regimental buckles, a turnkey and worm, a brush and

wire, brushes and combs as ordered, polishing buff." Seton, "Infantry Recruiting Instructions in England," 90.

5. Kopperman, "British High Command and Soldiers' Wives," 26.

6. Lawrence, *Autobiography*, 17.

7. Ibid., 56.

8. John Kincaid claimed that in six years of campaigning he "slept at least half the period under the open canopy of heaven." Kincaid, *Random Shots*, 189.

9. Douglas, *Douglas's Tale*, 49.

10. Lawrence, *Autobiography*, 71–74.

11. Anton, *Retrospect of a Military Life*, 121.

12. Harris, *Recollections* (1970 ed.), 42.

13. Robinson, "Peninsular Brigadier," 164–65.

14. Browne, *Napoleonic War Journal*, 193.

15. Steppler, "Coldstream Guards at Waterloo," 66–67. Steppler's point is that the British soldier as depicted by military artists is a false image. The men's uniforms were ragged, patched, and faded; whether in the Peninsula or in Belgium, the men's appearance was exactly as Grattan and Surtees described. Surtees, *Twenty-five Years in the Rifle Brigade*, 22.

16. The 88th, which had acquired the nickname "the devil's own," had such a plundering reputation that Wellington once remarked to his surgeon general: "I hang and shoot more of your old friends for murder, robbery, etc. than I do all the rest of the army together. . . . One more thing I will tell you, however; whenever anything very gallant or desperate is to be done, there is not a corps in the army, I would sooner rely than your old friends, the Connaught Rangers." McGrigor, *Autobiography*, 259.

17. Grattan, *Adventures with the Connaught Rangers*, 81. Surtees confirmed this description: "Our clothing was literally all filth and dirt; our arms the colour of our coats with rust [from the rain] and our faces black as if we had come out of a coal pit." Surtees, *Twenty-five Years in the Rifle Brigade*, 22.

18. Morley, *Memoirs of a Sergeant*, 81.

19. See tables 35–39 in appendix A.

20. Anton, *Retrospect of a Military Life*, 35.

21. The soldiers of the 28th Regiment of Foot, on board transports destined for Portugal in the summer of 1808, celebrated this new general order from the Horse Guards by throwing their severed queues overboard. Cadell, *Narrative of the Campaigns*, 28.

22. Holmes, *Redcoat*, 274.

23. For examples, see table 79 in appendix C.

24. Douglas, *Douglas's Tale*, 63. He writes that rations were delivered the next evening and also comments that during the retreat the "pig shooting went on very briskly." Ibid., 62. George Hennell wrote of a similar incident of soldiers being without rations for an extended period during the Salamanca campaign. Hennell, *Gentleman Volunteer*, 63.

25. See table 79 in appendix C.

26. Wheeler, *Letters*, 49–50.

27. Leach, *Rough Sketches*, 95.

28. Green, *Vicissitudes of a Soldier's Life*, 155.

29. Lawrence, *Autobiography*, 164–65.

30. Cooper, *Rough Notes*, 60.

31. Bell, *Rough Notes*, 37.

32. *Soldier of the Seventy-first*, 77.

33. Sanger, *Englishmen at War*, 252.

34. Sherer, *Recollections of the Peninsula*, 105. John Aitchison provides a similar assessment of the government's reluctance to look after its soldiers: "What must be thought of a government so stinting in comfort—nay *bare justice*—to the defenders of their country, as to deny a General the means of easing the suffering of the Soldier when *worn out*, probably restoring him to service. . . . I do not hesitate to say that such Governors ought to be dismissed." Aitchison, *Ensign in the Peninsular War*, 220 (emphasis in the original).

35. Leach, *Rough Sketches*, 96.

36. Cooper, *Rough Notes*, 157.

37. Sherer, *Recollections of the Peninsula*, 131–32.

38. Knowles, *War in the Peninsula*, 25.

39. Kincaid, *Adventures in the Rifle Brigade*, 140.

40. Green, *Vicissitudes of a Soldier's Life*, 156.

41. Costello, *Peninsular and Waterloo Campaigns*, 71.

42. Donaldson, *Recollections of an Eventful Life*, 111.

43. Macfarlane, "Peninsula Private," 8.

44. Hamilton, *Hamilton's Campaign*, 52.

45. Lawrence, *Autobiography*, 84–85.

46. Green, *Vicissitudes of a Soldier's Life*, 149.

47. Lawrence, *Autobiography*, 82–83.

48. Lawrence makes this assertion again, referring to Wellington's method of punishing looters after Badajoz. Ibid., 118.

49. Douglas, *Douglas's Tale*, 23.

50. O'Neil, *Military Adventures*, 142–44. Lawrence once did the same in an identical situation, sharing a sheep with a lieutenant of his company. Lawrence, *Autobiography*, 139.

51. Sergeant Johnson, "Waterloo Journal," 36.

52. Macfarlane, "Peninsula Private," 10.

53. Harris, *Recollections* (1970 ed.), 130.

54. Roderick Floud provides an excellent study on heights and weights using body mass as a guide, going as far as 1800. He argues that the BMI for a male 26–30 years old in 1800 to 1819 was about 20.7, compared to today's number, approximately 25 or more. Floud, "Height, Weight and Body Mass," 20, 36. Along these lines, John Komlos has estimated that a 17-year-old West Point cadet in the 1800s was about 67 inches tall, with a BMI of just over 19, giving him a weight of about 126 pounds. Today a cadet of that height would have a BMI closer to 22 and weigh approximately 140 pounds. Komlos, "Shrinking in a Growing Economy?" 787.

55. Floud, "Height, Weight and Body Mass," 35.

56. Two different approaches were used to approximate the average caloric needs of the British common soldier. Both methods depended on calculating the total energy expended (TEE) in a day, using a current formula that represents the TEE of modern adults with no particularly active lifestyle. TEE in megajoules can be calculated using the following equation: TEE = 7.377 – (0.073 × age) + (0.0806 × wt) + (0.0135 × ht) – (1.363 × sex), where age is in years, weight is in kilograms, height is in centimeters, and sex is zero for men and one for women. One megajoule equals approximately 239 nutritional calories. Vinken et al., "Equations," 923. This calculation should be a reasonable estimate of the British ranker's needs, if somewhat low. See appendix C. Komlos has surmised that adult males in America circa 1839 needed approximately 3,300 calories for a workday that included eight hours of heavy work. Komlos, "Shrinking in a Growing Economy?" 787. Jonathan Roth calculated a similar number in his analysis of the nutritional needs of the Roman legionary. He notes that while the present U.S. Army recommendations state that a 16- to 19-year-old soldier needs 3,600 calories and 70 grams of protein a day, the smaller stature of the Roman soldier would reduce these numbers to 3,000 calories and 60 grams of protein. Roth, *Logistics of the Roman Army at War*, 12.

57. Table 79 in appendix C.

58. Harris complained that carrying the fully weighted kit any measurable distance made a man "half-beaten before the scratch [fight]." Harris, *Recollections* (1970 ed.), 13.

59. Douglas grumbled that "our bread and rice ration [2 ounces] could be held with ease in one hand." Douglas, *Douglas's Tale*, 29. The inclusion of rice in the daily ration was sometimes the result of officers' efforts to keep the men healthy by adding to their diets. Rice was not part of the standard issue meal.

60. Like the Spanish soldiers and sailors, the Venetian oarsmen, being freemen, may have supplemented their diets out of their own pockets. As Guilmartin has noted in his seminal work on Mediterranean warfare of the early Renaissance, the carbohydrate-rich but protein-deficient diet of the galley slaves had unexpected consequences. While the high proportion of carbohydrates enhanced muscular endurance, the fat and protein deficiencies resulted in a high vulnerability to sickness and death, especially in cold weather. Personal communication, November 2004.

61. All the food items described in historical sources were matched with the closest equivalent in the U.S. Department of Agriculture, Agricultural Research Service, *USDA National Nutrient Database*. All data on the composition of various foods can be accessed using the search engine provided on this page and the specific name given in the text. Individual URLs for compositions of various foods are not available, so individual footnotes are not included in the table. The U.S. Army currently provides each soldier in the field a minimum of 3,750 calories in the form of an MRE (Meal, Ready-to-Eat). Defense Supply Center Philadelphia, Subsistence Operational Rations Business Unit, Frequently Asked Questions, 4 February 2008, http:///www.dscp.dla.mil/subs/rations/faqs.pdf (accessed 4 February 2008).

62. This endeavor translated to approximately 3,000 to 5,000 hours of hard labor per legion. Peddie, *Roman War Machine*, 77.

63. These men no doubt also turned to theft in order to increase their daily caloric intake.

64. Roth, *Logistics of the Roman Army*, 12.

65. Cooper, *Rough Notes*, 157.

66. The potential weight loss information in table 4 assumes that a pound of body fat contains about 90 percent fat and 10 percent water and that fat generates 9 calories of energy per gram.

67. Shorter march rates would, of course, reduce caloric expenditure. Even if the soldiers only walked 10–12 miles a day, which was closer to the norm, and occasional rest days were figured in, the caloric loss would still be unsustainable over time, given the caloric content of the available rations.

68. Men often commented on the lack of rations. Robert Knowles states that Camp Ello in Portugal had only 20 cottages to quarter 700 men and that fatigue parties were sent into the woods to search for acorns as a substitute for bread. He goes on to write, "You will agree with me when I say that few men in England would envy our situation." Knowles, *War in the Peninsula*, 42. Douglas complains that "not a toothful in the shape of eatables was served out" during the march from Ciudad Rodrigo to Campillo. Douglas, *Douglas's Tale*, 63. George Hennell wrote of a similar incident during the Salamanca campaign. Hennell, *Gentleman Volunteer*, 63. Captain Alexander Gordon of the 15th Hussars offers further confirmation, stating that on the retreat to Corunna "the army was seldom supplied with rations above once in three days, and the cavalry were sometimes four or five days without getting any." Gordon, *Journal of a Cavalry Officer*, 146–47. Surgeon Walter Henry gave a humorous but telling account of the end of a rationless day. When a rabbit scurried through the camp, the men sprang after it; the hare was in the camp-kettle in less than five minutes. Henry, who rarely mentions the men in his care, found the incident amusing; he had the means to purchase supplemental foodstuffs, so he did not share the men's privations. Henry, *Trifles from My Port-folio*, 1:143–44.

69. Additional examples are included in table 79 in appendix C.

70. For the exact dietary breakdowns by soldier type, see appendix C. For a current comparison, Major Peter Hart related that he lost 12 pounds in two weeks while at Ranger School, subsisting on one MRE a day. Personal communication, 12 September 2008. While the British soldier was not stressed to the extent that Rangers are each day during training, the long-term effects of existing on less than 2,500 calories daily, week in and week out on march and in battle, would have resulted in the same sort of body weight loss. Ranger training is just short of nine weeks in duration, which is less than the campaign season in the Peninsula. The average loss per Ranger in the 62-day course was about 15.9 percent of body weight. Committee on Military Nutrition Research, *Military Strategies for Sustainment of Nutrition*, 29.

71. Beers and Berkow, *Merck Manual of Diagnosis and Therapy*. All the micronutritional deficiency effects came from the same source but different subsites.

72. This list of medical ailments was suggested by Columbus physician Dr. Alex Kuskin. Personal communication, March 1999. Major Reva Rogers was also consulted regarding the correlation of alcohol with vitamin A deficiencies and respiratory problems. According to Rogers, "In the early 1820s the Surgeon General began petitioning Congress to remove rum from the American Military Ration; his efforts were not successful until 1832." Personal communication, 5 December 2007. Finally, Lieutenant Colonel Steven Tobler, U.S. Army physician, confirmed the stated relationships between nutritional deficiencies and disease. Personal communication, 10 April 2008.

73. Reva Rogers, "The Evolution of Army Rations" (unpublished paper), 1–2. She cites the following source: Office of Dietary Supplements, National Institutes of Health, *Dietary Supplement Fact Sheet: Vitamin A and Carotenoids,* http:///dietary-supplements.info.nih.gov/factsheets/vitamina.asp.

74. Marcos et al., "Changes in the Immune System," S66–S68.

75. Calder and Kew, "Immune System," S169. Also see Morgan, "What, If Any, Is the Effect of Malnutrition?"; and Keusch, "History of Nutrition."

76. Merino, "Immune and Hormonal Changes," 1034, 1036. Merino cites evidence in Zhang et al., "Changes in Immune Parameters," 6.

77. Kramer et al., "Effects of Food Restriction," cited in Merino, "Immune and Hormonal Changes," 1034.

78. Brenton et al., "Adaptation to Chronic Stress." Also see the committee's conclusions related to nutrition, soldier health, and immune function. Committee on Military Nutrition Research, *Military Strategies for Sustainment of Nutrition,* 126–27, 170–71. The entire study supports the relationship between immune response and caloric intake.

79. Davis and Taylor, *Stress in Combat,* 2, 9–12. The pituitary gland, stimulated by stress, secretes the adrenocorticotropic hormone (ACTH), which stimulates the adrenal glands to release corticoids; these alter the rates of physiological processes.

80. Hodges, "Impact of Nutritional Care," 158.

81. Keys et al., *Biology of Human Starvation,* vol. 2, 1010. Chapters 43–49 deal with the physiological effects.

82. The Chapman study was cited by Barrocas, "Nutritional Support of the Medical Patient," 7.

83. Russell, "Importance of Patients' Nutritional Status," 542. Also see Shikora, "Approaches to Nutritional Support," 314–16.

84. Cantlie, *History of the Army Medical Department,* 1:306–308, 354.

85. All these figures come from Army Medical Department sick returns. Yearly averages were as follows: 1810 (23.79 percent), 1811 (18.8 percent), 1812 (29.42 percent), and 1813 (23.96 percent). Ibid., 1:504–505. Surgeon Charles Boutflower offers supporting information, noting that in October of 1811 sick rates in his regiment (the 40th Foot) were running almost exactly 50 percent. Boutflower, *Journal of an Army Surgeon,* 113.

86. Cantlie, *History of the Army Medical Department,* 373, 293. The Waterloo campaign saw another 12,574 hospital admissions. Ibid., 387. In addition, 4,000 men were lost to Walcheren fever in the disastrous expedition to Scheldt in 1809. For insight into the efforts and travails of the army medical corps, see Blanco, *Wellington's Surgeon General.*

87. Dehydration no doubt also played a significant role in felling soldiers on the march. Because the connections between dehydration and heat exhaustion, muscle fatigue, loss of coordination, and heat stroke were unknown at the time, almost no records exist pertaining to water allocation, officers advocating hydration, or the numbers of soldiers lost because of the lack of water.

88. Cantlie, *History of the Army Medical Department*, 2:298. Cantlie also brings to light an 1813 order stating that a full hospital diet included one pound each of bread and meat, five ounces of rice, some sugar, salt, vegetables, and half a pint of wine. Had the troops in the field been fed this well, sick rates would have been drastically reduced. Ibid., 506.

89. For a vivid description of the efficacy of British medical treatment, see Green's experiences after he was shot in the side on 31 August 1813. It is astounding that he survived the wound and his medical care. Green, *Vicissitudes of a Soldier's Life*, 191–204.

90. Donaldson, *Recollections*, 165. Donaldson goes on to say: "The medical department of the French army was much superior to ours in every respect."

91. Anton, *Retrospect of a Military Life*, 155.

92. Keys et al., *Biology of Human Starvation*, 2:786.

93. Harris, *Recollections* (1970 ed.), 148–61; *Soldier of the Seventy-first*, 28; Porter, *Letters from Portugal and Spain*, 256; Donaldson, *Recollections*, 145, 178–80; Aitchison, *Ensign in the Peninsular War*, 64.

94. Keys et al., *Biology of Human Starvation*, 2:822, 828. See his table outlining these symptoms from semistarvation (weeks 12 and 24) through rehabilitation (rehab weeks 12, 20, and 33) for specifics. Ibid., 822. Keys also describes the attitudes of the men toward physical exertion as "ambivalent" at best: any such activity was something to be avoided if possible, due to their debilitated state.

95. Ibid., 793.

96. Ibid., 784, 823.

97. Such physical responses to starvation may be based in part on feelings of helplessness; as Stephen Rosen has shown, such feelings result in the body's release of cortisol, which causes depression and would engender the symptoms described. Rosen, *War and Human Nature*, 100, 105, 113.

98. As an example of this, Keys cites the general behavior pattern of many near-starving women. Even though nutritional deficiencies work physiologically to decrease the sex drive, the number of women in such situations offering themselves for food increases. Keys et al., *Biology of Human Starvation*, 2:785, 789.

99. Ibid. In addition to theft and increased violence, Keys mentions other symptoms of "personal and social deterioration," including child abandonment, prostitution, and even cannibalism. His charts outlining the intensity of symptoms and the percentage of deviate behavior related to starvation are worthy of a more detailed study than can be included here. Ibid., 790, 912–13.

100. Cited in ibid., 801. Also see Keys's work regarding personality traits and the effects of rehabilitating nutrition on personality. Ibid., 864–79.

101. Haythornthwaite, *Armies of Wellington*, 61. Also see Kopperman, "British High Command and Soldiers' Wives," 23. Kopperman cites Benjamin F. Stevens, ed., *General Sir William Howe's Orderly Book, at Charlestown, Boston, and Halifax, 17 June 1775 to 26 May 1776* (London, 1890) 235.

102. According to Captain Browne, the wives also became proficient at stripping the dead and plundering after a battle. He noted that "they had no hesitation in engaging themselves three and four deep to future husbands." Buckley rightly notes that the women's "behavior resulted directly from the bitterly harsh conditions and the uncertainty of military life, particularly when on active service." Browne, *Napoleonic War Journal*, 174, 345.

103. Donaldson, *Recollections*, 216.

104. Kopperman, "British High Command and Soldiers' Wives," 17.

105. Lynn, *Giant of the Grand Siècle*, 185.

106. Surtees, *Twenty-five Years in the Rifle Brigade*, 39, 90.

107. Green, *Vicissitudes of a Soldier's Life*, 115–16, 158.

108. Costello, *Peninsular and Waterloo Campaigns*, 58.

109. Lawrence, *Autobiography*, 85–86. But even this real threat was ignored when the men became famished. Costello writes of a time when, after two days without rations, he and his mates ended up in a firefight with Spanish troops who were guarding a wagonload of bread. Desperate, Costello and his comrades won the load of bread and shared it among the men. He summed up their point of view by succinctly stating that "the sufferings of our men were such that many considered death a happy relief." Costello, *Peninsular and Waterloo Campaigns*, 115.

110. Lawrence, *Autobiography*, 71–72, 84, 100. As with any vocation, Lawrence learned the trade from an accomplished mentor. He watched his friend "Pig" Harding, a scrounger with few peers. Pig had acquired his name due to the thoroughness of his searches. In the bacon theft with Pig, Lawrence mentions sharing the find with comrades who were not in the initial search party. One of his reasons, besides loyalty, was getting rid of excess plunder to avoid detection. Ibid., 98–99.

111. Knowles, *War in the Peninsula*, 72, 45.

112. Douglas, *Douglas's Tale*, 21.

113. Harley, *Veteran*, 2:59. Harley acknowledged the danger to Dolan, but circumstances forced him to continue relying on Dolan's ability to steal the food they needed. Another officer, Thomas Browne, admitted that he was once a member of a party of officers that set off after a soldier who was in possession of half a pig, which had been gained by plunder. The soldier dropped the carcass during the pursuit; Browne and the other officers recovered the remains and divided the pork among themselves, because they all were famished. Browne, *Napoleonic War Journal*, 194.

114. Fortescue, *History of the British Army*, 4:935. Holmes adds that it was not until 1847 that an order was passed requiring all soldiers to receive no less than one penny per day (one-twelfth of a shilling), regardless of the amount of stoppages owed. Holmes, *Redcoat*, 309.

115. Costello, *Peninsular and Waterloo Campaigns*, 30.

116. Douglas, *Douglas's Tale*, 12. This exchange took place in 1809.

117. Gunn, "Memoirs," 109.

118. Grattan, *Adventures with the Connaught Rangers*, 296–97. Browne also mentions an episode when hungry soldiers, retreating to Rodrigo, came upon a herd of swine feeding on acorns in a wood. The rankers immediately began firing at the pigs; the shooting reached such a volume that it resembled a skirmish. Wellington issued an order to put an end to such escapades, attaching the death penalty to his edict. Browne, *Napoleonic War Journal*, 194.

119. Blakeney, *Boy in the Peninsular War*, 103.

120. Macfarlane, "Peninsula Private," 11.

121. Cooper, *Rough Notes*, 119.

122. See Grattan, *Adventures with the Connaught Rangers*, 71; and Harris, *Recollections* (1970 ed.), 154, for two examples.

123. Grattan, *Adventures with the Connaught Rangers*, 71.

124. Harris, *Recollections* (1970 ed.), 154.

125. *Soldier of the Seventy-first*, 37.

126. Costello, *Peninsular and Waterloo Campaigns*, 127–29, 132–33.

127. Lawrence, *Autobiography*, 32, 34 (sharing prize money with widows), 83 (a few additional examples).

128. Ibid., 164. In this instance, Lawrence had just eaten and claimed that "I was not hungry myself." Given his pattern of behavior and his regard for his comrades, it is doubtful that the outcome would have changed had he been famished.

129. Ibid., 137–38. This is but one example of the culture of mutual support that was such a crucial part of British army life.

130. Larpent, *Private Journal*, 1:164.

131. Oman, "Courts Martial of the Peninsular War," 1711, 1712–13.

132. Henry, *Trifles from My Port-folio*, 1:192.

133. Lawrence, *Autobiography*, 98. Lawrence does state that drunken soldiers of the Fifth Division may have murdered a few of their own in the frenzied aftermath of the siege of Badajoz. Ibid., 118.

134. There were of course exceptions to this general rule. John Cooper, a British light infantryman, remembered a "brutal sergeant of ours" who killed a French soldier he had captured, shooting the man in cold blood. Esdaile, *Peninsular Eyewitnesses*, 110.

135. Henry, *Trifles from My Port-folio*, 1:168–69.

136. Sherer, *Recollections of the Peninsula*, 132.

137. Oman, *Wellington's Army*, 212–13.

138. Donaldson, *Recollections*, 176, 158–59.

139. Sherer, *Recollections of the Peninsula*, 179–80.

140. Cooper, *Rough Notes*, 15.

141. *Soldier of the Seventy-first*, 15–17, 60.

142. Lawrence, *Autobiography*, 134–35.

143. Donaldson, *Recollections*, 72.

144. Green, *Vicissitudes of a Soldier's Life*, 33.

145. Westbrook, "Potential for Military Disintegration," 247.

146. Stouffer et al., *American Soldier*, 174–75, 179, 181.

147. Cited in McGuffie, "Recruiting the Ranks of the Regular British Army," 130.

148. Green, *Vicissitudes of a Soldier's Life*, 128. The men were indeed enterprising when it came to drink. Costello relates the humorous tale of Tom Crawley, whose rum ration had been stopped because he woke his captain while loudly narrating a ghost story to his mates. At the next meal Crawley "accidentally" dropped his bread ration in the rum barrel. In slowly extricating it (after pushing it to the bottom of the barrel to ensure it soaked up as much rum as possible), Crawley brazenly turned and complained to the commissary officer about his "misfortune" in having lost his only hot meal for the next four days. The kindly commissary gave him an extra half-loaf, which Crawley "instantly squeezed against the wet one, lest a drop of precious liquor should fall to the ground." He then went away and happily devoured both loaves. Costello, *Peninsular and Waterloo Campaigns*, 46. While entertaining, Crawley's antics hint at a certain kind of desperation and perhaps even a dependence on alcohol. He was without question fond of his alcohol ration.

149. WO 90/1, cited in Buckley, *British Army in the West Indies*, 221. Also see Linch, "Recruitment of the British Army," 202–33, for a complete analysis of desertion.

150. Hughes, " 'Vive la république! Vive l'empereur!' " 380. Hughes notes that enlisted men did not often mention glory, rewards, or their feelings about Napoleon in their writings. He argues that the French soldier resigned himself to service and developed the same fatalistic attitude as did the British ranker. Ibid., 384–93.

151. Ibid., 398. French deserters were usually fined or forced to provide labor for public works. Only in the worst cases when theft of army property was involved did the French deserter face "the penalty of the bullet."

152. Surtees, *Twenty-five Years in the Rifle Brigade*, 134, 136.

153. Gilbert, "Why Men Deserted," 560.

154. Harris, *Recollections* (1970 ed.), 41. Harris's view of the soldiers' expectations about the officers' backgrounds reveals the attitude of optimistic subservience held by most men regarding the capabilities of high-born officers.

155. Ibid., 124. Donaldson described a similar couple dying in each other's arms on the retreat to Salamanca, remarking: "our reflections were bitter." Donaldson, *Recollections*, 121, 123.

156. Blakeney, *Boy in the Peninsular War*, 67. Few officers seemed to grasp that privation and hopelessness were the real root causes of the soldiers' alcoholic excesses; in this case Blakeney's assumption failed to identify the circumstances that led to the family's demise.

157. Surtees, *Twenty-five Years in the Rifle Brigade*, 39.

158. Robinson, "Peninsular Brigadier," 159.

159. In his work on the subject of soldier motivation, Lynn delineates sustaining motivation as a separate factor acting on soldiers, different from the initial enthusiasms that brought them into the army and vastly different from the forces that act on men during combat. Lynn, *Bayonets of the Republic*, 35.

4. A STICK WITHOUT A CARROT

1. Glover, *Wellington's Army*, 36–37.

2. Roger Buckley argues that officers came from four classes: "upper gentry and nobility; lesser gentry, distinguished families now involved in trade or profession, the clergy and surviving yeoman farmers; sweepings from a wide distribution across the first two groups and a significant minority of foreigners . . . ; and subaltern officers . . . promoted from the ranks." Browne, *Napoleonic War Journal*, 313. The second group produced the most officers.

3. Anglesey, *History of the British Cavalry*, 1:169.

4. Anton, *Retrospect of a Military Life*, 103. Coffee and tea were even beyond his means as a sergeant.

5. Larpent, *Private Journal*, 1:46, 52, 77. These purchases were all in 1812 and January 1813.

6. Hunt, *Charging against Napoleon*, 113.

7. Hennell, *Gentleman Volunteer*, 41–42. Prices were for Madrid in August 1812. Hennell's description of his leisurely life as a moneyed officer provides a great contrast to the day of the common soldier, who was struggling to survive. Ibid., 72.

8. Fitzgerald, "With the Tenth Hussars in Spain," 100.

9. For a complete breakdown of compliance types, see Westbrook, "Potential for Military Disintegration," 247.

10. Cited in Oman, *Wellington's Army*, 41.

11. Wheeler, *Letters*, 187.

12. Cooper, *Rough Notes*, 63.

13. Oman, *Wellington's Army*, 41.

14. Cooke, *Narrative of Events in the South of France and America*, 47–48.

15. Kincaid, *Random Shots*, 186.

16. Holmes, *Acts of War*, 343, citing Costello, *Peninsular and Waterloo Campaigns*.

17. Harris, *Recollections* (1970 ed.), 23, 118.

18. See John Lynn's work on the development of *esprit* and the role of small group cohesion in the armies of Louis XIV. Lynn, *Giant of the Grand Siècle*, 439–50.

19. Oman, *Wellington's Army*, 149.

20. Watson, "United States and the Peninsular War," 865.

21. Wellesley Papers, British Museum [B.M.] Add. MSS 37295: Liverpool to Wellington, 15 June 1810, and Perceval to Wellesley, 23 July 1810. Liverpool Papers, B.M. Add. MSS 38245: Wellington to Liverpool, 23 May 1810. Liverpool Papers, B.M. Add. MSS 38325: Liverpool to Wellington, 20 February 1811. Cited by Watson, "United States and the Peninsular War," 864.

22. The Duke of York, the army commander-in-chief in London, also had no direct control over the commissariat or the ordnance branch. Fortescue, *History of the British Army*, 6:190.

23. Ward, "Quartermaster-General's Department in the Peninsula," 137. The complete issue of equipment for the army was also the quartermaster-

general's responsibility, even issuing blankets and shirts to artillerymen, who normally were supplied by the Ordnance Department. Road and bridge maintenance and fortification repair were also under the purview of the quartermaster-general.

24. Ibid.

25. Ibid., 136.

26. Haythornthwaite, *Armies of Wellington*, 119.

27. See Schaumann, *On the Road with Wellington*, for an appreciation of the difficult life of a commissariat officer.

28. Commissariat officers were so pressed to come up with supplies that they sometimes took advantage of the locals. The potential for graft was also a temptation. Larpent comments in January 1813 about four cases against commissariat clerks accused of defrauding local Spaniards under the pretense of acting for the army commissariat. The accused were buying and selling goods and keeping the profits. Larpent notes that he had 37 complaints pending against commissariat men for shortchanging peasants or outright theft. Larpent, *Private Journal*, 1:79.

29. Aitchison, *Ensign in the Peninsular War*, 213. Rifleman Kincaid also recorded a fractious interaction between a line officer and a commissary officer: General Craufurd threatened to arrest the commissariat officer if he proved unable to supply bread to Craufurd's Light Division. Kincaid, *Random Shots*, 50, 144. Robert Blakeney recalled another such episode wherein General Henry Paget berated a paymaster in charge of bullocks, threatening to have the man hanged. Blakeney, *Boy in the Peninsular War*, 80.

30. Kincaid, *Random Shots*, 50, 144.

31. Larpent, *Private Journal*, 1:46.

32. Arthur Wellesley to Castlereagh, 21 August 1809.

33. Wellington to Henry Wellesley, 3 May 1812.

34. Wellington wrote on 8 January 1812 that pay was six months in arrears and that the war chest was empty. Wellington, *Dispatches*, 11:425, 427. In June he wrote to Lord Liverpool, stating that the troops were four months behind in pay, the staff six months, and the muleteers almost a year. Wellington complained that "we are in debt for every article of supply, of every description." Ibid., 9:263–64. Walter Henry mentions that the army was six months in arrears before the siege of Badajoz in 1812 as if this was an ongoing problem, which it was. Henry, *Trifles from My Port-folio*, 1:77. Larpent admitted that by 1813 the army was 16 months in arrears in pay; by October of that same year it was 20 months behind. Larpent, *Private Journal*, 2:69, 110.

35. Wellington, *Dispatches*, 9:582.

36. Ibid.

37. Mills, *For King and Country*, 264.

38. Aitchison, *Ensign in the Peninsular War*, 228 (emphasis in the original).

39. Ibid., 227 (emphasis in the original).

40. Ibid.

41. Larpent, *Private Journal*, 1:110.

42. George Woodbury of the 10th Regiment of Foot and 18th Hussars wrote that Wellington was "very much displeased with the insubordination

of the regiment.... Numbers of them he saw plundering in the streets; he was likewise very much displeased with several officers who were there likewise." As an important side note, Woodbury added that he was in such a state of starvation that he was forced to steal a sheep to survive. Hunt, *Charging against Napoleon*, 110.

43. Green, *Vicissitudes of a Soldier's Life*, 170.

44. Hunt, *Charging against Napoleon*, 164–65.

45. Robinson, "Peninsular Brigadier," 163.

46. Lawrence, *Autobiography*, 48.

47. The sergeant's halberd, officially called a pike, was actually a spontoon, which had replaced the real halberd in 1792. Scurfield, "Weapons of Wellington's Army," 146.

48. Lawrence, *Autobiography*, 49.

49. Also see Harris, *Recollections* (1970 ed.), 138.

50. See Richard Glover's comments regarding his characterization of British regulars as "appalling thugs" who required flogging to be controlled. His description is only the most vocal assessment of many similar opinions (outlined in chapter 1). Glover, *Peninsular Preparation*, 174–76.

51. Lawrence, *Autobiography*, 50.

52. Holmes, *Redcoat*, 320. Holmes goes on to point out that while civilian attitudes toward corporal punishment were changing, Eton headmaster Dr. J. Keate still caned as many as 80 boys a day in 1832.

53. Cleaver, *Under the Lash*, 4.

54. Flogging as a military punishment was first mentioned in an essay by a Lieutenant Colonel Dalrymple, published in 1761. British dragoon regiments used the punishment of being suspended by one wrist with one foot balancing on the tip of a rounded-off wooden cone as late as 1803–1804. Ibid., 11.

55. Steppler, "British Military Law," 859.

56. WO 71, cited in ibid., 860.

57. The soldiers were tried under the Article of War clause: "disorders and neglects, which officers and soldiers alike may be guilty of, to the prejudice of good order and military discipline." Ibid., 863.

58. Ibid., 876.

59. Cited in Wheeler, *Letters*, 3.

60. O'Neil, *Military Adventures*, 8, 48. O'Neil later petitioned the Duke of York at the Horse Guards, seeking permission to allow soldiers to attend services of their own denomination, and was gratified when this request was granted.

61. The British use of ceremony to enhance the effects of flogging stands in stark contrast to the way in which Napoleon used ceremonies to enhance morale.

62. The men were more frequently tied to three crossed sergeant's spontoons that had been driven into the ground.

63. Blanco, "Attempts to Abolish Branding and Flogging," 139.

64. Cleaver, *Under the Lash*, 74.

65. Green, *Vicissitudes of a Soldier's Life*, 15. In a drunken state, the soldier in question had struck an officer. His sentence was remarkably light

given the offense: such conduct usually resulted in either the gibbet or more than 1,000 lashes.

66. Cooper, *Rough Notes*, 14.

67. Morris, *Memoirs of a Soldier*, 38.

68. Larpent, *Private Journal*, 1:142–43.

69. Haythornthwaite, *Armies of Wellington*, 69–70. The man who mutilated himself was then punished for his efforts to avoid the lash. Haythornthwaite does not mention whether that was in addition to the flogging for the original crime.

70. Morris, *Memoirs of a Soldier*, 5.

71. Donaldson, *Recollections of an Eventful Life* (Glasgow, 1824), 196, 84.

72. Surtees, *Twenty-five Years in the Rifle Brigade*, 91. Harris concurred that Craufurd's iron discipline was necessary at times, particular when the brigade was hard pressed, such as during the hellish retreat to Corunna. Harris argued that if he "flogged two, he saved hundreds from death by his management. I detest the lash, but I am convinced the British army could never go on with it." Harris, *Recollections* (1970 ed.), 138. He was referring to an incident in which General Craufurd flogged two men for straggling in order to ensure that no men fell out during the last struggles of the retreat to Corunna. Harris's position, while seemingly odd, can probably be explained by noting that he had no other frame of reference by which to judge flogging: such corporal punishment was all he had ever known in civilian and army life. In this case, he saw that hard discipline might have saved lives under these special circumstances. It should be noted that Harris also lamented the tyranny of sergeants and officers who tormented the men with "trifles" and related punishments, a practice "very injurious to a whole corps." Ibid., 102.

73. Costello, *Peninsular and Waterloo Campaigns*, 13.

74. Costello notes that Plunkett soon got over the lashing, perhaps in part because he received only a portion of the sentence. Still, being humiliated and physically abused in front of peers is not a way to engender individual or unit pride. While flogging may have united the men, who despised its use, it was not the primary mechanism that shaped their behavior.

75. O'Neil, *Military Adventures*, 48.

76. Donaldson, *Recollections*, 146.

77. Ibid., 54.

78. Ibid., 104, 148, 104, 146. Donaldson made an additional statement, describing the effects of the lash on a man's character: "I have observed that it changed a man's character for the worse; he either became broken hearted and useless to the corps, or shameless and hardened." Ibid., 147.

79. Morris, *Memoirs of a Soldier*, 45.

80. Bell, *Rough Notes*, 1:121.

81. As proof that not every officer used flogging as a regular tool of coercive discipline, Costello writes proudly that his commanding officer, Major Cameron, was "not only a brave and gallant officer, but a shrewd man." He states that in six years not more than six men of his battalion had been flogged. Costello, *Peninsular and Waterloo Campaigns*, 118.

82. Buckley, *British Army in the West Indies*, 203.

83. Wheeler recalled having his division formed into an open square in order to witness an execution. The two deserters faced inward, with the firing party stationed only a few paces away as the court-martial was read and spiritual assistance was offered. The condemned men were blindfolded and forced to kneel. The soldiers in the square watched as the officer in charge dropped his handkerchief. The execution party fired, with the muzzles of the muskets held close to the kneeling men so that the soldiers could not miss. A flintlock was then discharged into the head of each man. The command "Eyes left" was issued, and the soldiers were required to view their dead comrades as the division was marched past the bodies. Wheeler wrote, "I shall not attempt to describe the frightful appearance of the mangled bodies." Wheeler, *Letters*, 68–69.

84. Holmes, *Redcoat*, 324. In his work on courts-martial for the period 1809 to 1814 Charles Oman noted three general offenses involving plundering, with tiers of related punishment. He found 50 cases of straight plundering, which merited 300–700 lashes; 30 convictions for theft of valuables, which brought 700–1,000 lashes; and 57 armed robbery cases, which resulted in 24 soldiers being hung and the rest receiving 600–1,200 lashes. Oman added that "some of the executed had taken comparatively little from the peasants whom they plundered, and had not severely injured them: no more than a blow with the butt-end of a musket had been given in many cases. . . . But the moment that the element of violence was added to the theft, Wellington became inexorable, and only pardoned on the rarest of occasions." Oman, "Courts Martial of the Peninsular War," 1710–13. Assaults did occur, although they appear to be far fewer than has been suggested. Those caught, as Oman contended, were quickly and severely punished.

85. Horse Guards circular, 25 March 1812, cited in Haythornthwaite, *Armies of Wellington*, 69.

86. Larpent, *Private Journal*, 1:127, 143–44. That same week a commissariat clerk found guilty of fraud committed suicide rather than face a flogging.

87. Holmes, *Redcoat*, 324. The maximum number of lashes for all branches was lowered to 100 in 1832. The number of flogging offenses was then reduced in 1833, and the total allowable lashes dropped to 100 at the regimental level and 200 for general courts-martial offenses. By 1847 the maximum was 50 lashes, and by 1879 it was 25. Holmes notes that by 1829 about 2 percent of the soldiers were lashed each year, which fell to approximately 0.5 percent by 1845.

88. Private Wheeler, for example, wrote that his unit received four extra hours a drill for a month for performing poorly on a field exercise. Wheeler, *Letters*, 36. McGuffie also mentions a "Disgrace Squad" in London for men whose behavior was "irregular and unsoldierlike." These men wore their tunics reversed and were constantly drilled. They also had all privileges suspended. McGuffie, "The 7th Hussars in 1813," 9. Both these instances, however, occurred while the army was not in the field, which may have allowed officers to consider punishments more carefully. Wheeler's case is also a collective rather than an individual punishment, and the "Disgrace Squad" appears to have been for men who committed very minor offenses.

89. *United Service Journal* 3 (1834): 413. Wellington added that "discipline, subordination, and good order" combined so that soldiers viewed NCOs and officers "as their best friends." Considering Wellington's attitude toward the men and his advocacy of the lash, this comment reveals his belief that properly trained soldiers could work with, not against, leadership. His words also reflect his views regarding the effects of coercive external discipline on soldier behavior. Men do not tend to respect or have positive feelings, however, toward superiors who beat them harshly or regularly.

90. Henry, *Notes of Conversations with the Duke of Wellington*, 13.

91. Larpent, *Private Journal*, 1:93.

92. *Colburn's Army and Navy Review* (May 1863): 32. Also cited in Ward, *Reign of Queen Victoria*, 1:272.

93. Blanco, "Attempts to Abolish Branding and Flogging," 145.

94. *Examiner*, 7 November 1868, 705.

95. As an example, Henry J. Temple (better known as Lord Palmerston, MP, secretary of war from 1809 to 1827, and later prime minister) wrote that corporal punishment "was essential to the very existence of the Army." Thomas Below, MP, added in 1855 that "he could not believe that the retention of the punishment . . . was at all likely to be injurious to the service or society." Sidney Herbert agreed, defending its use by explaining: "Those we get are the young, the heedless, the thoughtless, the wild." The *Manchester Guardian* countered by describing flogging "as being the last refuge of barbarism in this country." Blanco, "Attempts to Abolish Branding and Flogging," 138–39. Even William Wilberforce, usually an advocate of the common soldier, succumbed to the notion that flogging had always been done and was still needed. He commented that "when he considered what a huge and multifarious body an army was, he should be afraid of adopting suddenly so material a change in what was deemed to be so essential to its discipline, on which depended entirely the management and government of it." *Parliamentary Debates* 21 (1812): 1287.

96. Cleaver, *Under the Lash*, 1. Rowland Hill, one of Wellington's most competent commanders, was not among the advocates of the lash. Know as "Daddy" Hill to his men, he considered it unnecessary for preserving discipline. Instead he looked after the men's needs, exposed himself to the same dangers and hardships faced by the soldiers, and led by inspiration rather than by fear.

97. McPherson, *For Cause and Comrades*.

98. Lynn, *Bayonets of the Republic*, 119–62. Michael Hughes's very detailed analysis of Napoleon's efforts to use normative and remunerative compliance to improve soldier morale is the essential work on how Napoleon endeavored through written pleas, songs, and rewards to convince his soldiers to do his bidding by whatever means. Hughes, " 'Vive la république! Vive l'empereur!' " Also, for an interesting analysis of the national identities of British soldiers, see Pockett, "Soldiers of the King," 8–13.

99. Elting, *Swords around a Throne*, 601–602.

100. Hughes, " 'Vive la république! Vive l'empereur!' " 215. Hughes points out that these songs were probably intended for the civilian population as well.

101. Camon, *La Guerre Napoleonienne*, 5.

102. Gougaud, *Journal*, 2:119.

103. Elting, *Swords around a Throne*, 602.

104. Chandler, *Campaigns of Napoleon*, 155.

105. Ibid., 157.

106. Elting, *Swords around a Throne*, 598. This number includes 1,200 crosses that went to civilians. The Légion d'Honneur had various grades, making it a continuously attractive award. Also see Hughes, "'Vive la république! Vive l'empereur!'" 48–51.

107. Ibid., 601. Hughes's work on French army festivals provides the most complete description of the variety and purposes of these fêtes. Ibid., 32–51.

108. This was also possible in the British army.

109. Elting, *Swords around a Throne*, 421, 596.

110. Wellington, *Dispatches*, 9:425–26.

111. Macfarlane, "Peninsula Private," 14.

112. O'Neil, *Military Adventures*, 256.

113. Lawrence, *Autobiography*, 246, 249.

114. Cited in Costello, *Peninsular and Waterloo Campaigns*, 16. Plunkett was forced to reenlist to survive. After he was invalided out again, he and his wife, who had lost part of her face when an ammunition wagon exploded at Quatre Bras, tried settling in Canada on a small parcel of land allotted to pensioners. When he located his land, he was dismayed to find it mostly covered by swamp. Plunkett and his wife returned to England, where he was reduced to selling matches and needles; he soon died a pauper.

115. Ibid., 162. Costello married his wife, who was French, against orders. Thus, she was left behind when he sailed for England. Through much travail, they were reunited in England, only to discover that life on sixpence a day was impossible.

116. Harris, *Recollections* (1970 ed.), 189.

117. In 1829 George IV issued a royal warrant regulating pensions based on 21 years of service for infantry and 24 for cavalry. Disability pensions were more complex, based on the severity of the wound and a minimum of 14 years' service. Financial and land grant pensions for soldiers, while Roman in origin, were reintroduced by the American Congress for the Continental Army. Congress initially offered $10 and 100 acres of land for an enlistment in 1776. By 1779 the cash bonus had increased to $200, while the land grant remained at 100 acres for a private. Higher ranks were apportioned larger land shares. Teipe, *America's First Veterans*, 219–20. I am indebted to Josh Howard for pointing out this material and source.

118. This passage is meant to compare only the French and British treatment of discharged soldiers. Across time, nations as a whole (both European and American) have poor track records when it comes to taking care of soldiers once they are released from active duty.

119. Glover's footnote in Hennell, *Gentleman Volunteer*, 148.

120. Hughes, "'Vive la république! Vive l'empereur!'" 232.

121. This is not to imply that the French army was always well provisioned. It was not, and the sufferings of the men at time equaled those of the British soldiery.

122. Bartov, *Hitler's Army.*

123. The accounts of British soldiers caring for their French counterparts after battles are numerous, and one example suffices to show the British rankers' lack of enmity toward French soldiers. Rifleman Costello wrote about shooting a French soldier near a village and immediately feeling remorse. "An indescribable uneasiness came over me," he recalled. "I felt almost like a criminal. I knelt to give him a little wine from a small calabash." For the British common soldier, the French were the enemy but were regarded with professional respect. Costello, *Peninsular and Waterloo Campaigns*, 56.

124. Haythornthwaite, *Armies of Wellington*, 73.

125. Ibid.

126. Holmes, *Redcoat*, 408.

127. Costello, *Peninsular and Waterloo Campaigns*, 11.

128. The type of medal is never mentioned in Costello's account. This ceremony was conducted after the battalion returned to England. Several years later, after Waterloo, Costello encountered Plunkett during an inspection in Ireland, and he was wearing two medals: the Waterloo medal and probably the one in question. Ibid., 16.

129. Ibid., 8.

130. Donaldson, *Recollections*, 112.

131. Discipline and pride in their military training and accomplishments also kept the men fighting; the redcoats' capacities to withstand hardship and expertly perform required tasks on the battlefield worked in concert with faith in their leaders to provide additional impetus to soldier on. Although it does not surface often in primary source accounts, ethnic pride on the part of soldiers in regiments that were predominately Irish, Scottish, or English might also have played a role. Such pride (whether in an ethnic group, regiment, or army) only strengthened the bonds of the small groups that were forged under conditions of extreme hardship.

5. ORDEAL BY FIRE

1. Charles Esdaile, "Wellington Triumphant: An Analysis of British Battlefield Invincibility in Spain and Portugal, 1808–1814" (unpublished), 2. I am indebted to my long-time friend for sharing this preliminary version of his essay.

2. For a substantive examination of the problems underlying the combat limitations of the British cavalry, see Coss, "Misadventures of Wellington's Cavalry." For a counterargument, see Fletcher, *Galloping at Everything.*

3. Esdaile's "Wellington Triumphant," 3–7, provides a detailed analysis of these variables.

4. Six incidents (at Vimeiro, Talavera, Badajoz, Campo Mayor, Maguilla, and Waterloo) exemplify this tendency.

5. *Elucidation of Several Parts of His Majesty's Regulations*, 35. How these factors combined to create a force prone to uncontrollability is an interesting and complex story. Coss, "Misadventures of Wellington's Cavalry." Lieutenant-Colonel William Tomkinson's first-person experiences and anal-

ysis pinpoint the training and leadership deficiencies. Tomkinson, *Diary of a Cavalry Officer*, 135–36.

6. Fletcher, *Galloping at Everything*, xvi.

7. Wellington went on to acknowledge the gallantry and bravery of the cavalry and admits that they "have generally got themselves out of their own difficulties by sheer pluck." Gronow, *Reminiscences and Recollections*, 74.

8. See Calvert, *A Dictionary of Battles*.

9. Foy, *History of the War in the Peninsula*, 196–97. Foy's analogy, comparing British infantry to the *triarii* of the early Roman Republic army, is sound. The *triarii*, armed with long spears, formed the last tactical line and were meant to break pursuing formations.

10. Howie Muir, "Order of Battle: Customary Battle-Array in Wellington's Peninsular Army," in Muir et al., *Inside Wellington's Peninsular Army*, 84–171. Muir provides a detailed analysis of the patterns and purposes of Wellington's method of troop deployment.

11. Esdaile, "Wellington Triumphant," 16. All references to British infantry tactics include, in a general sense, the large numbers of Portuguese troops in the British army. They lived, trained, and fought in the same manner as did the British army, as Esdaile points out, and were often led by British officers. Ibid., 15.

12. Nosworthy, *With Musket, Cannon, and Sword*, 334–35.

13. See Gunther Rothenberg's figures representing column deployment (as well as that of *l'ordre mixte*) for accurate visuals. Rothenberg, *Art of Warfare in the Age of Napoleon*, 116–17.

14. Arnold, "Reappraisal of Column versus Line in the Peninsular War," 538–42. French infantry drill had its origins in the *Règlement* of 1791. This manual established the theoretical foundation of Revolutionary army tactics and heavily influenced those adopted by the armies of Napoleon. The regulations included descriptions of nine column formations, but only one was intended for tactical assault: the attack column. John Lynn convincingly argues that the regulations were altered in the field, where a "closed column with a front of two companies" superseded the attack column, with its wider intervals. This, he contends, allowed shock assault in column to emerge "as the decisive element in offensive tactics." He cites 42 examples of divisional columns in battle, with 35 of the cases being engagements in which the column was used in the attack. This emphasis on column assault helped transform Revolutionary zeal and group cohesion into a dominant battlefield tactic; French élan was put to use with *arme blanche*, a phrase denoting the white gleam from edged weapons, to create the Cult of the Bayonet. As Lynn points out, however, the French tactical system consisted of much more than bayonet charges. Revolutionary army tactics were theoretically founded on a series of coordinated attacks involving skirmishers, artillery, and infantry. Lynn, *Bayonets of the Republic*, 185–93, 252–54.

15. Ney, "Instructions for the Troops Comprising the Left Corps," 190, cited in Arnold, "Reappraisal of Column versus Line in the Peninsular War," 539.

16. The testimony originates from Lieutenant Charles Griois of the 1st Legère (Griois, *Mémoires du général Griois*, 308–13); General Jean-Louis Re-

ynier (Reynier, *Correspondance*); a French staff officer (Pelet, *French Campaign in Portugal*, 179); a French captain named Lapène (Beresford, *Refutation of Colonel Napier's Justification*, 170); a British officer at Waterloo (Ross-Lewin, *With the 32nd in the Peninsula*, 279); Captain H.W. Powell (Siborne, ed., *Waterloo Letters*, 255); another British officer (Bunbury, *Narratives of the Great War with France*); a British writer (Boothby, *Under England's Flag*); and a British ensign (Anderson, *Recollections of a Peninsular Veteran*). Sources originally cited in Arnold, "Reappraisal of Column versus Line in the Peninsular War," 546; and Chandler, *On the Napoleonic Wars*, 142.

17. Chandler, *On the Napoleonic Wars*, 143. Chandler writes: "It was axiomatic that the columns were intended to deploy into line before their final attack." Ibid., 139.

18. It might be argued that this reverse slope method also prevented the British infantry from firing too early, although this does not seem to have been a problem.

19. The OODA loop (Observe, Orient, Decide, and Act) concept was created by air force colonel and military strategist John Boyd. For a detailed analysis, see Frans Osinga, *Science, Strategy and War*.

20. Arnold, "Reappraisal of Column versus Line in the Peninsular War," 539.

21. Chandler, *On the Napoleonic Wars*, 136.

22. *Journal of the Royal Artillery Institution* 34 (1907). For an excellent summary of the evolution and perpetuation of Oman's misinterpretation, see Arnold, "Reappraisal of Column versus Line in the Peninsular War," 535–52. Arnold points out that seven other eyewitness accounts, never referenced by Oman, describe the French forming into a line just before the attack. Ibid., 543.

23. Oman, *Studies in the Napoleonic Wars*, 333. This is a reprint of Oman's Woolwich lectures. Oman did admit his mistake in a footnote in *Wellington's Army* but allowed his lectures to be printed without correction. See Arnold, "Reappraisal of Column versus Line in the Peninsular War," 543.

24. Chandler, *On the Napoleonic Wars*, 142. For Fortescue's support of Oman, see Fortescue, *History of the British Army*, 5:347.

25. Guibert, *Ecrits militaires*, 130, cited in Arnold, "Reappraisal of Column versus Line," 197.

26. The Brown Bess, British Short Land Pattern musket, was the preferred musket of manufacture for the British Army. The Board of Ordnance created the India Pattern version originally for the Honorable East India Company in the 1770s. The New Land Pattern variation was approved in 1803 but not manufactured before 1811; only 20,000 were made before Waterloo. The musket had a 39-inch barrel, as opposed to its predecessor's 42-inch length. This musket type was used as late as 1850 by some regular and militia units. Scurfield, "Weapons of Wellington's Army," 145.

27. Chandler, *On the Napoleonic Wars*, 135.

28. Hughes, *Firepower*, 27. Hughes is citing a French test made in 1800 wherein the French musket was fired at a target measuring 1.75 meters by 3.00 meters. At a range of 75 meters, 60 percent of the rounds struck the target; at 150 meters, the success rate fell to 40 percent. The estimated mean

error of rounds fired at the 150-meter distance was 75 centimeters in height and 60 centimeters laterally. A Prussian test firing at a sheet of canvas 6 feet tall by 100 feet wide returned similar results: 40 percent hits at 150 yards and 60 percent at 75 yards. Holmes, *Redcoat*, 198.

29. Nosworthy points out that the armies of most nations, including the French, tended to lack fire discipline and often made the tactical error of firing too soon. Nosworthy, *With Musket, Cannon, and Sword*, 190–92, 208–209, 243–44.

30. Thus, the most effective fire was usually the first, as the rounds were loaded before men's nerves and the stressors of the battlefield worked to lower firing efficacy.

31. Ibid., 73, 198.

32. The Brown Bess had a muzzle velocity of 1,500 feet per second, which was greater than American Civil War rifles. Nosworthy, *Bloody Crucible of Courage*, 33.

33. William Surtees of the 95th wrote that of this effect, noting that French shots were often high, coming down well behind his battalion. Surtees, *Twenty-five Years in the Rifle Brigade*, 121.

34. Nosworthy, *With Musket, Cannon, and Sword*, 205.

35. Hughes, *Firepower*, 27. Nosworthy provides an excellent analysis of casualties-per-shots-fired ratios using data supplied by various military writers, most of whom saw combat during the period in question. These rates range from .01 to 3–5 percent. Nosworthy, *With Musket, Cannon, and Sword*, 204–205. The accuracy problems stemmed not from firepower but from the space between ball and barrel and the irregular shape of rounds.

36. Hughes, *Firepower*, 133.

37. Muir, *Tactics and the Experience of Battle*, 82. Surtees provides an estimate that matches Muir's lower estimate exactly; Surtees then goes on to claim that 1 in 20 shots caused a casualty when fired from a rifle. Surtees, *Twenty-five Years in the Rifle Brigade*, 290.

38. Cited in Adkin, *Waterloo Companion*, 166.

39. For an excellent analysis of all the formation strengths, deficiencies, and tactical permutations of infantry combat during this period, see Muir, *Tactics and the Experience of Battle*, 68–104.

40. Lawrence, *Autobiography*, 210–11. Lawrence comments on the futility of the repeated French cavalry attacks against formed squares: "I must say here that I cannot think why those charges of cavalry were kept up against our unbroken squares. . . . It is murder to send cavalry against disciplined infantry unless they have artillery to act in conjunction with them." Ibid., 212.

41. Ibid., 211.

42. The Portuguese troops, under General Beresford, and the King's German Legion fully adopted British tactical methods.

43. The British could also resort to three- and even four-rank lines when the terrain and the situation demanded. Richard Master of the 1st Regiment of Guards described how his battalion formed a line four deep at Waterloo, with the men in the last two rows handing muskets to those in the front ranks. The 1st Guards, in concert with Lieutenant-General Sir Charles Al-

ten's brigade and artillery, repulsed the French Imperial Guard that day. In this case the British Guards, numbering well over 1,000, were forced to double the line in order to fit between adjacent Allied units. Firepower was no doubt the deciding factor in this instance. Master, "Ensign at War," 140. The Imperial Guard attempted to deploy into line about 50 yards from the British Guards. Ross-Lewin, *With the 32nd in the Peninsula*, 279. Josh Howard has pointed out that the Americans fought in a two-rank line in 1812. Personal communication, 6 October 2008.

44. Holmes, *Redcoat*, 33.

45. Chandler, *Military Maxims of Napoleon*, 72 (Maxim XLVIII).

46. Elting, *Swords around a Throne*, 537.

47. See Houlding, *Fit for Service*, 257–81, 426–27.

48. Haythornthwaite, *Armies of Wellington*, 89.

49. Browne, *Napoleonic War Journal*, 13.

50. Cited in ibid., 14.

51. Adkin, *Waterloo Companion*, 196.

52. Lawrence, *Autobiography*, 147–48.

53. Ibid., 149.

54. See Stouffer et al., *American Soldier*, 222–23.

55. Anton, *Retrospect of a Military Life*, 107–108.

56. Macfarlane, "Peninsula Private," 6.

57. Cited in Sherer, *Recollections of the Peninsula*, 110.

58. Gomm, *Letters and Journals*, 278.

59. Costello, *Peninsular and Waterloo Campaigns*, 125.

60. Aitchison, *Ensign in the Peninsular War*, 56.

61. Carss, "2nd/53rd in the Peninsula," 5–6.

62. Grattan, *Adventures with the Connaught Rangers*, 33.

63. *Soldier of the Seventy-first*, 17–18.

64. Gleig, *Subaltern*, 181–82, 190.

65. *Soldier of the Seventy-first*, 18.

66. Aitchison, *Ensign in the Peninsular War*, 57.

67. Patterson, "Line Regiment at Waterloo," 61. Patterson also complains that on the morning of Waterloo "still that rascally commissary did not bring us any provisions." Ibid., 63.

68. Cited in Marmont, *Mémoires*, 5:105. Another French account reproduces the same effects of British close-range musketry described by Bugeaud and a sudden charge on French troops. Although less dramatic, this 1824 anecdote from General G. Chambray ends with the same French surprise, disorder, and flight. Griffith, *Forward into Battle*, 36.

69. Esdaile, "Wellington Triumphant," 22. These regiments were the 43rd, 52nd, 60th (5th Battalion), 68th, 75th, and 90th Foot, in addition to the 95th and 71st.

70. Ibid., 23.

71. Griffith, *Forward into Battle*, 39.

72. Muir, *Tactics and the Experience of Battle*, 81.

73. Nosworthy reaches the same conclusion: "There is little evidence or no basis for the notion that British troops somehow defeated the French utilizing a continuum of well-orchestrated volleys." He contends that the

British tactic of the "determined charge" was the essential factor. Nosworthy, *With Musket, Cannon, and Sword*, 220–21.

74. Hibbert's highland private later commented on the difference between the attitudes and demeanor of French and British troops during an attack. The French, he noted, came on shouting, the "men vociferating . . . in a fury." The British were restrained, "as still as death." *Soldier of the Seventy-first*, 60.

75. Muir, *Tactics and the Experience of Battle*, 86.

76. Duffy, *Military Experience in the Age of Reason*, 245.

77. The Brown Bess bayonet was 17 inches long, while the Charleville musket bayonet was 15 inches.

78. Arnold, "Reappraisal of Column versus Line," 540.

79. Nosworthy, *With Musket, Cannon, and Sword*, 227.

80. Muir attests that "British troops were unusually good at holding their fire" and notes that "other armies placed less emphasis on close-range musketry." Muir, *Tactics and the Experience of Battle*, 81.

81. Lynn, *Bayonets of the Republic*, 185–93.

82. For a description of such attacks, see Nosworthy, *Anatomy of Victory*, 190–91. Matt Spring offers an important observation on the evolution of this technique, noting that the British were already practicing the volley and charge technique during the Seven Years War (French and Indian War in America) and the American Revolutionary War. General James Wolfe employed this method during the Battle of the Plains of Abraham (Battle of Quebec) in September 1759, and it was similarly and routinely used by British infantry during the battles of the American Revolution (personal communication, 1 December 2008). I am indebted to him for this insight.

83. Richard Holmes writes of the 31st Regiment of Foot firing a single volley at point-blank range and then charging a Sikh emplacement. The men uttered a "dreadful, sobbing, throaty roar," the "regiment breaking up into little knots of men laying on with bayonet and butt." Holmes, *Sahib*, 14.

84. Chandler, *On the Napoleonic Wars*, 132.

85. McNeill, *Keeping Together in Time*, 1–4.

86. The role of shared campaign experiences becomes clearer when days in the field are compared with days of combat. The 20 years of the Napoleonic Wars included only about 200 days of pitched battles. Holmes, *Acts of War*, 75.

87. Olmstead, *Small Group*, 19–20. In previous research, Roger Little included sharing, humility (the lack of bragging), dependability, and group allegiance in the form of not showing favoritism or having only one buddy among the most important group norms. Little, "Buddy Relations and Combat Performance," 200–201.

88. Behaviors that preserved life, from plundering and sharing to exhibiting steadiness in the face of danger, evolved to become the standards that shaped conduct. Such norms were less dependent on trickle-down principles (societal masculinity codes) than they were on the practicalities of campaign survival and the demands of combat. Contrary to Robert Nye's assertions, the French chivalric codes of *"prousées, loyauté, largesse, courtoisie,* and *franchise"* are unlikely to have percolated down and affected the creation of group

standards by common soldiers. Rather, the contingencies influencing soldier life during campaign and battle more probably became the catalysts that determined which values were adopted as meaningful and which were considered inconsequential to group survival. Nye, *Masculinity and Male Codes of Honor*, 15–30. As Michael Hughes points out, Nye and George Mosse (*Images of Man*) contend that the norms of courage and honor, valued by European aristocracy, were slowly being transferred from males of the upper levels of society (especially members of the bourgeoisie) to lower socioeconomic classes throughout Europe. Cited in Hughes, " 'Vive la république! Vive l'empereur!' " 180. Thucydides, however, wrote about Spartan and Athenian conceptualizations of honor, courage, and sacrifice that appear no different in substance or definition than the values of the same name as described by Nye and Mosse. It would seem that such concepts of masculinity existed in Western Europe and were esteemed by civilians and soldiers alike well before the nineteenth century. Perhaps this discrepancy helps explain why neither author can describe the process through which such ideals were supposedly assimilated by Europeans of the lower socioeconomic levels during the Napoleonic period, a failing that Hughes pinpoints in his work on soldier motivations.

89. Tiger, *Men in Groups*, 219.

90. Cited in Holmes, *Redcoat*, 154.

91. War has always had this effect, as the words of the fourteenth-century knight Jean du Beuil confirm: "You love your comrade so much in war. . . . A sweet feeling of loyalty and of pity fills your heart on seeing your friend so valiantly exposing his body. And then you are prepared to go and die or live with him, and for love not to abandon him. And out of that arises such a delight." Keegan, *Soldiers*, 19.

6. BANDED BROTHERS

1. In their quantitative analysis of the American Civil War soldiers, Dora Costa and Matthew Kahn discovered that when it came to combat motivation, "group loyalty was more than twice as important as ideology and six times as important as leadership. In contrast, during World War II group loyalty was almost three times as important as ideology and fourteen times as important as leadership." Costa and Kahn, *Heroes and Cowards*, 118–19. They also contend that social networks affected desertion rates, prisoner of war survival, and even "migration choices after the war." Ibid., 144, 153, 216.

2. Cooley's description of the effects of the group on the individual, and how the group molds the individual's perceptions to create a collective rather than an individual perspective, provides clarifying insight into the workings of primary group processes: "The result of intimate association, psychologically, is a certain fusion of individualities in a common whole, so that one's self, for many purposes at least, is the common life and purpose of the group. Perhaps the simplest way of describing this wholeness is by saying that it is a 'we.' " Cooley, *Social Organization*, 23–24, 26–28.

3. Omer Bartov has presented another viewpoint, arguing that draconian discipline and the capacity to vent anger and frustration on enemy com-

batants and civilians, particularly Jews or nationalities considered to be sub-human, kept small groups in the Wehrmacht intact. Bartov, *Hitler's Army*, 6, 28. "Cohesion," he contends, "came to depend on a perversion of the moral and legal basis of martial law." Ibid., 6. Bartov's ideological considerations would have had little impact on primary group cohesion during combat. Rather, they fall under John Lynn's category of sustaining motivations and apply to keeping men going between battles. Lynn, *Bayonets of the Republic*, 35. Paul Savage and Richard Gabriel reached the same conclusion regarding the impact of ideology on combat unity. In their work on unit cohesion and disintegration, they found that the willingness of German officers in World War II to share risk and hardship with their men was a key ingredient that helped cement unit cohesion. They explicitly state that "leadership did not hinge upon a dedication to the 'cause'—Nazi ideology or even national-ism." Savage and Gabriel, "Cohesion and Disintegration in the American Army," 343.

4. Stouffer et al., *American Soldier*, 130–31 (emphasis in the original).

5. Ibid., 149. In his appraisal of the inner workings of combat motiva-tion, Anthony Kellett notes that psychologist Stanley Schachter has experi-mentally demonstrated that as risk increases, so does the human desire to be in the company of others sharing the same danger. Kellett, *Combat Motiva-tion*, 287. Perhaps this originates from the subconscious understanding that survival probability is enhanced by collective action.

6. Stouffer et al., *American Soldier*, 98. John Keegan has attempted to distill Stouffer's discoveries regarding combat motivation down to three cate-gories, which he labels "inducement," "coercion," and "narcosis." Keegan's conceptualization falls short, in large part because he does not fully de-scribe the narcosis element. Keegan, "Towards a Theory of Combat Motiva-tion," 3–11.

7. Shils, "Primary Groups in the American Army," 27. Shils make it clear that the foundation for the entire Stouffer study on men in combat was the workings of primary groups, or "informal groups" as they are often called in *The American Soldier*. He argues that the value of the Stouffer et al. study lies in its analysis of how primary groups shape the behavior of soldiers. Stouffer et al. refer to this process as enhancing the soldier's "sense of power and security." Stouffer et al., *American Soldier*, 149.

8. While there is little doubt that Marshall conjured up his numbers regarding the percentages of men who actively participated in combat, the value of his work is not in his questionable numbers but in his recognition that not every man fights during combat and that the presence of comrades was the principal motivating reason why men were more likely to fight.

9. Shils and Janowitz, "Cohesion and Disintegration in the Wehr-macht," 281. The essay, published in 1948, investigated the relationship be-tween criminality and asocial behavior as indicators of a proclivity to sur-render. In their analysis Shils and Janowitz made the first military use of the term "primary social group." John Guilmartin has suggested that the Shils and Janowitz study was circulating through army channels during the war at the time when Marshall was conducting his interviews, conceivably shaping

his attitudes to some degree. Guilmartin, "Military Experience, the Military Historian, and the Reality of Battle," 12–13.

10. Holmes, *Acts of War*, 204.

11. In his analysis of group relations and men under fire in the Korean War, Roger Little concluded that "the primary basis for solidarity . . . was the recognition of mutual risk" and that "relationships were established to enhance effectiveness and survival." Little, "Buddy Relations and Combat Performance," 218. Some recent work on group processes reinforces this contention. A study by Roger Nibler and Karen Harris revealed that "cohesive effects were more likely to emerge in the process of decision making rather than in outcome." Nibler and Harris, "The Effects of Culture and Cohesiveness," 627.

12. Marshall, *Men against Fire*, 42.

13. The work of Shils and Janowitz supports the hypothesis that a soldier's capacity to withstand the stresses of combat has its roots in group dynamics. They argue: "It appears that a soldier's ability to resist [fear] is a function of the capacity of his primary group to avoid social disintegration. When the individual's immediate group, and its supporting formations, met his basic needs, offered him affection and esteem from both officers and comrades, supplied him with a sense of power . . . [then] the element of self-concern in battle, which would lead to disruption of the effective functioning of his primary group, was minimized." Shils and Janowitz, "Cohesion and Disintegration in the Wehrmacht," 281.

14. Du Picq, *Battle Studies*, 122. Colonel du Picq surveyed his fellow French officers and tallied their responses concerning battlefield morale. He recognized that individual morale was based on group unity and used the term "cohesion" (in regard to *esprit de corps*) in describing how combat required men to share a binding unity, a "moral cohesion." Du Picq was killed at Metz in 1870.

15. Rosen, *War and Human Nature*, 100, 105, 113, 121.

16. Ibid., 31, 35. See Rosen's second chapter, "Emotions, Memory, and Decision Making," 27–70, for a complete look at how strong emotions affect cognition and decision-making during times of stress.

17. Marshall, *Men against Fire*, 179.

18. David Grossman has offered several suggestions on why many soldiers are predisposed against shooting at other human beings. He identifies societal prohibitions against killing and poor training that does not prepare soldiers for the psychological shock of killing as possible reasons why some of them find it difficult to fire weapons at human beings. This initial resistance comes into conflict with the demands of the battlefield and, according to Grossman, leads to post–traumatic stress disorder (PTSD). I have had numerous conversations with soldiers who disagree with all or part of Grossman's premise. From their point of view, the action of killing an enemy who has the intent to do the same to the soldier or his comrades carries with it little remorse or psychological trauma. It would appear that the memories of seeing their pals horribly mutilated or killed have the greatest long-term emotional impact. Grossman, *On Killing* and *On Combat*. The army has

done some recent studies analyzing the effects of desensitizing soldiers to combat realities, combined with stress management techniques, on post-combat stress. "Virtual Reality Stress Inoculation Training" (slide briefing), U.S. Army Aeromedical Research Laboratory, United States Army Medical Research and Materiel Command (USAMRMC).

19. Little, "Buddy Relations and Combat Performance," 203.

20. Shils, "Primary Groups in the American Army," 26.

21. Dinter, *Hero or Coward*, 41. Marshall adds confirmation: "Man is a gregarious animal. He wants company. In his hour of greatest danger his herd instinct drives him toward his fellows. It is a source of comfort to be close to another man; it makes danger more endurable." Marshall, *Men against Fire*, 141.

22. Dinter, *Hero or Coward*, 40.

23. Stouffer et al., *American Soldier*, 174–75, 179, 181.

24. Wong et al., *Why They Fight*, 12. Another soldier explained why this was the case: "We eat, drink, [and go to the bathroom] together—everything—together. I think that it should be like that . . . I really consider these guys my own family, because we fight together, we have fun together. . . . We are to the point that we even call the squad leader 'dad.' " Ibid., 13.

25. Ibid., 12. According to the interviews conducted with captured Iraqi soldiers, "fear of retribution and punishment by [the] Baath Party or *Fedayeen Saddam*" kept the soldiers on the battlefield, if not particularly motivated. Fear of immediate officers turned out to be minimal; it was these external threats that most concerned enlisted Iraqi soldiers. Ibid., 6–7. External coercion rarely, if ever, makes soldiers fight effectively.

26. According to Mark Adkin, the death rate for wounded men reaching any of the makeshift field hospitals after Waterloo was a surprisingly low 9 percent. This number was 1 percent less than the death rates for hospital care in World War I. By World War II the rate was down to 4 percent. Adkin, *Waterloo Companion*, 312.

27. Moskos, *American Enlisted Man*, 145.

28. Harris, *Recollections* (1929 ed.), 86–87. Harris's comrade did return to the fighting; he died shortly after reaching his mates, when a cavalry saber cleaved his head almost in two.

29. Ibid., 40–41.

30. Costello, *Peninsular and Waterloo Campaigns*, 132.

31. Harris, *Recollections* (1929 ed.), 81, 85. Mayberry did indeed reclaim the esteem of his comrades before his death.

32. Lawrence, *Autobiography*, 112–13, 119, 122–24.

33. For further analysis of this topic, see Meier, *Military Psychology*, 57.

34. Green, *Vicissitudes of a Soldier's Life*, 76–79. Green detested the street-sweeping detail, noting that the Portuguese townsfolk "are the dirtiest people in this place I ever saw . . . [and] deposit filth of every kind in the streets."

35. Costello, *Peninsular and Waterloo Campaigns*, 131, 64. The connection between soldiers was ever present. Rifleman Kincaid amusedly recalled soldiers almost fainting with fatigue on the march being revived by the camaraderie of fellow soldiers during the few minutes of allotted rest time per

hour. The men "invariably grouped themselves in card-parties." The communal activity restored to a small degree the men's will to go on. Kincaid, *Adventures in the Rifle Brigade*, 146.

36. Costello, *Peninsular and Waterloo Campaigns*, 64. Burke was killed at Quatre Bras in 1815.

37. Grattan, *Adventures with the Connaught Rangers*, 219–22.

38. Bell, *Rough Notes*, 1:57.

39. Costello, *Peninsular and Waterloo Campaigns*, 153.

40. Wheeler, *Letters*, 57.

41. Douglas, *Douglas's Tale*, 66.

42. Donaldson, *Recollections*, 180–81.

43. Wheeler, *Letters*, 115, 170.

44. Lawrence, *Autobiography*, 126, 127.

45. Cited in Dyer, *War*, 127.

46. Grattan, *Adventures with the Connaught Rangers*, 308, 322.

47. Harris, *Recollections* (1929 ed.), 13. This incident took place during the relief of Copenhagen at the time of the Danish expedition of 1807.

48. Bell, *Rough Notes*, 1:57.

49. Costello, *Peninsular and Waterloo Campaigns*, 53, 54.

50. Anton, *Retrospect of a Military Life*, 193.

51. Lawrence, *Autobiography*, 193.

52. Ibid., 207, 222.

53. Ibid., 223. Charles Oman provides insight into the attitudes of Wellington and the British high command on cowardice. They seemed to punish it much less harshly than desertion. When the Spanish shot 27 of their men for cowardice after Talavera, Wellington is said to have appealed for their lives. As Oman notes, "Evidently the British army then believed that while an occasional, or even habitual, lack of courage was disgraceful, it should not be a capital offence." Oman, *History of the Peninsular War*, 2:515.

54. Bell, *Rough Notes*, 12.

55. Lawrence, *Autobiography*, 207, 224.

56. Costello, *Peninsular and Waterloo Campaigns*, 121.

57. Anton, *Retrospect of a Military Life*, 78, 140–41.

58. Little, "Buddy Relations and Combat Performance," 203.

59. Kindsvatter, *American Soldiers*, 73.

60. Ebert, *Life in a Year*, 111. Cited in Kindsvatter, *American Soldiers*, 73. Kindsvatter recommends Ebert's chapter on the experiences of new soldiers ("cherries" or "FNGs"), "Being New." Ebert's chapter does in fact provide excellent insight into the topic.

61. Wheeler, *Letters*, 142.

62. Replacements, not yet assimilated into a group, resorted more to prayer than to fear of letting down comrades as an aid during trying times on the battlefield. Interestingly, such men were prouder of their companies than were the veterans. This directly related to their aspirations to belong to the unit. Stouffer et al., *American Soldier*, 183–84, 278–79.

63. Little also notes that group norms often put the group at odds with the authority system, as group survival override external attempts to establish behavioral codes. This is a good description of the process whereby the

British ranker became an unrivaled looter on campaign, despite Wellington's orders against plundering. It also explains why nothing Wellington could do, short of providing adequate provisions, stopped the men from "reconnoitering" and sharing what they uncovered. Little, "Buddy Relations and Combat Performance," 195.

64. Lest such considerations seem archaic or applicable only to certain armies in isolated circumstances, we should note that today's U.S. Army sometimes struggles with the same dilemma. The current counterinsurgency doctrine espouses an approach to warfare that is a "combination of offensive, defensive, and stability operations." In a given locale "the exact mix varies depending on the situation and mission." Field Manual 3-24, *Counterinsurgency* (Headquarters Department of the Army, 2006), 1–19. One of the key considerations in this fluid environment is the use of appropriate force. The threat level during any mission may unexpectedly elevate; the commander must then make an immediate decision as to how much combat power is required to eliminate the danger. This choice must be predicated on the mission, commander's intent, and circumstances. A squad, feeling imperiled, may resort to instant and overwhelming force, regardless of the effects of such kinetic response on operational or strategic objectives. In this situation, group norms based on survival issues override mission requirements and army needs. The challenge is to inform, train, and trust subordinates in order to align group mores with mission goals. I am indebted to Major Steve Martinelli, who discussed in depth the challenge of coordinating mission requirements with the needs of small groups to protect their members, even when such actions threaten mission success. Personal communication, 5 December 2007.

65. WO 90/1, cited in Buckley, *British Army in the West Indies*, 221. In the BSC sample, which covers all the war years, 19.7 percent of soldiers whose records listed a final disposition were categorized as deserters (see table 14 in appendix A). The category of disposition appears to list only soldiers who died on duty, mustered out due to wounds, or deserted.

66. For an examination of this dichotomy, see Westbrook, "Potential for Military Disintegration," 248.

67. Because of their byzantine nature, the interconnections among these variables cannot be definitively parsed and individually weighed. Carl von Clausewitz noted the difficulty in quantifying the morale aspects of cohesion, writing that forces contributing to morale "will not yield to academic wisdom. They cannot be classified or counted. They have to be seen or felt." Clausewitz, *On War*, 184.

68. Leadership and group cohesion appear to be two factors that act as both sustaining and combat motivations. On the role of exterior factors affecting unit effectiveness, see Moskos, *American Enlisted Man*, 147.

69. See Rush, *Hell in Hürtgen Forest*, for specifics on how severe losses affect cohesion; and Stouffer et al., *American Soldier*, 285, for the effects of extended time in combat.

70. The vast majority of references to combat in this chapter focus on infantry in battle. While group cohesiveness remains the fundamental motivating factor, its effect on men in the different branches varies. Cavalry troop-

ers were usually required to summon up their courage for a single charge, or perhaps two. They were usually not required to stand under direct fire and await an attack, as cavalry was a proactive shock weapon. Artillery crews had a different dynamic entirely; their responsibility was to work their guns until danger was imminent. Then they usually fled as a group to the nearest infantry formation for protection. These differences in combat responsibilities by branch do not, however, negate the underlying force that keeps the soldiers of each branch functioning. For each, the catalyst for action remained the cohesion of the primary group.

71. "Primary group cohesion," Lynn writes, "is probably a universal military phenomenon; however it is crucial to consider the pattern of the group formed in a specific army at a specific time. The character, intensity, and significance of primary group cohesion are to a large degree determined by the group's structures, practices, relationships, and standards." Lynn, *Bayonets of the Republic,* 32–33. He adds: "Relationships between men are at the same time defined by the group's structure and practices and shaped by the religious, ethnic, class, and other societal attributes typical of the men themselves." Ibid., 33. Janowitz and Little echo similar sentiments in their work on the connections between sociology and the military establishment: "The goals and standards or norms that primary groups enforce are hardly self-generated; they arise from the larger environment and from the surrounding civilian society. Consequently, the empirical study of primary groups must extend beyond the factors that contribute to social cohesion in the smallest tactical groups." Janowitz and Little, *Sociology and the Military Establishment,* 94.

72. Wellington, *Dispatches,* 10:5.

73. Ward, *Wellington's Headquarters,* 200–201. James Gunn of the 42nd confirmed that the original kettle served 10 men. Gunn, "Memoirs," 97. Larpent, the army's judge advocate general, writes that Wellington had the kettles distributed one for every six soldiers and comments that the French still had no tents as of 1813. Larpent, *Private Journal,* 1:226 and 2:63.

74. As a side note, General Robert Craufurd had advocated the switch to smaller kettles in 1810, most likely because the lighter kettles would have enabled his division to travel faster, always a prime consideration for the Light Division. Aitchison, *Ensign in the Peninsular War,* 236–37.

75. Moyle Sherer, an officer in the 34th, pointed out that the French messed in groups of twos and threes. The effect this arrangement had on overall cohesion is unknown. Sherer, *Recollections of the Peninsula,* 132.

76. The men of each *contubernium* always slept in the same tent, further separating them from other groups.

77. The *ordinaire* of the French Revolutionary army was composed of 14 to 16 men, not unlike the size of current infantry squads. Lynn, *Giant of the Grand Siècle,* 441. The numbers in a group, however, greatly affect how group members interact, as members pair off differently depending on group size. The larger the group grows, the more the individual subgroups groups disconnect from each other. The soldiers in an *ordinaire* likely broke down into smaller subgroups of six to eight men each.

78. Aitchison, *Ensign in the Peninsular War*, 236. Aitchison thought that each man should be given his own small kettle, in lieu of the soup dish they carried.

79. An awareness of the value of keeping comrades together was already extant by this period. The British *Regulations for the Rifle Corps* (1800) stipulated that mates were to be quartered together in barracks or the field, stand together in battle, mess together, and share duties. Holmes, *Acts of War*, 294. John Lazenby, citing Xenophon's Cyrus, revealed that the Spartans also recognized the cohesive value of having men mess together. Cyrus writes that those who messed together were far less likely to desert and that the strongest phalanx was one composed of friends. Lazenby, "Killing Zone," 107.

80. Richardson, *Fighting Spirit*, 13.

81. Little, "Buddy Relations and Combat Performance," 200.

82. Marshall, *Men against Fire*, 18.

83. It is of course impossible to know how well Wellington's army would have fared against a contingent of equal size from Napoleon's Grande Armée of 1805, when the French army was at its peak. The French army of Austerlitz, for example, routinely employed *l'ordre mixte*. Linked brigades would advance in this fashion, the formation providing firepower and sufficient depth for assault. *L'ordre mixte*, however, was a tactical combination that required extensive training to maintain proper intervals between the three formations. By the time of the Peninsular War, especially the later years, the loss of so many French veterans and officers forced commanders to rely on independent columns to move and fight, with some of the columns changing to line formation in an attempt to provide firepower in addition to the shock capacity of the column. Thus, while it is entertaining to conjecture about the outcome of a meeting between Wellington's Peninsular army and Napoleon's army of 1805, such a clash never occurred. We are left with the actual encounters of the Peninsula campaign, which present us with a series of British victories. John Lynn, personal communication, 10 May 2005.

84. Bell, *Rough Notes*, 1:165.

7. INTO HELL BEFORE DAYLIGHT

1. Additionally, one soldier was also assigned to each section of the gun pit to pick off any defenders who exposed themselves along the walls or attempted to crew the fortress guns. Lawrence, *Autobiography*, 91.

2. Ibid., 102, 109.

3. At Badajoz Wellington had ten brass and four iron cannons. He also had four howitzers. His siege train was significantly better at Ciudad Rodrigo, where it contained thirty-five 24-pounders and three 18-pounders. Cocks, *Intelligence Officer in the Peninsula*, 162.

4. Aitchison, *Ensign in the Peninsular War*, 147. Richard Holmes comments that the purpose of this custom requiring surrender before the assault was to prevent the slaughter that always ensued once the attacking force gained entry to the city. Holmes, *Redcoat*, 381. Napoleon's edict changed this dynamic and ensured that high casualties for attacker and defender would be the norm.

5. The Forlorn Hope was followed in by designated regiments. At Badajoz, for example, the 43rd and 52nd were the primary assaulting units. They suffered casualties of 347 and 383 men and officers, respectively, or well over half the strength of each regiment. Holmes, *Redcoat*, 390.

6. Costello also comments bitterly on the way the French rewarded their stormers, while the British army all but ignored theirs. Costello, *Peninsular and Waterloo Campaigns*, 94–95, 134.

7. Surtees, *Twenty-five Years in the Rifle Brigade*, 152. William Grattan perceptively noted that the men also expected their officers to act appropriately regarding the honor of being chosen; he commented that the rankers did not approve of officers who sat around writing letters before the assault. Grattan explained that the men expected something more martial and task oriented and gave the example of General Picton. Though the men did not love Picton, they respected him due to his fearlessness and positive manner before siege attacks. Grattan, *Adventures with the Connaught Rangers*, 196, 207.

8. O'Neil, *Military Adventures*, 175.

9. Lawrence, *Autobiography*, 111.

10. For an overview of siege warfare in the Peninsula, see Fletcher, *In Hell before Daylight*. The title of this chapter is a slightly modified version of Fletcher's title.

11. Cooper, *Rough Notes*, 75–76.

12. Smith, *Autobiography*, 64, cited in Fletcher, *In Hell before Daylight*, 60.

13. Lawrence, *Autobiography*, 112–13. As previously mentioned, Harding died after receiving seven shots through the body, while Bowden expired after having both his legs blown off. Lawrence survived the wounds he took while climbing a ladder during the breach assault. Ibid., 119.

14. Charles Esdaile states that 4,670 British soldiers were lost at Badajoz, with 3,713 falling during the storming of the breach. Esdaile, *Peninsular War*, 387.

15. All the siege casualty numbers come from Napier, *English Battles and Sieges in the Peninsula*: (Christoval) 107, (Ciudad Rodrigo) 132, (Badajoz) 155, (Burgos) 217, (San Sebastian) 343.

16. Surtees, *Twenty-five Years in the Rifle Brigade*, 144.

17. O'Neil, *Military Adventures*, 177, 190.

18. Costello, *Peninsular and Waterloo Campaigns*, 82.

19. Harley, *Veteran*, 2:97–98. Harley also comments that the French never plundered a town that fell into their hands. Instead they demanded a "contribution" from the inhabitants, which was paid in lieu of being sacked.

20. Costello, *Peninsular and Waterloo Campaigns*, 98.

21. Commentary by Buckley in Browne, *Napoleonic War Journal*, 343. While he never directly refers to primary group allegiance, Buckley's observations indirectly identify group loyalty as one of the mechanisms that shape soldier behavior.

22. Lawrence, *Autobiography*, 108. Given Lawrence's height of 73 inches, the Frenchman must have been very tall indeed.

23. In today's terms it might be suggested that Lawrence suffered some degree of post–traumatic stress syndrome.

24. Lawrence, *Autobiography*, 99. Also see Hennell, *Gentleman Volunteer*, 17. Grattan also attests to the men's animus toward Badajoz civilians who had been unfriendly toward British troops before the civilians' active participation in the defense of the fortress. With barely contained glee, he writes that the men "contemplated with delight the prospect of having it in their power to retaliate upon the inhabitants their treatment of our men." Grattan, *Adventures with the Connaught Rangers*, 175.

25. Wellington to Henry Wellesley, 23 October 1813, cited in Esdaile, *Peninsular War*, 469. The town leaders did in fact encourage cooperation with the French defenders.

26. Aitchison, *Ensign in the Peninsular War*, 146–47.

27. Letter to Lord Canning, written in 1820, cited in Oman, *History of the Peninsular War*, 5:260.

28. Robinson, "Peninsular Brigadier," 167–68. Robinson also argues that the fire that destroyed so many houses was set by the French just before the assault. While such a tactic may seem an odd behavior for defenders intent on safeguarding a fortress, it possibly reveals French certainty that the British assault, once initiated, would inevitably succeed. Thus, the French started burning houses to deny the British an intact citadel. Ibid., 168.

29. Costello, *Peninsular and Waterloo Campaigns*, 96.

30. Lawrence, *Autobiography*, 110. As a testament to the close-action dynamics of breach assaults, Lawrence notes that all the French soldiers had been felled by bayonet wounds.

31. Kincaid, *Adventures in the Rifle Brigade*, 102.

32. Grattan, *Adventures with the Connaught Rangers*, 159–60, 170. Also Surtees, *Twenty-five Years in the Rifle Brigade*, 147.

33. Donaldson, *Recollections*, 162. John Harley recalled a similar scene after San Sebastian, describing soldiers coming out of a theater all dressed in costumes, while others paraded about in clerical attire. Harley, *Veteran*, 2:83.

34. Cited in Harley, *Veteran*, 2:101.

35. Ibid., 102.

36. Cited in Hennell, *Gentleman Volunteer*, 17.

37. Surtees, *Twenty-five Years in the Rifle Brigade*, 149. Major-General George Bell reiterates this explanation regarding the men's expectations, writing that the soldiers looked at the looting of a town as their reward for the dangerous exertions required of them during the storming of the fortress. Bell, *Rough Notes*, 34.

38. Browne, *Napoleonic War Journal*, 154. The complaining soldier was referring to soldiers who had not participated in the attack taking plunder, which the drunken redcoat thought should belong exclusively to the assault parties.

39. Aitchison, *Ensign in the Peninsular War*, 147.

40. Browne also mentions that a soldier bayoneted and killed an officer who was trying to stop him from looting. Browne, *Napoleonic War Journal*, 153.

41. Lawrence, *Autobiography*, 118.

42. Browne, *Napoleonic War Journal*, 153.

43. Costello, *Peninsular and Waterloo Campaigns*, 99.

44. Ibid., 97–98. Charles O'Neil confirms that many men lost their

lives "in vain attempts to check the cruelty and lust and drunkenness of their own comrades." O'Neil, *Military Adventures,* 190. Again, the degree to which O'Neil may have exaggerated the offenses committed and the number of lives lost is impossible to determine.

45. Fletcher, *In Hell before Daylight,* 108. The town of Ladysmith became a focal point in the Boer War, during which the Boers laid siege to the small city. The British defense of Ladysmith was reported in the popular press in England, with the conduct of the men being held up as an example of national grit in the face of adversity. The successful defense merited a distinct bar on the South Africa–Boer War campaign medal.

46. In the *Diagnostic and Statistical Manual of Mental Disorders* (DSM-IV-TR) the terms "psychopathy" and "sociopathy" are considered obsolete. The correct designation for this mental illness is antisocial personality disorder (APD). It is estimated that perhaps 1 percent of the general population has this disorder. See Hare, *Without Conscience.*

47. I could uncover no accounts by survivors among the vanquished defenders or townspeople, meaning that their perspectives, unfortunately, are left unheard.

48. Blakeney was the officer mentioned in the previous chapter who saw the soldier and his family lying dead in the snow. He writes that "exhaustion, depravity, or a mixture of both" led to their deaths. Blakeney, *Boy in the Peninsular War,* 67.

49. Ibid., 273–74.

50. Henry, *Trifles from My Port-folio,* 1:43–44, cited by Esdaile, *Peninsular War,* 187.

51. Cited in Fletcher, *In Hell before Daylight,* 99.

52. Swabey, *Diary of the Campaigns in the Peninsula,* 70–71.

53. Lawrence, *Autobiography,* 117–18.

54. Costello, *Peninsular and Waterloo Campaigns,* 97–98.

55. Gleig, *Subaltern,* 56.

56. Grattan, *Adventures with the Connaught Rangers,* 207–208.

57. Cooper, *Rough Notes,* 80–81.

58. Lawrence, *Autobiography,* 104, 116.

59. Grattan, *Adventures with the Connaught Rangers,* 211–12.

60. Costello, *Peninsular and Waterloo Campaigns,* 99.

61. Harley, *Veteran,* 2:92–93.

62. Costello, *Peninsular and Waterloo Campaigns,* 98.

63. Donaldson, *Recollections,* 176–77, 158–59.

64. Oman, *Wellington's Army,* 212–13.

65. Esdaile, *Peninsular War,* 469–70.

66. Boutflower, *Journal of an Army Surgeon,* 122.

CONCLUSION

1. Lynn, "Preface," in *Battle,* xv.

2. Westbrook, "Potential for Military Disintegration," 247.

3. Atkinson, " 'Infamous Army,' " 48.

4. Cited in Hynes, *Soldiers' Tale,* 17.

EPILOGUE

1. Lawrence, *Autobiography*, 195.

2. In sailing to Jamaica, a few of the sailors had smuggled a young woman on board. It was Lawrence's duty as sergeant of the watch to escort her ashore at Port Royal. Noting that the young woman was "nearly broken-hearted," Lawrence paid for her lodging out of his own pocket, commenting: "I could do no more for her under the circumstances." Ibid., 198.

3. Ibid., 199.

4. Siborne, *Waterloo Letters*, 398–405.

5. Lawrence, *Autobiography*, 210.

6. Siborne, *Waterloo Letters*, 400. Colonel S. Stretton states that the 40th had an effective strength of 720 enlisted soldiers.

7. Lawrence, *Autobiography*, 206, 210.

8. Ibid., 216.

9. Ibid., 213. Even then, danger was not far afield. During the search for kindling, a man of Lawrence's company named Rouse was cutting the top off a French powder barrel when he inadvertently struck a piece of metal, which caused the barrel to explode. Rouse was blown into the air; he landed, burned and blackened from head to toe, wearing only one shoe and nothing else. Lawrence wrote of his surprise at Rouse's survival but then, resignedly, added that Rouse was taken to a Brussels hospital, where he died a few days later, "raving mad." Ibid.

10. The French soldier ran off before Lawrence returned with the food. Ibid., 214–15.

11. Ibid., 219.

12. Lawrence notes that this French woman, who won his heart, went by the name of Clotilde because Napoleon had made a proclamation that no woman other than his wife was to be known as Marie Louise. Ibid., 226.

13. Apparently Lawrence learned to speak French fairly quickly, for he writes about speaking French to Clotilde because she could not understand English. This was in the winter of 1817. Ibid., 234–36.

14. Ibid., 228–29.

15. Ibid., 243–44.

16. Ibid., 245.

17. Ibid., 246.

18. Ibid., 249. Lawrence provides no details about how long he and Clotilde were together or when she died.

APPENDIX A

1. T.H. McGuffie noted these same inconsistencies within regimental description books. McGuffie, "Recruiting the Ranks of the Regular British Army," 123.

2. Fortescue, *County Lieutenancies and the Army*, 292.

APPENDIX B

1. See, for example, Gayer et al., *Growth and Fluctuation of the British Economy*, 1:9, 29.

2. Mitchell and Deane, *Abstract of British Historical Statistics*, 498.

3. Gourvish, "Note on Bread Prices in London and Glasgow."

4. Tucker, "Real Wages of Artisans in London," 21–35. It should be noted that while data on wages are extremely difficult to find, many economic historians have attempted to construct an index of prices during this period. One of the most representative and reasonable of these is the index of wholesale prices in Gayer et al., *Growth and Fluctuation of the British Economy*. Tucker's price data are almost perfectly collinear with Gayer et al.'s index; other price indices are also very similar. This enhances confidence in the use of Tucker's series.

5. Ibid., 25.

6. Gilboy, "Cost of Living and Real Wages," footnote on 14.

7. Ibid.

8. For a summary of the relevant Poor Laws and their impacts, see chapter 2.

9. François Crouzet dates the periods of serious enforcement of the Continental System as "late 1807–early 1808, end of 1810–mid 1812," but the system was in place from late 1806 on. In the midst of Britain's agricultural crises, however, licenses were granted for the export of French grain to Britain. François Crouzet, "The Impact of the French Wars on the British Economy," in *Britain and the French Revolution, 1789–1815*, ed. H.T. Dickinson, 192–93, 195.

10. Gayer et al., *Growth and Fluctuation of the British Economy*, 1:94, 119.

11. Ibid., 11, 32, 66, 87, 119.

12. Ibid., 32, 67, 89–90.

13. Along these lines, Gayer et al. attribute a sharp rise in prices in the first half of 1806 to fear of the blockade and anticipation of a harvest failure; this pressure was somewhat relieved when the harvest was not as poor as initially feared, but such psychological factors may still have played a role in decision-making throughout this period. Ibid., 63.

14. Ibid., 72, and see the information on machine breaking in chapter 2.

15. For a discussion of the end of the volunteer system, see chapter 2.

16. Tucker, "Real Wages of Artisans in London," 21–35.

17. Gayer et al., *Growth and Fluctuation of the British Economy*, 1:11, 32, 66–67, 87, 89–90, 119.

18. Since each independent variable is separately statistically significant, there are no initial signs of collinearity problems. This was confirmed by looking at the correlations of the independent variables. The independent variables are not highly correlated with each other either pairwise or as one variable compared against the other two. This indicates that the variances of the model are not inflated due to collinearity. There is no reason to suspect a pattern in the residuals correlated with one or more of the in-

dependent variables (heteroskedasticity), and the Breusch-Pagan test for such patterns was negative.

APPENDIX C

1. U.S. Department of Agriculture, *USDA National Nutrient Database.* All data on the composition of various foods can be accessed using the search engine provided on this page and the specific name given in the text (individual URLs for compositions of various foods are not available). All nutritional data were verified in May 2008.

2. U.S. Food and Drug Administration, *How Folate Can Help Prevent Birth Defects.*

3. Kaplan, *Bakers of Paris,* 63, 72–73, 65.

4. *Energy and Protein Requirements,* 114.

5. Food and Nutrition Board, *Dietary Reference Intakes.*

6. Roderick Floud provides an excellent study (going back as far as 1800) on heights and weights using body mass as a guide. He argues that the BMI for a 26- to 30-year-old male in 1800 to 1819 was about 20.7, compared to 25 or more today. Floud, "Height, Weight and Body Mass," 20, 36.

7. TEE in megajoules can be calculated using the following equation: $TEE = 7.377 - (0.073 \times age) + (0.0806 \times wt) + (0.0135 \times ht) - (1.363 \times sex)$, where age is in years, weight is in kilograms, height is in centimeters, and sex is zero for men and one for women. One megajoule equals approximately 239 nutritional calories. Vinken et al., "Equations," 923.

8. This assumes that a pound of body fat contains about 90 percent fat (and 10 percent water) and that fat generates 9 calories of energy per gram, according to the usual Atwater factors for energy values of protein, carbohydrate, and fat, drawn from *Energy and Protein Requirements.*

9. METS are drawn from Ainsworth, *Compendium of Physical Activities Tracking Guide.* The METS used are 6.5 for "marching, rapidly, military" and 8.0 for "running, 5 mph," and a 60-kg soldier (about 130 lbs.) is taken as the average. The same assumptions are used for all calculations unless indicated otherwise. It should be noted that expenditures for marching are included on top of the normal daily expenditure; there may in fact have been some overlap here (for example, a limited amount of marching would have been included in the normal daily expenditure), but any resulting overestimate would be more than equaled by the extra expenditures of the soldiers in carrying heavy loads on their marches and marching over varied terrain, which have been specifically added into the calculations. It is estimated that the British soldier's pack weighed about 59 pounds. For a detailed breakdown of its contents, see Cooper, *Rough Notes,* 85–86. Green confirms the weight of the pack, stating that it was about "four stones weight" (56 pounds). Green, *Vicissitudes of a Soldier's Life,* 63. The ranker's musket weighed an additional 9 pounds. The weight of the British soldier's pack far exceeds the limit arrived at by S.L.A. Marshall in his study of the relationship between fatigue and fear. He recommended that a soldier weighing 154 pounds should carry a combat load of no more than 40 pounds, excluding his weapon. Marshall, *The Soldier's Load,* 71–73.

10. This was the rate of the Roman legionary. The Romans maintained 20 miles daily, day in and day out. Webster, *Roman Imperial Army*, 121. John Peddie hazards a guess of about 15 miles a day (3 mph), but his numbers are less certain. Peddie, *Roman War Machine*, 75. British accounts often mention similar march distances of 16 to 20 miles and more.

Bibliography

ARCHIVAL COLLECTIONS, JOURNALS, AND MEMOIRS

United Kingdom. War Office. Description book of the 1st Foot, 1st Battalion. WO 25-308.
——. Description book of the 6th Foot. WO 25-329.
——. Description book of the 8th Foot. WO 67-7.
——. Description book of the 25th Foot, 2nd Battalion. WO 25-352.
——. Description book of the 28th Foot, 1st Battalion. WO 25-357.
——. Description book of the 32nd Foot, 2nd Battalion. WO 25-368.
——. Description book of the 34th Foot. WO 67-14.
——. Description book of the 42nd Foot, 1st Battalion. WO 25-382.
——. Description books of the 53rd Foot, 1st Battalion. WO 25-412 and WO 25-413.
——. Description books of the 58th Foot. WO 25-435 and WO 25-436.
——. Description book of the 79th Foot. WO 25-477.
——. Description book of the 88th Foot. WO 25-516.
——. Description book of the 3rd Lt. Dragoons. WO 25-276.
——. Description book of the 18th Lt. Dragoons. WO 25-292.
——. Description book of the 19th Lt. Dragoons. WO 25-283.
——. Description book of the 20th Lt. Dragoons. WO 25-285.
——. Description book of the Grenadier Guards. WO 25-874.
——. Description book of the Scots Guards. WO 67-1 and WO 67-3.
——. Description books of the artillery pool. WO 54-303, WO 54-305, and WO 54-307.

Aitchison, John. *An Ensign in the Peninsular War: The Letters of John Aitchison.* Ed. W.F.K. Thompson. London, 1994. Reprint of 1981 edition.

Anderson, Joseph. *Recollections of a Peninsular Veteran.* London, 1913.

Anton, James. *Retrospect of a Military Life.* Edinburgh, 1841.

Bell, Major-General George. *Rough Notes by an Old Soldier.* 2 vols. London, 1867.

Beresford, Major William. *Refutation of Colonel Napier's Justification of His Third Volume.* London, 1834.

Blakeney, Robert. *A Boy in the Peninsular War.* Ed. Julian Sturgis. London, 1899.

Boothby, Charles. *Under England's Flag from 1804–1809.* London, 1900.

Boutflower, Charles. *The Journal of an Army Surgeon during the Peninsular War.* Manchester, 1912.

Browne, Captain Thomas. *The Napoleonic War Journal of Captain Thomas Henry Browne, 1807–1816.* Ed. Roger Buckley. London, 1987.

Bunbury, Sir Henry. *Narratives of the Great War with France.* London, 1854.

Cadell, Charles. *Narrative of the Campaigns of the Twenty-eighth Regiment since Their Return from Egypt in 1802.* London, 1835.

Caldwell, George, and Robert Cooper. *Rifle Green in the Peninsula.* Leicester, 1998.

Carss, John. "The 2nd/53rd in the Peninsula, Contemporary Letters from an Officer of the Regiment." Ed. S.H.F. Johnson. *Journal of Army Historical Research* 26.105 (1948): 2–17.

Cocks, Edward. *Intelligence Officer in the Peninsula: Letters and Diaries of Major the Hon. Edward Charles Cocks 1786–1812.* Ed. Julia Page. New York, 1986.

Colección Navarrete. Museo Naval, Madrid (compiled under the direction of Teniente de Navio Fernández de Navarrete ca. 1789–95; originally in 44 volumes, of which 29 survive along with 3 additional volumes of reconstituted fragments; index).

Colección Sanz de Barutell (Simancas). Museo Naval, Madrid (compiled under the direction of Teniente de Navio Don Juan Sanz de Barutell ca. 1789–95; 6 *Artículos* of 1–4 volumes each; index); also *Colección Sanz de Barutell (Barcelona)*, Biblioteca de la Academia Nacional, Madrid (dealing with the maritime affairs of the Kingdom of Aragon prior to the union with Castile).

Cooke, John. *A Narrative of Events in the South of France and America.* London, 1835.

Cooper, John. *Rough Notes of Seven Campaigns.* London, 1914. Reprint of 1869 edition.

Costello, Edward. *The Peninsular and Waterloo Campaigns.* Ed. Anthony-Brett James. Chatham, 1968.

Creevey, Thomas. *The Creevey Papers.* Ed. John Gore. London, 1934.

Dallas, Robert. "A Subaltern of the 9th in the Peninsula and at Walcheren." Ed. C. T. Atkinson. *Journal of Army Historical Research* 28.105 (1950): 59–67.

Donaldson, Joseph. *Recollections of the Eventful Life of a Soldier.* Philadelphia, 1845. This appears to be a much revised reprint of the 1824 edition with significant reorganization.

Douglas, John. *Douglas's Tale of the Peninsula and Waterloo.* Ed. Stanley Monick. London, 1997.

An Elucidation of Several Parts of His Majesty's Regulations for the Formations and Movements of Cavalry. London, 1808.

Esdaile, Charles. *Peninsular Eyewitnesses.* Barnsley, South Yorkshire, 2008.

Fitzgerald, Edward Fox. "With the Tenth Hussars in Spain: Letters of Edward Fox Fitzgerald." Ed. Captain D.J. Haggard. *Journal of Army Historical Research* 44.178 (1966): 88–112.

Foy, Maximilien. *A History of the War in the Peninsula under Napoleon.* London, 1827.

Gleig, George. *A Subaltern: A Chronicle of the Peninsular War.* London, 1825.

Gomm, Field Marshal Sir William. *Letters and Journals of Field Marshal Sir William Maynard Gomm, G.C.B, Commander-in-Chief of India, Constable of the Tower of London, etc., etc., from 1799 to Waterloo, 1815.* Ed. F. Carr Gomm. London, 1963.

Gordon, Alexander. *The Journal of a Cavalry Officer in the Corunna Campaign.* Ed. Colonel H. Wylie. London, 1913.

Gougaud, General G. *Journal.* 2 vols. Paris, 1899.

Grattan, William. *Adventures with the Connaught Rangers, 1809–1814.* Ed. Charles Oman. London, 1902.

Green, John. *The Vicissitudes of a Soldier's Life.* Cambridge, 1996. Reprint of 1827 edition.

Griois, Charles. *Mémoires du général Griois, 1792–1822.* Paris, 1909.

Gronow, Captain Rees. *The Reminiscences and Recollections of Captain Gronow.* London, 1964. Reprint of the 1892 edition.

Guilbert, Comte de. *Ecrits militaires.* Paris, 1976.

Gunn, James. "The Memoirs of Private James Gunn." Ed. Dr. R.H. Roy. *Journal of Army Historical Research* 49.198 (1971): 90–120.

Hamilton, Anthony. *Hamilton's Campaign with Moore and Wellington.* Troy, 1847.

Harley, Captain John. *The Veteran, or Forty Years in the British Service.* 2 vols. London, 1838.

Harris, John [Benjamin]. *The Recollections of Rifleman Harris.* Ed. Henry Curling. New York, 1929.

——. *The Recollections of Rifleman Harris.* Ed. Christopher Hibbert. Hamden, 1970.

Hathaway, Eileen. "Introduction." In *A Dorset Rifleman* by Benjamin Harris. Dorset, 1995. Revision of *The Recollections of Rifleman Harris* (1929).

Heeley, Edward. "The Journal of Edward Heeley." Ed. David Chandler. *Journal of Army Historical Research* 44.258–59 (1986): 94–117.

Hennell, George. *A Gentleman Volunteer: The Letters of George Hennell.* Ed. Michael Glover. London, 1979.

Henry, Philip, Earl of Stanhope. *Notes of Conversations with the Duke of Wellington, 1831–1851.* London, 1998. Reprint of 1886 and 1888 editions.

Henry, Walter. *Trifles from My Port-folio, or Events of a Military Life.* Ed. P. Edward. 2 vols. London, 1970. This is a reprint of the 1839 edition.

Hunt, Eric, ed. *Charging against Napoleon: Diaries and Letters of Three Hussars, 1808–1815.* London, 2001.

Johnson, Sergeant. "A Waterloo Journal." Ed. A.T. Atkinson. *Journal of Army Historical Research* 38.153 (1960): 30–42.

Journal of the House of Commons 64 (1809): 640–48.

Kincaid, Captain John. *Adventures in the Rifle Brigade, in the Peninsula, France, and the Netherlands, from 1809 to 1815.* New York, 1929.

——. *Random Shots from a Rifleman.* London, 1835.

Knowles, Robert. *The War in the Peninsula: Some Letters of Lieutenant Robert Knowles.* Ed. Sir Lee Knowles. Bolton, 1913.

Larpent, F. Seymour. *The Private Journal of F. Seymour Larpent, during the Peninsular War, from 1812 to Its Close.* Ed. Sir George Larpent. 3 vols. London, 1853.

Lawrence, William. *The Autobiography of Sergeant William Lawrence.* Ed. George Bankes. London, 1886.

Leach, Lieutenant-Colonel John. *Rough Sketches of the Life of an Old Soldier.* Cambridge, 1986. Reprint of 1831 edition.

Macfarlane, John. "Peninsula Private." Ed. Major Eric Robson. *Journal of Army Historical Research* 32.129 (1954): 4–14.

Marmont, Marshal A.F.L.V. *Mémoires du Maréchal Marmont, duc de Raguse, de 1792 à 1841.* 9 vols. Paris, 1857.

Master, Richard. "Ensign at War: The Narrative of Richard Masters, First Guards." Ed. General Sir David Fraser. *Journal of Army Historical Research* 66.267 (1988): 127–56.

McGrigor, James. *The Autobiography of Sir James McGrigor Bart., Late Director-General of the Army Medical Department.* London, 1861.

Mercer, General Cavalie. *Journal of the Waterloo Campaign.* New York, 1995. Reprint of 1827 edition.

Mills, John. *For King and Country: The Letters and Diaries of John Mills, Coldstream Guards, 1811–1814.* Ed. Ian Fletcher Staplehurst, Kent, 1995.

Morley, Stephen. *Memoirs of a Sergeant of the 5th Regiment of Foot.* London, 1842.

Morris, Thomas. *Memoirs of a Soldier in the 73rd.* Ed. John Shelby. London, 1967.

Ney, Marshal Michel. "Instructions for the Troops Comprising the Left Corps." Reprinted in the *Memoirs of Marshal Ney.* Philadelphia, 1834.

O'Neil, Charles. *The Military Adventures of Charles O'Neil.* Staplehurst, 1992. Reprint of the 1851 edition.

Patterson, Frederick. "A Line Regiment at Waterloo." Ed. Brigadier B.W. Webb-Carter. *Journal of Army Historical Research* 42.174 (1965): 60–66.

Pelet, Jean. *The French Campaign in Portugal, 1810–1811: An Account.* Ed. Donald D. Horward. Minneapolis, 1973.

Porter, Sir Robert. *Letters from Portugal and Spain under Moore.* London, 1809.

Reynier, Jean-Louis. *Correspondance du General Reynier, commandant le corps d'expedition dans les Calabres, 1806–1807, Registre No. c/31, Archives de l'Armée.* Vincennes.

Robertson, Frederick. "Reminiscences of a Woolwich Cadet." Ed. Lieutenant-Colonel J.H. Leslie. *Journal of Army Historical Research* 5.19 (1926): 1–14.

Robinson, Major-General Sir F.P. "A Peninsular Brigadier: The Letters of Major-General Sir F. P. Robinson." Ed. A.T. Atkinson. *Journal of Army Historical Research* 34.140 (1956): 153–70.

Ross-Lewin, Major Harry. *With the 32nd in the Peninsula.* London, 1834.

Sajer, Guy. *The Forgotten Soldier.* New York, 1972.

Sanger, Ernest. *Englishmen at War: A Social History in Letters, 1450–1900.* Dover, 1993.

Scarfe, Norman, ed. *Letters from the Peninsula: The Freer Family Correspondence 1807–1814.* Leicester, 1953.

Schaumann, A.L.F. *On the Road with Wellington: The Diary of a War Commissary in the Peninsular Campaigns.* London, 1999. Reprint of 1924 edition.

Seton, Colonel Sir Bruce. "Infantry Recruiting Instructions in England in 1767." *Journal of Army Historical Research* 4.16 (1925): 84–90.

Shakespear, Arthur. "Waterloo Arthur." Ed. C. T. Atkinson. *Journal of Army Historical Research* 36.147 (1958): 124–29.

Sherer, Moyle. *Recollections of the Peninsula.* Staplehurst, Kent, 1996. Reprint of 1824 edition.

Siborne, Major-General H.T. *Waterloo Letters.* Mechanicsburg, 1993. Reprint of 1891 edition.

Smith, Sir Harry George Wakelyn. *The Autobiography of Harry Smith.* London, 1999. Reprint of 1910 edition.

A Soldier of the Seventy-first. Ed. Christoper Hibbert. London, 1975.

Steppler, Glenn, ed. "The Coldstream Guards at Waterloo: A Quartermaster's Tale." *Journal of Army Historical Research* 67.270 (1989): 66–67.

Stevenson, John. *Twenty-one Years in the British Foot Guards.* London, 1830.

Stothert, Captain William. *A Narrative of the Principle Events of 1809, 1810, and 1811.* London, 1812.

Surtees, William. *Twenty-five Years in the Rifle Brigade.* London, 1833.

Swabey, William. *Diary of the Campaigns in the Peninsula for the Years 1811, 12, and 13.* Ed. F. Whinyates. London, 1984.

Tomkinson, Lieutenant-Colonel William. *Diary of a Cavalry Officer.* London, 1894.

Vallée, Gustave, and George Pariset, eds. *Carnet d'étapes du dragon Marquant.* Paris, 1898.

Wellington, Duke of. Arthur Wellesley to Castlereagh. 21 August 1809. US WP 1/273, Wellington Papers, University of Southampton.

——. *The Dispatches of Field Marshal the Duke of Wellington, KG, during His Various Campaigns.* Ed. J. Gurwood. 13 vols. London, 1837–39.

——. *Supplementary Despatches and Memoranda of Field Marshal Arthur Duke of Wellington KG.* Ed. A.R. Wellesley, second Duke of Wellington. 15 vols. London, 1858–72.

——. Wellington to Henry Wellesley, 3 May 1812. U.S. WP 1/347, Wellington Papers, University of Southampton.

——. Wellington to Henry Wellesley, 23 October 1813. U.S. WP 1/347, Wellington Papers, University of Southampton.

Wheeler, William. *The Letters of Private Wheeler.* Ed. B.H. Liddell Hart. Cambridge, 1951.

BOOKS AND ARTICLES

Adkin, Mark. *The Waterloo Companion.* Mechanicsburg, 2001.

Ainsworth, B.E. *The Compendium of Physical Activities Tracking Guide.* Prevention Research Center, Norman J. Arnold School of Public Health, University of South Carolina, 2002.http:///prevention.sph.sc.edu/tools/docs/documents_compendium.pdf (accessed 13 January 2005).

Alder, Ken. *The Measure of All Things: The Seven-Year Odyssey and Hidden Error That Transformed the World.* New York, 2002.

Alexander, Don. *Rod of Iron: French Counterinsurgency Policy in Aragon during the Peninsular War.* Wilmington, 1985.

Anderson, Fred. *A People's Army: Massachusetts Soldiers and Society in the Seven Years' War.* Chapel Hill, 1984.

Anglesey, Marquess of. *A History of the British Cavalry 1816–1850.* 8 vols. Hamden, 1973.

Arnold, James. "A Reappraisal of Column versus Line in the Napoleonic Wars." *Journal of Army Historical Research* 60.244 (1982): 196–208.

——. "A Reappraisal of Column versus Line in the Peninsular War." *Journal of Military History* 68 (2004): 535–52.

Atkinson, C. T. "An 'Infamous Army.'" *Journal of Army Historical Research* 32.130 (1954): 48–53.

Bailey, Brian. *The Luddite Rebellion.* New York, 1998.

Baines, Edward. *History of the Cotton Manufacture in Great Britain.* London, 1959.

Barnett, Correlli. *Britain and Her Army, 1509–1970.* London, 1970.

Barrocas, A. "Nutritional Support of the Medical Patient." *Hospital Material Management Quarterly* 7.3 (1986): 1–15.

Bartov, Omer. *Hitler's Army: Soldiers, Nazis, and War in the Third Reich.* Oxford, 1992. Reprint of the 1991 edition.

Beattie, J.M. *Crime and the Courts in England 1660–1800.* Princeton, 1986.

Beers, Mark, and Robert Berkow, eds., *The Merck Manual of Diagnosis and Therapy.* 17th ed. (Merck Research Laboratories: Whitehouse Station, 1999), http:///www.merck.com/mrkshared/mmanual/sections.jsp (accessed 20 January 2005).

Bertaud, Jean-Paul. *La révolution armée: Les soldats-citoyens et la Révolution française.* Paris, 1979.

Best, Geoffrey. *War and Society in Revolutionary Europe, 1770–1870.* Guernsey, Channel Islands, 1998.

Beyerchen, Alan. "Clausewitz, Nonlinearity, and the Unpredictability of War." *International Security* 17.3 (1993): 59–90.

Blanco, Richard. "Attempts to Abolish Branding and Flogging in the Army of Victorian England before 1881." *Journal of Army Historical Research* 46.187 (1968): 137–45.

——. *Wellington's Surgeon General: Sir James Blanco.* Durham, N.C., 1974.

Botham, F.W., and E.H. Hunt. "Wages in Britain during the Industrial Revolution." *Economic History Review* n.s. 40 (1987): 380–99.

Bowen, H.V. *War and British Society, 1688–1815.* Cambridge, 1998.

Bowley, A.L. "The Statistics of Wages in the United Kingdom during the Last Hundred Years (Part I): Agricultural Wages." *Journal of the Royal Statistical Society* 61 (1898): 702–22.

——. "The Statistics of Wages in the United Kingdom during the Last Hundred Years (Part II): Agricultural Wages." *Journal of the Royal Statistical Society* 62 (1899): 140–50.

——. "The Statistics of Wages in the United Kingdom during the Last Hundred Years (Part III): Agricultural Wages." *Journal of the Royal Statistical Society* 62 (1899): 395–404.

——. "The Statistics of Wages in the United Kingdom during the Last Hundred Years (Part IV): Agricultural Wages." *Journal of the Royal Statistical Society* 62 (1899): 555–70.

——. "The Statistics of Wages in the United Kingdom during the Last Hundred Years (Part VI): Wages in the Building Trades—English Towns." *Journal of the Royal Statistical Society* 63 (1900): 297–315.

——. "The Statistics of Wages in the United Kingdom during the Last Hundred Years (Part VII): Wages in the Building Trades—Continued. Scotland and Ireland." *Journal of the Royal Statistical Society* 63 (1900): 485–97.

——. "The Statistics of Wages in the United Kingdom during the Last Hundred Years (Part VIII): Wages in the Building Trades—Concluded." *Journal of the Royal Statistical Society* 64 (1901): 102–12.

——. "The Statistics of Wages in the United Kingdom during the Last Hundred Years (Part IX): Wages in Worsted and Woollen Manufactures of the West Riding of Yorkshire." *Journal of the Royal Statistical Society* 65 (1902): 102–26.

——. "The Statistics of Wages in the United Kingdom during the Last Hundred Years (Part XI): Engineering and Shipbuilding. B. Statements of Wages from Non-Trade Union Sources in General Engineering." *Journal of the Royal Statistical Society* 68 (1905): 373–91.

Bowley, A.L., and George Wood. "The Statistics of Wages in the United Kingdom during the Last Hundred Years (Part V): Printers." *Journal of the Royal Statistical Society* 62 (1899): 708–15.

——. "The Statistics of Wages in the United Kingdom during the Last Hundred Years (Part X): Engineering and Shipbuilding. A. Trade Union Standard Rates." *Journal of the Royal Statistical Society* 68 (1905): 104–37.

——. "The Statistics of Wages in the United Kingdom during the Last Hundred Years (Part XII): Engineering and Shipbuilding. C. Statements of Wages from Non-Trade Union Sources in Shipbuilding and Engineering at Shipbuilding Centres." *Journal of the Royal Statistical Society* 68 (1905): 563–614.

——. "The Statistics of Wages in the United Kingdom during the Last Hundred Years (Part XIII): Engineering and Shipbuilding. D. Dockyards and Railway Centres." *Journal of the Royal Statistical Society* 68 (1905): 704–15.

——. "The Statistics of Wages in the United Kingdom during the Last Hundred Years (Part XIV): Engineering and Shipbuilding. E. Averages, Index Numbers, and General Results." *Journal of the Royal Statistical Society* 68 (1905): 104–37.

Brenton, E., D. Hoover, R. Galloway, and K. Popp. "Adaptation to Chronic Stress in Military Trainees: Adrenal Androgens, Testosterone, Glucocorticoids, IGF-1, and Immune Function." *New York Academy of Science Annual* 774 (1995): 217–31.

Brereton, J.M. *The British Soldier: A Social History from 1661 to the Present Day.* London, 1986.

Brett-James, Anthony. *Life in Wellington's Army.* London, 1972.

Briggs, Asa. *Age of Improvement 1783–1867.* London, 1959.

Brown, Henry Phelps, and Sheila Hopkins. *A Perspective of Wages and Prices.* London, 1981.

Brown, Richard. *Society and Economy in Modern Britain 1700–1850.* London, 1991.

Bruce, Robert, Iain Dickie, Kevin Kiley, Michael Pavkovic, and Frederick Schneid. *Fighting Techniques of the Napoleonic Age 1792–1815.* New York, 2008.

Brundage, Anthony. *The English Poor Laws, 1700–1930.* New York, 2002.

Bryant, Arthur. *The Great Duke.* New York, 1972.

——. *Years of Victory.* London, 1945.

Buckley, Roger. *The British Army in the West Indies.* Tallahassee, 1998.

——. "The Destruction of the British Army in the West Indies: A Medical History." *Journal of Army Historical Research* 56.226 (1978): 79–92.

Caffrey, Kate. *The Twilight's Last Gleaming: Britain vs. America, 1812–1815.* Briarcliff Manor, 1977.

Calder, Philip, and Samantha Kew. "The Immune System: A Target for Functional Foods?" *British Journal of Nutrition* 88 (2002) S165–76.

Calvert, Brigadier Michael. *A Dictionary of Battles, 1715–1815.* New York, 1979.

Camon, General. H. *La Guerre Napoléonienne: Les systèmes d'opérations.* Paris, 1907.

Cantlie, Lieutenant-General Sir Neil. *A History of the Army Medical Department.* 2 vols. London, 1974.

Carlyle, Thomas. *The French Revolution: A History.* London, 1837.

Chambers, J.D., and G.E. Mingay. *The Agricultural Revolution, 1750–1880.* New York, 1966.

Chandler, David. *The Campaigns of Napoleon.* New York, 1966.

——. *The Military Maxims of Napoleon.* New York, 1988.

——. *On the Napoleonic Wars: Collected Essays.* London, 1994.

Clark, Gregory, Michael Huberman, and Peter Lindert. "A British Food Puzzle, 1770–1850." *Economic History Review* n.s. 48 (1995): 215–37.

Clausewitz, Carl von. *On War.* Ed. and trans. Michael Howard and Peter Paret. Princeton, 1976.

Cleaver, Scott. *Under the Lash: A History of Corporal Punishment in the British Armed Forces.* London, 1954.

Clinton, Ned. *Ned Clinton; or the Commissary.* 3 vols. London, 1825.

Cockerill, A.W. *Sons of the Brave.* London, 1984.

Colley, Linda. "The Reach of the State, the Appeal of the Nation: Mass Arming and Political Culture in the Napoleonic Wars." In *An Imperial State at War: Britain from 1689 to 1815,* ed. Lawrence Stone. London, 1994.

Colquhoun, Patrick. *Treatise on the Wealth of the British Empire.* London, 1814.

Committee on Military Nutrition Research, Food and Nutrition Board, Institute of Medicine. *Military Strategies for Sustainment of Nutrition and Immune Function in the Field.* Washington, D.C., 1999.

Cookson, J.E. "The English Volunteer Movement of the French Wars, 1793–1815: Some Contexts." *Historical Journal* 32 (1989): 867–91.

Cooley, Charles H. *Social Organization.* New York, 1909.

Cornwell, Bernard. *Sharpe's Company.* London, 1983.

Corvisier, André. *L'armée française de la fin du XVIIe siècle au ministère de Choiseul: Le soldat.* 2 vols. Paris, 1964.

Coss, Edward. "The Misadventures of Wellington's Cavalry, from the Peninsula to Waterloo." *Journal of the Waterloo Committee* 10 (April 1988): 18–28.

Costa, Dora, and Matthew Kahn, *Heroes and Cowards: The Social Face of War.* Princeton, 2008.

Crafts, N.F.R. *British Economic Growth during the Industrial Revolution.* Oxford, 1985.

———. "British Economic Growth, 1700–1831: A Review of the Evidence." *Economic History Review* n.s. 36 (1983): 177–99.

———. "National Income Estimates and the British Standard of Living Debate: A Reappraisal of 1801–1831." *Explorations in Economic History* 18 (1981): 176–88.

———. "Some Dimensions of the 'Quality of Life' during the Industrial Revolution." *Economic History Review* 50 (1997): 617–39.

Crafts, N.F.R., and Terence Mills. "Trends in Real Wages." *Explorations in Economic History* 31 (1994): 179–80.

Crouzet, François. "Wars, Blockade, and Economic Change in Europe, 1792–1815." *Journal of Economic History* 24 (1964): 567–88.

Darvall, Frank. *Popular Disturbances and Public Order in Regency England.* New York, 1969.

Davies, Godfrey. "Recruiting in the Reign of Queen Anne." *Journal of Army Historical Research* 28.116 (1950): 146–59.

———. *Wellington's Army.* Oxford, 1954.

Davis, S.W., and J.G. Taylor. *Stress in Combat.* Chevy Chase, 1954.

Deane, Phyllis, and W.A. Cole. *British Economic Growth, 1688–1959: Trends and Structure.* Cambridge, 1962.

Dickinson, H.T., ed. *Britain and the French Revolution, 1789–1815.* New York, 1989.

Dinter, Elmar. *Hero or Coward.* London, 1985.

Dollard, John. *Fear in Battle.* New Haven, 1943.

Duffy, Christopher. *The Military Experience in the Age of Reason.* London, 1987.

Duffy, Michael. "The British Army and the Caribbean Expeditions of the War against Revolutionary France 1793–1801." *Journal of Army Historical Research* 62.250 (1984): 65–104.

Dupin, C. *View of History of the Actual State of the Military Forces of Great Britain.* London, 1822.

Dyer, Gwynne. *War.* New York, 1985.

Ebert, James. *A Life in a Year: The American Infantryman in Vietnam.* Novato, 1993.

Elting, John. *Swords around a Throne.* New York, 1988.

Emsley, Clive. *British Society and the French Wars, 1793–1815.* London, 1979.

Energy and Protein Requirements. Report of a Joint FAO/WHO/UN Expert Consultation. World Health Organization Technical Report 724, WHO. Geneva, 1985.

Esdaile, Charles. *The Duke of Wellington and the Command of the Spanish Army, 1812–1814.* London, 1990.

——. *Fighting Napoleon: Guerrillas, Bandits and Adventurers in Spain, 1808–1814.* New Haven, 2004.

——. *The French Wars.* London, 2001.

——. *The Peninsular War.* New York, 2003.

Esteban, Javier Cuenca. "British Textile Prices, 1770–1831: Are British Growth Rates Worth Revising Once Again?" *Economic History Review* n.s. 47 (1994): 66–105.

Fagan, Brian. *The Little Ice Age: How Climate Made History, 1300–1850.* New York, 2000.

Feinstein, Charles. "Pessimism Perpetuated: Real Wages and the Standard of Living in Britain during and after the Industrial Revolution." *Journal of Economic History* 58 (1998): 625–58.

Fletcher, Ian. *Badajoz 1812.* Oxford, 1999.

——. *Galloping at Everything: The British Cavalry in the Peninsular War and at Waterloo, 1800–1815.* Mechanicsburg, 1999.

——. *In Hell before Daylight.* Staplehurst, 1994. Reprint of 1984 edition.

Flinn, M.W. "Trends in Real Wages 1750–1850." *Economic History Review* 27 (1974): 395–413.

Floud, Roderick. "Height, Weight and Body Mass of the British Population since 1820." *Historical Paper 108: National Bureau of Economic Research* (1998): 1–44.

——. "A Tall Story? The Standard of Living Debate." *History Today* (May 1983): 36–40.

Floud, Roderick, and Donald McCloskey. *The Economic History of Britain since 1700.* 2nd ed. Cambridge, 1994.

Food and Nutrition Board, Institute of Medicine, National Academies. *Dietary Reference Intakes (DRIs) for Energy, Carbohydrate, Fiber, Fat,*

Fatty Acids, Cholesterol, Protein, and Amino Acids (2002). Institute of Medicine, http:///www.iom.edu/Object.File/Master/21/372/0.pdf (accessed 8 May 2008).

Forest, Alan. *Conscripts and Deserters: The Army and French Society during the Revolution and Empire.* Oxford, 1989.

——. *Napoleon's Men.* London, 2002.

Fortescue, John. *The County Lieutenancies and the Army, 1803–1814.* London, 1909.

——. *A History of the British Army.* 13 vols. London, 1899–1930.

Frankel, Jeffery. "The 1807–1809 Embargo against Great Britain." *Journal of Economic History* 42 (1982): 291–308.

Frey, Silvia R. *The British Soldier in America: A Social History of Military Life in the Revolutionary Period.* Austin, 1981.

Fry, Fiona Somerset. *A Soldier in Wellington's Army.* East Sussex, 1987.

Furet, François, and Mona Ozouf. *Reading and Writing: Literacy in France from Calvin to Jules Ferry.* Cambridge, 1982.

Gabriel, Richard. *No More Heroes: Madness and Psychiatry in War.* New York, 1987.

Gates, David. "The Transformation of the Army, 1783–1815." In *The Oxford History of the British Army,* ed. David Chandler. Oxford, 1994.

Gayer, Arthur, W.W. Rostow, and Anna Jacobson Schwartz. *The Growth and Fluctuation of the British Economy, 1790–1850: An Historical, Statistical, and Theoretical Study of Britain's Economic Development.* 2 vols. New York, 1975. Reprint of 1953 edition.

Gilbert, Arthur. "An Analysis of Some Eighteenth-Century Army Recruiting Records." *Journal of Army Historical Research* 54.217 (1976): 38–47.

——. "Ethnicity and the British Army in Ireland during the American Revolution." *Ethnic and Racial Studies* 1 (1978): 475–83.

——. "Why Men Deserted from the Eighteenth-Century British Army." *Armed Forces and Society* 6 (1980): 553–67.

Gilboy, E.W. "The Cost of Living and Real Wages in Eighteenth-Century England." In *The Standard of Living in Britain in the Industrial Revolution,* ed. Arthur J. Taylor. London, 1975.

Glover, Michael. *Wellington as Military Commander.* London, 2001. Reprint of 1968 edition.

——. *Wellington's Army.* London, 1987.

Glover, Richard. *Britain at Bay: Defence against Bonaparte, 1803–1814.* London, 1973.

——. *Peninsular Preparation.* Cambridge, 1963.

Goldsworthy, Adrian. *The Roman Army at War, 100 BC–AD 200.* Oxford, 1996.

Gourvish, Terence R. "A Note on Bread Prices in London and Glasgow, 1788–1815." *Journal of Economic History* 30.4 (1970): 854–60.

Graham, John. *The Forlorn Hope.* London, 1989.

Griffith, Paddy. *Forward into Battle: Fighting Tactics from Waterloo to the Near Future.* Marlborough, 1990.

——. *Wellington Commander: The Iron Duke's Generalship.* Sussex, 1985.

Grinker, Roy, and John Spiegel. *Men under Stress.* Philadelphia, 1945.

Grossman, David. *On Combat: The Psychology and Physiology of Deadly Conflict in War and Peace.* Millstadt, Ill., 2004.

——. *On Killing: The Psychological Cost of Learning to Kill in War and Society.* Boston, 1995.

Guilmartin, John, Jr. *Gunpowder and Galleys: Changing Technology and Mediterranean Warfare at Sea in the Sixteenth Century.* Cambridge, 1974.

——. "Military Experience, the Military Historian, and the Reality of Battle." Paper presented at the Shelby Cullom Davis Center for Historical Studies, Princeton University, 8 October 1982.

——. "Student Study Guide and Workbook History 580.01: European Warfare from the Renaissance through 1870." Columbus, 2005.

Hall, Christopher. *British Strategy in the Napoleonic War, 1803–1815.* Manchester, 1992.

Hanson, Victor Davis. *The Western Way of War.* London, 1989.

Hare, Robert. *Without Conscience: The Disturbing World of the Psychopaths among Us.* New York, 1999.

Hay, Douglas. "War, Dearth, and Theft in the Eighteenth Century: The Record of the English Courts." *Past and Present* 95 (1982): 117–60.

Hay, Douglas, Peter Linebaugh, John G. Rule, E.P. Thompson, and Cal Winslow. *Albion's Fatal Tree: Crime and Society in Eighteenth-Century England.* London, 1975.

Haythornthwaite, Philip. *The Armies of Wellington.* London, 1998. Reprint of 1994 edition.

——. *Die Hard! Dramatic Actions from the Napoleonic Wars.* London, 1996.

Heckschler, Eli. *The Continental System: An Economic Interpretation.* Gloucester, 1964.

Henderson, Wm. Daryl. *Cohesion: The Human Element in Combat.* Washington, D.C., 1985.

Hendin, Herbert, and Ann Haas. *Wounds of War: The Psychological Aftermath of Combat in Vietnam.* New York, 1984.

Herodotus. *The Histories.* Trans. Walter Blanco, ed. Walter Blanco and Jennifer Roberts. New York, 1992.

Hess, Earl. *The Union Soldier in Combat.* Lawrence, 1997.

Hodge, William. "On the Mortality Arising from Military Operations." *Journal of the Statistical Society of London* 19 (1856): 219–71.

Hodges, Lieutenant-Colonel Patricia. "Impact of Nutritional Care upon Return-to-Duty Rates." *Military Medicine* 158 (1993): 157–60.

Holderness, B.A. "Prices, Productivity, and Output." In *Agrarian History of England and Wales, 1750–1850,* ed. G.E. Mingay. Cambridge, 1989.

Holmes, Richard. *Acts of War: The Behavior of Men in Battle.* New York, 1985.

——. *Redcoat: The British Soldier in the Age of Horse and Musket.* London, 2001.

——. *Sahib: The British Soldier in India.* London, 2006.

Horner, Thomas. "Killers, Fillers, and Fodder." *Parameters, Journal of the US Army War College* 12.3 (1982): 27–34.

Horrell, Sara, and Jane Humphries. "Old Questions, New Data, and Alternative Perspectives: Families' Living Standards in the Industrial Revolution." *Journal of Economic History* 52 (1992): 849–80.

Houlding, J.A. *Fit for Service: The Training of the British Army, 1715–1795.* Oxford, 1981.

Hueckel, G. "Relative Prices and Supply Response in English Agriculture." *Economic History Review* n.s. 29 (1976): 401–14.

——. "War and the British Economy." *Explorations in Economic History* 10 (1973): 365–96.

Hughes, Major-General B. P. *Firepower: Weapons Effectiveness on the Battlefield, 1630–1850.* New York, 1974.

Hughes, J.R.T. "Measuring British Economic Growth." *Journal of Economic History* 24 (1964): 60–82.

Hughes, Michael. " 'Vive la république! Vive l'empereur!': Military Culture and Motivation in the Armies of Napoleon, 1803–1808." Diss., University of Illinois, 2005.

Hynes, Samuel. *The Soldiers' Tale: Bearing Witness to Modern War.* New York, 1997.

Janowitz, Morris, and Roger Little. *Sociology and the Military Establishment.* Beverly Hills, 1974.

Jones, David. *Crime, Report, Community, and Police in Nineteenth-Century Britain.* London, 1982.

Kaplan, Steven Laurence. *The Bakers of Paris and the Bread Question, 1700–1775.* Durham, 1996.

Keegan, John. *The Face of Battle.* New York, 1976.

——. *Soldiers: A History of Men in Battle.* New York, 1986.

——. "Towards a Theory of Combat Motivation." In *A Time to Kill,* ed. Paul Addison and Angus Calder. London, 1997.

Kellett, Anthony. *Combat Motivation: The Behavior of Soldiers in Battle.* Boston, 1982.

Kennedy, Paul. *The Rise and Fall of the Great Powers: Economic Change and Military Conflict from 1500 to 2000.* New York, 1987.

Keusch, Gerald. "The History of Nutrition: Malnutrition, Infection, and Immunity." *American Society for Nutritional Sciences* 133 (2003): 336S–40S.

Keys, Ancel, Josef Brozek, Austin Henschel, Olaf Mickelsen, Henry Longstreet Taylor, Ernst Simonson, and Angie Skinner. *The Biology of Human Starvation.* 2 vols. Minneapolis, 1950.

Kindsvatter, Peter. *American Soldiers: Ground Combat in the World Wars, Korea, and Vietnam.* Lawrence, 2003.

Kinealy, Christine. "Living with the Memory of the Great Hunger." In *Ireland's Great Hunger: Silence, Memory, and Commemoration,* ed. David Valone and Christine Kinealy. New York, 2002.

King, Peter. *Crime, Justice, and Discretion in England, 1740–1820.* Oxford, 2000.

Kohn, Richard. *Eagle and Sword: The Federalists and the Creation of the Military Establishment in America, 1783–1802.* New York, 1975.

——. "The Social History of the American Soldier: A Review and Prospectus for Research." *American Historical Review* 86 (1981): 553–67.

Komlos, John. "Shrinking in a Growing Economy? The Mystery of Physical Stature during the Industrial Revolution." *Journal of Economic History* 58 (1998): 779–802.

Kopperman, Paul. "The British High Command and Soldiers' Wives in America, 1755–1783." *Journal of Army Historical Research* 60.241 (1982): 14–34.

Kramer, T.R., R. Moore, R.L. Shippee, K.E. Friedl, L. Martinez-Lopez, M.M. Chan, and E.W. Askew. "Effects of Food Restriction in Military Training on T-Lymphocyte Responses." *International Journal of Sports Medicine* 18 (1997): 584–90.

Landes, David. *The Unbound Prometheus.* London, 1969.

Lane, Frederick C. "Venetian Merchant Galleys, 1300–1334, Private and Commercial Operation." *Speculum* 38 (1963): 179–205.

Latimer, Jon. *1812: War with America.* Cambridge, 2007.

Lazenby, John. "The Killing Zone." In *Hoplites: The Classical Greek Battle Experience,* ed. Victor Davis Hanson. London, 1991.

Lees, Lynn. *The Solidarities of Strangers: The English Poor Laws and the People.* Cambridge, 1998.

Lendon, J.E. *Ghosts & Soldiers: A History of Battle in Classical Antiquity.* New Haven, 2005.

Linch, Kevin. "The Recruitment of the British Army, 1807–1815." Diss., University of Leeds, 2001.

Linderman, Gerald. *Embattled Courage.* New York, 1987.

Little, Roger. "Buddy Relations and Combat Performance." In *The New Military,* ed. Morris Janowitz. New York, 1964.

Lock, Ron, and Peter Quantrill. *Zulu Victory.* London, 2002.

Longford, Elizabeth. *Wellington: The Years of the Sword.* New York, 1969.

Lorenz, Konrad. *On Aggression.* New York, 1963.

Lynn, John. *Battle: A History of Combat and Culture.* Boulder, 2003.

——. *The Bayonets of the Republic: Motivation and Tactics in the Army of Revolutionary France, 1791–94.* Boulder, 1996. Reprint of 1984 edition.

——. *Giant of the Grand Siècle: The French Army, 1610–1715.* Cambridge, 1997.

Lyons, Martyn. *Napoleon Bonaparte and the Legacy of the French Revolution.* New York, 1994.

Mantoux, Paul. *The Industrial Revolution in the Eighteenth Century: An Outline of the Beginnings of the Modern Factory System in England.* New York, 1947.

Marcos, A., E. Nova, and A. Montero. "Changes in the Immune System Are Conditioned by Nutrition." *European Journal of Nutrition* 57, Supplement 1 (2003): S66–S69.

Margo, Robert, and Richard Steckel. "Heights of Native-Born Whites during the Antebellum Period." *Journal of Economic History* 43 (1983): 167–74.

Marshall, S.L.A. *Bringing Up the Rear: A Memoir.* San Rafael, 1979.

——. "Commentary on Infantry Operations and Weapons Usage in Korea, Winter of 1950–51." ORO-R-13, dated 27 October 1941. Operations Research Office, Johns Hopkins University.

——. *Men against Fire*. New York, 1946.

——. *The Soldier's Load and the Mobility of a Nation*. Quantico, 1980.

McGuffie, T.H., ed. *Rank and File: The Common Soldier at Peace and War, 1642–1914*. New York, 1964.

——. "Recruiting the Ranks of the Regular British Army during the French Wars." *Journal of Army Historical Research* 34.138 (1956): 123–32.

——. "The 7th Hussars in 1813." *Journal of Army Historical Research* 46.169 (1964): 4–15.

McNeill, William. *Keeping Together in Time: Dance and Drill in Human History*. Cambridge, 1995.

McPherson, James. *For Cause and Comrades: Why Men Fought in the Civil War*. Oxford, 1997.

Meier, Norman. *Military Psychology*. New York, 1943.

Merino, Danielle. "Immune and Hormonal Changes following Intense Military Training." *Military Medicine* 168 (2003): 1034–38.

Miller, William. *The Mystery of Courage*. Cambridge, 2000.

Mitchell, B.R., and Phyllis Deane. *Abstract of British Historical Statistics*. Cambridge, 1971.

Mokyr, Joel. "Has the Industrial Revolution Been Crowded Out? Some Reflections on Crafts and Williamson." *Explorations in Economic History* 24 (1987): 302+.

Mokyr, Joel, and Eugene Savin. "Stagflation in Historical Perspective: The Napoleonic Wars Revisited." *Research in Economic History* 1 (1976): 198–259.

Moran, Lord. *The Anatomy of Courage*. London, 1945.

Morgan, Gareth. "What, If Any, Is the Effect of Malnutrition on Immunological Competence?" *Lancet* 349 (1997): 1693–95.

Moskos, Charles. *The American Enlisted Man: The Rank and File in Today's Military*. New York, 1970.

Mosse, George. *The Images of Man: The Creation of Modern Masculinity*. New York, 1998.

Muir, Rory. *Britain and the Defeat of Napoleon, 1807–1815*. New Haven, 1996.

——. *Tactics and the Experience of Battle in the Age of Napoleon*. New Haven, 1998.

Muir, Rory, Robert Burnham, Howie Muir, and Ron McGuigan. *Inside Wellington's Peninsular Army, 1808–1814*. Barnsley, South Yorkshire, 2006.

Murphy, Audie. *To Hell and Back*. New York, 1983.

Myatt, Frederick. *British Sieges of the Peninsular War*. New York, 1987.

——. *The Soldier's Trade*. London, 1974.

Napier, General Sir George. *Passages in the Early Life of Gen. Sir G.T. Napier*. London, 1884.

Napier, Lieutenant-General Sir William. *English Battles and Sieges in the Peninsula*. London, 1990. Reprint of 1855 edition, with the narrative extracted from his *History of the War in the Peninsula and the South of France, from the Year 1807 to the Year 1814*. 6 vols. London, 1832.

——. *War in the Peninsula*. 6 vols. London, 1828–40.

Neuberg, Victor. *Gone for a Soldier: A History of Life in the British Ranks from 1642*. London, 1989.

Nibler, Roger, and Karen Harris, "The Effects of Culture and Cohesiveness on Intragroup Conflict and Effectiveness." *Journal of Social Psychology* 143 (2003): 613–35.

Nicholas, Stephen, and Richard Steckel. "Heights and Living Standards of English Workers during the Early Years of Industrialization, 1770–1815." *Journal of Economic History* 51 (1991): 937–57.

Nosworthy, Brent. *The Anatomy of Victory: Battle Tactics, 1689–1763*. New York, 1990.

——. *The Bloody Crucible of Courage: Fighting Methods and Combat Experience of the Civil War*. New York, 2003.

——. *With Musket, Cannon, and Sword: Battle Tactics of Napoleon and His Enemies*. New York, 1996.

Nye, Robert. *Masculinity and Male Codes of Honor in Modern France*. London, 1998.

O'Brien, Patrick Karl. "The Impact of the Revolutionary and Napoleonic Wars, 1793–1815, on the Long-Run Growth of the British Economy." *Review: Fernand Braudel Center for the Study of Economies, Historical Systems, and Civilizations* 12 (1989): 335–95.

O'Brien, Patrick Karl, and Caglar Keyder. *Economic Growth in Britain and France, 1780–1914: Two Paths to the Twentieth Century*. London, 1978.

Olmstead, Michael. *The Small Group*. New York, 1978.

Oman, Sir Charles. "Courts Martial of the Peninsular War, 1809–1814." *Journal of the Royal United Service Institution* 56 (1912): 1699–1714.

——. *A History of the Peninsular War*. 7 vols. London, 1902–30.

——. *Studies in the Napoleonic Wars*. New York, 1930.

——. *Wellington's Army, 1809–1814*. London, 1913.

Osinga, Frans. *Science, Strategy and War: The Strategic Theory of John Boyd*. Abingdon, 2007.

Park, S.J., and George Nafziger, *The British Military: Its System and Organization, 1803–1815*. Cambridge, Ontario, 1983.

Parker, Geoffrey. *The Military Revolution: Military Innovation and the Rise of the West, 1500–1800*. Cambridge, 1988.

Partridge, Richard, and Michael Oliver. *The Napoleonic Army Handbook*. London, 2000.

Peddie, John. *The Roman War Machine*. Stroud, Gloucestershire, 1994.

Peel, Frank. *The Rising of the Luddites*. London, 1968.

Petersen, Christian. *Bread and the British Economy, c1770–1870*. Aldershot, 1995.

Picq, Ardant du. *Battle Studies*. Trans. Colonel John Greely and Major Robert Cotton. Harrisburg, 1946. Reprint of the 1870 edition.

Pockett, Christopher. "Soldiers of the King: British Soldiers and Identity in the Peninsular War, 1808–1814." Thesis, Queen's University, Kingston, Ontario, 1998.

Prebble, John. *Mutiny: Highland Regiments in Revolt, 1743–1804*. London, 1975.

Radzinowicz, Leon. *History of English Criminal Law*. 3 vols. London, 1948.

Rambaud, Patrick. *La bataille.* Paris, 1997.

Richardson, Major-General F.M. *Fighting Spirit.* New York, 1978.

Rodger, N.A.M. *The Wooden World: An Anatomy of the Georgian Navy.* New York, 1986.

Rogers, Colonel H.C.B. *The British Army of the Eighteenth Century.* New York, 1984.

——. *Wellington's Army.* London, 1979.

Roper, Michael, and John Tosh. *Manful Assertions: Masculinities in Britain since 1800.* London, 1991.

Ropp, Theodore. *War in the Modern World.* London, 1959.

Rose, Michael. *The English Poor Laws, 1780–1930.* New York, 1971.

Rosen, Stephen. *War and Human Nature.* Princeton, 2005.

Roth, Jonathan. *The Logistics of the Roman Army at War.* Boston, 1999.

Rothenberg, Gunther. *The Art of Warfare in the Age of Napoleon.* Bloomington, 1980.

Rudé, George. *Criminal and Victim.* Oxford, 1985.

Rush, Robert. *Hell in Hürtgen Forest: The Ordeal and Triumph of an American Infantry Regiment.* Lawrence, 2001.

Russell, Linda. "The Importance of Patients' Nutritional Status in Wound Healing." *British Journal of Nursing* 10 (2001): 542–48.

Sarkesian, Sam C., ed. *Combat Effectiveness: Cohesion, Stress, and the Volunteer Military.* Beverly Hills, 1980.

Savage, Paul, and Richard Gabriel. "Cohesion and Disintegration in the American Army." *Armed Forces and Society* 3 (1976): 343–70.

Schofield, R. "Dimensions of Literacy, 1750–1850." *Expectations in Economic History* 10 (1973): 437–54.

Schwarz, L.D. "The Standard of Living in the Long Run: London 1700–1860." *Economic History Review* 38 (1985): 24–41.

Scott, Samuel. "Les soldats de l'armée de ligne en 1793." *Annales historiques de la Révolution française* 44 (1972): 493–512.

——. *The Response of the Royal Army to the French Revolution.* Oxford, 1978.

Scurfield, R. "The Weapons of Wellington's Army." *Journal of Army Historical Research* 36.148 (1958): 144–51.

Shay, John. *Achilles in Vietnam.* New York, 1994.

Shikora, Major Scott. "Approaches to Nutritional Support for Battle Casualties and Trauma: Current Military Practice and Lessons Learned from the Civilian Sector." *Military Medicine* 160 (1995): 312–17.

Shils, Edward. "Primary Groups in the American Army." In *Continuities in Social Research: Studies in the Scope and Method of "The American Soldier,"* ed. Robert Merton and Paul Lazarsfeld. Glencoe, 1950.

——. "A Profile of the Military Deserter." *Armed Forces and Society* 3 (1977): 428+.

Shils, Edward, and Morris Janowitz. "Cohesion and Disintegration in the Wehrmacht in World War II." *Public Opinion Quarterly* 12 (1948): 280–315.

Spiers, Edward. *The Army and Society, 1815–1914.* New York, 1980.

Steckel, Richard. "New Light on the 'Dark Ages': The Remarkably Tall Stature of Northern European Men during the Medieval Era." *Social Science History* 28 (2004) 211–29.

Steppler, Glenn. "British Military Law, Discipline and the Conduct of Regimental Courts Martial in the Later Eighteenth Century." *English Historical Review* 102 (1987): 859–86.

——. "The Common Soldier in the Reign of King George III, 1770–1793." Diss., University of Oxford, 1984.

Stouffer, Samuel, Arthur Lumsdaine, Marion Lumsdaine, Robin Williams, M. Brewster Smith, Irving Janis, Shirley Star, and Leonard Cottrell. *The American Soldier: Combat and Its Aftermath.* Vol. 2 of *Studies in Social Psychology in World War II.* 3 vols. Princeton, 1949–50.

Strachan, Hew. *Wellington's Legacy: The Reform of the British Army, 1830–54.* Manchester, 1984.

Strawson, John. *Beggars in Red.* London, 1991.

Teipe, Emily. *America's First Veterans and the Revolutionary War Pensions.* New York, 2002.

Thucydides. *History of the Peloponnesian War.* Trans. Rex Warner. Harmondsworth, Middlesex, 1971.

Tiger, Lionel. *Men in Groups.* New York, 1970.

Tucker, Rufus S. "Real Wages of Artisans in London, 1729–1935." In *The Standard of Living in Britain in the Industrial Revolution,* ed. Arthur J. Taylor. London, 1975.

Tunzelman, G.N. von. "Trends in Real Wages 1750–1850 Revisited." *Economic History Review* 32 (1979): 33–49.

U.S. Department of Agriculture, Agricultural Research Service. *USDA National Nutrient Database for Standard Reference, Release 20,* Nutrient Data Laboratory Home Page, http:///www.ars.usda.gov/ba/bhnrc/ndl (accessed 8 May 2008).

U.S. Food and Drug Administration. *How Folate Can Help Prevent Birth Defects,* http:///www.fda.gov/fdac/features/796_fol.html (accessed 20 January 2005).

Urban, Mark. *Wellington's Rifles: Six Years with England's Legendary Sharpshooters.* New York, 2004.

Vinken, A.G., G.P. Bathalon, A.L. Sawaya, G.E. Dallal, K.L. Tucker, and S.B. Roberts. "Equations for Predicting the Energy Requirements of Healthy Adults Aged 18–81 Years." *American Journal of Clinical Nutrition* 69 (1999): 920–26.

Ward, S.G.P. "The Quartermaster-General's Department in the Peninsula, 1809–1814." *Journal of Army Historical Research* 43.172 (1964): 133–94.

——. *Wellington's Headquarters: A Study of the Administrative Problems in the Peninsula, 1809–1814.* London, 1957.

Ward, Thomas, ed. *The Reign of Queen Victoria.* 2 vols. London, 1921. Reprint of 1887 edition.

Watson, G.E. "The United States and the Peninsular War, 1808–1812." *Historical Journal* 19 (1976): 859–76.

Watteville, Colonel H. de. *The British Soldier: His Daily Life from Tudor to Modern Times.* New York, 1955.

Webster, Graham. *The Roman Imperial Army*. Whistable, 1985.

Weigley, Russell. "Foreword." In *American Soldiers* by Peter Kindsvatter. Lawrence, 2003.

Weller, Jac. *Wellington at Waterloo*. London, 1992. Reprint of 1967 edition.

———. *Wellington in India*. London, 1993. Reprint of 1972 edition.

———. *Wellington in the Peninsula*. London, 1992. Reprint of 1962 edition.

———. "Wellington's Peninsular Logistics." *Journal of Army Historical Research* 42.172 (1964): 197–202.

Wells, Roger. *Wretched Faces: Famine in Wartime England, 1793–1801*. Gloucester, 1988.

Westbrook, Steven. "The Potential for Military Disintegration." In *Combat Effectiveness: Cohesion, Stress, and the Volunteer Military*, ed. Sam C. Sarkesian. Beverly Hills, 1980.

———. "Sociopolitical Alienation and Military Effectiveness." *Armed Forces and Society* 6 (1980): 170–89.

Western, J.R. "The Volunteer Movement as an Anti-Revolutionary Force, 1793–1801." *English Historical Review* 71 (1956): 603–14.

Williams, F.D.G. *SLAM: The Influence of S.L.A. Marshall on the United States Army*. Washington, D.C., 1994.

Williams, J.E. "The British Standard of Living, 1750–1850." *Economic History Review* n.s. 19 (1966): 581–606.

Winter, Jay, and Emmanuel Sivan, eds. *War and Remembrance in the 20th Century*. Cambridge, 1999.

Wong, Leonard, Thomas Kolditz, Raymond Millen, and Terrence Potter. *Why They Fight: Combat Motivation in the Iraq War*. Carlisle, 2003.

Wood, George. "The Statistics of Wages in the United Kingdom during the Last Hundred Years (Part XV): The Cotton Industry." *Journal of the Royal Statistical Society* 73 (1910): 128–63.

———. "The Statistics of Wages in the United Kingdom during the Last Hundred Years (Part XVI): The Cotton Industry." *Journal of the Royal Statistical Society* 73 (1910): 128–63.

———. "The Statistics of Wages in the United Kingdom during the Last Hundred Years (Part XVII): The Cotton Industry." *Journal of the Royal Statistical Society* 73 (1910): 283–315.

———. "The Statistics of Wages in the United Kingdom during the Last Hundred Years (Part XVIII): The Cotton Industry." *Journal of the Royal Statistical Society* 73 (1910): 411–34.

———. "The Statistics of Wages in the United Kingdom during the Last Hundred Years (Part XIX): The Cotton Industry." *Journal of the Royal Statistical Society* 73 (1910): 585–633.

Woolgar, C.M. "Writing the Dispatch: Wellington and Official Communication." *Wellington Studies* 2 (1999): 1–25.

Wright, J.F. "British Economic Growth, 1688–1953." *Economic History Review* n.s. 18 (1965): 397–412.

Young, Peter, and Richard Holmes. *The English Civil War*. London, 1974.

Zhang, Q., X.D. Zhou, and T. Denny. "Changes in Immune Parameters Seen in Gulf War Veterans But Not in Civilians with Chronic Fatigue Syndrome." *Clinical Diagnostic Laboratory of Immunology* 6 (1999): 6–13.

Index

References to illustrations appear in italics.

Adkin, Mark, 334n26
Aitchison, John, 131, 133–35, 169–70, 220, 310n34
Alcohol, 41, 117–19, 221, 283, 292n37, 313n72, 317n148; plundering of, 18, 20, 27, 35, 115, 218–19, 223–25, 230–33; soldiers' rations of, 6, 91, 103, 121, 274, 277, 286–87
Alexander, Alex, 76
Alten, Charles, 328n43
American Civil War, 4, 8, 14, 145, 299n37, 328n32, 331n1
American Revolution, 295n33, 297n10, 330n82
Anderson, Fred, 68
Anton, James, 19–20, 89, 105, 168, 204
Arnold, James, 159, 174
Atkinson, C. T., 41–42, 237, 293n2
Auerstadt, 159

Bankes, George, 12
Bartov, Omar, 150–51, 331n3
Baste, Pierre, 23
Bathurst, Henry (earl of Bathurst), 30
Beattie, J. M., 82
Beckwith, Thomas, 152, 200
Belgium, 240, 309n15; Quatre-Bras, 171, 324n115, 335n36; Waterloo, 12, 30, 44, 56, 84, 90, 149, 155–56, 164, 171, 174, 191, 205, 238, 240–41, 290n13, 296n46, 306n178, 313n86, 325n4, 327n26, 328n43, 334n26
Bell, George, 18, 92, 142–43, 200–201, 203, 205, 210, 340n37
Bell, William, 166
Below, Thomas, 323n95
Beresford, William, 32, 126, 296n38, 297n57, 328n42
Bertaud, Jean-Paul, 54–56, 71

367

Best, Geoffrey, 60, 64

Beuil, Jean du, 331n91

Blakeney, Robert, 27, 110, 227–28, 319n29, 341n48

Blanco, Richard, 139

Blücher, Gebhard Leberecht von, 43

Bonaparte, Joseph, 111, 135, 198

Bonaparte, Napoleon. *See* Napoleon

Boutflower, Charles, 234, 313n85

Bowden, George, 198, 214, 216, 339n13

Bowen, H. V., 84

Boyd, John, 327n19

Brazil, 87

Brenier, Antoine-Francois, 170

Brereton, J. M., 302n100

Briggs, Asa, 302n108

Britain, 11, 13–14, 292n40, 307n188, 308n199, 343n9; administrative acts, 56, 64–65, 71–72, 304n138, 305n141; effects of Industrial Revolution on, 51–52, 59–61, 63–67, 75, 79–86, 94, 109, 140, 148, 160, 238–39, 241–42, 265, 301n79; hospitals at Chelsea and Kilmainham, 109, 148, 241–42

British Army: Coldstream Guards (2nd Foot Guards), 90, 133, 245; Grenadier Guards (1st Foot Guards), 245–46, 328n43; Horse Guards, 59, 140, 144, 148, 309n21, 320n60, 322n85; Royal African Corps, 80; Royal Artillery, 52, 76, 160, 245–46, 318n23; Royal Marines, 52; Royal West Indian Rangers, 80; Royal York Rangers, 80; Scots Greys, 96, 124; Scots Guards (3rd Foot Guards), 131, 169, 220, 245–46; 1st Foot (Royal Scots), 91, 110, 117, 121, 201, 245–46, 297n9; 3rd Light Dragoons, 245–46; 5th Foot, 151, 180; 6th Foot, 245–46, 259, 297n9; 7th Foot (Royal Fusiliers), 92, 94, 215, 230; 7th Light Dragoons, 59; 8th Foot, 96, 245–46, 291n20, 297n9; 9th Light Dragoons, 297n57; 10th Foot, 43, 319n42; 17th Foot, 299n38, 308n4; 18th Foot, 297n9; 18th Light Dragoons, 25, 43, 124, 135, 245–46, 319n42; 19th Light Dragoons, 245–46, 291n20; 20th Light Dragoons, 245–46, 261; 24th Foot, 25; 25th Foot, 245, 291n20, 297n9; 27th Foot, 297n9; 28th Foot, 75, 110, 139, 214, 217, 245–46, 297n9, 309n21; 29th Foot, 177; 31st Foot, 330n83; 32nd Foot, 245, 291n20, 297n9; 33rd Foot, 171; 34th Foot, 39, 92–93, 114, 142–43, 203, 245–46, 297n9, 337n75; 36th Foot, 27; 40th Foot, 20, 51–52, 167, 178, 239–43, 313n85, 342n6; 42nd Foot, 19, 89, 105, 110, 168, 245–46, 297n9, 337n73; 43rd Foot, 44, 94–95, 200–201, 216, 329n69, 339n; 44th Foot, 137; 45th Foot, 228; 51st Foot, 91, 138, 200; 52nd Foot, 329n, 339n5; 53rd Foot, 23, 42, 169, 245–46, 291n20, 297n9; 56th Foot, 18; 58th Foot, 245–46, 259–60, 297n109n, 298n113, 303n119; 60th Foot, 329n69; 68th Light Infantry, 92, 107, 199, 329n69; 71st Foot (Highland Light Infantry), 94, 115, 149, 151, 168, 170, 329n69; 73rd Foot, 140; 75th Foot, 329n69; 78th Foot, 297n9; 79th Foot, 245–46, 297n9; 85th Foot, 170; 87th Foot, 297n9; 88th Foot (Connaught Rangers), 18, 90, 111, 166, 168–70, 200, 203, 222, 245–46, 258, 297n9, 309n16; 90th Foot, 329n69; 91st Foot, 297n9; 92nd Foot (Gordon Highlanders), 77, 297n9; 93rd Foot (Sutherland Highlanders), 143; 94th Foot, 22, 76, 86, 181, 201, 222; 95th Foot (The Rifles), 18, 23, 45, 47, 89, 94, 108, 111, 119, 126, 128, 131, 141, 149, 151, 172, 197–98, 203, 214, 216, 222, 225, 229, 292n34, 302n105, 308n3, 328n33, 329n69; 96th Foot, 298n13, 303n119; 101st Foot, 297n9

Browne, Thomas, 224, 292n33, 315n113, 316n118, 340n40
Browne, William, 228, 232
Bryant, Arthur, 41
Buckley, Roger, 80–81, 143, 166, 219, 293n57, 295n33, 306n177, 306n178, 315n102, 318n2, 339n21
Bugeaud, Thomas, 171–72, 329n68
Burgoyne, John, 87
Burke, Private, 200–201, 335n36

Calder, Philip, 103
Campbell, Archibald, 42
Canada, 324n114
Cantlie, Sir Neil, 314n88
Carlyle, Thomas, 295n26
Carss, John, 23, 42, 169
Castles, Johnny, 225
Chandler, David, 146, 159, 161, 174
Chapman, Gayle, 104
Charles I, 72
Charles II, 72
Civilians, 7, 14, 20, 37–40, 47, 80, 84, 94–95, 100, 112, 129–30, 145–46, 149, 185, 218, 222–23, 297n57, 324n117, violence against, xviii, xx, 21–26, 37, 41, 82, 100, 111–16, 118, 137, 150–51, 213, 226–33, 237, 293n53, 293n58, 295n23, 309n16, 316n118, 340n24
Clausewitz, Carl von, 336n67
Coates-Wright, Philip, 306n167
Cockerill, A. W., 56, 85, 298n19, 299n40
Colbert, August, 152
Colborne, Sir John, 114, 233
Cole, W. A., 304n131
Colley, Linda, 48
Colquhoun, Patrick, 307n188
Cooke, John, 127
Cooley, Charles H., 5–6, 191, 331n2
Cooper, John, 92–93, 98–99, 110, 115, 126–27, 139, 215, 230–32, 316n134
Cornwell, Bernard, 295n32
Corvisier, Andre, 54–56, 66, 70–71, 298n18, 299n27, 304n129

Costa, Dora, 331n1
Costello, Edward, 94, 108, 111–12, 127, 141, 149, 152, 166, 168–69, 198, 200, 203–206, 214, 218, 221, 225, 229–32, 308n3, 315n109, 317n148, 321n74, 321n81, 324n115, 325n123, 325n128, 339n6
Crafts, N. F. R., 304n131
Craufurd, Robert, 17, 33, 96–97, 127–28, 141, 319n29, 321n72, 337n74
Crawley, Tom, 317n148
Creevey, Thomas, 43
Cromwell, Oliver, 72
Crouzet, Francois, 343n9
Czech Republic, Austerlitz, 148, 238

Darvall, Frank, 67, 302n102
Deane, Phyllis, 265, 304n131
Denmark, 335n47
Desertion, 4–5, 17, 33–36, 58, 78, 80, 198, 201, 207–208, 245, 247, 290n5, 335n57, 336n65, 338n79; punishment for, 21, 118–19, 137, 205, 292n42, 317n151, 322n83
Dinter, Elmar, 195
Dolan, Pat, 109, 315n113
Donaldson, Joseph, 22–23, 76, 86, 94, 115–17, 141–42, 201, 222, 232, 314n90, 317n155, 321n78
Douglas, John, 91, 96–97, 109, 201
Drouet, Jean-Baptiste (comte d'Erlon), 155
Duffy, Christopher, 173
Duffy, Michael, 306n176
Dundas, Sir David, 165–66, 295n17

Egypt, 174
Elting, John, 145–46
English Civil War, soldiers' diets during, 98–100, 272, 274–75, 279
Enlistment, 5–6, 11–14, 50–87, 244–69, 291n20, 297n9, 302n100, 302n105, 324n117
Esdaile, Charles, 21, 24, 47, 154, 172, 233, 297n56, 326n11, 339n14

Executions, xviii, 20–22, 35, 81, 113, 131, 225, 231, 241, 247, 293n58, 307n181, 322n84, 335n53

Ferguson, William, 45
Fitzgerald, Edward, 124–25
Fletcher, Ian, 215
Flinn, M. W., 65, 67
Flogging, 12, 26, 76, 152, 197–98, 201, 205–206, 231, 293n2, 305n151, 320n50, 321n69, 321n74, 321n81, 322n86, 322n87, 323n95; of British soldiers, 14, 16–17, 30, 39–42, 128, 135–45, 320n54, 320n61, 321n72
Floud, Roderick, 310n54, 344n6
Forest, Alan, 9–10
Forlorn Hope (company), 151, 200, 213–16, 339n5
Fortescue, John, 79, 160, 305n160
Foy, Maximilien, 43, 156
France, 110, 205, 241
Franco-Prussian War, 333n14
Frederick, Duke of York, 143, 209, 295n17, 318n22, 320n60
Frederick the Great, 173
Frederick II (of Prussia), 174
French Army, xvii–xviii, xx, 3, 9, 13–15, 20, 31–32, 37–39, 43, 45–48, 54–58, 60–61, 70–71, 91, 103, 107, 110, 114, 116–19, 126, 129, 135, 137, 141–42, 201–205, 208, 211–13, 217–22, 235–45, 291n28, 293n57, 293n64, 298n13, 303n114, 314n90, 316n134, 317n150, 324n107, 324n121, 325n123, 326n14, 327n22, 337n75, 337n77; tactics of, 145–76, 327n22–328n29, 328n40; treatment of civilians, 21–27, 293n49
French Revolution, xvii–xviii, 4, 38, 60, 157–58, 174, 295n26, 298n13, 337n77
Frere, J. H., 32
Frey, Silvia, 81, 295n33
Furet, Francois, 8–9

Gabriel, Richard, 331n3
Gayer, Arthur, 267
George III, 11, 88, 143
Germany, 64, 238
Gilbert, Arthur, 69, 80–81, 119, 297n10, 303n119
Gilboy, Elizabeth, 267
Gleig, George, 229–30, 232
Glover, Michael, 123, 150, 293n2, 295n27
Glover, Richard, 41, 320n50
Gomm, William, 168
Gordon, Alexander, 47–48
Gordon, George (duke of Gordon), 77
Gordon, James, 131
Gordon, Major, 110
Goya, Francisco, 24
Grattan, William, 18, 20, 90, 110–11, 169–70, 200–203, 222–23, 230–32, 309n15, 340n24
Green, John, 92, 95, 107, 116–17, 135, 139, 199, 201, 314n89
Griffith, Paddy, 173
Griois, Charles, 326n16
Grossman, David, 333n18
Gudin, Charles Etienne, 159
Guilmartin, John, 311n60, 332n9
Gunn, James, 110, 337n73

Hamilton, Anthony, 94–95
Hamilton, Inglis, 96
Hanger, George, 162
Hanoverian army: King's German Legion, 154, 172, 222, 328n42; Brunswick-Oels Jagers, 172
Harding, "Pig," 198, 212, 214, 216, 315n110, 339n13
Harley, John, 109, 123, 218, 231–32, 315n113, 339n19, 340n33
Harris, John (Benjamin), 47–48, 89, 96, 111, 120, 127, 149, 197–98, 203, 290n14, 311n58, 317n154, 321n72, 334n28
Harris, Karen, 333n11
Hart, John, 197
Hart, Peter, 312n
Hathaway, Eileen, 293n2

Hay, Douglas, 65, 82
Haythornthwaite, Philip, 77, 130, 166, 293n2, 300n54, 305n158, 308n195
Heeley, Edward, 25
Hennell, George, 124, 309n24, 312n68, 318n7
Henry, Walter, 113–14, 228, 232, 312n68, 319n34
Herbert, Sidney, 323n94
Hervey Felton, 155–56
Heyland, Arthur, 240
Hill, Rowland, 17, 127, 168, 323n96
Hippolyte, Jacque Antoine (comte de Guibert), 160–61
Hodenburg, Charles von, 222–23
Holderness, B. A., 64
Holmes, Richard, 193, 315n114, 320n52, 322n87, 330n83, 338n4
Hudson, Major, 138
Hughes, B. P., 162, 327n28
Hughes, Michael, 25, 118–19, 291n28, 317n150, 323n100, 324n107
Hugo, Abel, 293n58
Hynes, Samuel, 9, 290n17

India, 156, 327n26; siege of Lucknow, 176
Industrial Revolution, 59–67, 270
Iraq, Operation Enduring Freedom, 196, 334n25
Irish Rebellion (1798), 73
Italy, 160; Elba, 149, 239

Jacobite Rebellion (1745–46), 174
James II, 72
Janowitz, Morris, 4, 6, 192, 290n5, 332n9, 333n13, 337n71
Jenkinson, Robert (Lord Liverpool), 34–35, 82
Johnson, Sergeant, 96
Jones, David, 83
Jourdan, Jean-Baptiste, 135
Junot, Laure, 24

Kahn, Matthew, 331n1
Keegan, John, 297n2, 332n6

Kellett, Anthony, 332n5
Kennedy, Arthur, 25
Kew, Samantha, 103
Keys, Ancel, 106, 314n98, 314n99
Kincaid, John, 45, 94, 126–27, 131, 222, 309n8, 319n29
Kindsvatter, Peter, 206, 335n60
Knowles, Robert, 94, 108, 312n68
Komlos, John, 300n, 310n54, 311n56
Kopperman, Paul, 106, 315n101
Korean War, 195, 206, 333n11
Kuskin, Alex, 313n72

Larpent, F. S., 20, 113, 124, 131, 134, 140, 143–44, 319n28, 319n34, 337n73
Larrey, Dominique-Jean, 173
Latimer, John, 300n67
Lavaux, Francois, 23
Lawrence, Sir Henry, 176
Lawrence, William, 12–13, 20, 51–56, 67, 70–72, 74, 85–89, 95, 108, 112–13, 116, 135–36, 149, 164, 166–67, 198–99, 201–202, 204–205, 211, 214, 216, 219, 225, 229–30, 232, 239–43, 290n15, 297n5, 310n48, 310n50, 315n110, 316n128, 316n133, 328n40, 339n13, 339n22, 339n23, 340n30, 342n2, 342n9, 342n12, 342n13, 342n18
Layton, G. B., 106
Lazenby, John, 338n79
Leach, John, 39, 92–93
Lennox, Charles (duke of Richmond), 32
Le Roy, Claude, 13
Linch, Kevin, 297n8, 298n20, 299n42, 302n100, 304n126
Lindert, Peter, 304n124
"Little Ice Age," 57–58, 299n32
Little, Roger, 195, 330n87, 333n11, 335n63, 337n
Longford, Elizabeth, 43
Louis XIV, 147–48, 318n18
Louis XV, 54, 70
Louis XVIII, 43

Louis, Claude (comte de Saint-Germaine), xvii, 13
Lowe, John, 197–98
Lynn, John, 13, 50, 107, 235–36, 291n25, 302n97, 317n159, 318n18, 331n3

Macfarlane, John, 75, 94, 149, 168
Mackey, Corporal, 170
Manchester, William, 202
Mann, James, 199
Marquant, Francois, 24
Marshall, S. L. A., 192–94, 210, 332n8, 332n9, 334n21, 344n9
Marten, Private, 164
Massena, Andre, 23, 43
Master, Richard, 328n43
Mayberry, Private, 197–98, 334n31
McGrigor, James, 35–36
McGuffie, T. H., 46, 118, 303n120, 306n169, 322n88, 342n1
McNeill, William, 175
McPherson, James, 145
Melito, Andre Miot de, 293n54
Merino, Danielle, 103–104
Mills, John, 133
Mitchell, B. R., 265
Moore, Sir John, 17, 21, 45, 47, 125, 151, 154, 172
Morris, Thomas, 140, 142
Moskos, Charles, 197
Mosse, George, 330n88
Muir, Rory, 162, 173, 326n10, 328n37
Murray, John, 34
Murray, Sir George, 130–31

Nafzinger, George, 292n40
Napier, Charles, 93
Napier, Sir William, 44, 296n47
Napoleon, 6, 9, 24–25, 29, 31, 43–46, 48, 51, 53, 59, 64–66, 81, 84, 88–90, 118, 129, 145–50, 157, 162, 165, 173–74, 204, 208, 210, 212, 220, 235–36, 239, 267–70, 272, 277, 283, 291n28, 296n46, 299n45, 300n49, 300n67, 305n143, 317n150, 320n61,

323n98, 326n14, 330n86, 338n4, 338n83, 342n12
Nelson, Horatio, 61, 268
Netherlands: Walcheren Campaign, 116–17, 313n86
Ney, Michel, 159–60, 171, 174
Nibler, Roger, 333n11
Nicholas, Stephen, 83, 290n13, 298n25
Nosworthy, Brent, 174, 328n35, 329n73
Nye, Robert, 330n88

O'Brien, Patrick, 303n118
Obrien, Private, 221
Oman, Sir Charles, 113–14, 127, 160–61, 233, 292n42, 306n178, 322n84, 327n22,
O'Neil, Charles, 75, 95, 108, 139, 141, 149, 214, 217, 308n4, 320n60, 340n44
Ozouf, Mona, 8–9

Paget, Lord Henry, 59, 319n29
Paget, Sir Edward, 152
Park, S. J., 292n40
Patterson, Frederick, 171, 329n67
Peddie, John, 345n10
Picq, Ardant du, 193, 333n14
Picton, Thomas, 17, 339n7
Pitt, William, the Younger, 82
Plundering, xviii, xix, 12–13, 18–19, 25–28, 31–46, 89–100, 105–108, 111–17, 129–35, 150–52, 196, 207–208, 214–18, 221–36, 292n44, 295n23, 309n16, 315n102, 315n113, 319n43, 322n84, 330n88, 335n63, 339n19, 340n38
Plunkett, Thomas, 141, 149, 152, 321n74, 324n114, 325n128
Porter, Sir Robert, 45–48
Portugal: Alemtejo, 297n57; Busaco, 168–69; Cascaes, 293n46; Castel Branco, 199; Portalegre, 95; Porto de Mos, 22; Redinha, 204; Santarem, 23; Vigo, 141; Vimiero, 168, 170, 197
Portuguese army, 23, 26, 32–34, 98,

115, 129, 154, 172–73, 223–24,
    326n11, 328n42
Powell, H. W., 326n16
Powers, Lieutenant, 231–32
Powers, Manley, 224

Rape, xviii, 20–25, 27, 37, 82, 110,
    114, 137, 150, 211, 218, 226–34
Rations (food, diet), xix, 6–7, 10–11,
    13, 17–20, 25, 32–33, 35–40, 45–
    47, 51–52, 58–61, 65, 73, 82–83,
    88–113, 115, 118–20, 123–25,
    129, 131–37, 153, 196, 204–205,
    218, 224, 234–37, 272–87,
    309n24, 312n68, 314n88, 315n109
Reynier, Jean-Louis, 326n16
Richard I, 136
Richardson, F. M., 46, 209
Robinson, F. P., 89–90, 120–21, 221,
    340n28
Rodger, N. A. M., 306n178
Rogers, Reva, 103, 313n72
Romana, Marqués de la, 21
Roman army, 4, 57, 324n117, 326n9;
    diet of, 98–100, 156, 209, 272,
    275, 278, 345n10
Ropp, Theodore, 300n49
Rosen, Stephen, 16–17, 193, 314n97
Roth, Jonathan, 98, 311n56
Rouse, Private, 342n9
Rowbottom, William 75
Rudé, George, 83
Russia, 91, 156, 174

Savage, Paul, 331n3
Schachter, Stanley, 332n5
Scott, Samuel, 39, 54–55, 57, 71,
    298n13
Scovell, Sir George, 25
Selway, Benjamin, 90
Seton, Sir Henry, 299n38, 308n4
Seven Years War, 174, 330n82
Sharpe, Richard, 295n32
Shelley, Percy Bysshe, 63
Sherer, Moyle, 39–40, 93, 114,
    337n75
Shils, Edward, 4, 6, 192, 195, 290n5,
    332n9, 333n13

Sikh Wars, 174, 330n83
Simmons, George, 23
Sivan, Emmanuel, 293n1
Slade, John, 117
Smith, Harry, 215–16, 225
Soult, Nicolas, 43–44, 126
South Africa, 225, 341n45
Spain: Albuera, 42, 126, 296n38; Al-
    caniz, 23–24; Avila, 293n58; Bada-
    joz, 26, 115, *188–90*, 197–200,
    202, 212, 214–17, 219–27, 229,
    231, 287, 310n48, 316n133,
    319n34, 325n4, 338n3, 339n5,
    339n14, 340n24; Burgos, 110, 212,
    339n15; Cacabellos, 152; Cadiz,
    209; Campillo, 91, 312n68;
    Ciudad Rodrigo, 26, 91, 119, 128,
    131, *182–87*, 199–200, 212, 217–
    20, 222–23, 226, 228–31, 234,
    312n68, 316n118, 338n3, 339n15;
    Cordoba, 23; Corunna, 21, 47–48;
    91, 96, 105, 118, 120, 141, 149,
    152, 154, 321n72; Fuentes
    d'Onoro, 111; Gamonal, 23;
    Huarte, 30; Madrid, 201, 318n7;
    Manzanares, 24; Matagorda, *181*,
    Maya, 114; Oropesa, 88; Pam-
    plona, 110, 167; Sahagun, 155; Sal-
    amanca, 121, 131, 155–56, 200,
    309n24, 312n68, 317n155; San
    Christoval, 212, 217, 339n15; San
    Sebastian, 26, 90, 200, 212, 217–
    18, 221, 226, 229, 231–33,
    339n15; Talavera, 32, 156, 169–
    70, 335n53; Vitoria, 111–12, 116,
    135, 156, 198, 287; sixteenth-
    century galley slaves' and sol-
    diers' diets, 98–100, 274–77, 280–
    82
Spanish army, 22, 24, 32, 47, 78, 132,
    154, 174, 220–22, 315n109,
    335n53
Spring, Matthew, 330n82
Stanhope, Charles (earl of Stan-
    hope), 31, 144, 294n7
St. Cyr, Guivon, 165
Steckel, Richard, 57–58, 83, 290n13,
    298n25

Steppler, Glenn, 12, 137, 298n14
Stewart, Robert (Lord Castlereagh), 82, 132
St. Helena (island), 44
Stothert, William, 287
Stouffer, Samuel, 191–92, 195, 332n7
Stuart, Charles (1st Baron Stuart de Rothesay), 32–33
Surtees, William, 18, 107, 119–20, 141, 292n34, 309n15, 328n37
Swabey, William, 228–29

Taggert, Lieutenant, 216
Tandy, Tom, 18
Temple, Henry J. (Lord Palmerston), 323n95
Tobler, Steven, 313n72
Tomkinson, William, 325n5
Torrens, Henry, 34
Trafalgar (Battle of), 61, 268
Tucker, Rufus, 59, 66, 265–67

Uniacke, John, 127, 166
Urban, Mark, 302n105

Venetian galley oarsmen: diets, 98–100, 274–75, 281

Wallace, Alexander, 170
Wallace, Kit, 203
Ward, S. G. P., 130
War of 1812, 59, 62, 64, 239, 265
Weigley, Russell, 297n2
Wellesley, Arthur (duke of Wellington), 3–4, 8, 16–17, 20–22, 26–43, 46, 48, 84, 91–92, 96, 108, 113, 115, 120–21, 123–35, 144–45, 154–56, 159, 168, 173–74, 179, 209–13, 217, 220, 223–27, 231–33, 235, 237, 264, 269, 289n2, 291n20, 293n2, 293n46, 294n7, 294n8, 295n23, 295n32, 297n56, 304n138, 306n178, 309n16, 310n48, 316n118, 319n34, 319n42, 322n84, 323n89, 323n96, 326n7, 326n10, 335n53, 335n63, 337n73, 338n3, 338n83
Wellesley, Henry, 132
Wells, Roger, 61
Westbrook, Steven, 14, 117, 237
West Indies, 80, 143, 219, 239, 305n157, 342n2
Wheeler, William, 91, 200–201, 206–207, 322n88
Wilberforce, William, 323n95
Williamson, Jeffrey, 304n124
Winter, Jay, 293n1
Wolfe, James, 330n82
Wolseley, Viscount Garnet, 144
Women, 10, 16, 22–25, 27, 39–40, 52, 58, 65–66, 73, 77, 82, 89, 106–107, 111, 118, 125, 149, 201, 218, 222–23, 227–34, 241–43, 311n56, 314n98, 315n102, 324n115, 342n2, 344n9
Wood, George, 301n77
Woodbury, George, 43, 124, 319n42
World War I, 4, 334n26
World War II, 4, 105–106, 150–51, 191, 195, 202, 290n9, 331n1, 331n3, 334n26